RED ★ SKY MORNING

THE EPIC TRUE STORY
OF TEXAS RANGER COMPANY F

JOE PAPPALARDO

ST. MARTIN'S GRIFFIN
NEW YORK

For Amber, who keeps getting better

Published in the United States by St. Martin's Griffin, an imprint of St. Martin's Publishing Group

RED SKY MORNING. Copyright © 2022 by Joseph Pappalardo. All rights reserved. Printed in the United States of America. For information, address St. Martin's Publishing Group, 120 Broadway, New York, NY 10271.

www.stmartins.com

Designed by Omar Chapa

The Library of Congress has cataloged the hardcover edition as follows:

Names: Pappalardo, Joe, author.
Title: Red sky morning : the epic true story of Texas Ranger
     Company F / Joe Pappalardo.
Other titles: Epic true story of Texas Ranger Company F
Description: First Edition. | New York : St. Martin's Press, [2022] |
     Includes bibliographical references and index.
Identifiers: LCCN 2022003909 | ISBN 9781250275240 (hardcover) |
     ISBN 9781250275257 (ebook)
Subjects: LCSH: Texas Rangers. Frontier Battalion. Company F—History. |
     Law enforcement—Texas—History—19th century. | Sabine County (Tex.)—
     History—19th century. | Conner family.
Classification: LCC F391 .P22 2022 | DDC 976.4/061—dc23/eng/20220127
LC record available at https://lccn.loc.gov/2022003909

ISBN 978-1-250-88737-5 (trade paperback)

Our books may be purchased in bulk for promotional, educational, or business use. Please contact your local bookseller or the Macmillan Corporate and Premium Sales Department at 1-800-221-7945, extension 5442, or by email at MacmillanSpecial Markets@macmillan.com.

First St. Martin's Griffin Edition: 2023

10 9 8 7 6 5 4 3 2 1

CONTENTS

Truly the universe is full of ghosts, not sheeted churchyard specters, but the inextinguishable elements of individual life, which having once been, can never die, though they blend and change, and change again forever.

—*H. Rider Haggard*, King Solomon's Mines

Don't bother about being modern. Unfortunately it is the one thing that, whatever you do, you cannot avoid.

—*Salvador Dalí*

Red sky morning, I know it's real
Red sky morning, go for my steel
Fight gonna come, I got a black cat bone
When the morning comes, I'm gonna stand alone

—*"Red Sky Morning," Gangstagrass*

INTRODUCTION

THE RECRUIT
January 15, 1883

James Brooks takes in Cotulla and sees progress where others would only see squalor. It's grown since his last visit, two years ago. The town is now a backwater of twenty or so one- or two-room wooden shacks connected by muddy trails just wide enough for a wagon. The truly desperate dwell in lean-tos.

However, there's also a brand-new building on Front Street, the heart of the emerging community. The recently opened La Salle Hotel, the only structure of any size in Cotulla, is also the only inn of any repute. In comparison, reflective of Cotulla's priorities and his own, there are three saloons in Cotulla when Brooks arrives there in January 1883.

He's a reasonably tall man at five foot ten inches, but with shoulders that drop as if weighed down by heavy hands. Under his worn trail hat, Brooks has a slightly pinched nose and oddly cool blue eyes. His frame is lean from years wandering Texas, hardened by outdoor work and time riding livestock trails.

Since his arrival in 1877, Texas hasn't shown him a path to stability. At age twenty-seven, he's already been a rancher, hired hand, mineral prospector, sheep farmer, aspiring groom—and nothing worked out. Brooks has no wife, no family in the state, and no steady job. He drinks too much whiskey, as befitting a man born in Bourbon County, Kentucky. He's essentially a man with nothing to lose. A place like Cotulla could revive or ruin him.[1]

The town is the brainchild of Polish immigrant and rancher Joseph Cotulla, who, in 1881, successfully wooed the International & Great Northern Railroad to his shady hamlet with free land. The freshly minted municipality is now selling new lots to the west of a freshly built train depot. Cotulla, already holding the reputation for being rowdy—conductors announce arrival there by calling out, "Cotulla! Everybody get your guns ready!"—is poised to become a booming cattle town.[2]

Brooks certainly isn't put off by Cotulla's reputation, and had a memorable time there during a previous visit. "Liquored up" in a Cotulla saloon in 1881, he witnessed Texas Ranger Lee Hall face off against six armed men—and back them down bloodlessly through nerve alone.[3]

This vivid encounter is undoubtedly on his mind on January 15, 1883, when he sits down with Lieutenant Charles "Girlie" McKinney, acting commander of the Texas Rangers' Company F, stationed in Cotulla. He's filling in after the resignation of Captain Tom Oglesby in November, but that doesn't stop him from accomplishing one of a captain's main duties: finding new Rangers.

Brooks finds his own expectations rattled by his recruiter. He certainly doesn't fit the expected picture of a grim-faced, death-dealing

---

1 Born November 20, 1855. Physical descriptions, from newspapers to his service records, agree on these stats and match photographic records. See Brooks's reenlistment papers via State Library and Archives Commission: https://www.tsl.texas.gov/apps /arc/service/storage/service_media/pdfs/FB/b/br/bro2477.pdf.

2 John Leffler, "Cotulla, TX," *Handbook of Texas Online,* Texas Historical Research Association, https://www.tshaonline.org/handbook/entries/cotulla-tx.

3 Paul Spellman, *Captain J. A. Brooks, Texas Ranger* (Denton: University of North Texas Press, 2007).

Texas Ranger. McKinney is charismatic, quick-witted, and a natural storyteller. And his looks are not what you would call steely.

"McKinney had the prettiest pink-and-white complexion, the mildest and softest blue eyes, golden hair which curled in little ringlets all over his head, a Cupid's bow of a mouth, and an expression of feminine innocence—except when he was on the warpath," describes author N. A. Jennings, who knew him. The Rangers are the ones who nickname McKinney "Girlie," but Jennings also notes that "the man who attempted to impose upon Charley McKinney because of his innocent appearance invariably regretted it."[4]

The Texas Rangers are already legendary in 1883, but few then—as now—have a grasp on what they actually *do*. A Ranger of the time, Jennings sums up the organization's mystique and tendency to be misunderstood at the turn of the century: "Nearly everyone has heard of the Texas Rangers at some time in his life, but how many know what the Rangers really are, or what are their duties? In a general way, everyone knows they are men who ride around on the Texas border, do a good deal of shooting, and now and then get killed or kill someone. But why they ride around, or why they do the shooting, is a question which might go begging for an answer for a long time without getting a correct one."[5]

Part of the confusion comes from a tortured history of the term *Texas Ranger*. The moniker had been, even by 1883, applied to a myriad of volunteer militia, mounted police officers, and military units. *Texas Rangers* could mean members of the Ranging Corps (1836–1845), the Rangers, Mounted Volunteers, and Minute Men (1846–1861); the Mounted Regiments and Frontier Regiments during the Civil War (1861–1865); the Frontier Forces (1870–1873); or the short-lived Frontier Men (1874). Each

---

4 N. A. Jennings, *A Texas Ranger* (New York: Charles Scribner's Sons, 1899).

5 This books seeks to answer that very question about the Texas Rangers of the late 1800s.

name came with a different mandate and historical imperative based on who needed protection and who the state deemed in need of shooting.

The Frontier Battalion forms in 1874 as the first permanent force of Texas Rangers. Their first foes are Comanche and Kiowa, and the Rangers get bloody putting them down. But by the mid-1870s, the Indian presence has largely been crushed and tribal lands ceded to the United States. The Rangers fixate on a new target—criminals—and by necessity transform from military cavalry militia into roaming, mounted police officers.

When Brooks sits down with Girlie McKinney, the Rangers' chief concerns are politically motivated fence saboteurs, violent strikers, and opportunistic thieves. The governor responded to the increasing constituent requests for law and order by deploying the Texas Rangers, who are expected to bring results when the local law is ineffectual either because of a fear of the criminals or sympathy for them. As outsiders, they rely on both guile and deadly force to do their jobs, a mix that antagonizes locals. "Who are the Texas Rangers?" asks one turn-of-the-century magazine. "By many he is regarded as a sort of legalized vigilante, ruling through the right evolved of necessity in the realm where the six-shooter is the only arbiter."[6]

When it comes to the Texas Rangers, James Brooks likes what he hears. It's a life that will satisfy his rootless disposition, and at forty-five dollars a month. McKinney must see the potential in the quietly experienced man. Companies routinely recruit teenagers, but someone with years spent riding the range brings more valuable skills, higher endurance, and better judgment. Brooks signs up as a private with Company F on the spot.[7]

---

6 Earl Mayo, "Texas Rangers: The Most Efficient Police Force in the World," *Frank Leslie's Popular Monthly,* October 1901. It's a portrait of the organization just before a massive overhaul.

7 "Adjutant General Service Records," Texas State Library and Archives Commission, https://www.tsl.texas.gov/apps/arc/service/.

There is a sink-or-swim mentality when it comes to breaking in tenderfoots. Ranger hires are often done spur of the moment, and acceptance of a sudden lifestyle change is the recruit's first test. Brooks's first assignment comes that same week he joins. He's going to crash a wedding.

The targets are men who clipped eight miles of fence in Frio County.[8] Fences are more than pieces of wood and metal; they are symbols of the death of opportunity for smaller-scale cattlemen. Some fences are direct challenges, when they block access to public land and water. Barbed wire, taken as a whole, is also an existential threat since it brings with it a new way of handling animals that is designed to kill the very idea of the open range. Therefore, cutting fences is an act of insurrection, a way to lash out against economic change. Nipping, as it was called, is only a misdemeanor that draws a small fine, so it's not too much of a risk to participate.

Brooks is one of five Rangers dispatched to Frio County to make arrests. The Rangers, under the leadership of Corporal Brack Morris, quickly learn that all four cutters will soon gather at a wedding, ready to be scooped up at once. His corporal's bold plan makes Brooks excited and edgy—how will the men react? What if their friends are carrying pistols on their belts or have rifles slung on their saddles? What if the wedding becomes a riot? Just what is he getting himself into?

Stomping into the festivities, Brooks finds that the defiant men submit without a fight. "Those old Texans were proud of what they had done," he later writes in a journal. "That their fathers had fought Indians, bled and died for that land, and no Yankees could come here and fence the livestock from the water holes and lakes."[9]

The party continues as the Rangers ride away, prisoners in tow. His

---

8 Paul Spellman, *Captain J. A. Brooks.*

9 Brooks's notebook, courtesy of Texas Ranger Hall of Fame and Museum, Waco, TX.

first case shakes Brooks's conventional understanding of who criminals are and the motives that drive them.

Brooks is paid ninety dollars every two months, so his first paycheck, issued on February 28, 1883, is forty-five dollars.[10] New recruits often borrow money from the organization to pay for a horse, saddle, Winchester rifle, and Colt pistol, an amount subtracted from their initial paycheck. Brooks appears to pay nothing; as an experienced trailhand and horseman, he seems to have most of this gear already. The coming miles of travel will wear on his horse, but his fellows tell him that the state reimburses for any mount killed or used up during Ranger service. This, he learns, is an opportunity to generate some supplemental income. "I never heard of the state paying less than $100 for a dead horse," says Jennings. "And I never knew a Ranger to pay more than $40 for a live one."

There's clearly more to this profession than just aiming guns at people. Brooks dives into his new job with quiet fervor. His age and dependability earn him respect within the company. James Brooks is no longer just a wandering soul, lost amid the saloons, rail lines, and roundups. He's a Texas Ranger.

CORONER'S PARTY
December 6, 1883

Dr. J. W. Smith rides toward Holly Bottom with a bad feeling that only grows with each hoof step. His destination, best known for providing access to a bayou well-suited for rooting pigs, is ten miles southeast of the town of Hemphill. That's where a pair of bodies have been found shot to death and left in the rain.

Hemphill may only be an isolated, deep East Texas hamlet of 350

---

10 In January 1900, all active Texas Rangers had to reregister during a reorganization, and filled the paperwork with the Adjutant General's Office. Accessed via https://www.tsl.texas.gov/apps/arc/service/storage/service_media/pdfs/FB/b/br/bro2477.pdf.

people, but it's a beacon of civilization compared to the bordering primordial forest. Each minute heading southeast brings the doctor and his three fellow travelers deeper into shadowed hills and impenetrable thickets. "Sabine is a small county and the lower end of it is sparsely populated," one newspaper describes at the time. "The people of the upper part of it know nothing of the country."[11]

John Wesley Smith, despite being from Hemphill, has a better-than-average knowledge of southern Sabine County. The thirty-nine-year-old is a county native who has served as a doctor here for seven years. Being summoned from his office, or even bedroom, to handle unexpected backwoods emergencies is a fundamental part of the job.

Just such an opportunity presented itself this afternoon in the form of Sabine County judge J. A. Whittlesey, who summoned him for this grim, unexpected ride. Whittlesey's in charge of the impending double-murder inquest since, among his other civic functions, he's the county's de facto coroner. Wisely, since he has no medical training, the judge enlisted Smith to provide his pathological expertise.

Two other men of Hemphill ride with the judge and doctor. Store owner J. O. Toole is a man on the rise, already well-to-do and poised to do better. He operates a shop on the town's courthouse square and has expanded his operation by marrying the daughter of his competition. His father-in-law and now business partner, Hampton Pratt, is also a man of some stature, having served as a colonel with the First Texas Infantry during the Civil War.

Larkin Morris, the final member of what a court will later call "the coroner's party," is a forty-year-old carpenter. He's another Confederate States Army (CSA) veteran, being a former private from Company G of the Twenty-Second South Carolina Infantry.[12] Morris has family in

---

11 *Temple Weekly Times*, April 16, 1887.

12 Sabine County Census, 1880, places him in Hemphill. His grave lists his CSA service, confirmed via National Park Service.

Sabine County, and he heads there to start a postwar life. He and his wife, Mary, married in 1867, have four children left; their daughter Mollie died two years ago, a few days after birthing a daughter who bears her name. Life goes on: Morris's own son Thomas just arrived on November 25. Maybe the new father is happier out here in the somber woods, where at least it's quiet.

The doctor, the carpenter, and the merchant have combined under the judge's fiat to become a coroner's jury. These quasi-judicial bodies preside over an inquest that decides if there's enough evidence to justify a murder charge. Members collect evidence, interview witnesses, and testify to what they find in court.

The first box for a coroner's jury to check, legally, is cause of death. From what they've heard from the search party that reported the grisly discovery, both men have obviously been shot to death. But Whittlesey still wants every step taken to gather evidence and build a case. He knows a talented doctor, like Smith, can infer things about how the killings occurred by examining the wounds.

The coroner's party is on the only trail between the Housen Bayou and Holly Bottom. It winds through the gloomy hills and over murky creeks made quick with the recent rain. Sunlight filters softly between the canopy of longleaf pines and creates odd patterns on the dirt path. There are swine prints along the trail. It's December, and herds of pigs are gathering in the lowlands to feast. Hoofprints of horses, ridden by the pigs' various owners, are stamped into the ground along the path, as well. *With the temperature dropping*, Smith thinks moodily, *it will soon be slaughtering time.*

A gathering of empty horses and solemn men stands along the path. *Guess we're at Holly Bottom*, Smith thinks grimly. Somewhere beyond the search party members are the bodies of twenty-four-year-old William Christopher "Kit" Smith and twenty-two-year-old Eli Low.

The men of Hemphill dismount and offer condolences all around, starting with Eli Low's father, Jack Low. William McDaniel is also understandably distraught—as a youth, Kit Smith lived with his uncle Billy after his mother died, along with his widower father, Irving Smith, and his brother, Joe.

How would Smith feel if it were one of his boys out here, shot down in the woods like a feral hog? The answer is reflected on the shocked and infuriated faces of the members of the search party, all friends and family, gathered around the corpses. Jack Low, William McNaughton, Billy McDaniel, Bob Ener, and Alex McDaniel found the bodies earlier that day after a trail-by-trail search.

Smith already knows who the main suspects are. Like everyone else in the county, he's heard about the animosity between the Conner family and both victims. He also knows of their family connections—in Sabine County, everyone seems related to everyone by blood or marriage.

This includes Dr. Smith. His family tree becomes a bit of a tangle after Smith marries his cousin Caroline in 1866. Caroline (Smith) Smith dies in 1871 at age twenty-eight during the birth of their second son, Cornelius Franklin Smith. The aspiring, bereaved doctor is left with newborn Frank and two-year-old Tom.[13] Smith doggedly pursues medicine and begins practice in Hemphill that same year. His life stabilizes; two years later, he marries Jane Cicero Cogburn, and they produce four children.

He's related to the dead man Kit Smith if you crawl up the family tree far enough to reach the fork between brothers William (Kit's branch) and Obadiah Smith (J. W.'s branch), both early Sabine County pioneers. But he's also obliquely tied to Leander Conner, part of the family under suspicion, who is married to his late wife's cousin Marthy.

The doctor's familial connections are nothing compared to the close ties between the Lows, Smiths, and Conners. For starters, both victims can name a Conner man as a brother-in-law. A bloody feud between

---

13 The birth date of Frank Smith and the death date of his mother—March 25, 1871—are the same, as listed on their headstones. She's buried at the Deas-Mason-Smith Cemetery, and he in Hemphill Cemetery, both in Sabine County.

these clans would literally tear those families apart and take Sabine County with them.

It doesn't take too long for Smith to realize that the situation is worse than he feared, as Jack Low relates fresh, accusatory news. Just days ago, he traded some harsh words with Willis Conner and his son Frederick during an encounter at Six Mile Creek, which runs between their homesteads. The younger Conner, whom everyone calls "Fed," specifically threatened the victims—who weren't even there—after accusing them of pestering the family's hogs. The argument almost escalated into a gunfight, Low says.

Whittlesey reads the mood of the crowd and gets the inquest underway. He wants actual justice to begin before frontier justice can foment. It's time for the doc to get to work examining the bodies. The friends and family back away, unwilling to leave but unable to watch.

The corpses lie ten feet apart. Kit Smith lies on his back, his feet tucked unnaturally beneath him. This is where and how the search party found him. However, they found Eli Low on the side of the trail, partially submerged in rainwater. Jack Low couldn't stand that sight and asked the men to get the body to dry ground. They fished him out and placed him facedown; the doctor will soon see why.

Dr. Smith does a preliminary check of both men's stiff limbs. Considering the evident rigor mortis, they've been here about twenty-four hours, shortly after they were last seen. The December weather has only slowed the microbial decay. Smith is a little further along than his companion, who was in the water, although Low's exposure to the air is already accelerating the process, with results the coroner's jury members can't help but smell.[14]

---

14 Smith's diagnoses and all the pathological details are detailed in court records, *Reports of Cases Argued and Adjudged in the Court of Appeals of Texas*, vol. XVII, 1885. For a trove on waterlogged forensic pathology, see W. Lawler, "Bodies Recovered from Water: A Personal Approach and Consideration of Difficulties," *Journal of Clinical Pathology* 45, no. 8 (1992): 654–659.

The doctor examines Kit Smith first. There's a catastrophic but single head wound in his left temple, seemingly a gunshot. It's enough to kill, but until he sees more of the body, he won't immediately declare it the cause of death. The wound in the man's blood-soaked right side needs to be considered. He begins to strip the body with clinical poise. A sudden flash on the dead man's vest—a blue-and-white piece of homespun patching—catches Smith's eye. If this material is wadding for the handcrafted ammunition used by the killers, it is a piece of evidence left at a scene that has precious little. He hands the cloth to Larkin Morris, who puts it in an envelope.

The stripped corpse reveals a galaxy of shotgun pellet wounds in the side of his right shoulder and, as Smith tips the stiff torso forward, another spread across his back. He digs out a few pellets: all buckshot. These wounds may have killed Kit Smith from blood loss eventually, but the doctor already knows they didn't have the chance. He takes a steel rod and inserts it into the hole in Smith's left temple. A single bullet channel plunges down into his throat, almost reaching his chest. He considers the probe's angle. Someone stood above the prone, wounded man, aimed a gun at his inclined head, and fired straight into it. When Smith digs out the bullet, he confirms that it has come from a rifle.

Dr. Smith walks to the body of Eli Low, his jury companions following, and starts a new examination. He turns the corpse over and winces. One eye is gone, the socket now a gory entry wound. The victim's hands are drawn up near his face, as if reaching out to block the incoming gunshot. In one cold hand, he holds a piece of white patching, which is also preserved as evidence. This, too, could be wadding used in the homemade ball that seemingly killed him. It would be tucked between the casing inside the cartridge to seal the explosive gases in all directions but one, maximizing the projectile's speed.

Now the dreaded part. Smith probes the eye wound's channel with the rod and finds another downward trajectory. Another execution while the man was on the ground.

Low's clothes now removed, the doctor clearly sees a pattern of shotgun wounds in Low's shoulder and, in his back, two smaller shots placed five inches apart. He digs out two pistol balls from the twin holes. Doing a similar excavation shows the shotgun blast is a mixed load of buck and squirrel shot that impacted in the same spread. Given the difference in loadout between victims, it's likely that different men wielded the shotguns.

Morris collects the balls and pellets and seals them in an envelope. He'll pass the envelope to Whittlesey right away, and the next day, Whittlesey hands both patches of wadding over to W. T. Arnold, clerk for the grand jury.

Smith finishes his examination as night falls. As for the cause of death, multiple gunshots are the obvious conclusion. But the narrative told by the bodies is sure to further incite the county: This wasn't much of a fight. Kit Smith and Eli Low were shot in their backs by multiple gunmen using shotguns and a pistol.[15] The unhorsed, wounded men were then finished off with head shots while lying helplessly on the ground.

The inquiry is over, and the findings point to a cold-blooded double murder at Holly Bottom. Dr. Smith can imagine what the friends and family of Smith and Low, some of them milling nearby in frustrated grief, will think of that when they hear it. The only suspects live just three miles away. Now the question cannot be avoided: What is to be done about the Conner family?

---

15 The horses are found the morning after the discovery of the bodies. Low's has shotgun wounds; Smith's is unscathed and wanders back to Kit Smith's field on its own. Details from *Reports of Cases Argued*.

1

RESTLESS BEINGS

FOREVER IN THE SADDLE
May 19, 1886

The trio of Texas Rangers wake in their temporary campsite in the Washita Valley, inside the Indian Territories. They handle this Saturday morning's[1] work the way Rangers always do, with each man responsible for a specific task. One prepares food, the other makes a fire, another tends to the horses.

Being a Ranger means getting used to staples of life on the trail, which are enshrined in the 1874 law that created the Frontier Battalion: bacon, corn, meal, fresh beef, beans, peas, green coffee, potatoes. There's always plenty of salt, pepper, and vinegar.[2] Breakfast is made, served, and eaten within a half hour. The morning fire is then doused and stamped

---

1 Contrary to some published reports, this was a Wednesday, not a Saturday. Data via dateandtime.com at https://www.timeanddate.com/calendar/index.html?year=1886 &country=1.

2 April 10, 1874, "An Act to Provide for the Protection of the Frontier of the State of Texas in 1874," most easily accessed online via Texas Ranger Hall of Fame and Museum, https://www.texasranger.org/texas-ranger-museum/researching-rangers/laws -1874/. This menu is virtually unchanged the next time such a list is enshrined into law in 1901. In the twentieth century, the Rangers start to get pickles.

out. Camp-grimed overalls are replaced by buttoned shirts and vests. Blankets are rolled and stowed in saddles.

The campsite efficiency comes with professionalism, not urgency. Still, their pace is brisk. Sergeant James Brooks, freshly promoted at age thirty, doesn't want to send the wrong message to the two privates. Rangers are *always* expected to ride hard.

Brooks is easy to respect but harder to like. When not obscured by a hat, Brooks's pronounced forehead bulges slightly under his steadily receding hairline. Brooks's mustache forms a tight inverted V under his nose, hiding the corners of his mouth. The facial hair makes his default expression seem like a scowl.

Or maybe that's just because he doesn't talk all that much. A reporter for *Harper's* will one day meet Brooks and offer his idealized impression of the Ranger and his men. "They were somewhat shy with strangers, listening very intently but speaking little, and then in a slow, gentle voice," he writes. "As they spoke so seldom, they seemed to think what they had to say was too valuable to spoil with profanity."[3]

Brooks has a reputation for being tough, but he doesn't project much flash or swagger. He prefers a quiet demeanor coupled with definitive action. Later in life, he'll say, "We only performed our work as best we saw it, and all this 'hell in boots' stuff is tommy-rot."[4]

Each Ranger's waist is ringed with a three-inch-wide leather belt festooned with twin rows of bullets for pistol and rifle, which use the same ammunition. This example in commonality comes courtesy of hard lessons learned by prior Rangers who jammed their rifles with pistol cartridges during gunfights. The "scout belts" are folded so they can hold money and the L-shaped tools used to tighten the screws of their fire-

---

3 Richard Harding Davis, "The West from a Car Window," *Harper's Weekly,* March 5, 1892.

4 "Yes, Captain Brooks Loves Peace," *Corpus Christi Caller-Times,* November 22, 1935.

arms; some Rangers have rusted the screws with salt water to hold them fast against the repeated impacts of long rides on horseback.[5]

The rifles are stowed for the ride but kept within reach. There's a Winchester '73 in Brooks's saddle scabbard. A Colt Frontier Six-Shooter rests easily on his belt.[6] It's holstered high on his right side, a typical strong-side carry. If the target is close enough to grapple, a savvy lawman will fend off any advances with the weak hand and use the dominant, unobstructed one to pull his pistol.

Brooks has young privates Dee Caldwell and Henry Putz with him. There are not many ranks within the Ranger organization, so privates come with a wide range of experience. "The recruit is not subjected to any examination as to his fitness beyond that which the captain of the company may insist upon," observes writer Earl Mayo after visiting the Rangers in 1901. "The membership of this unique organization has consisted always of those restless beings in whom the spirit of adventure is the compelling motive."[7]

These two privates are still early in their service, which is measured in one-year commitments. Captain William Scott only signed Caldwell to Company F in March.[8] Brooks has quiet doubts that he has what it takes to stay a Ranger very long.

Henry Putz is more experienced, having joined the previous

---

5 William Sterling, *Trails and Trials of a Texas Ranger* (Norman: University of Oklahoma Press, 1959).

6 Another name for the Colt Single Action Army, used from 1872 to 1940. "Colt Single Action Army," Texas Ranger Hall of Fame and Museum, https://www.texasranger .org/texas-ranger-museum/museum-collections/firearms/colt-single-action-army/.

7 Earl Mayo, "Texas Rangers: The Most Efficient Police Force in the World," *Frank Leslie's Popular Monthly*, October 1901.

8 "Adjutant General Service Records," Texas State Library and Archives Commission, https://www.tsl.texas.gov/apps/arc/service/. The organization has digitized much of

September, and Brooks has seen him in action during manhunts. The nineteen-year-old Ranger was with him when they got the drop on the remaining pair of the Wade Gang and brought them to a Dallas jail, all without bloodshed.[9] But Putz doesn't fit the picture of a quiet but deadly Ranger. He's quick to open his mouth, and what comes out is often glib, a bad mix for a deliberate, soft-spoken man like Brooks.

As a tenderfoot just the previous year, Putz can sympathize Caldwell's attempts to keep up. "I was not used to the saddle and by the time I had negotiated the thirty-five miles on the back of a mount whose movements suggested nothing of the rocking chair, I was sore head to foot and ready to drop with fatigue," Putz later recalls of his first days with Company F. "Next morning Capt. Will Scott ordered me to return the horse to Sheriff Baylor and gave me a pack mule to take along and ride back. From the back of the horse to the back of the mule was decidedly a change for the worse and when I got back to camp I was more dead than alive. I fell on a blanket, sound asleep, only to be rudely disturbed by Sgt Brooks, who said we were to go on a scout."[10]

That day featured a new recruit's other hurdle: hazing. "We set out at a gallop but had proceeded only a few miles when my right stirrup gave way. Some of the men had cut the laces that fastened the stirrup to the leather as a practical joke. I had no time to stop and repair my saddle but had to gallop on with my leg rubbing against my Winchester at every leap of my horse."

Brooks and Putz, guided by a deputy sheriff, caught two horse

---

its offerings, including Ranger service records of various eras. A searchable database can be accessed at the organization's website.

9 "Ranger Forty Years Ago Had No Easy Life; Henry Putz, Who Enlisted at 18, Tells of Their Exploits," *Dallas Morning News*, October 3, 1926. Putz is likely from Wichita Falls, Texas, and worked at a gunsmith's shop as a teen. See chapter 9 for details.

10 Ibid.

thieves that night. As soon as they returned to camp, more orders came for the pair to track a man running horses across the Rio Grande. "And thus it went," Putz says. "One hard ride after another—forever in the saddle."[11]

The current hard ride in the Washita Valley brings Brooks and his Rangers outside of the borders of Texas. Nine days ago, the sergeant received orders from Captain Scott, who in turn was responding to a direct request from the governor's office. Governor John Ireland, the self-styled foe of all desperadoes, was rankled by yet another report of out-of-state lawbreakers operating in northern Texas. A crew of Anglo cattlemen, including a man named Sam Gopher, came to Texas seeking horses and mules, stiffed a local merchant named O. P. Wood[12] on a deal, and high-tailed it back to the Indian Territories with two unpaid mules in tow.[13]

Word of this reaches Austin and prompts a telegram from the governor's office to Captain Scott, whose Company F is camped in Wilbarger County but deployed to Fort Worth in response to a chaotic railroad strike. Scott literally waves the governor's telegram at Brooks with orders: He's to take two privates, go back to Wilbarger, and then

---

11 Ibid.

12 Probably Oliver Wood of O. P. Wood Banking and Mercantile.

13 Brooks, in memoirs written many years later, says the men took "18 horses and a pair of mules" from the settlers on land owned by Wilbarger County School District. Court records don't contain these details and only identify O. P. Wood as the aggrieved party in the disputed deal. He paints the picture of a hunt for horse thieves, while the records describe more of a sternly enforced settlement of a deal over a mule team gone wrong. Robert Owen also later testifies that the Rangers "were after two mules brought out from Texas" and mentions no horses. Brooks does mention that Scott showed him the governor's telegram. Memoir courtesy of the Armstrong research center at the Texas Ranger Hall of Fame and Museum. It's on display, but a transcript is available at https://www.texasranger.org/wp-content/uploads/2019/08/JA-Brooks-notebook-transcription.pdf.

head north into the Indian Territories. They are to return with either the mules or the money.

The territories are a patchwork of relocated tribes, each managing large swatches of land mostly in what is modern-day Oklahoma. The Cherokee, Choctaw, Chickasaw, Creek, and Seminole formed the official territories, but the U.S. government has deposited scores of others in nearby, adjoining land.

Cattle is a big moneymaker in the Indian Territories, like everywhere else in the West with a patch of land. Mixed families of Anglo and Indian ranchers are taking full advantage of the beef boom. Those traditionalist Native American families who have no interest in ranching can rent their land to cattlemen driving their hungry herds north from Texas to the railroads.

The mortal threat hanging over these operations are shaky lease licenses, which are tangled by unclear federal regulations and legal rulings. There is a steady push to seize the Indian lands outright, and squatters, tacitly encouraged by state politicians in Oklahoma, are setting up illegal settlements. The open range makes this even messier, as massive herds drift from Texas and Oklahoma into the territories to mix and mingle, causing all manner of disputes and confrontations.[14]

Brooks needs a local guide to steer through this terrain, so the Rangers' first stop in Indian Territory was Fort Sill to ask U.S. Indian agent Robert Owen for backup. Lieutenant Thomas Knight, of the United States Indian Police, drew the assignment. He's the fourth man in the Ranger camp that spring morning.

The five-foot, ten-inch, 165-pound Cherokee lawman is the eldest member of the quartet at forty-one, but the seasoned campaigner has no problem keeping up. He was a university student at Baptist Mission School in Cherokee territory before the Civil War, and like the bulk of the Cherokee Nation, he supported the Confederacy. Knight joined

---

14 William Savage Jr., *The Cherokee Strip Live Stock Association* (Norman: University of Oklahoma Press, 1973).

the First Regiment Cherokee Mounted Volunteers at the war's start and served four years, taking part in a handful of set-piece battles and, more commonly, guerrilla tactics aimed at other tribes that supported the Union. Some of their efforts tied up thousands of soldiers, and others led to the slaughter of fellow Native Americans.[15]

The territories bounced back from the Civil War on the back of cattle and mining. Like many veterans, Knight became a small rancher and farmer. In 1870, he married Rachel Sixkiller, the sister of Sam Sixkiller, the well-known captain of the U.S. Indian Police, federal lawmen with jurisdiction across the territories. Knight resisted the pull of law enforcement until 1884, when he moved to the town of Vinita and joined his brother-in-law's ranks.[16]

Armed with Knight's local knowledge, the hunt for Sam Gopher shouldn't be a hard one. The man lives on Red Alexander's farm, the only landmark around. Alexander owns the only store and runs the only post office for miles. People have taken to calling the small, unincorporated town springing up around the store "Alex." It's only fifteen miles from the Rangers' overnight campsite.

The four men mount up. The Indian Territories remind Brooks of an earlier time in Texas cattle history, of the raw and wild edge that is elsewhere being dulled by stock farming and barbed wire. It makes Brooks reflect on his earlier life, of professions and moneymaking schemes attempted and failed, of long rides watching over herds of animals.

He feels an equal lack of regret over all of them because he is right

---

15 In March 1862, the First Regiment Mounted Rifles covered the Confederate retreat after the Battle of Pea Ridge, achieved victory at Newtonia on September 30, and lost the Battle of Fort Wayne in October. Knight's physical stats come from later court records.

16 H. F. Obeirne, *The Indian Territory: Its Chiefs, Legislators and Leading Men* (Saint Louis, MO: C. B. Woodward, 1892).

where he belongs. J. A. Brooks only found a skin that fit when he became a Texas Ranger.

THE KENTUCKIAN
January 1, 1877 (eight years and seven months before Brooks's deployment to the Indian Territories)

James Brooks steps off the Galveston, Harrisburg and San Antonio Railway train at Marion, Texas. From this humble wooden platform, the twenty-one-year-old is ready to take on the whole state.

Brooks has taken the Sunset Route train line as far as it'll go, disembarking at this camp for railroad workers twenty-five miles outside San Antonio proper. The wooden depot just opened for service in spring 1876, with passengers taking hack coaches or their own horses to the town. The Sunset Route is slowly extending passenger service into South Texas and won't reach downtown until February 5, 1877, sparking the boom of "Alamo Town" into a major city.

The allure of endless plains, high adventure, and steep profits stands in sharp contrast to Brooks's youth in Kentucky. It starts well, at least. His father, John Strode Brooks, is a respected doctor who owns a small parcel of land and a few slaves in Bourbon County. He has one younger sister, Lillie, and his mother is healthy, being fifteen years younger than her husband.

But the Brooks family's reality shatters in twin blows when the Civil War breaks out in 1861 and John Strode Brooks dies in 1863. The young boy shoulders a lot of extra weight. "When eight years of age Jim would take old Red and Blue, two oxen, hitched to a sled and haul fodder in over snow-covered fields," a reporter for *The Corpus Christi Times* describes, based on details from an interview with Brooks. "In the spring, when the sap began to flow, he would press old Red and Blue into service again, bringing the valuable yield from the maple trees to his big pans."[17]

The Civil War brings hardship to his literal doorstep. "When the

---

17 "Yes, Captain Brooks Loves Peace," *The Corpus Christi Caller-Times*, November 22, 1935.

Yankees came through our part of Kentucky they killed and ate all of our sheep," he recalls to the newspaper. "But they couldn't eat the wool." The slaves gather the discarded wool, spin it into cloth, and weave some into Brooks's first pair of long pants.[18]

At the war's end, the freed slaves stay on to work the Brookses' small farm. J. A. Brooks grew up outdoors and on horseback, in the land that produced some of the nation's finest riders. A former slave who grew up with Brooks became a famous racehorse rider, according to *The Corpus Christi Times*, but the man's name is not mentioned. The area also produces the nation's best whiskey, and like a good Kentucky boy, Brooks learns its taste at a young age.

Brooks knows that when he turns twenty-one in November 1876, he'll be leaving Kentucky. Like so many, the frontier of Texas draws him in. This is partially by design—the state has proactive offices in the United States and abroad to entice immigrants. It's not a place, it's a buzzword for ambition and adventure.[19]

The young man bids farewell to his mother and sister on Christmas Day and boards a train for Chicago, the easiest route to his ultimate destination. After touring the city, Brooks takes another train, heading south. He watches anxiously as the landscape changes from endless plains to arid desert. He arrives in Marion on New Year's Day.[20]

Texas proves itself thick with opportunity and disappointment. Cow punching makes the most sense as an initial profession. He rides the Chisholm Trail to Kansas, but he finds it both risky and dull. Sickness nearly kills him in Kansas, and he returns to Texas, forever from then

---

18 Ibid.

19 "If you gotta fight Texas, a mother has no chance."—Attributed to Katie Elder, comparing the appeal of the state's wild promise to that of a seductive woman's, in the film *The Sons of Katie Elder* (1965).

20 *Galveston Daily News*, January 2, 1877.

on his adopted home. He tries his hand as a miner, gold speculator, and ranch hand. No luck.

Brooks tries settling down at a homestead. In 1878, he owns acreage on the headwaters of Wilson Creek, valued at $300. His belongings, listed in tax records that year, include one horse, one wagon, forty-nine head of cattle, and four hogs. He also races horses, courts women, and suffers when they choose other men or spurn his advances toward the altar.[21] Brooks's romantic streak, seemingly at odds with his preference for travel and hard drink, endures his entire life. "I don't know which I think is prettier, a fine racehorse or a pretty girl in a hoop skirt dancing the Virginia Reel," he will later remark.[22]

Ranching doesn't take, and neither does family life. Brooks then throws himself back into the frontier, seeking opportunity while on the move. In 1880, for example, he drives a herd of sheep northward through Texas, from the town of San Diego to the city of San Antonio.[23] Across the years, he makes many temporary business partners, some of whom would find fame later in life. His only steady company is alcohol.

The future lawman makes an irresponsible cowboy. C. V. Terrell, a state treasurer and railroad commissioner, tells a rare story about Brooks's early years in a 1948 memoir. Brooks rides into Decatur to purchase supplies and gets into a bottle of moonshine whiskey. When the Decatur marshal begins to arrest him, a grocer known as "Uncle Charley" Cates talks the officer out of it, and Brooks gallops unsteadily out of town. He wakes in the saddle, standing on the property of a bemused settler, his horse slurping from a water barrel. The Hobson family, who lives there, must be a charitable one, because they take him in for breakfast and

21 Paul Spellman, *Captain J. A. Brooks, Texas Ranger* (Denton: University of North Texas Press, 2007).

22 *Corpus Christi Caller-Times*, November 20, 1938.

23 Ibid.

decline his offer to pay for the hospitality. "Not a cent," settler Nemi Hobson tells him. "Just don't drink any more."[24]

By the end of 1882, Brooks is scouring the spreading web of train lines, seeking opportunity in the rowdy boomtowns that spring up along these routes. He aims for the town of Cotulla, and his fateful January 1883 meeting with Lieutenant Charles McKinney. Now he's a private stationed in a wild boomtown.

"Girlie" McKinney, who was in temporary command, soon retires to become sheriff with jurisdiction over Cotulla. Brooks then works for Captains Joe Shely and William Scott. He considers them both influential mentors, men who fill the void left by his late father, but has a closer connection with Scott. "While Lieut. Wm Scott was in charge of the eastern detachment of old Co. 'F' stationed in DeWitt County, Scott encouraged young Ranger Brooks to be a real worthwhile Texas Ranger, under all circumstances," Brooks will say.

As the fence cutting rises to crisis levels in 1883, Brooks is sent on a mission that will directly lead to a new, violent phase of the Texas Rangers' struggle against it.

Late that year, Governor John Ireland's gaze falls on Gonzales County, near his home constituency, where cowboys in Lee County are destroying fences. Scott needs a Ranger to go to Austin and report to Adjutant General Wilburn King, who has the assignment straight from the governor. It's a testament to Scott's trust in Private Brooks that he selects him to go.

Brooks and Lee County deputy sheriff William Scurry head into adjacent Bastrop County to hunt for "nipper" suspects. As usual, the cutters are not exactly shy. They operate with a sense of immunity that comes from community support and toothless criminal charges. The pair of lawmen generate the names of twenty-eight fence cutters.

Faced with the results of this investigation, and hearing equal frustration from Scott in Gonzales County, the governor sees that misdemeanors

24 C. V. Terrell, *The Terrells: Eighty Five Years in Texas from Indians to Atomic Bomb* (Dallas: Wilkinson Printing, 1948).

are not deterring these self-righteous bands. Ireland calls a special session of the legislature to meet on January 8, 1884; fence cutting becomes a felony punishable by one to five years in prison.[25] Cutters who would earlier have surrendered can now be counted on to fight.

Back in Cotulla, the usual mix of thieves, killers, and drunks keeps the Rangers busy. Brooks spends the next two and a half years there with Company F, where he is promoted to corporal and then to second sergeant. Commanders applaud his mix of intimidating calm and deliberativeness. He has plenty of chances to prove himself as the city grows fast and wild. "El Paso, Tombstone, Tascosa and the other widely publicized frontier towns could not equal the deadliness of this cattle center on the Nueces River," says writer W. W. Sterling, Brooks's friend and fellow Ranger. "In most of the rough places, a noted officer could make his play stand up on the strength of his reputation. This was not the case in Cotulla."[26]

The rowdy town hardens Brooks, although he never kills anyone. His reputation as a tough man grows quickly in the Rangers' ranks and on the muddy streets. Rangers love shooting competitions, and Brooks is unnaturally fast. This mystique actually helps keep his pistol in its holster. Sterling writes that Private Brooks's "steely blue eyes, square jaw and panther quick movements were the marks of a good man to let alone . . . After sizing him up, the array of local gunmen decided to take him at his face value. He quickly became a veteran."

Austin politicians are foes the Rangers can't outride or outshoot. Budgetary maneuvering brings unwelcome change to the Rangers as the state legislature's cuts force the Frontier Battalion's reorganization. In

---

25 Ibid. and Wayne Gard, "Fence Cutting," *Handbook of Texas Online,* Texas State Historical Association, https://www.tshaonline.org/handbook/entries/fence-cutting. See also: Gard, "The Fence-Cutters," *Southwestern Historical Quarterly (51),* July, 1947 via https://texashistory.unt.edu/ark:/67531/metapth101119/m1/91/.

26 Sterling, *Trails and Trials.*

October 1885, all companies are slashed by six men each, and Company A is mustered out of the battalion permanently.

The reorg chart becomes a ladder for Brooks, who is promoted to first sergeant that October. Shortly after his promotion, Company F is sent to Wilbarger County, on the Red River border, across from the Chickasaw Nation.

THE DARK-HAIRED COWBOY
May 19, 1886

Alex isn't yet a town. It's a collection of frontier settlements scattered in proximity to the road connecting Chickasha and Erin Springs. In time, these roots will support a thriving population, but for now, the place is a crude, remote outpost in Chickasaw territory.[27]

The area is no Cotulla, but its isolation breeds little respect for the law. Early Alex resident John Looney notes that "difficulties were usually settled out of court, generally with guns."[28]

There's only one draw here: Red's Store, the only trading post in Pickens County. William "Uncle Red" Alexander is a former Confederate soldier who served with the Second Cherokee Regiment under General Stand Watie. He marries Chickasaw Rebecca Colbert and thereby gains the right to own Indian Territory land. She dies, and he remarries New York state native Martha Davies in 1874 and keeps the land rights, and the couple settles down in the Washita Valley in 1878. In 1881, he opens the store.

---

27 The town is officially incorporated in 1910. On November 16, 1907, Oklahoma becomes the forty-sixth state, and the town of Alex in the Pickens District of the Chickasaw Nation, Indian Territory, becomes Alex, Grady County, Oklahoma. "Alexander Credited with Birth of New Town," Alex, Chickasaw Nation, Indian Territory, Oklahoma, http://www.alexoklahoma.net/alexhistory/prestatehood/prestatehood.html.

28 Quote from Sue Moore, *Chickashaw Star-Express*, 2007, in ibid.

Alex should be quiet, but as Brooks and his trio of accompanying riders enter town, they can see handfuls of cowboys milling around the store, dressed ready for the trail. It doesn't take a master sleuth to quickly find out that a driver named Obadiah Love is organizing a roundup about a dozen miles to the north. The store will soon be the focal point for dozens of cowboys provisioning for the job.

Brooks tasks the privates with bringing the horses somewhere out of the way and instructs Caldwell to watch over them. They set off to find a quiet spot under the shade of some trees.

Sam Gopher isn't at Red's Store or farm. "When we got there we made an inquiry of Mr. Gopher," Knight recalls. "A man said he was on a roundup near there. We found one of the mules in a team, we took possession of that."[29]

Now they have one mule but need the other and the man who took them. It should only be a matter of time before he shows up back at Red's. Knight and Brooks sit by the front porch, watching the cowboys and locals mill around. Just before 3:00 p.m., none other than Sam Gopher gallops up to the store. The lawmen show him the order regarding the mules. They won't return to Texas without the animals or the money.

Gopher has his own version of the events in Texas. He says he and O. P. Wood had done hundreds of dollars' worth of business prior but had a falling-out. "I went to him after a load of corn and he said, bill-of-sale me a span of mules and see if you can pay me for it," Gopher says. "Then he brings out the whole claim, the whole account. He had me charged for the whole hundred dollars . . . I thought he was trying to get me a game, I thought I would get him one."[30] So he crossed the Texas border, heading for home, with the mules.

---

29 Trial transcript, Arkansas, Criminal Case Files, 1866–1900, NARA, via Ancestry .com. COVID-19 closed offices, making any documents hard to find. Luckily, Ancestry.com includes this document.

30 Ibid.

It's not uncommon for the Rangers to find disputed stock and either take them or a fair payment, no questions asked. This is what happens here, with Gopher agreeing to give them one mule and pay the balance.

This is his beat, so Knight continues to chat with Gopher as Brooks turns his attention back to Red's Store. He's just in time to see three young cowboys dismounting from their horses in front of the store. One of them is tall, with long, dark hair. Brooks and the dark-haired cowboy exchange looks.[31]

Brooks sees a man six foot five and clearly strong. Stringy black hair falls down his neck, to the top of wide shoulders. He's wearing a blue shirt and a vest. The Ranger reflexively scans the man's weapons—pistol on one hip, knife on the other, and two cartridge belts slung over his shoulder.

For his part, the dark-haired cowboy is staring at alert blue eyes, shadowed by a wide-brimmed, light-colored cowboy hat. The man is wearing a road-weary, conservative, buttoned shirt—and a holstered pistol. Clearly not a cowboy, but no Indian Police agent, either. There is no badge on his breast; Texas Rangers of the era don't wear them.

The two men nod silently at each other as the cowboy steps onto the porch.[32] Then he wordlessly enters Red Alexander's store, his two companions following. The other two men, Brooks sees, are not wearing weapons.

Knight turns to Brooks with news: The dark-haired cowboy is trouble. Just three weeks earlier, Knight had a run-in with him right here in

---

31 Ibid. "Lt. Knight and I mixed with the crowd trying to locate the leader of the thieves," Brooks will later write in his unpublished memoirs, written by hand as an old man. "One of the ranchers thought he had seen one of them, a tall long black haired man." This is not backed up by Knight's later testimony in court or even his own. Brooks does say he and Albert St. John acknowledge each other in passing.

32 Ibid.

Alex, warning him not to carry weapons in town, and it did not go well.
Now he is back, flouting the law.

Openly carrying a weapon is illegal in many parts of the Indian Territories. The patchwork of tribes creates inconsistent laws, however, and here
in Chickasaw territory, it's not illegal to openly carry weapons, as it is in
Cherokee Outlet.[33] But the territories are again in turmoil. Drifting cattle
from Texas and Oklahoma have brought scores of cowboys to chase them
down in roundups. Some have been in the area for weeks, waiting for the
work to begin. A formula for drunken troublemaking, in other words. U.S.
Indian agent Robert Owen in April decreed that the cowboys can't wear
their weapons in town, only on the trail, "because I didn't want any conflict
between the cow men and Indian Police," as he later puts it.[34]

U.S. Indian agents are roundly disrespected. There are not enough
of them around, and their beat is awash with well-armed, transient men,
who, generally speaking, hate Native Americans. There are reports of
outlaws who get into gunfights with state lawmen, only to apologize later
saying they thought the targets were Indian Police. There are no federal
laws protecting the Indian Police agents from violence, despite the pleas
of the commissioner of Indian Affairs to change this.[35]

When Knight last saw the dark-haired cowboy, the man certainly
took the opportunity to put the unarmed Indian Police officer in his
place. The cowboy squared up, towering over Knight in defiance. "If any

---

33 The disparate laws can be found on Library on Congress' collection of "Native
American Constitutions and Legal Materials." Via https://www.loc.gov/collections
/native-american-constitutions-and-legal-materials/?dates=1800/1899. There you can
find: Homer, Davis, *Constitution, and laws of the Chickasaw nation*, The Foley Railway Printing Company, 1899, and *Laws and joint resolutions of the Cherokee Nation*,
Cherokee Nation, 1887.

34 Trial transcript, Arkansas, Criminal Case Files.

35 *Annual Report of the Commissioner of Indian Affairs, for the Year 1886* (Washington,
D.C.: United States Government Printing Office, 1886).

Indian agent wants my pistol," he told him, "by God, he'll have to buy it from me."

Knight backed down, and the defiant cowboy rode away. Now here he was again, wearing that pistol in full defiance of the law.

The Indian Police agent shows Brooks the letter with his orders to disarm cowboys. It mostly pertains to moving intruding cattle from the territories, so the Ranger skips down to the pertinent section toward the bottom: "You will direct all persons not acting officially to lay aside all deadly weapons under penalty of confiscation and, if necessary, arrest and expulsion."[36]

Knight's sure the man didn't see him; he can be surprised in the store where it won't cause as much of a scene. He asks Brooks to back him up as he disarms the man, and, as Brooks says, "I accepted the invitation."

Just then, Putz returns from a quick town scout, looking for Gopher. Brooks quickly fills in the private and orders him to come along. Putz loosens the "retreating strap," a belt loop hooked over the hammer of the pistol on his belt. This keeps a gun in its holster during a ride, but one thing the veteran Rangers drill into recruits is the necessity of removing this before going into a potentially sticky situation. The Ranger nickname for them is a reminder of the Ranger axiom: "If you forgot to loosen them before a fight, you had better retreat."

The older men stride into the store, and Putz follows them inside. So much for a quiet Saturday afternoon.

GRANDSON OF TEXAS
May 19, 1886 (earlier that day)

Albert St. John rides into Alex on Wednesday afternoon with Price Fulton at his side. The pair of cowboys are looking for their boss's horse.

The duo have known each other off and on for two years, coworkers verging on friends. They're both in the immediate employ of trail boss

---

36 Trial transcript, Arkansas, Criminal Case Files. In his unpublished memoirs, Brooks mistakenly recalls that "Lt. Knight took three warrants" for St. John's arrest with them into Red's Store. The trial mentions no warrants.

Obadiah Love, who is organizing a roundup of scattered stock belonging to cattleman B. R. Grimes.

Fulton, from the cow town of Caldwell, Kansas, reunited with St. John last month at a cowboy camp on the Washita River in the Cherokee Strip. They'd both been working in the area for months, albeit for different cattlemen. When Fulton stops working for the Oklahoma Ewing family (who will bring their Dallas-associated name to North Texas in the next decade), he joins the roundup of Grimes's stock.[37]

There, he sees St. John already at work, living in a cowboy camp called Roaring Springs. He recognizes his long, dark hair right away.

Roundups have become annual events during late spring or early summer. It's straight-up open-range work: trekking across miles of terrain, gathering up cattle, and herding them into pens. There they separate the animals by brand and mark any new calves. It takes a lot of hands to get this done—dozens are involved in Love's—and a circuit of sorts has formed across the territories for cowboys to work roundup to roundup.

Albert St. John left his South Texas hometown of Refugio four years ago. The twenty-five-year-old is still finding his way in a land of adventure, ambition, and frontier freedom. St. John may look like just another cowboy, but he is actually one step from Texas royalty. His family's story in Texas mirrors the state's history of settlement and independence.

In 1833, a man named James Power arrives in Tipperary, Ireland, with a bold scheme to colonize a section of northern Mexico. He collects payments to bring 350 people across, most of the families selling their entire belongings for the chance at a new life.

One of them is Edmond St. John, at age forty. His wife, thirty-two-year-old Julia, and their children, William, James, and five-year-old Edward, join their father on an epic trek bedeviled by shipwreck and

---

37 Ibid.

plague.[38] The resilient St. John is granted his land—"Edmondo San Juan received a Mexican land grant of 1 league and 1 labor of land"—and with it a stake in the future of Texas.[39]

As the St. John boys grow, so does the Anglo Texans' drive to declare independence. Edmond St. John gets caught up in the movement. At Nuestra Señora de Loreto Presidio on December 20, 1835, Edmond St. John becomes one of ninety-one signers of the Goliad Declaration of Independence, a revolutionary document declaring Texas a "free, sovereign, and independent State," and pledging the signers "lives, fortunes, and honor" to the cause. It predates Steve Austin's pronouncement at Velasco by two days and the Texas Declaration of Independence by seventy-three.

When Hugh McDonald Fraser, the elected captain of the pro-independence Refugio Militia, asks for volunteers on February 2, 1836, Edmond and sons James and William enlist—Edward (who will one day father a dark-haired son named Albert) is too young at age eight—as do more than thirty other South Texans. Fraser's militia company reports to Colonel James Walker Fannin Jr., a plantation owner and member of a slave-trade syndicate. Fannin's men face the Mexican Army but are captured and executed as prisoners at Goliad, but the three St. John men get lucky. About half of Fraser's militia had been tasked with evacuating civilians or acting as couriers when the fleeing Texans were pinned down by the Mexican Army.[40] The St. Johns are among them, sparing their lives.

Edmond's youngest son, Edward, is left in Refugio for the duration but experiences the turmoil of the revolution's aftermath. After a series

---

38 "Edmond St. John, of Tipperary, Ireland," St. John Genealogy Origin and Ancestry DNA Database & Electronic Archive, https://cpanel.stjohngenealogy.com/getperson.php?personID=I105550566&tree=OSA0001.

39 Land Office, Refugio County Deed Records, vol. 45. One league equals 4,428 acres and one labor equals 177 acres.

40 84 Cong. Reg. (August 1939) (Remarks of Joseph Mansfield of Texas).

of cross-border raids from Mexico, in October 1841, he joins a company of armed minutemen—locals meant to augment a company of Rangers assigned to protect the area. He serves for two weeks, as long a term as any other private in the short-lived militia.

With Texas incorporated into the United States in 1845, the St. John family focuses on the future. Edmond St. John excels to become what one newspaper calls "a prominent public man."[41]

Edward St. John weds Blume Amanda Kokernot in Refugio on September 9, 1857. His son, Albert St. John, is born on May 1, 1861, the same day Robert E. Lee orders Stonewall Jackson to remove the weapons and equipment from the arsenal at Harpers Ferry.[42]

Albert St. John's father's family is well respected, but his mother's side is *rich*. His grandfather is D. L. Kokernot, another wellspring of true blood, Texas respectability, and wealth. David Levi Kokernot emigrated from Amsterdam in late 1805, helping his father as a trader even as he apprenticed to become a ship's pilot. In 1830, the younger Kokernot became a commissioned warrant officer in the U.S. Revenue Cutter Service. His career is best known for wrecking a cutter near the Sabine estuary while hunting smugglers.[43]

In 1832, he takes the gamble and buys property on the San Jacinto River. He opens a floating shop, stocking it with goods he could buy from (and some of them stolen by) contacts in New Orleans.[44] One of his regular customers and friends is Sam Houston. The pair stoke each other's revolutionary fervor, and Kokernot supplies Houston with updates on friend and foe in South Texas.

---

41 "Edmond St. John Buried at Refugio," *Victoria Advocate*, March 28, 1937.

42 *Fort Worth Gazette*, May 28, 1886.

43 Alan Barber, *David Kokernot: Rogue Solider of the Texas Revolution* (Sandpoint, ID: Kullyspel Press, 2012).

44 Ibid.

Kokernot joins Fannin's company, stationed in Gonzales, during the Texas Revolution. He becomes a trusted agent of Houston's, one part scout and one part spy. In April 1836, Houston sends him to warn President David Gouverneur Burnet that the Mexican Army is surging through Texas. At that meeting, Burnet gives him leave to evacuate his family to New Orleans, keeping Kokernot from the loss at Goliad and the victory of San Jacinto. He returns to Texas just after those climactic battles and receives inglorious orders to seize the cattle and horses of those who didn't aid the cause. His neighbors never forgive Kokernot for his zeal in carrying this out—it leads to lawsuits and a charge of larceny, which by-then U.S. senator Sam Houston defends him against.

Despised by his neighbors in South Texas, Kokernot moves to Gonzales County in 1853. The Civil War derails his business plans, as it does everyone else's. The elder Kokernot serves briefly with the CSA home guards, while his son Levi Moses serves in the Eighth Texas Cavalry Regiment, Terry's Rangers. The cattle boom resumes with the war's end, and the Kokernots ride the wave. By the 1880s, the herd sizes have grown bigger than anyone could have imagined.

By the time the tall, dark-haired Albert St. John leaves home, his famous grandfather is one of the richest ranchers in the state. And the empire is still growing as his sons, Levi and John, establish large cattle operations in Gonzales, Pecos, Jeff Davis, and Brewster Counties.

With such an illustrious family, it would have been logical for the young cowboy to have stayed in Refugio or head to the San Antonio area, where his mother's family had the most connections. His brother Edmond, for example, sticks around Refugio to become a stockman-style rancher.

Instead, St. John heads north on his own at age twenty-one, leaving the fences and family behind. (His widowed mother, Blume Amanda St. John, a brother, and a sister live in Refugio, and another sister is married in Victoria.)[45] This is not the first or last case of a young man escaping the shadow of his esteemed, heroic family with bold, independent action.

---

45 Siblings: Ellen, Clara, and Edmond.

St. John rattles around until he finds himself nestled within the turmoil and promise of the Indian Territories. There is still work here for cowboys and the chance for an independent operator to make his own stake. The Indian lands are "the cattleman's last frontier in a fast-changing era that saw the rise and fall of the open-range cattle industry."[46]

Albert St. John seems no less determined to make his own way than was J. A. Brooks as a young man, five years earlier. His family seems to admire young Albert's work ethic and hold out hope he will succeed in the north. "By hard work and close economy he was succeeding very well, and had already accumulated sufficient funds to secure a half interest in a small bunch of cattle," the *Victoria Advocate* states, relaying information from his mother. She identifies his business partner as Albert Weber.[47]

The German-born Weber runs a meat market in Plymouth, Indiana, where he operates as a beef broker. He appears in Indiana newspapers, promising to convince prospective buyers "that he can sell better and cheaper meat than any other man." Another says that "farmers having good cattle to sell can get the highest cash price by calling on Albert Weber." He lives with his three children and wife, Johanna, until January 1884, when the family is rocked by the death of the eldest child, fourteen-year-old Charles. It's the first loss in a life that will be defined by them—burying his wife, losing his business, and spending his final days in an insane asylum.[48] But in 1886, he appears to be a diligent, striving businessman.

---

46 Jimmy Snodgrass, "Cherokee Strip Live Stock Association," *Encyclopedia of Oklahoma History and Culture,* https://www.okhistory.org/publications/enc/entry.php?entry=CH025.

47 *Victoria Advocate,* June 5, 1886.

48 See his ads in *The Weekly Republican,* March 13, 1879, and March 20, 1879. The Plymouth newspaper also bluntly covered his later commitment to an asylum: "Albert Weber Is Insane," *Weekly Republican,* September 21, 1911.

Part of Weber's job is finding good deals on beef, whether in the markets of Chicago or in Kansas at the end of the Chisholm Trail. Cowboys would be needed to scout opportunities in the territories and then gather the animals; Weber and St. John go a step further by pooling resources and splitting the share of a small cattle stock. Everything seems aboveboard.

But there seems to be a darker side to this cowboy's ambitions. There are those in the territories who label St. John, in the words of one Indian Affairs report, "a notorious desperado and reputed cow thief."[49] The ones who made that designation are the board of directors of the Cherokee Strip Live Stock Association.

The association formed in 1883 around an alliance of cattlemen in Kansas who lease acreage from the tribe. The association serves as a guild, regulates roundups, and keeps a record of brands to resolve issues of stray cattle.[50] Unlike other similar associations, the CSLA is also formed to ward off the political influence of a homesteader lobby that is eager for the federal government to open Indian Territories to white settlement. The ranchers therefore defend the integrity of the relocated Indian's new lands, since that protects their own interests.

The association does what it can by designating staff as investigators to wander the territories to identify desperadoes. They give this information to the Indian Police and anyone else who might want it. Albert St. John has found a spot on the list of suspect cowboys, and trail bosses have fired him because of his reputation.

If true, he would certainly not be the only legitimate cowpuncher with one boot in the criminal world. Cowboys can easily convert the skills they learn on the open range to become rustlers. But the opposite

---

49 *Annual Report of the Commissioner of Indian Affairs, for the Year 1886.*

50 The Cherokee Strip is a belt of land sixty miles wide containing more than 6.5 million acres.

is also true; rustlers can easily double as cowboys, and so legitimate work can double as scouting missions for thieves.[51]

Or maybe St. John just wants to raise a little hell. Even his friends admit he's got a combative nature. He's a big man, at six foot five, and broad shouldered. On top of this physical size is a tendency to act tough and run with rough cowboys of a similarly wild mindset. He's quick to threaten violence.

St. John's current employers don't seem to harbor any mistrust. Certainly, Obadiah Love doesn't consult with the Cherokee Strip Live Stock Association when he hires his hands. The trail boss will refer to himself as "a personal friend of Albert St. John." That description comes after the young cowboy makes his own mark on Texas history, just not in any way he would expect—or want.

As the roundup begins, Love asks St. John and Fulton to fetch a horse Love has left in the pasture at Alexander's store. After a morning of "throwing cattle" on Saturday, St. John suggests heading into Alex right away to get it.

Price Fulton knows this could be a bad idea. He reminds St. John that there's a good chance he will run into Indian Police agents there, which could lead to trouble given that he's armed with a rifle and pistol. Less than two weeks ago, St. John sassed an Indian Police officer in Alex who objected to the pistol on his belt.

The others with St. John are not wearing guns—following a recent order to leave weapons out of towns—but the dark-haired cowboy seems determined to carry his. Choices like this are what makes Fulton expect St. John to one day get himself killed.[52]

---

51 Investigators with the Texas and Southwestern Cattle Raisers Association have told the author that this kind of insider casing remains common in the modern era.

52 He will express this to friends later this very day. Trial transcript, Arkansas, Criminal Case Files.

"Let's go to the pasture and see about that horse," Fulton says, trying one last time to steer away from possible trouble.

But St. John wants to go to the heart of the Alex community, such as it is. "Nah," he says. "Let's go to the store."[53]

"THE THING WAS DONE SETTLED"
May 19, 1886

The interior of Red's Store is made smaller by counters, shelves, and display cases. One corner is reserved as a post office; the store has been a mail drop since 1885, and it's the only one between Purcell and Fort Sill. There is a row of barrels containing flour and similar supplies, standing in a line running the length of the store. It's a hospitable place where customers can take a rest, share a cup of hard cider, and swap the latest news.

Brooks takes in the surroundings. There's not a lot of room for tactics. He fixes the target, the dark-haired cowboy with the pistol, sitting with one ass cheek on the counter, feet dangling, speaking to a store clerk named Ridge Whitlock. The dark-haired cowboy is separated from his unarmed companions, who are chatting up other customers.

A pair of customers are standing near the southside counter. Two other customers, Bill Long and Fleming "Clem" Stanford, are jawing sociably near the hard cider barrel, cups in hand, near the post office in the northwest corner.

Knight doesn't delay, which Brooks appreciates. The best way to do these things is quickly and forcefully. The Indian agent stalks up to the tall cowboy, striding through the lane formed by the counter and the barrels, with Brooks and Putz walking on the other side of them. The Rangers are each within five feet of their man when Knight makes his move.

In their previous encounter, when the Indian agent was alone and unarmed, this dark-haired cowboy showed blatant disrespect. Now Knight takes the opportunity to show a little flash when he disarms

---

53 Ibid., according to testimony of Price Fulton during cross-examination.

him. "Young man," he quips, putting a hand on the cowboy's knee. "I'll buy that six-shooter from you now."

The reaction to this challenge is immediate; the man drops a hand to his gun and says, "Let it alone." Knight also reaches for the cowboy's pistol, stopping him from drawing it, the agent's left hand producing his own gun as a struggle begins.

Brooks and Putz see trouble and draw their pistols, done in smooth motions earned from long days of practice and shooting competitions with fellow Rangers. An experienced gunman always cocks the hammer during the draw, so the weapon is ready to fire with a curl of the finger.

"Hold up," Brooks cries to the cowboy. "Hold up!"

The cowboy sees the dark eye of Brooks's gun pointed at him. It's terrifying. He reaches out with his left hand to grab at it or at least slap it away. For some adrenaline-fueled reason, the dark-haired cowboy cries something that sounds like, "Let 'er pop!"

What happens during the next few seconds will be debated for years. There's a series of four rapid gunshots, blasting nearly on top of each other. The small store immediately fills with billowing, acrid black powder smoke.

The tall cowboy staggers on his feet for a few steps, toward the cider barrel, before collapsing onto the floor. He rolls onto his back, gasping and writhing. Blood soaks through his vest, which now has two holes, one over the collarbone and another over the chest. Another stain blooms slowly on his leg.

When the dark-haired cowboy grows still, this chapter of the St. John family's epic saga in America ends abruptly.

The moment of silence in Red's Store after the shootings seems longer than it is. Then the customers clear out. An influx of fresh air from the front door displaces the gun smoke. Ridge Whitlock remains frozen in place. Red Alexander's oldest son, Perry, pokes his wary head from a storeroom, where he was throwing dice instead of minding the place for his father. He can see figures through the haze: the Rangers standing around a body bleeding motionless on the floor.

Knight's holding his still-warm pistol in one hand and the dead cowboy's in the other, having taken it from the man's hand as he stumbled away. "I thought he shot you," Brooks says, glancing at the slain man's six-shooter. "Hey watch out, it's half-cocked."

Knight secures the pistol. "It's a real shame," Knight says, looking down at the corpse. "He's a fine looking fellow."[54] Then he walks from the store.

He has two goals in mind. Knight first asks for someone to fetch a doctor, which he knows is good form but probably futile. But Knight also wants to make sure that none of the cowboy's unarmed friends take the dead man's rifle and use it to get immediate revenge. Witnesses watch as he takes the Winchester from the scabbard on the dead man's horse and goes back inside the store with it.

Love's roundup cowboys Thomas Burke and Henry Witt race from Alexander's house when the gunshots rang out and enter the store after him to see Brooks throwing empty shells from his six-shooter. They identify the dead man and ask if St. John shot his pistol. Brooks says he thought so but asks Knight to show everyone the chambers of the six-shooter in question. It is unfired, and all bullets are accounted for—there are only five, since St. John, like many cowboys, rode with an empty chamber as a safety measure. This is something the Rangers don't do; when they pull, they are always ready to shoot immediately.

Brooks asks if Witt and Burke will tend to the body, and they say they will. The pair create a makeshift litter from some wooden planks and hoist the corpse to a nearby warehouse. Burke can see the blood still seeping through the fabric covering St. John's leg, chest, and collar. They lay him down and place his limp head on a coffee sack.

Witt and Fulton ready themselves to leave, wanting to report the shooting to their boss, Obadiah Love. Before Witt leaves, he offers Knight some advice that almost sounds like a threat. "His crowd is out

---

54 Ibid., various corroborating witness testimony.

there," he tells the Indian agent, gesturing in the general direction of the
Roaring Springs cowboy campsite. "You better get out of here."[35]

Fulton, Witt, and Burke gallop away, ensuring all the cowboys in
the area will hear what happened. Now the Rangers are in a tight situation. Even a cowboy unknown to St. John could be easily incensed by
the news of a fellow hand being gunned down as he loitered inside a
store. It could be any of them next, if a retaliatory message isn't sent to
the intruding lawmen.

Brooks and his two privates are far from home, with only a solitary
Indian agent for backup. It's time to get the hell out of Alex and the
Indian Territories.

Even as he gauges the growing threat to his men, Brooks feels someone at his arm. It's Sam Gopher. "I agreed to pay the mortgages and this
thing occurred before I paid it," Gopher says later. "The thing was done
settled and then after the shooting I gave him a check for the money."[36]

The four lawmen fetch the horses and ride out of town before the
sun sets. The Rangers take a cautious, looping route toward Pauls Valley
and stop for the night, not daring to build a fire. "We camped on a creek
where there were a lot of large trees," Brooks recalls in his unpublished,
handwritten memoirs. "About midnight sixteen armed men crossed the
creek: they were on our trail. We were glad they passed without discov-
ering where we were. The four of us were not anxious for a fight when
there was four to one against us."[37]

55 Ibid., Witt testimony on cross-examination.

56 "Seeing that we wanted him and the mules, or the amount of money for the mort-
gage called for, he forked over the money and we set him free," Putz will later
summarize to *The Dallas Morning News,* a likely reference to the Sam Gopher mule
caper. Maybe not so oddly, given the controversy around it, he doesn't recount the
shooting in that interview.

57 Brooks's handwritten memoirs, courtesy of Texas Ranger Hall of Fame and Museum.

The next morning, the four men arrive at the PO supply store in Pauls Valley. Officials there are sympathetic to the lawmen's plight and help steer them from danger. "The postmaster told his clerk to get his horse and guide us another way back," says Brooks.

They arrive at the I. B. Ranch near Fort Sill and report to Indian agent Owen. Knight, Henry Putz, and Brooks are interviewed for affidavits regarding the shooting, and then the three Rangers shake hands with the Indian Police agent and part ways. "We spent two days at the Suggs Ranch where we learned that those same desperate cowboys had been giving them trouble," Brooks writes in his memoirs. "Two days later we were safe back in Texas." The Rangers' assignment is over, but the specter of St. John still trails them.

Back in Alex, anger is mounting. Trail boss Love arrives in Alex within hours of the shooting but after the Rangers have left. He and his men show up wearing their guns. He's outraged by the death. He makes it a point to be there when the dead cowboy is stripped and pays close attention to the number and location of the wounds.

Love quickly starts a campaign to build the case against Brooks, Putz, and Knight. When he informs the deceased's family what happened in a letter, he makes sure to use language designed to inflame: "Albert was killed at this place yesterday evening—shot four times, two of them mortal. He never spoke. He was murdered in cold blood and it can be proved."[58]

Weber also stirs the pot. According to a newspaper article that ran just after the murder, he also writes the St. John family in Refugio explaining "the particulars of the killing, which he designates as entirely unprovoked, announcing that he intends selling the partnership stock, and after forwarding one half the sum received, will expend the balance in prosecuting the murderers."[59]

By May 26, two days after Brooks returns to Texas, Love writes a

---

58 Included in the trial records, Western Arkansas District, 1887, Fort Worth.

59 *Victoria Advocate*, June 5, 1886.

letter addressed to Montgomery Sandels, the district attorney for the federal court at Fort Smith, Arkansas. It's direct and without prose: "Albert St. John was murdered at Alex on the 19th of this month by T. R. Knight, J. A. Brooks and two unknown men. The murder was cold blooded as the eye-witnesses below will attest." At the bottom are signatures from Stanford, Burke, Long, and Fulton.[60]

Five days later, a federal court files the charges. They allege the Rangers "feloniously, willfully, premeditatedly and of their malice aforethought killed and murdered Albert St. John." This wayward, blue-blood grandson of Texas is not going to the grave without a final fight.

INVERTED ICONS
June 4, 2020

Seven faceless men gather around the metal statue standing in the main terminal at Dallas Love Field Airport. This is the age of OSHA, so they are all wearing eye protection and yellow hard hats. It's also the age of the COVID-19 virus, so all are wearing masks.

The statue towers above them, a lean man in a wide-brimmed cowboy hat. There's a pistol on his belt, and one hand seems to linger over it with a dangerous promise. The other hand is held out, palm down, as if soothing a rowdy crowd. The pedestal says, "One Riot. One Ranger."

The seven men loop straps around the statue's shoulders and hoist the figure from the anchors holding it to the pedestal. The hovering Texas Ranger sways slightly as the workers position a four-wheeled trolly below. It takes some manhandling to set the statue down, faceup, and secure it with a strap across the sternum. Then they wheel it away.

The expressions on the faces of bystanders are inscrutable, hidden by surgical masks. If they reflect divided public sentiment, some see this as another knee-jerk effort to get on the racial sensitivity bandwagon, while others see it as a long-overdue reckoning with the Texas Rangers' checkered history.

The statue is being removed in the aftermath of the death of a man

---

60 "Love to Sandels, May 26, 1886," trial records, Western Arkansas District.

named George Floyd, arrested for passing a bad check, who pled for medical assistance as a police officer knelt on his neck for more than eight minutes. The wave of protests that follow is fierce, and the reaction in the United States proves significant. Police reform efforts, including defunding, gains serious traction. Uniformed leadership quit command positions in protest. Mainstream companies hire media firms to create Black Lives Matter ad campaigns. Law-and-order voters display American flags with a blue stripe to support cops. The BLM initials appear on Major League Baseball mounds and city-sanctioned murals.

And statues fall.

Typically, those eyed for removal are Confederate heroes, making the airport statue of a Texas Ranger an outlier. The toppled Texas Ranger statue lying on the dolly is modeled after Captain Jay Banks, who served in the Rangers in the 1950s. The pedestal doesn't say his name, just the famed slogan "One Riot, One Ranger," which has nothing to do with him.[61] Still, Banks's likeness is deemed unwelcome due to his staunch refusal to help racially integrate schools after the landmark *Brown v. Board of Education* ruling.

One could argue that the statue represents more than just Banks, but that position doesn't spare it from removal since the national conversation in 2020 is focused on historic Texas Ranger atrocities. Doug Swanson's book *Cult of Glory: The Bold and Brutal History of the Texas Rangers* is released that year, during the initial surge of the Black Lives Matter movement. The newly published book, and an excerpt in *D* magazine,

---

61 "The often cited 'One Riot, One Ranger' appears to be based on several statements attributed to Capt. Bill McDonald (another of the four 'great ranger captains') by Albert Bigelow Paine in his *Captain Bill McDonald Texas Ranger*. Now there was a Ranger who could bluster a mob into submission—or a nervous politician. When sent to Dallas to prevent a prizefight, the mayor met McDonald at the train station with a panicked, 'Where are the others?' McDonald supposedly replied, 'Hell, ain't I enough?'" Mike Cox, "A Brief History of the Texas Rangers," Texas Ranger Hall of Fame and Museum, https://www.texasranger.org/texas-ranger-museum/history/brief-history/.

places Banks's bigotry as just one incident in a long line of earlier Texas Ranger misdeeds.

The worst atrocities were aimed at Mexicans in the 1910s, when the quickly augmented Rangers were acting as paramilitaries. "They burned peasant villages and slaughtered innocents," Swanson writes of the so-called Special Ranger force of the time. "They committed war crimes. Their murders of Mexicans and Mexican Americans made them as feared on the border as the Ku Klux Klan in the South."[62] This rough hyperbole is backed by solid documentation, especially state representative José Canales's 1918 investigation that exposed thousands of deaths and prompted a major overhaul of the Texas Rangers that steered the organization back into professional law enforcement work.

For all the twenty-first century's new appraisal of the Rangers' worst moments, there has been less attention paid to their actual crime fighting.[63] J. A. Brooks and Company F are mercifully spared from the worst of the Rangers' history, having come in too late for Indian fighting and too early for the Mexican Revolution. You won't even find J. A. Brooks, John Rogers, William Scott, or most of the other central figures of this book in the index of *Cult of Glory*.

Similarly, even the Texas Rangers' Wikipedia page skips from 1877 to 1910, basically from atrocity to atrocity, and glosses over a prime era of Texas Ranger outlaw hunting. Everyone seems to acknowledge the effectiveness of their abilities as lawmen, taking it as a given and moving on to more divisive discussions.

It's a strange common ground. Supporters use the Rangers' long legacy of battling criminals as a hedge against sporadic examples of brutality. This is a version of the "bad apples" argument, saying the overall history of the Texas Rangers is positive enough to not taint the entire

---

62 Doug Swanson, *Cult of Glory* (New York: Viking, 2020).

63 The exception that proves the rule is the mythologized hunt for Bonnie Parker and Clyde Barrow.

bushel. Detractors, by ignoring this crime-fighting era, also give the Rangers the benefit of the doubt, as if to say that the good efforts to arrest cattle rustlers and bank robbers are a given, but do not excuse them for their extremes in the early 1900s and intolerance of the 1950s.

Between these two arguments—and the desire to make them heroes or villains—there hasn't been much unbiased analysis of the Rangers' actual law enforcement work during the late 1800s. It's a particularly vital period, since they are acting for the first time as a permanent organization—and one under a law enforcement mandate rather than serving primarily as a home guard.

In the late 1800s, the Frontier Battalion is writing their own rule-book on how to stamp the state's influence on a changing, tumultuous landscape. Two of the men of Company F will become "legendary Texas Rangers Captains," celebrated as the most influential in the organization's history. Between 1886 and 1888, these future influential men are in the early, formative phases of their careers.

Mexican revolutionaries and Indian war bands are not the challenges in 1886 and 1887. On top of a never-ending rogue's gallery of bank robbers and stage-coach heisters, Company F's foes are radical fence cutters supported by local police, feuding families defending their turf, and cowboys who, but for a few choices, could have been J. A. Brooks.

In 1886, the proper role of the Texas Ranger is being messily crafted in the freshly tamed parts of Texas. However, race is not the predominant dividing line. One Company F member, John Rogers, tellingly remarks to a reporter that the most "desperate" people he encounters during manhunts are Caucasians. "They make the best citizens and most dangerous criminals of them all," he puts it.[64]

Indeed, Rangers of this era are not shy about gunning down people—like St. John—who look like themselves. Everyone Company F kills between 1886 and 1888 is white, and the backlash against their actions correspondingly comes from sections of the Anglo establishment.

---

64 "The Man Who Knows No Fear Leaves the Rangers," *El Paso Herald,* February 4, 1911.

Company F hunts criminals within familiar cowboy and ranching communities, enabling undercover operations and running informants. Being subjected to that sort of detective work leads locals, including police and district attorneys, to cry foul.

The status of the Texas Ranger as the "determined outsider" will one day be instrumental in cleaning up crooked oil towns and taking down public officials turned criminal, but in the late 1800s, the concept is new. The reactions and recollections of residents on the receiving end of their justice present alternative views that often paint the lawmen as interlopers. Hard lessons are about to be learned about the limits of the Rangers' methods, both in terms of their efficacy and political liability.

The legal aftermath caused by the shooting of Albert St. John may feel familiar to a twenty-first-century reader. The story's arc fits a familiar pattern of split-second decision-making followed by years of disagreement in the courts over what happened. Brooks, Putz, and Knight are not the last officers of the law to find themselves on the defendant's side of the courtroom after a shooting they felt was justified. Nor will this be the only fatal incident to be used as a political football, as this case is destined to become.

This era can't be understood just by erecting or dismantling a piece of public art. There is social currency in identifying heroes and villains, but history is not made by statues. The unvarnished, balanced truth of Company F's violent years of 1886 and 1887 is not a tale about icons of either oppression or justice. It's a story of people—brave, dangerous, unyielding, duplicitous people—making fateful choices that end in collisions of gunfire and blood.

In a secluded county in deep East Texas, a series of decisions like that are being made that will alter the fates of the men of Company F forever.

2

HOMEGROWN OUTLAWS

THIS WHOLE CONNER TROUBLE
February 8, 1886

James Irvine Perkins composes his thoughts in his office in downtown Hemphill, steadying himself for the step he's about to take. The thirty-nine-year-old district judge doesn't want to write this letter, but the situation in Sabine County, located on the Louisiana border 140 miles northeast of Houston, has gotten so out of hand that he needs Governor John Ireland to fix it.

This is a harsh personal admission for him as a local, born in neighboring San Augustine County, as well as an unwelcome political one. Representative John Reagan next year may run for U.S. Senate, vacating his seat in Texas's Second District. One newspaper will note that "it's an open secret" that Perkins has his eye on the office in Austin.[1]

But the judge is desperate for help. A family feud, ignited by the double murder of Christopher "Kit" Smith and Eli Low in 1883, is disrupting the population. The Conner family have gone outlaw after breaking out of jail and vanishing into the local piney woods and swamps.

There are parts of the county that are still wild, even to most locals, and that's just where the Conners reign. "The streams breaking into the

---

1 "For Reagan's Vacant Seat," *Galveston Daily News*, February 3, 1887.

Sabine bottom make it hilly, and thickets almost impenetrable run in the hills and bottoms crosswise," one local newspaper describes. "And these Conners know every stock trail for 20 miles below them."[2]

Willis Conner and his six sons have evaded capture for eleven humiliating months. Their continued freedom has roiled the county and attracted statewide media attention. Judge Perkins is the foremost vestige of law and order in Sabine County, a place that is being shaken by a flagrant disregard for it.

The jurist isn't a man who is easily rattled. At age seventeen, Perkins enlists in Colonel Walter Lane's regiment and as a private fights to repel the Union's abortive Red River campaign, that epic combined gunboat-infantry incursion through Louisiana and toward Texas.[3] Perkins also sees the Confederacy fail firsthand at the battles of Mansfield, Pleasant Hill, and Yellow Bayou.

While on the road to a new command, he hears of the Confederate surrender at Appomattox, and Perkins immediately returns home to Texas. Farming doesn't work out, and two years later, he heads to law school. He spends a busy 1870 at the University of Virginia getting a degree and is examined by O. M. Roberts, the future Texas governor. Then it's back to his native East Texas to hang a sign and build a future.

In 1873, a high-profile case makes his name and changes his fortunes. Perkins, who grew up on his family's slave plantation, defends five Black men accused of murdering a prominent white man. His colleagues advise against it, but Perkins doesn't back away. Four of his clients are acquitted; one admits to the crime and is hanged. Perkins's stature rises, as do his fees and allure as a prospective groom. He marries Myrta Blake, daughter of Nacogdoches judge Bennett Blake, on March 21, 1876.

Three years later, he's appointed district attorney for the Third

---

2 *Temple Weekly Times*, April 16, 1887.

3 Cherokee County Historical Society, *Cherokee County History* (Denton: University of North Texas Libraries, 2001).

District, and in 1884, Governor Ireland appoints him as its judge. He's elected to the office later in 1884 . . . just in time to preside over the double-murder case, *State of Texas v. Willis Conner, John Conner, Charles Conner, Fed Conner and William Conner*. Now it's nearly 1886, and the aftermath of the murders are still upending the county.

The Conners have offered their conditional surrender directly to the judge, in a letter written by lawyer, former newspaperman, aspiring doctor, and fellow outlaw L. L. Loggins. The wanted men are willing to come in from the wilderness "on certain conditions he [Perkins] would have this whole Conner trouble settled in court and in a civilized way."[4]

That Loggins is their emissary is in itself an insult. The judge has nothing but distaste for the man, who is on the lam after being indicted for forgery, jailbreak, and murder. Loggins also has humiliated Perkins personally with taunts in the local newspapers.

Perkins doesn't respond to Loggins's offer. The Conners have gone too far to negotiate. The local police can't tame them, local family and friends still support them with impunity, and the sporadic deployments of one or two Texas Rangers have foundered in the brush. But the judge won't capitulate, not when he has another card to play.

He has heard the family is unhappy with their former defense attorneys, W. W. Weatherred and James Polley. Someone even snuck into Weatherred's home and left the imprint of a pistol on his pillow. That, Perkins knows, is a mistake. It's not a good idea to threaten a former state senator who counts as his friend the state's adjutant general.

Perkins writes to Governor Ireland that Weatherred is coming and that he supports the demand for action. With the former state senator pushing in Austin, the judge expects a whole company of Texas Rangers to come to Sabine County.

---

4 Henry Fuller, *A Texas Sheriff: A. J. Spradley* (Whitefish, MT: Literary Licensing LLC, 2011); originally published in 1931 by Baker Printing Co., Nacogdoches, TX. This biography is really a collection of newspaper clips and autobiographical material collected and coauthored by Fuller, Spradley's friend.

"UNDISPUTED CONTROL OF THE RANGE"

July 15, 1878 (five years before the killings of Kit Smith and Eli Low)

Willis Conner stands in the East Texas piney woods, head cocked to one side. He's using more than his eyes to scan his surroundings. The trees are alive with crazed barks and howls of his dogs, sweeping from his left to his right. Willis Conner has loosed four mixed-breed Texas bulldogs into the woods where the wolves have been spotted, prowling near the family's herds of pigs. They even now are driving the prey his way, and he needs to choose the ideal place to intercept it, using the topography to predict the creature's likely route.

Conner knows it's a wolf by the way his animals are reacting. None of these hunting dogs would dare make such a fuss over a racoon. His dogs are specialists trained "for each branch of business—some for cattle, some for hogs, some for deer, some for varmints, etc.," describes one local newspaper. "Each set of dogs understand fully their business, and they claimed and owned for many years undisputed control of the range."[5]

The same accolade can be said of Willis Conner at age fifty-six.[6] After a lifetime of striving to find a home, he's found one in this remote section of East Texas. It's a place many settlers travel through but very few decide to stay.

The El Camino Real de los Tejas, an old Spanish road, remains a major route for settlers crossing into Texas from Louisiana well into the 1800s. The road enters Texas in Sabine County and extends south-west to San Antonio and over the decades brings streams of new Texans into the interior, where there are good opportunities for farming, cattle, and mining. Getting to this promised land of open plains and mineral-rich mountains means traversing an ocean of thickly forested hills and swamplands collectively known as the Big Thicket. It's the kind of

---

5 "East Texas Outlaws," *Galveston Daily News*, April 7, 1887.

6 Willis Conner, born March 15, 1822.

untamable wilderness that fills the 1800s mindset with an almost super-stitious dread and hostility.

Willis Conner is not from the Big Thicket, but it suits him. It re-minds him of Tattnall County, in southeast Georgia, where he was born and raised. Only a hardy stock dares settle in Sabine County. Those who do are mostly from the southeastern states and bring a deep-seated, frontier culture with them. That's shorthand for small farms, subsistence hunting, and belief in common land use. "Free range meant a great deal more than the simple right to range one's stock on others' land," writes East Texas researcher Thad Sitton. "People fenced out woods from their cotton, cane and corn fields, but outside the fences the hogs and cattle from many families mixed and merged on the open range . . . A perim-eter fence around one's property was an un-neighborly act."[7]

Since his arrival in 1859, Willis Conner mastered life and death among these towering trees and deep-set bogs. But lifestyle and time are both taking their toll on his body. His black hair is starting to go gray, with his facial whiskers leading that particular charge. He sports a full beard but cuts it short on the sides. A *Galveston Daily News* article says he "talks fast, [is] quick in his movements, about 5 foot 10 inches high, weight about 160 pounds, wears no. 9 shoes, has blue eyes and wears spectacles generally, and two fingers off on one hand, think it is the left."[8] It won't be long until his hair color and grizzly reputation earn him the persistent nickname "Old Man Conner" among Sabine County residents.

The bays and barks of the dogs move left to right, typical of a wolf hunt since the animals tend to run in several-mile circles when steadily pursued. The chase, seen from above, would appear as a tightening spiral. Willis Conner is right where his auditory senses tell him the wolf will pass—through a dry creek bed with sloped sides.

---

7 Thad Sitton, *Big Thicket People: Larry Jene Fisher's Photographs of the Last Southern Frontier* (Austin: University of Texas Press, 2009).

8 "All at Large," *Galveston Daily News,* September 11, 1885.

Even though he expects it, part of Willis Conner is still surprised when the smear of silvery-red fur speeds into view. Hesitation lasts a mere moment before he readjusts his aim to compensate for the animal's movement and empties one barrel. The wolf stumbles as if pushed by an invisible force, flips over once, and then collapses in a heap.[9]

The gun smoke hangs heavily in the air as Willis Conner walks to the corpse. The tight cluster of shot took the animal through the shoulder and neck, a much preferable way to die than being torn apart by dogs.

He has a horn he can blow to call the dogs—a command that supersedes all ongoing chases or fights—but they appear on their own, panting with exertion and shuddering with excitement. Human figures carrying shotguns also appear to his left and right, responding to the gunshots. These are Willis Conner's sons, regrouping from their own selected wolf ambush sites. Their chagrined looks say it all. Naturally, the old man figured out the best one and claimed the kill.

Like any litter of pups from the same mother, all his kids have different markings. The oldest is Frederick, or Fed, at age thirty. He's solidly built at five foot seven but seems shorter because of his stooped shoulders. His eyes are a cool bluish gray, and a sharp Roman nose rises above his short but thick beard. Willis's eldest has a chronic cough that usually only manifests when he speaks.[10]

Charles Conner, the second son, is twenty-eight years old. He's got dark hair but fair skin, and stands six feet even at 160 pounds. He's considered the least intelligent of them; his own father sometimes

---

9 This hunt is based on methods used by wolfers, including a description of a wolf hunt by Theodore Roosevelt, "Hunting the Grisly and Other Sketches," Full Text Archive, https://www.fulltextarchive.com/page/Hunting-the-Grisly-and-Other-Sketches3 /#p34, and one from the 1960s by Jack Olsen, "Sounds and Hounds of a Texas Wolf Hunt," *Sports Illustrated,* September 14, 1964. The 1960s article calls the rather barbaric hunt "a living fragment of a wild past."

10 "All at Large," *Galveston Daily News.*

refers to him as an "idiot."[11] Leander, twenty-six, is still tall but just a hair shorter, and has black hair and a sallow complexion. There are a pair of scars etched into his chin. And twenty-four-year-old Alfred, called "Alfie" or "Bubba," is shorter still, a five-foot, ten-inch Conner man with dark hair, gray eyes, and a facial scar, this one gouged into his upper lip.[12]

The younger sons, the unmarried ones, appear last. William Conner is twenty-two, with distinctive auburn hair, mustache, and whiskers, all of which he reflexively twirls with a finger while he talks. When he speaks, he speaks slowly, but he's got the height and hotheaded temper of Fed and his father. His most unfortunate feature are his eyes, which not only bulge from his face like a frog's, but one is slightly larger than the other.

John Conner, twenty, is the shy one. Part of it might be his weight, being the same height but heavier than his brothers. He's got the auburn hair gene, and his hair is as light as his father's is dark. A newspaper will remark that he "has a bashful look and is timid in conversation; has a pleasant countenance and very fair complexion."[13]

The Conner boys are beaming with satisfaction; this is the third wolf they've taken down today, as well as many other targets of opportunity. This banner day of hunting even makes the local newspapers: "Willis Conner and his sons, last week in one day, killed ten deer, three wolves, three opossums and one rattlesnake."[14]

The hunters head for their respective houses, a cluster of separate

---

11 Mark Dugan, *Judge Not* (unpublished, 1982); Willis Conner to friend and neighbor Bob Ener, according to Ener's son.

12 Rusk Prison Records, *Convict and Conduct Registers, 1875–1945*, Texas State Archives, Austin, TX.

13 "All at Large," *Galveston Daily News*.

14 This item from *Saxon* ran in *The Galveston Daily News* on July 20, 1878.

log cabin homesteads. They are a successful, stubbornly independent family. The secluded, sparsely populated confines of East Texas appeal to their independent spirit. But the path from Georgia to Texas has been a rocky one.

Willis and his wife, Piercy Douglas, have three children—Frederick Monroe Conner, born 1846, Charles Wilson Conner, born 1849, and Leander Jackson Conner, born 1850—when the Conner family leaves Georgia for Florida. Oral tradition in Sabine County holds the move is prompted by a business dispute. It's true that the Conner family, in the form of Willis's uncle Wilson, had been implicated in the illegal import of slaves, with three forcibly seized by authorities in 1818.[15] But the reasons for the exodus from Georgia, decades later, remain obscure.

But when the Conners leave, the whole family goes, father William and mother Nancy included. Census records show Willis adding to the Conner family in the wilderness town of Alligator, Florida: Alfred Horton is born there in 1852, William Conner in 1854, and Catherine Conner arrives in 1857.

As Willis Conner's family grows and he puts down roots, Florida is inflamed by conflict. There have already been decades of fighting with Seminole Indians over the land, and violence again flares in 1855. Dubbed the Third Seminole War, the conflict motivates Willis Conner to travel one hundred miles from his swampland home to enlist. In March 1857, Willis Conner's name appears on the roster of Bullock's Company of the Florida Mounted Volunteers.

The role of volunteers during the Third Seminole War is certainly a mixed bag. One lieutenant said the volunteers "usually had well selected officers, but the majority of the companies were made up of the rough-

---

15 "Governor's Proclamation," May 14, 1818, Georgia Department of Archives and History, Atlanta, GA.

est element. Very often they would include in their attacks Indian men, women and children and take very few prisoners."[16]

Captain Robert Bullock is stationed at Fort Gatlin, near modern Orlando, far away from the fighting. The men of the Florida Mounted Volunteers are drawing full pay for doing nothing. Bullock, Willis Conner's commander, wants to keep it that way. He earns scorn from First Lieutenant A. L. Magilton, the regular army officer in charge there, who complains to his commanding officer: "Your order requiring the company to move . . . has been received and given him; since which time he had received other orders which he thinks excuses him from complying with the first order. I informed him of the contrary." This is not a bureaucratic mix-up but craven foot-dragging. "Were it not that it might look that I took delight in ferreting out things outrageous," he writes, "I could perhaps tell a tale."[17] The unit will go on to make several scouts but sees no action.

On June 1, Willis Conner has a fateful conversation with William Dees in Providence, a tiny town between Tampa and Orlando. *The Florida Peninsular*, a Tampa newspaper, provides details of what happens next:

> A young man by the name of William Dees was killed last week, near Providence in this county, in an affray with one Willis Conner. There had been some previous difficulty between the

16 Oliver Howard, "Autobiography of Oliver Otis Howard," in *History of the Third Seminole War*, ed. Joe Knetsch, John Missall, and Mary Lou Missall (Philadelphia: Casemate Publishers, 2018).

17 "A.L. Magilton to F.N. Page," April 22, 1857, USACC HQFLS, M-1084, Roll 8, in *History of the Third Seminole War*, ed. Knetsch, Missall, and Missall. As a colonel, Magilton assumed command of an entire brigade at the battle of Antietam. He resigned from service shortly after Fredericksburg and taught infantry tactics at the Philadelphia Free Military School for officers of Colored Troops. He lived in Philadelphia and was deputy collector of U.S. revenue until his death from liver disease at age forty-nine; "Albert Lewis Magilton," Antietam on the Web, http://antietam.aotw.org/officers.php?officer_id=899.

two, and on the eve of that day of young Dees' death, Conner
went to the young man's home and called him out: and after a
half an hour's conversation they got into a fight. There was no
deadly weapon used but Dees was killed by strangulation and
one or two severe kicks given him in his side as Conner was
being pulled off. The young man lived until carried into the
house, when after one or two struggles for breath he expired.
Some three or four others have been included in the verdict of
the Coroner's Jury as accomplices, which verdict was for willful
murder. Conner, the principal, has not yet been taken.[18]

The crime doesn't seem to interrupt his military career—Willis
Conner's name continues to appear on Bullock's roster of men, and he
even reenlists for a second term of service in September. He receives a
furlough to visit home before that service starts but never returns and is
eventually charged with desertion.[19]

His visit home becomes an escape. As he learns that authorities are
looking for him, Willis uproots the entire family. In October, the Conners flee Florida for Texas. They are several steps ahead of the law: Governor Madison Perry only puts a one-hundred-dollar bounty on Willis
Conner's head in February 1858. The bounty includes a description: "Said
Conner is about five foot six or seven inches high, dark complexion,
rather quick spoken, a finger on his right hand shot off, about 34 or 35
years of age."[20]

---

18 "A Man Killed," *The Florida Peninsular,* June 6, 1857. Many researchers put this incident later in the year, but this article shows a more complicated time line.

19 Dugan, *Judge Not,* citing service records provided by Conner family descendants.

20 Madison Perry, "$100 Reward," February 9, 1858. It ran in *The Florida Peninsular* on
February 27, 1858, and identifies the victim as "William Deas."

An article in *The Galveston Daily News*, which runs after the Conners go outlaw, indicates that the locals in Texas know of Willis Conner's violent past: "Old Willis Conner killed a man in Georgia and fled, and settled down in that country [Sabine County] on account of its obscurity and remoteness from civilization."[21]

The Big Thicket is certainly a great place to hide, but Willis Conner also chooses to move here because he has family nearby. His distant cousin Lewis Conner has moved from Columbia County, Florida, to Newton County, a neighboring county to the south of Sabine, just a few years prior to Willis's fatal fight.

It takes a special personality to see the opportunity in deep East Texas. Swampy Sabine County isn't a popular place to create a future. There are 2,498 residents there in 1850, 942 of them slaves; in 1860, the total population will be just 2,750 people.

The Conners settle down in the northern end of the county, alongside a bewilderingly winding waterway called Bull Bay Creek. It looks and feels like Georgia, with the familiar knolls, hollows, and pines. He and his sons know how to wrest money and sustenance from this land, and that's all it takes to claim it as their own.

"Very few of the descendants of the old settlers own any land," notes John Caplen, from Georgia, describing the attitude he found across the Big Thicket during a trip in the late 1880s. "The people have been in the habit of using every man's land for their own for so many years that they have come to believe the land has no owners."[22]

Willis Conner does pay taxes, however, and the rolls in 1858 show he has no property except for the two slaves he brought with him, both of

---

21 "East Texas Outlaws," *Galveston Daily News*.

22 Quoted in Sitton, *Big Thicket People*.

whom he sells by the next year. Just three years later, he owns 350 acres of land and 350 head of cattle.[23]

The Conner family may be new to the area, but they don't take long to become embroiled in the hot-button issue of Sabine County, the location of the county seat. Sabine is an original Texas county, one of the first to form during the revolution. Since this glory-soaked inception, the county seat has been the town of Milam, in the north. This is eleven miles away from Willis Conner's homestead—a perfect distance that preserves his privacy but also enables him to sell hogs, resupply what he can't make, and file official useful paperwork, like pig ear notch registration.

But starting as early as 1850, families in southern Sabine have been petitioning for a centrally located county seat. These families included the Lows and Smiths, prosperous clans with roots in the southern Sabine County since the early 1800s.

The fight comes down to math. The argument for a new seat holds that Milam is more than five miles from the geographic crossroads of the county, and a new town should be formed closer to the county's mathematically derived center. Willis Conner's name appears on petitions to keep the seat in Milam. It is the first time he and the Smith family are on opposing sides, and it happens nearly immediately on the Conners' arrival in Texas.[24]

In August 1858, an election is held, and 160 out of 260 votes are cast in favor of relocation. However, without an official survey proving Milam's actual distance, the results are thrown out. A new survey is performed that finds Milam is six and three-quarter miles from the center

---

23 Sabine County Tax records. The family may also own pigs, which didn't yet have to be registered. Author Mark Dugan helpfully found, consolidated, and listed the family's tax records in *Judge Not*.

24 Weldon McDaniel has traced the Conners' movements in the county and documented the Milam-Hemphill political battle. He feels that the bad blood between families started there.

of the county, and so a new election is scheduled. On November 11, 1858, a majority of Sabine residents again vote for relocation.

The acting Sabine County Court—which includes J. A. Whittlesey and John H. Smith (of the Fairmount Smiths, so a forebear of Kit Smith)—before year's end decree a new town be created to be the county seat, located at the center of the county. They name the new town Hemphill, in honor of the sitting United States senator John Hemphill. Hemphill was elected senator in 1858 to replace his friend Sam Houston, who left office maintaining Texas didn't have the right to secede.

This is definitely not Hemphill's position, who is elected to rebel. He is one of fourteen senators who, on January 6, 1861, recommend the immediate withdrawal of the Southern states. On February 4, 1861, the Secession Convention elects him one of seven Texas delegates to the convention of Southern states. This leads to his expulsion from the U.S. Senate.[25]

John Conner is born in 1861, just before the Civil War breaks out. Texas is not really a contested state as a whole, but a lot of what action the state sees happens in East Texas. The Union invades Galveston but loses control of the city in January 1863. Later that year, in September, the Union army invades the mouth of the Sabine River at the Texas-Louisiana border. Local, overwhelmed Confederates wage an epic defense and drive back the Union troops. Galveston remains the only sizable port to remain in Southern hands at the war's end.

The war effort literally passes through Sabine County, since a Confederate cattle supply trail crosses it on the way to Natchez, Mississippi.

---

25 Matthew Hayes Nall, "Sabine County," *Handbook of Texas Online*, https://www .tshaonline.org/handbook/entries/sabine-county. As a jurist, Hemphill is remembered for expanding women's rights. He dies in Richmond, Virginia, on January 4, 1862, and his body buried in Texas State Cemetery in Austin. Some refer to him as "the John Marshall of Texas for the significant role he played in the development of Texas jurisprudence." See Thomas Cutrer, "John Hemphill," *Handbook of Texas Online*, https://www.tshaonline.org/handbook/entries/hemphill-john.

The real direct impact on the area is a drain of young men. Entire households are abandoned as fathers and sons answer the rebel call.

The Conners are not swept up into the war; their lifestyle is well suited to ride out the crashing cotton economy. None of the sons serve; the eldest, Fed, is fifteen years old when it starts. However, on January 15, 1863, Willis Conner appears at a Confederate recruiting camp, where he joins Captain J. M. Burroughs's Sabine County Volunteer Infantry, Company G. Willis Conner is a private again; he serves three months of home guard duty.[26]

The Texas legislature creates these local frontier defense forces to keep order in the state during the war's chaos. The largest fear was that Mexican and Native Americans would seize the opportunity and strike settlements. There are many incarnations that all fit under the heading of Texas State Troops (TST). Organized like military units, these groups are not actually part of the Confederate States Army. Their part in the greater war effort is building breastworks and keeping up morale at home.[27]

Burroughs's group is one such TST formed in 1863, dubbed the Frontier Organization. It appears to be a short-lived unit—most members, including Willis Conner, perform three months of duty and see no action. But it means that he was once, briefly, part of a proto-organization of what will later be called the Texas Rangers.[28]

The war ends in 1865, and the economy starts to recover. For the Conner family, whose herds grew during the conflict, peacetime means

---

26 National Park Service, "The Civil War Soldiers and Sailors System," and Texas State Archives, Austin, TX.

27 Christina Stopka, "Partial List of Texas Ranger Company and Unit Commanders," Texas Ranger Hall of Fame and Museum, https://www.texasranger.org/wp-content/uploads/2019/10/HISTORY_RangerCommanders2019.pdf.

28 Ibid. Burroughs appears in the leadership rosters of state organizations that preceded the Frontier Battalion of the late 1800s and the current Ranger organization. It may come as news to many that this was not officially part of the Confederate Army; veterans like Willis Conner have Confederate graves, and his tombstone says CSA TEXAS INFANTRY.

even more opportunity. The family is prosperous and growing; in October 1870, Willis's daughter Nancy is born. It's also time for Willis's sons to marry, build their own log houses, and create their own homesteads. But not on Bull Bay Creek.

Willis Conner relocates twenty miles to the south, to a spot on Six Mile Creek. It's just ten miles from the new county seat and six miles away from the Smith homesteads. The former political opponents are now neighbors.

The Smiths may not be thrilled, but the Low family is more accommodating. Or maybe it's just easier, since the Conner family is already settled on their range. Willis Conner builds his log cabin on the sprawling Low family land grant, which encompasses the Housen Bayou, sometime before 1870 when he appears there in a census listing. He buys the land—160 acres purchased in Piercy's name from Isaac Wright Low, future murder victim Eli Low's uncle—in February 1871. Establishing a homestead is an effective opening gambit in any East Texas property deal.

The Conner footprint near the Housen Bayou will only grow as the elder Conner sons marry local women from good families and move out. The single men continue to live with their father; the exception is Fed, who lives at home with his father despite marrying Nancy Pauline Travis around 1871.

Leander Conner is the first to set up his own place, buying 146 acres on a Low land grant in 1874. He marries Martha Caroline Smith; Marthy, as she's better known, is the daughter of John A. Smith and Amanda Low. Leander's homestead is just three miles from his father's. Over the ensuing years, the other boys will follow suit, giving birth to what has come to be called "the Conner Community." Leander Conner also doubles his land holdings by 1877.

One newspaper says of the Conners: "The country they live in is unfit for anything but stock country, and for many years they have made a living off their stock, and by hunting and fishing generally keeping among them twenty-five to thirty dogs."[29] This may inflate their canine ownership

---

29 "East Texas Outlaws," *Galveston Daily News.*

but understates their prosperity; the "unfit" land the reporter disparages provides ample opportunity to produce a profit for those who can tame it.

Southern Sabine County doesn't have much flat prairie to offer long-horns. Here, the "open range" is swampland and deep forest that are best suited for rooting swine. Large herds of pigs run the bayous and bottoms of Sabine County the same way cattle run the open-range plains elsewhere in Texas.

The first year that pigs appear in Sabine County tax records is 1877; prior to that, swine were not required to be listed. Between Willis and the boys, the family that year has 130 pigs registered compared to seventy-eight head of cattle.

Taken together, this represents a thriving hog business. "The largest pig herd at that time would've been maybe fifty sows," says swine expert Peter Schlichting, who earned his Ph.D. in wildlife biology from Texas Tech. "They would've probably weaned five or six pigs a litter with only one, sometimes two litters a year. So, they would've had 250 pigs a year at most. He would eat a few of them and sell the rest, either as breeding stock or as food."[30]

Pigs are easy in one sense: Let them loose and they forage on their own, eating everything between frogs and tree moss to survive. They predictably flock to the bottoms, making roundups easy, especially using trained dogs. The Conners' herds—and those owned by neighboring families—head to the Housen Bayou for a feast of acorns, worms, and the like. Older pigs are collected and crammed into log-walled fattening pens. The acknowledged system to identify open-range pigs is to cut unique ownership notches in their ears, the hog equivalent of a cattle brand. These are registered at the local county courthouse; the Conner family notches are still on file in Hemphill.[31] The butchery happens around winter, when it's easier to preserve the salt-cured meat and lard.

---

30 Interview with author.

31 Tom Robbins, "Pigs," National Park Service, updated April 14, 2015, https://www.nps.gov/grsm/learn/historyculture/pigs.htm; Weldon McDaniel, interview with author.

There is another way to regard pigs in Texas. "Because of the central place of pork in rural people's diet, average number of hogs per farm measures, in part, the degree of remaining self-sufficiency," says author Kyle Wilkinson, who crunched the numbers in 2008. He found that hog ownership plunged in Texas between 1870 and 1910, cut in half to an average of one hog per person.

However, East Texas is different; the hog-to-person ratio doesn't decline at all during that period. It's a bastion of frontier independence in a modernizing land, and Willis Conner is the pig-farming epitome of a freestanding Big Thicket backwoodsman.[32]

There is another way to make money in Sabine County—trees. The family selects and kills trees in the summer and harvests them in the winter. The boys then create rafts from the logs and float down the Sabine River to sell them, pitching a deck tent for shelter as they travel.[33] Alfie Conner has a particular penchant for logging, and he's the only son who doesn't own any hogs.[34]

Charles marries Julia Ann Scruggs in late 1874. He sets up shop in a log cabin on a 160-acre plot of public domain land, along a stream that stretches for miles through the county. Locals dub the waterway "Conner Creek."[35]

The boys sire many children, but a spate of tragic deaths rattle the growing families. Fed and Nancy's children, Millie Conner (born in 1873) and Monroe Conner (born in 1876), die of diphtheria within a week of each other in March 1877. One of Leander's children, two-year-old

---

32 Kyle G. Wilkison, *Yeomen, Sharecroppers, and Socialists: Plain Folk Protest in Texas, 1870–1914* (College Station: Texas A&M University Press, 2008).

33 Dugan, *Judge Not.* Elderly family and friends of the Conners recall their trips down the river.

34 Sabine County tax records.

35 McDaniel interview and various 1800s and current maps.

John Wesley, also dies that month. More tragedy awaits when Charles and Julia's first daughter, Mary Galen Conner, dies in 1878 at age two. Each are buried on a bare hilltop near Charles Conner's homestead, the first to find rest there, but far from the last.

Charles will soon commission a survey of the public land where the graveyard sits, the first step to claiming ownership. The state of Texas grants this in 1882, but as usual, the paperwork lags; land-use maps start listing the "C.W. Conner" land grant in 1879. Fed, after living near his in-laws closer to Hemphill for a few years, returns to the Conner Community to set up shop on seventy acres of his father's land.

For his seeming success and family stability, Willis Conner's violent streak has not left him. Even family friends will tell their children that Willis and Fed "are the most likely to knock the hat from your head."[36]

One local newspaper article—albeit published when his notoriety is at its peak—presents him as an extreme bully:

> All of his neighbors were afraid of him and his six sons. To illustrate his everlasting and unremitting tyranny: On one occasion one of his neighbors did something that he took umbrage at. He waited until he met him at a log-rolling or a road-working. He deliberately stepped off, cut a good hickory stick, trimmed it well and walked up to him and felled him and beat him unmercifully, and bid defiance to the crowd. Then told the victim of his hellish wrath that he must be at District Court next term to pay his fine and cost, and sure enough the victim came up at his bidding and paid as directed.[37]

By any account, Old Man Conner and his sons are rugged, intrepid, and dangerous. They are certainly not ones to butt heads with, especially

---

36 Dugan, *Judge Not,* quoting the late Norman Ener, son of Conner friend Bob Ener.

37 "East Texas Outlaws," *Galveston Daily News.*

in the secluded bayous and forests a dozen miles to the southeast of Hemphill.

ROAD TO HOLLY BOTTOM
January 19, 1882 (twenty-three months before the killings)

Melissa Cordelia Travis and Isaac Low gaze at each other as they exchange vows. He has a stout, wide face and thick, uneven ears. His hair is already thinning. Low takes in his bride's expansive forehead, broad nose, and prominently square chin. The tips of her mouth naturally curve into a resting frown.

When the ceremony ends, she's no longer Melissa Travis; she's Melissa Travis-Low. Her husband comes from a solid family and owns a good home. Still, there's a sadness clinging to him from being orphaned so young. Little Ike never talks about his early life, a sign of his sensitivity to it.

First his father, Isaac Hickman Low Sr., died in Louisiana while in the service of the Confederate Army. CSA veteran Elmore Harper, the deceased's friend and neighbor, returned from the war and married the widow Mary Ann. When she died shortly after, her widower promptly "separated the children by farming them out to various cousins to raise," according to the late local Sabine County historian Blanche Toole, and then remarries. The newlywed Harpers then have a son of their own, Elmer Harper.[38]

Isaac Low is "farmed out" to be raised by his father's nephew, Isaac Wright Low, a former sergeant in Texas's Eleventh Infantry Regiment.[39]

---

38 Ed Wetterman, "Ike Low and Melissa Travis," East Texas Generations, July 31, 2010, http://easttexasgenerations.blogspot.com/2010/07/ike-low-and-melissa-travis -122-and-123.html, quoting Low descendants, now deceased. Little Ike Low's reticence to speak of his childhood comes from here, too.

39 "Low, I.W.," National Park Service, Civil War Soldier Details, https://www.nps .gov/civilwar/search-soldiers-detail.htm?soldierId=0CB881B4-DC7A-DF11-BF36 -B8AC6F5D926A.

Everyone knew, in the words of one decedent, that "he would take any-body in."[40] Census records indeed show the veteran's family raised several area children on behalf of their families.

Ike Low grows up with his extended kin and, for convenience, takes on the nickname "Little Ike." Jack Low keeps him at a distance, but neighbors, including Willis Conner, lend a hand to help him get es-tablished. Now, the unwanted youth has grown to a man with his own property. And as of today, a wife.

The wedding is being held at the groom's home, a fairly roomy log cabin perched on a steep hill overlooking a slender creek. It doesn't have a well, requiring Low to continually refill a cistern with wagonloads of water from the nearby stream. Still, a family member recalls, "it was a real good house and it had a dog pen, a hall down the middle, and he had a kitchen making an L on one end of it."[41] Even now, guests are crowding both the front and back porches.

One of them is Melissa's sister Nancy. She and her husband, Fed Conner, are mingling with a couple of teenagers: Melissa's sister Theodosia "Docia" Travis and Milton Anthony, ages sixteen and fif-teen, respectively. If Docia is eyeing him up for betrothal, she could do worse. The Anthony family is as well established as the Lows and Smiths.

Milton Anthony's father is more than another farmer. Thomas B. Anthony is a battle-scarred Civil War veteran from Fairmount, and those who know the family are eager to see if the young man will grow out of

---

40 Ed Wetterman, "1990 Interview with Blanch Toole, Sabine County Historian," East
Texas Generations, August 1, 2010, http://easttexasgenerations.blogspot.com/2010
/08/1990-interview-with-blanch-toole-sabine.html. I couldn't be more appreciative
of Toole and Wetterman, both deceased, for her effort to capture oral histories and
for his to put them online. People like them make works like this possible.

41 Ibid.

his overbearing father's shadow.[42] The teenagers are certainly interested in each other—and as more than just neighbors.

This is an ideal setting for the youth to flirt and mingle. Like most rural weddings, the ceremony leads immediately to a dance, featuring musicians from the local community jamming together in groups of four or five. Polkas and traditional square dance tunes are the order of the day. Everyone preens in their best clothes and scuffs their boots on flat, dirt dance floors.

That's when guests Kit Smith and Charles Conner come head-to-head. They are only a year apart in age, brimming with masculine pride and ego. And they both want to play the fiddle during the dance, which sparks a spirited argument. The dispute over the instrument simmers through the festivities and erupts after it ends, when Kit and Charley come to blows.[43]

This is not unexpected from Kit Smith. He's a large man and prone to pushing people around. One neighbor and brother-in-law, Alex McDaniel, one day describes him to his son as "a very rough and overbearing man, very bad to cuss, blow and brag." Charles, also tall, isn't too bright and usually is shy, but not so much when provoked.[44]

McDaniel and Charley Conner are both connected to Kit Smith by their marriages to Scruggs girls. The story is an East Texas classic. When Dr. D. M. Cooper weds Gracie Harper, he's eager to marry off the three

---

42 Dugan, *Judge Not*. Thomas Anthony's personality and relationship with his son are described by now-deceased Sabine County residents.

43 Mea culpa. There is no evidence that Smith and Conner sparred at the wedding of Ike Low. Local lore, enshrined in Joseph Combs's book *Gunsmoke in the Redlands* (San Antonio, TX: Naylor, 1968), maintains there was a confrontation between the two at a "community dance" in the early 1880s. What better reason than a wedding to hold a dance, one attended by a wide number of interrelated figures involved in this drama? I couldn't resist and ask the reader's indulgence. It won't happen again.

44 Dugan, *Judge Not*.

daughters of his wife's previous union with Jesse Scruggs. Alex McDaniel marries Nancy Scruggs, Charley Conner ties the knot with Julia Ann Scruggs, and Kit Smith weds Mary Alma Scruggs.[45]

Christopher "Kit" Smith is born in Sabine County on December 5, 1858. His father, Irving, cuts a sad figure. The 1870 Sabine County Census reveals him as a widower living with sons Chris and Joe in the McDaniel home. The binds between the McDaniel and Smith families are obviously tight.

Kit Smith is building a homestead near the Conners, an area they consider their range. It sets up a clash typical of the open-range system—everyone's pigs mingle in the same places, inviting confrontation among their owners.

It's not just a single new settler that has the Conners stirred up. Kit Smith has a friend and ally who's also establishing a nearby farm; Eli Low, Little Ike's nephew. It seems that a whole new generation is establishing homesteads of their own east of Hemphill, just a handful of miles apart from each other.

Eli Low is another link that connects the newlyweds to the Conners, this time on the groom's side. He's the son of Jackson "Jack" Green Low, with uncles Isaac Hickman Low Sr. and Jesse Low.[46] Jesse Low's daughter married John Smith, and their daughter Marthy Smith married none other than Leander Conner.

Eli Low is close with the groom, Little Ike Low, since they lived with Isaac Wright Low together as children. They only have a year's

---

45 His wife's brothers run with the outlaw John Wesley Hardin, who stays with the family and will nearly be shot while fleeing Cooper's place in 1872 after he wounds a Sabine County deputy in Hemphill.

46 1860 Census, Sabine County, Texas. Born February 1, 1861.

difference between their ages. Eli Low is married to Sarah Tatom, and they have one child, Lee Low.[47]

Willis Conner isn't happy about these interlopers, even if they are relatives by marriage. "They just assumed that all the land around where he settled belonged to him," says a Texas Ranger from Company F, J. Allen Newton, who will have firsthand experience with the family. "Some men named Smith and Low bought some land in the middle of Conner's range, and started a hog and cattle ranch. They were warned by the Conners that it was right unhealthy for them to stay, but they did not move."[48]

The Galveston Daily News later paints them as resolute men who won't back down to bullies. "Kit Smith and Eli Low were as brave as brave could be and contested that they had as much right to the range as the Connors [*sic*] or anyone else and were determined to exercise that right," the newspaper says. "The Connors warned them not to go into the woods, but they did so."[49]

Others are not so charitable to Low and Smith. Nacogdoches sheriff A. J. Spradley all but accuses Smith and Low of being hog thieves: "The Conners were great hog ranchers and in the course of their prosperity in this line of industry, they were constantly missing hogs from their stock which ran at large in this open acorn range."[50]

Court witnesses will later testify that the Conners accused the Smith, Harper, and Low family members of cutting off their pigs' tails and riding them down with horses. A worse form of sabotage is trimming

---

47 Wetterman, "1990 Interview with Blanche Toole."

48 Sarah Ellen Davidge, "Texas Rangers Were Rough and Ready Fighters," *Frontier Times*, November 1935.

49 "East Texas Outlaws," *Galveston Daily News*.

50 Fuller, *A Texas Sheriff*.

off their ears, which destroys ownership notches. Messing with the pigs in any way is a challenge to the entire Conner family.

In June 1882, William Conner and Eli Low get into an altercation during the raising of a bridge over Six Mile Creek. Eli Low is a favorite of his father, Willis Conner, but his son feels no such connection. An eager crowd rings them, and the confrontation nearly ends in a fistfight. Fed is there but takes no part. The confrontation peters out before blows are landed, but the hotheaded William makes it plain that he is not "satisfied" and doesn't consider it over.

Incidents and tension continue to rise around the Housen Bayou. Weldon McDaniel, a living descendant of the Smiths, describes his forebears' reputation in Sabine as a family that "had a case of the yeah-yeah-yeahs, always stirring things up."[51] The belief in the county is that Kit Smith and his friends are at least partially responsible for escalating trouble with the Conners, but Spradley seems alone as a contemporary accusing them of thievery.

The stage has been set for a feud. "Willis Conner's house was something of a common headquarters of the Conner family," future court records describe, based on witness testimony. "The cursing and abuse of Eli Low and Kit Smith was common fireside talk."[52]

FUSSING IS BAD BUSINESS
December 4, 1883 (one day before the killings)

It's just another winter morning in the Housen Bayou for Jack Low, who is running hogs on horseback with his fifteen-year-old son. They are

---

51 Interview with author.

52 *Reports of Cases Argued and Adjudged in the Court of Appeals of Texas*, vol. XVII, 1885, citing *State of Texas v. Willis Connor, John Conner, Charles Conner, Fed Conner, William Conner*. The encounter at the bridge "six months before the murders" is documented in the appeals court case, too. The criminal trial records were destroyed in a fire in Hemphill, leaving the appeals case as its only description.

less than a mile from his home, crossing Six Mile Creek, when he runs into Willis and Fed Conner. The two men are on foot, appearing with no warning. And they both have shotguns. Jack Low has seldom been happier to have a Winchester resting on his lap.

The conversation starts abruptly and at a distance. "By God," Willis Conner cries. "Somebody has been bothering my hogs!"

"It wasn't me, Willis."

"If you have not, your boys have, and they must stop it," Old Man Conner responds, closing the distance. His son Fed says nothing as the older men spar verbally. After twenty-five minutes, it's clear the conversation is going nowhere. Old grievances are being aired.

"You and Eli ran over a hog of mine in the road six or eight years ago," Willis charges. "By God, you cannot deny that."

"If my boys are ever caught dogging or abusing the Conner stock, I'll pay any damages resulting," says an angry Jack Low. "Now, *you* watch *your* boys, while you're at it. I'll surely be watching them."

"It's no use to watch," Willis replies. "You may watch a wolf all summer, and yet he will eat the pigs in the fall."

Fed Conner finally speaks, but it's not to Jack Low or his son. "Fussing is bad business," he tells his father. "We had as well drop it and go on to the ones who have done it."

Willis ignores this and resumes the argument. "If anybody catches me bothering their stock, I want them to shoot me down like a wolf, and leave me in the woods," he declares. "And I intend to do the same, and to make it my rule."

"You carry on like that, innocent people are gonna get hurt," Jack Low retorts.

"When men dog my stock, I know whether they do it accidentally or on purpose," Willis says.

In response, Jack Low shifts his weight so that the muzzle of his Winchester is pointing toward the Conners. Willis jumps nervously and raises the shotgun half to his shoulder. "Take that gun off of me," he growls, his usually quick delivery now menacingly slow.

Jack Low complies wordlessly, and he and his son ride off.[53] It's a close call that shows him the precariousness of the situation. When he gets home, Jack Low puts the word out: Anyone who rides the Holly Bottom trail near the Conner fields could be accused at gunpoint of dogging pigs. That list of common travelers—and possible targets—includes his son Jack Low Alex McDonald, Elmore Harper, George Williams, Kit Smith, and Eli Low.

The next day, December 5, is overcast and promises rain. Sallie Lowe, Eli Low's wife, watches as her husband molds bullets with Kit Smith at their home, one mile away from Holly Bottom. The pair leave together after eating dinner. They take their guns with them and ride off on horseback. About fifteen minutes after they leave, a slight rain falls, halts for a few minutes, and turns into a sudden downpour.

Neither man is again seen alive.

On December 6, a search party of family and friends scouring the bayous finds the pair shot dead in Holly Bottom. The forensic evidence indicates a volley of gunfire from behind, followed by a close-range execution with head shots. Suspicions on the Conners is exacerbated by the fact that Willis and his sons stay silent on the killings and don't even attend the funerals of Kit Smith or Eli Lowe.[54] It reads to the community like an admission.

The Conners hire two high-powered attorneys, William W. Weatherred and James Polley, to defend them, but stay mute as to the murders. After a habeas corpus hearing, during which their family and friends testify but the Conner men do not, Willis, Fed, William, John, and Charles are all indicted. They submit without incident, traveling the dozen miles into Hemphill in their best clothes to surrender. In an uncomfortable de-

---

53 The trial of *State of Texas v. Willis Connor, John Conner, Charles Conner, Fed Conner, William Conner* is summarized in the case's appeal, *Fed and Charles Conner v. the State,* Court of Appeals of Texas, 1886 (No. 1759). It includes the dialogue above.

54 Ibid.

velopment, they're to be held in jail without bond. Their strategy hardens, trusting that staying silent will set them free. But there are unpleasant surprises awaiting.

TESTIMONY AND WADDING
September 1884

Octavine Cooper, at age nineteen, is more than just a star witness of a double-murder trial. She's a lit match setting fire to several family trees, with flames traveling along many intertwined branches.

She's tied to both sides of the feud. The witness's father, Dr. David Cooper, by marrying a Scruggs woman, is the stepfather-in-law to victim Kit Smith, state's witness Alex McDaniel, and accused murderer Charles Conner. Even more confusing, Jack Low married the sister of Octavine's aunt, making the late Eli Low her second cousin.

Octavine Cooper finds herself in the literal center of the feud when she moves into the home of her half sister and Charles Conner six weeks before the killing. There she works as a teacher to young Nancy "Miss Nan" Conner, Willis's girl.[55] From the family table and fireside discussions, she hears the Conner-Smith–Low feud heat up. Called by the prosecution, she testifies that William Conner complained to his brother that Eli Low had run his hogs out of Holly Bottom. Charles Conner responded that he'd help Billy protect his hogs and that Eli Low specifically "better not try that again."

Hearing the inner workings of the family is harmful enough, but Octavine's unique role in this trial comes from identifying a swatch of fabric found at the scene of the crime as coming from the Conners' loom.

Shown the colored wadding found on Eli Low's corpse, Octavine tells the courtroom that she saw Miss Nan with a new dress made of the exact green-blue-white fabric. The prosecutors are arguing that the cloth had been made in the loom, trimmed from the child's dress, and the excess used by the frugal Conners for their homemade ammunition.

---

55 Wetterman, "1990 Interview with Blanche Toole."

Wadding keeps shotgun pellets from hitting each other chaotically inside the barrel, which ruins spread, accuracy, and distance. In rifles, wadding is used to direct the explosive force inside the cartridge.

It's as close to physical evidence that the prosecutors can get, and even this is linked to the Conners based on testimony. The district attorney is building a case, but it is circumstantial. It will all come down to the state's witnesses to sell it to the jury. Young Octavine Cooper is not the only one within the Conner household who will be called to testify during *State of Texas v. Willis Connor, John Conner, Charles Conner, Fed Conner, William Conner*, Judge J. I. Perkins presiding.

A walking hard-luck story named Sam Everett, who lived at Charles Conner's place off and on for two years while working for the family, also takes the stand for the prosecution. Accused of housebreaking in Mississippi, he won a lawsuit for slander, but his attorney made off with all the proceeds, and he tells the jury that he's been left "flat." The Louisiana native is in Sabine County to get back on his feet.

During the trial, Everett provides details of the bridge-raising encounter and describes closed-door accusations about the Lows, the Smiths, and others chasing off pigs. Everett's testimony captures the flavor of the day-to-day interactions among the neighbors around Holly Bottom: "Sometime before the killing of Smith and Eli Lowe, Fed Conner remarked to witness: 'I asked McDaniel who threw his (McDaniel's) fence down, when Kit Smith up and answered, 'I don't know who in the hell it was.' Now, wasn't that a hell of an answer to make a white man?'"

Search party member George Williams takes the stand. He is a close friend of the Low family, one of those whom Sam Everett says the Conners cursed at home. His testimony isn't pivotal, but Williams does describe the unopened shot pouch on Eli Low's body, indicating he was not involved in a gunfight when he died.

Deeper harm is done to the Conners when another part-time ranch hand, an African American named John Marshall, testifies to damning details of the family's doings on December 5, 1883:

On Wednesday, the day of the killing, he was in the employ of Willis Conner, splitting rails. Witness, with Joe and Clark Ford, went to their work immediately after dinner on that day. They were at work about a quarter of a mile northeast from Willis Conner's house. Willis, Fed, John, Charley and Billy Conner passed witness and the Fords, where they were at work, a short time after dinner. They were traveling the trail, going in a northeast direction, when they passed out of the view of the witness. Willis, Fed, John and Charles Conner had guns. Billy had no gun.[56]

But the damage of these two men's testimony is dwarfed by that of Joe Ford, another African American man building the fence. He testifies to seeing the Conners ride out and confirms the Conners' visible loadout. He also adds that he saw Billy Conner put a pistol in his pocket earlier that day. The descriptions of the guns carried by the accused now match the wounds described to the jury by Dr. J. W. Smith. But Ford has a lot more to say.

Less than an hour after he saw the Conners pass, he details, a soft rain started to fall. It slacked off, but the sky remained gray. That's when he heard the gunshots. "The first two were fired in quick succession from shotguns," a court document summarizes his testimony. "A slight intermission was followed by two discharges from rifles. These guns were fired in the direction of the Holly Bottom."[57]

The rain restarts, harder now, and the men take shelter. Later that night, after the Conners drive some pigs back to their home for wintertime slaughter, Ford is told to get some supper from the kitchen, where

56 *Fed and Charles Conner v. the State.*

57 Ibid. A courthouse fire destroyed the original trial records, but it's summarized in the appeal.

he finds a perfect spot to eavesdrop on an incriminating husband-and-wife discussion between Piercy and Willis Conner.[58]

"Did you do what you went to do?" she asks.

"Yes, by God, I did," Willis replies.

"Are you sure they are dead?" she insists. "Are you sure you don't have to go back and make sure?"

"By God they are, and they won't steal any more of my hogs, nor dog any more of my stock."

As if that's not bad enough, Ford also catches conversations with the other family members as he hides behind a chimney. From there, he hears William Conner say: "I guess the damned son of a bitch won't curse me anymore. I took two pops at him with John's Smith & Wesson pistol, and he is as good as Mollie ever rubbed her leg over."

Ford testifies to hearing more boasting, saying he heard this from Willis Conner: "Eli begged mightily, but he was just a year too late. It didn't do any good. He had no business bothering my stock. He had warning not to go into my stock range."

The question implicitly raised by Dr. Smith's clinical testimony—who fired the execution-style rifle shot into Eli Low's eye as he reached out for mercy—has now seemingly and gruesomely been answered.

This brutal testimony is blunted by the fact that the details of these conversations were not included in Ford's initial testimony during the examining habeas corpus trial, where he appeared twice.[59] In court, Ford claims he was scared of the Conners, who were not then in jail. There are records showing he had to be fetched by a deputy to testify. This will raise eyebrows later, as rumors of witness tampering quietly circulate among the county residents.

No one knows what transpired at Holly Bottom for sure except the

---

58 Ibid. He quotes these family exchanges in his testimony, enabling me to do the same.

59 The focus of an examining trial is exclusively upon whether or not there was "probable cause" for an arrest to be made. There's no jury.

dead men and, presumably, the Conners. But Weatherred calls no defense witnesses; he is representing a family that simply won't give him ammunition to defend themselves. He lost the habeas corpus proceedings, despite testimony from female Conner family members and several neighbors. In the trial, all he can do is point out the changing nature of some of the witnesses' stories and question some of their backgrounds. (J. O. Toole testifies and no one brings up his charge of illegally carrying a pistol in town, but the laborer Sam Everett gets no such courtesy.)

The case is indeed circumstantial; even Judge Perkins acknowledges this during his jury instructions. But the twelve men hear slightly different language regarding Fed's case versus Charles's when the judge instructs them before their deliberations. By only mentioning the handling of "circumstantial evidence" when speaking about Charles, it could be argued that the jury felt the evidence against Fed was *not* circumstantial. It's a small slipup that no one notices at the time but will soon lead to additional legal wrangling that will change the trajectory of events in Sabine County.

The verdicts soon come down. Fed is guilty of first-degree murder and sentenced to life; Charles is convicted of murder in the second degree and sentenced to twenty-five years. Appeals are filed right away. The trials of John, William, and Willis await, and the family holds out no hope for acquittals. The county remains inflamed, either with hatred for the Conners or anger for their continued incarceration, and passions must have run high enough to spook Sheriff William Smith and Judge Perkins. They ship the family away from Hemphill's log-walled jail to be held in Nacogdoches, in neighboring San Augustine County.

Given some of the coming rhetoric, it's worth a moment to examine the case for signs of corruption and tampering, especially since it's grounded by so much circumstantial evidence. So first, what are the odds that the forensic report could have been set up?

It's not an idle question. Coroner's juries have mixed reputations, even by nineteenth-century standards. One journal around the time disparages "the rascally side of the present system" that "leads to a strong suspicion that 'fake' inquests may be more common than has been supposed." The journal article describes some nefarious doings: "An inquest really amounts to very little in the majority of cases; the jury contributes only an element of ignorance, and it is not surprising that an unprincipled ward-politician, such as many of our city coroners and coroner's deputies are, concludes occasionally to dispense with it and pocket its fees."

That description of graft and laziness does not appear to apply to the two murder inquest professionals with reputations at stake, Dr. Smith and Judge Whittlesey. They rode out to the scene with men they felt were impartial and performed the inquest immediately. Smith would have had to falsify the descriptions of the wounds to create a ghastly picture of an execution. Given Smith's fairly neutral position in the feud, overall professional reputation, and later candid comments about both sides to his family, it's hard to imagine him embroiled in a conspiracy.

Smith testifies to seeing the wadding collected as evidence. If he's to be trusted, it was there at the time of the field inquest. To plant this evidence, the search party would have to place cloth at the scene that they knew someone from inside the house—like Octavine Cooper—would be able to recognize as belonging to the Conners or agree to lie about identifying it. It would have taken some quick, conspiratorial thinking from aggrieved men to put together such a complex plan on the spot. Pressuring Octavine Cooper's testimony that placed the fabric at the Conners' is a more likely scenario if you're looking for tampering.

Joe Ford's inconsistent testimony deserves the most scrutiny because it does the most damage. He seems to be in the right place at the right time to see and hear the most incriminating things. His changing testimony can easily be attributed to fear, but of whom? It is just as believable that he would be scared to testify against a white man as it is that he could be pressured by well-off families into lying in court. Race relations in Sabine County have always been notoriously rough, and given his powerless situation, Ford was clearly in a tough bind.

Witness testimony can certainly be coerced, faked, or purchased. Indeed, some of his seems a little too perfect or at least dramatic. Rumors persist in private, and one claim of tampering survives by word of mouth. One of the Housen Bayou neighbors will one day tell a Conner friend that his father, George Williams, "was up to his neck in setting up the Conners."[60] Much later, in letters to Austin and under very different circumstances, Weatherred will also suggest that there is more to the case than meets the eye.[61]

There is no official version from anyone who was there of what transpired in Holly Bottom. However, the Conners did tell some people their version of the killings. One of them is an unlikely sympathizer: the sheriff of neighboring San Augustine County.

NACOGDOCHES SOJOURN
October 1, 1884

Sheriff A. J. Spradley walks stiffly past the courthouse in downtown Nacogdoches and heads to the front door of the one-story brick jail next door.[62] He's moving deliberately, wincing with the pain each step causes to a healing gunshot wound.

He wants to visit the prisoners from Sabine County being held inside, but not because he fears an escape. Spradley is fretting that the Conners are being railroaded.

Willis Conner and his sons have been shipped to his jail because authorities in Sabine County don't trust the local population to keep them inside. The jailed Conners are at risk of being lynched or set free;

---

60 Dugan, *Judge Not*, quotes Norman Ener (son of Conner family friend Bob Ener); his brother-in-law Ray Williams told him that his father, George Williams, and Jack Low set up the Conners by convincing the African American witnesses to lie on the stand.

61 I won't let a footnote serve as a major spoiler. This is discussed in detail later.

62 The excellent website "Tiny Texas Jails" found maps of the jail over many years, including 1885. "Nacogdoches County," Tiny Texas Jails, http://www.tinytexasjails .com/vanished/nacogdoches-county/.

what does either threat say about what's going on there these days? Besides, Spradley knows a little bit about family feuds and is prone to being sympathetic.

Andrew Jackson Spradley is born in Westville, Mississippi, the son of a successful but illiterate yeoman farmer. As a young man, he killed two men, reportedly in self-defense, either sparking or as part of a wider feud. He flees retaliation by heading to Texas in the mid-1870s and settles in Nacogdoches. His entire family follows, and he marries local Victoria Johnson on May 2, 1878.[63]

Spradley is known as a tough guy, unsurprisingly, and his violent résumé favors a career in law enforcement. In 1881, the Nacogdoches sheriff, Richard Orton, appoints Spradley as a deputy. Two years later, the deputy becomes sheriff.

In June 1885, Spradley confronts a drunk named Joe Rogers for disorderly conduct. Rogers draws a .44-caliber pistol and shoots the sheriff in the chest. The ball punches through his torso. As he drops, Spradley snaps off a pistol shot of his own into Rogers's arm.

Spradley "lingered on the verge of the grave for weeks," reads *The Galveston Daily News*. "But the most careful nursing, the assiduous attention of friends, cheerful company and nothing wanting to minister to his comfort, brought him through."[64]

His assailant, while wounded less severely, is still in peril. "Rogers was put in jail, and the weather being very hot, his wounded arm became inflamed and swelled to such an extent that the doctors insisted on amputating it," the newspaper says admiringly. "Rogers swore he would die first, and with calm fortitude bore his sufferings and awaited the end."

Spradley takes a deep breath as he enters the jail. He readies himself

---

63 Fuller, *A Texas Sheriff*. It's a collection of newspaper articles and single-source reminiscences from the lawman to his friend Fuller and as such can be considered Spradley's autobiography.

64 *Galveston Daily News*, April 9, 1885.

to hide his discomfort; there's no good reason why the prisoners should know he's ailing. Inside, he first curtly greets Rogers, who survived the arm infection and still awaits sentencing next year. He plans on pleading guilty and doing his prison time, as the newspaper notes, "with two good arms instead of one."[65]

He quickly moves on to his other prisoners: Rogers isn't going anywhere soon, but the Conner family won't be with him for much longer. Sabine County shipped them here until Charley and Fed's appeal is heard, scheduled for next week in Hemphill. The trials of the others will start in the spring, after the results of the appeals are heard. The Conners are all going back to the Sabine County jail to wait for the wheels of justice to slowly spin.

"Sheriff Spradley stated that never in all his career as an officer has it been his privilege to have in jail at Nacogdoches a better or obedient bunch of men," relates his friend and biographer, Henry Fuller. "They obeyed every rule without question, caused the Sheriff no trouble and were model prisoners in every sense of the word. Old man Connor [sic] told Mr. Spradley that he need have no uneasiness about him or his sons trying to escape, even if the jail doors were left unlocked at night."[66]

The lawman and prisoners must have spoken of the killings that landed them here, since Spradley offers details that don't appear in news coverage or court documents. "In order to catch the thieves, a close watch was kept on the hogs in the woods," Spradley recalls through his biographer. "One day, they came upon two men. A fight ensued and both men were killed." Spradley upbraids them for not reporting the shoot-out, calling it a mistake to not tell authorities their side.

Neighbors who heard "the whole story" from Willis Conner himself recall more details that explain the family's refusal to speak about Holly Bottom. In his version, Kit Smith and Eli Low have a confrontation

---

65 Ibid.

66 Fuller, *A Texas Sheriff.*

with William and John Conner in the Housen Bayou the day before the shootings. During that encounter, Smith holds a cocked shotgun on William while accusing the Conners of using their dogs to run off his pigs. The family is outraged, feeling the Smith family is the one sabotaging stock. Willis is especially disappointed in Eli Low, whom he's tried to help since his uncle Isaac and the youth's own father, Jack, seem disinterested in him.

The Conners maintain that Kit Smith and Eli Low ride to Willis's house on December 5, fully armed, to heap abuse on the family from horseback. After the pair gallop off, the Conners saddle their horses and follow. Charles tries to join but, as Willis puts it to his friend Bob Ener, "You know I didn't take Charley along, idiot that he is."[67]

Interestingly, the testimony of Joe Ford and John Marshall is what links Charles Conner to the crime, with their glimpses of the man riding out with his family that fateful day. (Octavine Cooper only testifies that he had a gripe against Eli Low for pushing William Conner around.)

Back to December 5, as Willis Conner told his neighbors it went down. When the Conners catch up with their quarry in Holly Bottom, Kit Smith draws his rifle. Willis Conner shoots Smith in the shoulder and again in the back as he falls. Fed shoots Eli Low as he rides away, incurring his father's wrath. Willis even claims to his friend Bob Ener that he almost shot Fed right there for the offense.[68] Not only is he attached to Low personally, but the family also just lost the only witness that can say that Kit Smith provoked a fight.

The part Willis Conner leaves out to Spradley and his neighbors is what happens after Smith and Low are down. He doesn't address what the pathological evidence, as presented by J. W. Smith, indicates is a double execution. Once the shots are fired, the die is cast. Silencing both witnesses is ruthless but also prudent.

---

67 Dugan, *Judge Not*.

68 Ibid., quoting Bob Ener's son.

Taking the Conners' version at face value still leaves the family arming themselves and pursuing the men on horseback—Kit Smith could easily have felt threatened by their appearance—and hangs Fed on the hook for a cold-blooded shot in the back. If this is the best case for the Conners, it doesn't look great.

No matter what version he hears, the prisoners' tale touches Spradley's contrarian spirit, and he becomes a consistent Conner sympathizer. That he sticks up for them years later speaks volumes about the sheriff's view of more than just the Sabine County feud. The idea of men bullied by the justice system matches his iconoclastic political personality as a Populist and Prohibitionist, for which he's later known. However, his own role in pursuing the Conners will go deeper than he lets on to his sympathetic biographer.

The Conner family leaves Nacogdoches the second week of October, heading for the jail in Hemphill ahead of their appeals. There, Fed's conviction is overturned. According to the appeals court, the judge's instructions to the jury mentioned the importance of the "circumstantial evidence," which could have made the jury "understand that the case of Fed Conner did not depend wholly upon that character of evidence, but was supported, in part at least, by direct evidence. This, we think, was in error. The charge upon circumstantial evidence should have been made applicable to the case of Fed as well as to the case of Charles . . . its omission from the charge, as has been repeatedly held, was error for which the judgment must be reversed."[69]

Charles's sentence is affirmed, and he's sent to prison. He enters Huntsville Penitentiary as convict number 2545 on November 25, 1884. He is thirty-six years old and is not expected to be released until 1909, when he's sixty-one.

Fed isn't off the hook. He's jailed for another trial. John, William, and Willis spend the winter likewise awaiting spring trials. It's time to butcher hogs and lay in meat for winter, but they're locked inside this

---

69 *Fed and Charles Conner v. the State.*

absurd log cabin. There is only so much the two remaining free sons can do to keep the family afloat.

Making matters worse, Catherine Conner Williams loses her husband on March 14, 1885, when he has a total mental breakdown and is hauled off in restraints. Two days later, a six-man jury declares him insane and ships him off to an asylum in Austin. Catherine is now left alone to raise four young children; her oldest, Thomas Williams, is just ten when her husband is committed.[70]

In the wilds south of Hemphill, Leander and Alfie Conner are enraged. So, too, are many of the people of Sabine County. They have been told that Charles Conner wasn't even in Holly Bottom that day and that the other Conners are being equally persecuted. To them, it's a case of men defending their livelihood and their very right to exist. The phrase *circumstantial evidence* is used a lot in seething homestead conversations and becomes "no evidence" in many minds.

The Conner brothers gather with their allies, prompted to action by a flamboyant former newsman and current fugitive, Lewis Loggins. Something, he agrees with them, must be done.

BREAKING OUT, BREAKING BAD
March 25, 1885

Lewis L. Loggins eyes the Hemphill City Jail with contempt. It's not a formidable fortress, as he well knows. The walls are made of logs, the ground soft and the guards nonexistent. He's proud of the men gathered downtown, not in them for standing up to authority in defense of their neighbors but in committing a brazen midnight jailbreak, which he successfully incited.

Loggins likes to be called "Pete." He has a dark complexion, a dark half-inch-long beard, and heavy dyed-black mustache "that he pulls when meditating," according to a newspaper description of him in 1885. "He is five feet ten inches high, spare built, a little stoop shouldered and

---

70 Dugan, *Judge Not*, citing Probate Book B, John H. Williams, pp. 340–341.

a little knock kneed or some people would say, tangle legged, but toes turned outward."[71]

Despite these unflattering details, others appreciate his looks. Wooing women is never a problem for Loggins. He has an occasional stammer, but despite this, he's a smooth talker.

Loggins has one of those ego-driven personalities that fills him with confidence that he can excel at anything. He attains positions at newspapers and as a lawyer, professions that garner him attention, but his real desire is to be a doctor. And he isn't letting the fact that he's a wanted man get in the way.

Loggins is an East Texas local, born in San Augustine County in 1848. His troubles start early. His parents, Martin and Susanna, had thirteen children, of which Lewis is born third to last.[72] "The quiet life on the farm and attendance at a country school had little attraction for the restless spirit of young Loggins, and after seriously shooting his cousin, a boy companion, he went into Jasper County."[73]

In 1871, he finds his foothold in the community by becoming an apprentice at a printing office. Loggins observes the publishing process of *The Jasper Newsboy* with an interested eye, but also uses the time at the print shop to study law.

Mary Elizabeth Gilbreath likes to be called "Mollie." She's the literate daughter of Alabama transplants to Sabine County, and she catches the eye of the aspiring young attorney Lewis Loggins. He woos her with a singular focus, and the pair marry while traveling near Dallas in February 1873.[74]

---

71 *Galveston Daily News,* September 3, 1885.

72 Prison records and *Western Historical Quarterly* 24, no. 1 (1993).

73 "The Journalistic Bigamist," *Daily Arkansas Gazette,* July 21, 1888.

74 "Texas County Marriage Index, 1837–1977," Family Search, 2013.

Loggins's life continues on an upward trajectory. He's admitted to the bar in 1874 and practices in Jasper, Shelby, Sabine, and San Augustine Counties. That year, his first son is born. More importantly, he runs for county attorney in Jasper County and wins the office in an election with 690 votes cast.

His duties include assessing stray cattle with W. H. Truett, the county clerk. As soon as his two-year term ends, he heads to Jasper to run *The Saxon*, a rival newspaper to *The Newsboy*. Loggins's fortunes seem to be on the rise as a public man. His family grows as well, with Lewis Loggins Jr. born in 1877.[75] The family loses two other children during infancy.

In 1880, Loggins announces his intention to run for representative of the Fourth District. "He says he relies on his personal merits," one local newspaper notes.[76] The voters don't respond, and he loses the bid.

Around this time, with a budding family and a land boom exploding around him, Loggins starts to chase the fortune that so far has eluded him. In 1881, he starts to assemble a deal for 1,107 acres in Sabine County, just over the Jasper County line. His partner is Abraham Smith, a Confederate veteran who served as a private with in the Twentieth Texas Cavalry, Company D.

The problem is that Loggins doesn't appear to own the land. "He attempted to set up title by forging the name of William Gibson of Louisiana," says the *Daily Arkansas Gazette*.[77] A Texas newspaper offers more details: "He sold it to Capt. Norseworthy, a prominent and worthy citizen of Jasper, who found in time . . . that the deed was forged. The

---

75 1880 United States Federal Census.

76 *Brenham Weekly Banner*, April 2, 1880.

77 *Daily Arkansas Gazetteer*, July 21, 1888.

witness by whom this deed purported to have been proven was one Abe Smith, a citizen from Sabine County."[78]

Now the scheme is unraveling. As the authorities are closing in on him for the alleged forgery, Loggins eyes an exit from Texas.

The first sign that Loggins is planning an escape comes when he quits his position at *The Saxon* in July 1882. The reaction from *The Galveston Daily News* doesn't describe a graceful exit: "The retiring editor bids his readers a feeling adieu, a pathetic part of which is an appeal to delinquents to pay their dues."[79]

It's actually a plea for traveling money. That summer, Loggins abandons his family and flees to Howard County, Arkansas. He's there to scout out a new place to rebuild, and it's not all business: "While there he came near marrying a very pretty young girl, and was only thwarted by some rumors of his land trouble in Texas, which gave him a sudden desire to again travel," a newspaper will later chronicle.[80]

Call it a lesson learned: If Loggins ever flees Texas again, he'll need to adopt an entirely new identity.

For now, it's time to head home. He finds the law ready to pounce—his accomplice, Abe Smith, has turned on him. Armed with Smith's information, Sabine County officials indict Loggins for forgery, jail him, and drag him in front of a grand jury in September 1882.

The Sabine County jailhouse is, like most structures in the area, made of wood. All that really stops a dedicated person from escaping is respect for the rule of law. Loggins, although a lawyer, shows very little regard for that. So, before the year ends, he escapes. There are some hints that he set a fire to cause an evacuation and slipped away during

---

78 "A Bad Man," *Fort Worth Daily Gazette,* April 8, 1888.

79 *Galveston Daily News,* January 11, 1882.

80 "The Journalistic Bigamist," *Daily Arkansas Gazette.*

the ensuing chaos, but the arson charges against him that back up this theory seem to fade in light of other, later crimes.[81]

In July 1883, he takes his Winchester and stalks Abe Smith. The ambush is ruthless and effective—he drops the informant with six rifle shots.[82] Some reports claim half as many bullets, but the fact remains that the man who crossed him is dead. It does nothing to quash the forgery case, and it makes him a wanted murderer, but Loggins makes his statement. It leaves Smith's wife, Martha, and his children, Ollie and Emma, to grieve as he's buried in Brookeland Cemetery.[83] Martha relocates to Houston and never remarries.[84]

That's when Loggins truly bonds with the Conners. It's a matter of fateful geography. Jim Sanders, his cousin, lives next to the Conner family and enjoys good relations. As Loggins seeks safe havens in the backwoods of Sabine County, still on the lam from prowling law enforcement, he finds the Conner Community to be friendly turf. It's an unlikely alliance between the illiterate farmers and the ambitious lawyer/newspaperman, but Loggins's mix of book smarts, medical knowledge, and woodcraft make him both useful and a novelty.

---

81 Newspaper reports covering the case—for example, *The Daily Arkansas Gazette* of July 28, 1892—cite "arson" as one of the Texas charges against L. L. Loggins.

82 Ibid. Reports claim he ambushed Smith at a sawmill. If true, it must not have been in Sabine County or it happened at one that closed. The Texas Forestry Museum (www .texasforestrymuseum.com) has a database of registered sawmills, and none appear to have opened in 1883. Howard & Craig sawmill opens in the town of Pendleton in 1884.

83 His cemetery stone in Brookeland Cemetery, in Sabine County, states his CSA enrollment; rank confirmed via the National Park Service's Find a Soldier database: "Smith, Abraham," National Park Service, Civil War Soldier Details, https://www .nps.gov/civilwar/search-soldiers-detail.htm?soldierId=3E99EBD1-DC7A-DF11 -BF36-B8AC6F5D926A.

84 In the 1930 Houston County Census, she is eighty-one and living with Ollie's family.

"He joined a band of bad characters, of which he virtually became leader, and for two years or more kept that whole section of country intimidated," says one newspaper biography of Loggins. It adds that Loggins enjoys the reputation as a dead shot with a Winchester, with which "he would go about openly defying arrest."[85] Loggins's loose association with the Conners—who are intimidating but not yet "bad characters" in the legal sense when Loggins first connects with them—doesn't help their case after the murders of Kit Smith and Eli Low.

Now the outlaw lawyer can only watch from the woods in dismay as the Conner family is hauled off, jailed, and, with Charley's departure, sent to prison. It's a time for action-oriented men to strike back, and Loggins considers himself one of those. The idea grows to break the Conner family out of jail.

There is a chance the Conners paid him to help organize tonight's jailbreak—Alfred Conner sells a piece of property in Sabine County for $200 on February 8, 1885.[86] Of course, that money is also meant to sustain the Conners when they go outlaw, but there's always a chance the wily Loggins took a piece of it for services rendered. After all, he is the county's most experienced jailbreaker.

Loggins also has the ability to use his lawyerly skills to whip up a mob of locals who see their neighbors being unfairly persecuted. The night of the jailbreak, these men meet at a local farmhouse before descending on downtown Hemphill en masse. There, what a reporter calls Loggins's "keen black eyes" scan the collection of men. They have more to lose than he does.

At this moment, he is the only criminal among them. The rest are crossing the Rubicon that night. That includes Conner boys—gaunt Leander and bug-eyed Alfie—who are not implicated in any feud violence

---

85 "The Journalistic Bigamist," *Daily Arkansas Gazette.*

86 This well-spotted, intriguing property deal was included in Dugan, *Judge Not.*

but have appeared to free their kin. Jim Sanders is also there to support his cousin and release his neighbors.

Those involved in the jailbreak are hardly the baddest men in the county. For example, counted among them is W. E. T. Ogletree, a thirty-seven-year-old schoolteacher. Not a seasoned outlaw, that one. The others are the farmers and laborers like Leon "Lem" Taylor, George Toms, Wade Noble, Sam Swan, and Ike Gary. Dutch Watkins is also here. He certainly has an opinion about frontier justice—he reportedly shot a man named Joseph Ford to death on December 10, 1876, during an argument over who won a horse race.[87]

Sterling Eddings, born 1851, has left a wife and child at home to release the Conners. His anger has seemingly been stoked by the investigation into his younger brother for rape.[88] The Eddings boys' father, Sterling Sr., was an early settler in Sabine. His boys married local girls: David K. Eddings, the accused, has a wife, Sarah, two children, and one grandchild. Sterling Eddings's role is seemingly a form of protest since his brother isn't even indicted yet and is not inside the jail.

The jail sits on the courthouse square, unguarded but locked. The jailbreakers mill around, pushing on the front door and thinking of ways to break through it. No one disturbs them. The ground is soft enough for digging, so the men start scraping out a hole under the raised pier-and-beam floor. Wade Noble holds the horses. They make quick work of it, but this can hardly be called a well-oiled, lightning operation.[89]

The most interesting member of the jailbreakers is Larkin Morris,

87 Ibid.

88 *Galveston Daily News*, September 18, 1885.

89 "The Lowe-Conner-Smith Feud Ends," East Texas Generations, July 31, 2010, http://easttexasgenerations.blogspot.com/2010/07/lowe-conner-smith-feud-ends .html, quotes a history compiled by local historian Ruth Sibley Davis called *Neighbor Against Neighbor: An East Texas Feud* that says the group "were forced to dig under the jail an opening large enough for the imprisoned men to be freed."

the member of the Smith-Low coroner's jury. There is no known reason why the Hemphill carpenter would join the throng; it certainly feeds the idea that the Conner family isn't getting a fair shake from the legal system. He's not known to be at the farmhouse and likely joined them downtown and supplied the jailbreak materials.

The hole is now wide and deep enough to accommodate a man. The jailbreakers pry open the floorboards between beams and then wait for the first prisoner to wriggle free. Willis Conner emerges, followed by Fed, William, and John. Another grimy figure slithers under the wall and out the hole. It's A. G. Click, who is being held for attempted murder. He's sees the opportunity; he's taking it.[90]

The men disperse into the night. Spradley calls the jailbreak "a mistake . . . made by the overzealous friends of the Conners." There is none more overzealous in his defiance of the law than L. L. Loggins, who slips away with the formidable, reunited family.

Now he and the Conners are equal. They are all outlaws.

BELL THE CAT
September 9, 1885

Judge James Perkins reads the newspaper and grits his teeth. *The Galveston Daily News* has an item about Sabine County's outlaws in today's edition that begins: "Loggins, Conners & Co. continue to agitate the public mind."

It gets worse as the outlaws flaunt their continuing freedom. The fugitive attorney wants everyone to know that he is ready to become a doctor. "Loggins, by messenger, notified Dr. F.H. Tucker, president of the board of medical examiners for this district, that he wishes him to propound in writing questions that he will be required to reply to in order to get a certificate to practice," the article relates. "He will send in his answers."

The public message includes a personal dig at Perkins, asking for

---

90 He ends up in the Indian Territories. Despite an 1887 extradition attempt, he bounces around Oklahoma and gets into the milling business and dies in 1941. *Chickasha Daily Express,* March 26, 1941.

"what suggestions he has to make. He says a personal interview with Judge Perkins or Dr. Tucker at this particular time would be very inconvenient to him."

Loggins's cheeky message seems clear: The Conner gang is in Sabine County, secure and unintimidated.

Willis Conner and all his boys have left their families, but in the end, they've only retreated to their own backyards—the wilds of Sabine County. There, they have a network of temporary camps hidden in the backwoods surrounding their homesteads. They're beyond the reach of the local lawmen and visiting detectives but remain plugged into their families and the Sabine community. Loggins, too, appears to have free rein—his wife, Mollie, is expecting again and due to give birth in October.[91]

A September 3, 1885, article in *The Galveston Daily News* notes that "75 men are scouring the country" and looking for "Loggins and his allies," and this posse "keeps him moving around." The reward for Loggins is $300, but the newspaper suggests the governor allocate larger amounts for him and the Conners. "What are we coming to!" the newspaper wails in closing.[92]

On September 14, 1885, the law strikes back. Sheriff William Smith has easily identified the jailbreakers after Wade Noble shoots off his mouth a week after the breakout. Noble tells Ada Toms, the wife of his neighbor, about the night's activities and mentions Dutch Watkins's involvement. Bad move—Toms is the daughter of Joseph Ford, slain by Watkins those many years ago. Maybe he thought that she'd remain quiet since her cousin George Toms is one of the jailbreakers. Instead, she identifies all those involved to the sheriff.

Eleven indictments land on the jailbreak gang, including Leander and Alfie Conner. Wade Noble and Jim Sanders are arrested, and Watkins turns himself in. George Toms is not indicted, likely a favor granted to Ada, the informant. L. N. Morris is indicted but not charged

---

91 Myrtle Loggins will be born in October 1885.

92 *Galveston Daily News*, September 3, 1885.

by the district attorney. When it's time to appear in court, Leander and Alfie Conner, Ogletree, Loggins, Sam Swan, and Sterling Eddings "are conspicuous by their absence" in the words of *The Galveston Daily News*. The paper notes that David K. Eddings has now been indicted for rape.

Sabine County is torn into two uneasy camps. There is some sympathy from locals who see the killings as part of something larger and better left alone. A segment of the population clearly feels the murder victims are not blameless. "It is stated by unbiased men who are good authorities that a deadly feud existed between the parties, and they were mutually hunting each other with the purpose of fighting it out to the death," notes *The Galveston Daily News,* at the time a usually reliable source for anti-Conner rhetoric.

The paper again bemoans the uproar in Sabine County: "If things go on in our section for the next two years as they have in the past two years, where will we land? Perhaps that place that the Prohibs call h_ll."[93]

Being outlaws is bad for the family business. In November 1885, Piercy Conner sells the 160 acres of land in her name, getting $500 for it. A neighbor and family friend, Redden Alford, witnesses the deal, since Willis Conner is a fugitive. Alford is one of the locals who meets the Conners in the woods to receive hams and wild game, which he brings to Hemphill to trade for goods that the outlaw family needs, like cornmeal and flour. It's a name worth remembering.

There are others who describe the Conners' tactics as more predatory and desperate. A Texas Ranger who will face them, J. Allen Newton, describes them as a menace: "People were afraid to light their lamps after dark. The gang would drive up to a farm, force the farmer to hitch up his team to his wagon, fill it full of corn, and then they would take it to their camp in the woods." It's hard to measure the accuracy of these details. This kind of fiery description, coming from the public officials in

---

93 *Galveston Daily News,* September 18, 1885. *Prohibs* is short for *Prohibitionists.*

Hemphill and repeated by Rangers, follow the Conners from the minute they break out of jail.[94]

The citizen-led manhunts are failures. Private detectives, sheriffs from three counties, and partial deployments of Texas Rangers (solo or in pairs, backed by deputies) all try their hands at tracking the Conners. None find success, and the outlaw family remains at large in Sabine County as the calendar switches to 1886.

Awkward family ties continue to be bound. In January 1886, Elmer Harper's son Elmore, who lived with Little Ike Low and stood accused by the Conners of pestering their pigs, marries Nancy "Miss Nan" Conner when she turns eighteen.[95] One can only imagine Old Man Conner's face when he hears of this betrothal. On that score, the outlaw life has not stopped Fed Conner from procreating; Fannie Conner, born in 1886, is conceived while Fed is an outlaw.

As for the local law, there's not much for the outlaws to worry about. "The people of Sabine County knew the situation and Sheriff Smith of that county made no effort to arrest the men he had known for years as his neighbors and friends," says the always-opinionated sheriff A. J. Spradley.[96]

Family lore grants a more sympathetic view of William H. Smith, whose family moved to Sabine County in the 1820s.[97] In 2011, J. Harris Smith, a retired police officer, writes details of his great-great-

---

94 Davidge, "Texas Rangers Were Tough." His narrative is also available via J. Allen Newton, "Early Days of the Texas Rangers," in the research room of the Texas Ranger Hall of Fame and Museum, Waco, TX.

95 Edna McDaniel White and Blanche Toole, *Sabine County Historical Sketches and Genealogical Records* (Pearl River, NY: LaBelle Printing, 1972).

96 Fuller, *A Texas Sheriff.*

97 William H. Smith, born December 29, 1835, in Arkansas, is the son of John Bailey Smith and grandson of John E. and Mary Smith, who arrived in San Augustine / Sabine County in the early 1820s.

grandfather's quandary in the comments of a genealogical website. "He didn't even own a gun when the feud started. He went to the general store and bought one," he relates. "He decided he wasn't gonna try to get the old man by himself. Everybody else was too scared to go help him."[98]

A darker version is given by Newton, who heard a story of pure intimidation while he was deployed in Sabine County:

> The sheriff at that time was named Smith. He was a big fellow, over six feet tall. He hunted the Conners and another fellow named Loggins, who had murdered a man. One day while driving through the woods he found them, as they were waiting for him with six-shooters. "You better start saying your prayers," they said. He begged them not to kill him, that he would go back and resign if would let him alone. Finally they decided to let him go. He kept his word and resigned. Oliver [sic] was the next sheriff. He wouldn't even try to go after the Conner gang.[99]

The Ranger is wrong; Smith didn't quit, but he did lose the 1886 election.[100] His replacement is S. H. Oliphint, from a well-to-do Hemphill family. Even as his tenure begins, it becomes obvious he's also not going to bring the Conners to justice without help.

Appeals from Judge Perkins and Sheriff Smith to Austin for a greater reward has fallen on deaf ears. But an incident in January 1886 brings a new, loud voice to the Conner trouble—their former attorney William Weatherred. Someone has, seemingly, violated his home.

---

98 Comments on "The Lowe-Conner-Smith Feud Ends," East Texas Generations.

99 Davidge, "Texas Rangers Were Rough."

100 Election records, Sabine County Historical Commission.

Many suspect the Conners have delivered a threat to their failed defense attorney.

Sabine County loves a conspiracy, and it *is* hard to imagine Willis Conner signing off on such an aggressive move when his family is in hiding. Those in Sabine County who believe the Conners were framed see the hand of Williams, Low, or even J. O. Toole at work.[101] But there is another player in the drama with a flair for the dramatic to add to the list: L. L. Loggins. It's not hard to see him stirring the pot, choosing a prominent local attorney—in his mind, a peer—as a target. Leaving a pistol imprint on a pillow indicates a level of theatricality that fits his personality. Loggins is also in a position to help put the Conners at odds with their attorney by describing how Weatherred botched the case, while hearing the way Loggins would have expertly handled it. Bad-mouthing in the wilds can quickly be interpreted as a threat once the word of it reaches Hemphill.

It doesn't matter who threatened Weatherred or even how. What matters in the end is that the former state senator gets involved in bringing a full company of the state's best gunmen to Sabine County. Maybe he was scared, maybe he was morally offended by the jailbreak, or maybe he was getting involved simply to assist his political allies in the county. Whatever the motivation, the defense attorney becomes a chief proponent of hunting down his former clients.

Perkins has the title of judge, but Weatherred has the political juice—he counts Adjutant General Wilburn King as a friend. On February 8, he boards a train for Austin, first telling Perkins that he'll be agitating for state help. The judge writes to Governor Ireland, telling him to expect Weatherred and asking for help "to effect the arrest of the outlaws Loggins and Conners who are not only still at large but . . . terrorizing the county."

The governor issues a new reward proclamation for the Conner family,

---

101 Dugan, *Judge Not*. Toole has an arrest in Sabine County for unlawfully carrying a weapon.

doubling the bounty to $200 apiece. The exception is Fed, who warrants $300. This lands them in the 1886 List of Fugitives from Justice, the so-called Ranger Bible, published in July.

The Conners' declared enemies in Sabine County now include leading public officials and esteemed men, as well as members of two vengeful backwoods families. All obsess over ways to bring down the Conners. "The general theme of conversation is how to bag them, and as usual everyone has his idea and can tell exactly how to do it," *The Galveston Daily News* holds forth on matters in Hemphill. "But then the question naturally suggests itself: Who will be the mouse to bell the cat?"[102]

In early fall 1886, that job falls to Company F.

---

102 *Galveston Daily News*, September 9, 1885.

3
BIG THICKET

THE OLE COMPANY
August 3, 1886

Captain William Scott gazes at the thick woods outside the perimeter of his camp, a few miles outside of Hemphill. It's healthy, clean forest dominated by individual pine trees growing 150 feet tall, with 5-foot diameters. They are wonderous, but if Scott had enough saws, he'd mow every one of them down like cornstalks. Those lovely trees represent nothing but dangerous hardships for Company F.

Scott's Rangers are recovering from yet another fruitless hunt for the Conner family, scouring dozens of miles of East Texas creek beds for signs of their campsites. They are following a lead generated by W. W. Weatherred, but have nothing to show for it but pests. "We have been going out every day and each man brings back ticks," Scott writes to fellow captain and Ranger quartermaster Liam Sieker. "Enough to keep him scratching and cussing all night."[1]

Scott led Company F for months as a lieutenant before his promotion to captain in late 1885, and by now, he wears leadership comfortably. His nine-year trail as a Texas Ranger has produced a litany of arrested men, quelled riots, averted gunfights, escorted prisoners,

---

1 "Scott to Sieker," July 31, 1886, Texas State Archives, Austin, TX.

political disputes with other Rangers, and townsfolk either appeased or aggrieved.

But East Texas is something different. The thick woods and wretched swamps make Scott long for the rest of Texas's open plains. He's been here before on scouts, looking for the Conners with small squads, and he knows exactly the threat that the terrain represents. Narrow trails, steep creek beds, and shadowy forests are frightening places to conduct a manhunt. Outlaws here seem to have all the advantages.[2]

Instead of focusing on the brooding surroundings, Scott fixes his attention on the Ranger camp around him. The collection of canvas tents is comfortably familiar, but not luxurious. "The Rangers' camps look much like those of gypsies," a *Harper's* reporter writes after a visit. "One wagon to carry the horses' feed, the ponies grazing at the ends of the lariats, the big Mexican saddles hung over the nearest barb fence, and the blankets covering the ground and marking the hard beds of the night before."[3]

But the company's camp also brings comforts, particularly in the form of teamster James Johnson, a Black man who joined Company F in September 1885, a few months after Scott took control as lieutenant.[4] Johnson is responsible for the heart of the Ranger camp—the chuck wagon that holds all the company's shared supplies and, more importantly, is the source of their meals. The teamster is cook, logistician, and inventory steward to a group of eleven men with incredibly erratic hours

---

2 He later shares these sentiments with family members in Dallas, as we shall see.

3 Richard Harding Davis, "The West from a Car Window," *Harper's Weekly*, March 5, 1892.

4 It's hard to give James Johnson his just due. Records identifying him don't exist beyond his service record pay stubs. His race is not listed. A Ranger who joins Company F the next year, J. Allen Newton, recalls Company F "wagons driven by negroes" in Sarah Ellen Davidge, "Texas Rangers Were Rough and Ready Fighters," *Frontier Times*, November 1935.

and travel schedules. He's the face of Company F's home, even if home is a campsite designed to be entirely uprooted at a moment's notice.

The mobile supply wagon is an invention for cattle drives, and it brings roundup-derived "Cookie" etiquette to a Ranger camp. The tenets are simple: Don't eat using the wagon's work space as a dining table. Riders should always approach and leave camp downwind. An unfinished plate is an insult to the cook. Anyone refilling his coffee is duty-bound to refill anyone else waving a cup.[5]

Scott's biggest comfort is the proximity of his Rangers. Here at camp, he can keep an eye on them. As Company F's captain, each of his ten men represents a unique responsibility. Scott must break in each one, train him to be deadly or judicious as needed, and back him up when he gets in trouble. He can't help surveying the ones nearby, just as a herd dog at rest will constantly keep an eye on the flock.

He spots private Henry Putz feeding Chico, the pack mule, a piece of candy. The company has three mules, but everyone is sweet on Chico. The mule earned their respect on the trail, following them without rope and leaping over fences even while bearing a heavy pack. She also earns treats that the Rangers buy for her in town.[6] Putz is nearing the end of his tenure, and Scott doubts he'll reenlist. Hopefully, the shooting in Alex won't follow him into retirement or force the end of Company F sergeant J. A. Brooks's career as a Ranger.

Lounging nearby, examining his legs for bloodsuckers, is T. S. Crowder, who most Rangers just call "Bob." He and his Winchester carbine lean against a tree trunk. He's been a Ranger since November 1884, a welcome transfer to Company F from Captain S. A. McMurray

---

5 Kathy Weiser, "The Chuck Wagon—The Real Queen of the Cattle Trail," *Legends of America*, March 2020, https://www.legendsofamerica.com/we-chuckwagon/.

6 Per a description of the animal by J. Allen Newton, who joined Company F the next year. Davidge, "Texas Rangers Were Rough."

in Company B in August 1886. Lean and somber, Crowder sports as full a mustache as Scott's sergeant, J. A. Brooks.

Crowder's sitting near another Company B refugee, Private John Rogers. The pair just missed each riding together amid transfers and reenlistments but still have a lot of comrades in common. Rogers is writing in his daybook, keeping a journal as so many Rangers do. These are generally lists of places and people, rather than diaries of innermost thoughts. Rogers keeps this journal in his vest pocket; his Bible resides in a saddlebag.

Rogers is just back from fetching the accused rapist Dave Eddings, brother of the jailbreaker Sterling Eddings. The man skipped town after his indictment, but the Rangers learned he was spotted, in a nearby hamlet appropriately called Pineland. Rogers brought him back to the Hemphill jail single-handedly.

Scott trusted him to get the job done, and not solely because Rogers is an experienced private. "He is modest, unassuming and dignified in his demeanor, as well as wearing apparel," according to the *El Paso Herald*. "He has long been reputed by his friends and associates as a man possessing all the gentleness and sympathy of a woman, but once aroused he is as courageous as a lion and forceful as a Bengal tiger."[7]

John Harris Rogers is a native of Texas, born on a farm nine miles east of Seguin on October 19, 1863. His father, Pleas Rogers, is a Mississippi native who moved to Texas after the Civil War, during which he enlisted at age sixteen. His son John attends a district school but has a penchant for work outdoors. The allure of Texas draws him away from the farm. A future writer describes: "When 18 years old he saddled his horse one bright spring morning, bade his parents goodbye and rode into Mitchell County where he got his first position, that of a roustabout on the ranch of W.N. Waddle. He got $15 a month."[8]

Rogers didn't leave home just to work on a ranch. He tells Waddle

7 "Man Who Knows No Leaves the Rangers," *El Paso Herald,* February 4, 1911.

8 Ibid.

that he wants to quit to join the Texas Rangers, and the rancher respects the choice enough to introduce him to Captain Bill McMurray and recommend him for the job. He's sworn in on September 5, 1882. He spends fifteen months with Company B before he resigns, "feeling homesick," and returns to Seguin.

The mistake becomes evident. Rogers only makes it a few weeks back on the family farm before he's riding to Cotulla to meet Company F captain Joe Shely and reenlist. But a stutter-start career haunts him a year later, when budget cuts cost him a position with the Rangers since he's the company's most junior member. After three months of boredom in Seguin, Shely calls him back to service. Soon after, William Scott takes the reins as Company F's head when Shely takes a job as sheriff.

In all his time as a Texas Ranger, Rogers never killed anyone, but no one doubts his ability to pull when needed. A religious teetotaler like he certainly sticks out in this outfit—his Kentucky-born sergeant is certainly no stranger to drink—but his deep Christian convictions feed a quiet righteousness as a lawman, and vice versa. "Christianity came to me gradually after much study of the question," Rogers will one day explain. "Years of religious reading gave me the conviction that Christianity should dominate a man's life, no matter in what occupation that he might be engaged."[9]

When it comes to breaking in tenderfoots, Scott relies on Rogers to set a good example. An example of how well this works is sitting on a blanket nearby—Private J. B. Harry. He joined last January, and by month's end, he was riding dozens of miles outside of town to arrest suspected home burglars with only Rogers as backup. Being a Ranger suits him; he's now a strong, stout man with a full mustache who's taken to wearing his hat cocked at a jaunty angle while in town.[10]

---

9 Harry Van Demark, "Religion and Bullets," *Texas Monthly*, March 1929.

10 Ranger service records, period photos; service records kept at the Texas Ranger Hall of Fame and Museum's Tobin and Anne Armstrong Ranger Research Center, Waco, TX. See: "About the Tobin & Anne Armstrong Texas Ranger Research Center,"

Resting nearby is another steady and extremely experienced private, thirty-year-old Jim Moore. Frank Moore, his uncle, was already a Confederate Civil War hero when he made his name again with the Texas Rangers, fighting Indians. After serving with Company F, he reenlisted as a second lieutenant in Company D and eventually became its captain. He retired in 1877 to operate a successful ranch in Kerr County but just couldn't leave law enforcement behind. The Ranger private's "Uncle Frank" is now sheriff of Kerr County and has been since 1882.

Many of his nephews follow Frank's lead and enter law enforcement, particularly the Texas Rangers. Jim Moore joins Company D of the Frontier Battalion in 1875 at age eighteen, transfers to Company C two years later, and then to Company F in March 1881. Having spent his entire adult life as a Texas Ranger, he's an extremely valuable private.[11] He's even been to Sabine County before, having accompanied a deputy sheriff during the arrest of unrepentant Conner family jailbreaker Ike Gary here last September.

Scott understands the impulse to follow family into law enforcement; his older brother Jack served in the Texas Rangers.[12] His brother had the good sense to retire outside of Dallas, near their sister Emily Virginia Bower, but William Scott just can't let go. But on an assignment like this one, he has to question his choices.

Maybe Dee Caldwell had the right idea. The young private left the service in March, just a few months into his first year. Ranger life isn't for everyone, and there's no point trying to force anyone to stay for their full-year commitment. Maybe being chased out of the Indian Territories

---

Texas Ranger Hall of Fame and Museum, https://www.texasranger.org/texas-ranger-museum/researching-rangers/.

11 Ranger service records, "Adjutant General Service Records," Texas State Library and Archives Commission, https://www.tsl.texas.gov/apps/arc/service/.

12 He may also have been "Shingle" Scott, the commander of a Black militia company.

and seeing a fellow private and sergeant accused of murder dampened his enthusiasm. His absence leaves Scott shorthanded as he ranges the depths of Sabine County.

The Ranger camaraderie is being stressed by the assignment and the ever-present ticks. Scott hears the men grumble and shares their frustration. Deep East Texas has robbed his Rangers of much that makes them so dangerous.

For one, speed. The Rangers catch horse and cattle thieves more with tenacity than aggressive gunplay. They move unnaturally fast, riding long hours to spring on their prey from behind or leapfrog ahead and intercept them as they approach. But what good is the ability to ride seventy miles a day in a land of darkened woods and swampy bogs? These Conners aren't trying to get much distance between themselves and the law; they are staying right where they are, where they know every obscure trail and twisted creek. They could be just a dozen feet away and stay concealed, making the vast forests of East Texas large enough for the outlaws to hide for years, maybe forever.

The art of tracking in the rest of Texas depends on following hoofprints across dry and sandy plains. The typical rules, learned by countless Rangers chasing countless stolen animals, apply. When the tracks are bunched up, the party is moving fast. Free horses leave different tracks from those being ridden; tenderfoots are taught how to age a trail based on its condition. Experienced Rangers claim to reporters that they can tell the racial makeup of a party by the tracks they leave behind but refuse to reveal how.[13]

None of those tracking skills can be applied to the Big Thicket. The Conners move without leaving a trace, making their ever-moving camp impossible to find. Their handful of mules leaves few lingering signs. Blundering through Conner country is more than exhausting, it's dangerous. It leaves his men vulnerable to ambush by the seasoned woodsmen.

---

13 Earl Mayo, "Texas Rangers: The Most Efficient Police Force in the World," *Frank Leslie's Popular Monthly*, October 1901.

"I had rather be a pack mule out west than be a million heir [*sic*] in this brush," he writes King. "It is sure rough country on man and beast, but I can stand it if I can only get back to the prairie alive."

What Scott really needs is someone on the inside. He has experience with this. After all, being an informant is what got him into the Texas Rangers to begin with.

WILL SCOTT, FREELANCE DETECTIVE
April 8, 1878 (nine years before Company F's Sabine County deployment)

William Scott follows just behind Billie Collins as he walks around the man's house, heading to the back. He's trying to hide his nerves. At twenty-four years old, fear is indistinguishable from excitement.[14] Every boot step brings him deeper into the inner circle of the wanted criminal Sam Bass.

Hopefully, tonight he will hear details of the outlaw's next score. Collins leads him to a barn, where a cluster of men have gathered. Scott swallows his surprise when he sees that the gang's all here.[15] Collins is sheltering them here in Dallas County, outside the North Texas town of Denton. They are fresh from a crime. In fact, that serves as Scott's signal to find them. When he hears about the heist of a stagecoach, he knows to seek them out.[16]

Billie Collins has schemed to bring the notorious outlaw to Dallas County to help Billie settle a grudge. It started when he joined a couple of rowdy farmhands, recent area transplants Sam Pipes and Albert Herndon, in causing a scene with some Duck Creek farmers at a dance. The merry scene erupted into a violent brawl, injuring some of the Duck Creek boys and putting a memorable cap on the night's festivities.

---

14 An 1870 census estimates his date of birth as 1854.

15 He means this literally. This phrase won't become famous until 1880 when *The Pirates of Penzance* debuts in New York City.

16 Charles Martin, *A Sketch of Sam Bass, the Bandit* (Dallas, TX: Worley, 1898).

The bad blood spilled over into prosecutions against Collins and company, articles in newspapers, and libel lawsuits.

Now it's a feud, and Collins wants the biggest, baddest guns in Texas to back him up. That means getting Sam Bass to come to Dallas County. He has the contacts to do it—his brother, Joel, rode with Bass during his successful train robbery in Big Springs, Nebraska. Never mind that Joel Collins also died up north, shot down by lawmen.

William Scott seeks out Billie Collins, figuring a family member of the outlaw's partner could know how to reach out to Sam Bass. Instead, he finds the sibling is also actively looking for the robber and his gang. The pair set off together to Bass's known haunt, the city of Denton.

His supporters are easy to find by visiting Denton taverns and law offices. People talk to Billie Collins; his brother's fatal connection to Bass gains him and Scott their first audience at Bob Murphy's farm. The gang is camped there, but Bass isn't. Some of the men are Bass's "regulars," who have been committing stagecoach and train robberies during an interstate crime spree.[17]

Scott stays there several days and is invited to meet at the Collins house after he hears about a nearby robbery. Because of his time at Bass's camp, he can recognize most of the men assembled here tonight.

Frank Jackson is a quiet and polite twenty-two-year-old and certainly doesn't seem a killer. Growing up poor and surrounded by wild cowboys, he took his first life as a youth, well before he joined the gang, when Jackson murdered a Black man over a dispute over a horse. Then came the big chance to straighten out: he relocated to Denton to be tutored by his employer, a doctor. Jackson's torn between civil living and the wild life, a battle that ends when he connects with Sam Bass in 1877. Serene, good-tempered, dependable, and a veteran of every Bass train robbery, he's now a trusted member of the gang.

Another is a tall, thin man with a feather in his cowboy hat. Seaborn Barnes, twenty-five, has a sharp, sloping nose and awkwardly jutting

---

17 Ibid.

Adam's apple that draws the eye. He's from a decent Texas family but is illiterate and, Scott quickly finds, has rough manners to go with the scraggly looks. He's got an attack dog's loyalty to the gang and has proven eager to shoot during robberies.

Scott then meets the small eyes, deep in their sockets, of Henry Underwood. The thirty-two-year-old has a dark complexion and a heavy, black mustache that matches his eye color. He's a good-size man, at five foot, nine inches tall. After serving in the Union Army in the Civil War as a youth, Underwood found the righteous, dull path of a wood hauler to be less appealing than gambling and drinking. Underwood left his wife and family and, in 1874, teamed up with Bass to race horses. The two are virtually inseparable; he and Bass beat up Black people, tangle with cattle vigilantes, and, in time, graduate to armed robbery. Underwood often complains about the time he was falsely arrested in Nebraska—twice—for being a man named Tom Nixon. Underwood had to break out of the Kearney jail after being accused of crimes he didn't commit, so could be free to commit his own.

A tall man Scott has never seen before is eyeing him warily. This is Arkansaw Johnson, the most frightening of the group. There is an air of violence around him that is palpable. Back when his name was Huckston, the one he was born with, he served with the Union Army. He and Underwood met in that Kearney jail and plotted the escape together. They rode back to Texas together in 1878 to join with Bass. Johnson's crimes run deeper than just banditry—he raped a girl during a home invasion in Arkansas after murdering her parents with an iron bar.[18]

Scott tonight faces Sam Bass himself, for the first time falling under the gaze of the twenty-six-year-old outlaw's dark brown eyes. He's five foot, eight inches, 140 pounds, with a pleasant face and trimmed mustache. When he laughs, which is often, he flashes an excellent set of white teeth. He looks, it has to be said, like more of a stage hero than villain. It's hard to believe that this man can have Scott killed and buried with a word.

18 Rick Miller, *Texas Ranger John B. Jones* (Denton, TX: University of North Texas Press, 2012).

When Bass went outlaw in 1874, Billie's older brother, Joel Collins, was right there with him. The pair drifted from North Texas to Nebraska, working cattle drives, but decided it was easier and more fun to rob stagecoaches. The big score came in September 1877 in Big Springs, when their gang of six robbed a Union Pacific train of $65,000 in gold coins and valuables. (That's about $1.4 million today.) Within a few weeks, Collins and two others were killed resisting arrest, but Bass got away and fled to Texas. Since then, his heists have proven to be dangerous and far from lucrative. He hopes the next one turns out better.

William Scott speaks up boldly. He suggests robbing a bank in Dallas, where he's from. They won't see it coming, unlike the train operators and passengers who often carry weapons in expectation of trouble.

Others suggest a bank in Weatherford. Bass's is the only vote that matters, and he wants to rob another train first. He announces the next target is the Texas & Pacific in the town of Mesquite. He dispatches Billie Collins, not a known outlaw, to reconnoiter the depot for places to stash horses, avenues of escape, and the like. Another meeting here will follow in a few days to finalize plans, Bass tells them.

Scott mulls the details of the caper as he rides away. He's got more at stake than the stolen proceeds and a budding reputation as an outlaw. The young man is playing a dangerous game of double agent without any legal sanction, aiming to bring down the infamous band—and claim his share of the reward money for the Union Pacific train robbery.

Scott, with siblings already in the profession, catches the law enforcement bug but approaches it in a rash way. He hatches a reckless plan to infiltrate the Sam Bass gang on his own and report their inner workings to the authorities.

Going undercover is a gamble that is clearly paying off, he thinks smugly as he rides away from the clandestine April 8 meeting. If Scott knew what some of the others are saying behind his back, he wouldn't be so proud. After meeting Scott for the first time that night, Arkansaw

Johnson "declares Scott a spy and urges the robber chief to put him out of his way."[19]

Bass heeds his own counsel and trusts the eager newcomer. It takes a couple of days for Collins to complete his scout, and when he does, the Bass gang holds their next meeting. William Scott is invited. Scott rides to the gang's Denton County camp. The critical moment that every undercover agent dreads nears: He's enmeshed in a violent crime, and he can either go along with it or arouse suspicions by refusing. Even worse, he's not even an agent of the law. He could be shot or arrested for robbery, should he go along.

Luckily for him, the supply of wannabe criminals in Texas is larger than the demand for them. The meeting is attended by too many for the Mesquite train job. It's more gunmen than he needs, Bass explains, and using everyone here would unacceptably reduce everyone's share of the take.

This is an easy out for William Scott, who removes himself from the impending caper. But farmhands Herndon and Pipes are committed. "Pipes was 'train struck' and would listen to no reason," notes one chronicle of the gang. "It is said that he formerly lived in Missouri near the rendezvous of the James and Younger brothers and that evil shadows had fallen across the bright beams of childhood fancy."[20]

With the core of five regulars, Bass only needs two Denton locals to come along. Billie Collins refuses to be left behind, and even mounts a horse to follow, but Bass coolly orders him to stay.

The heist goes down late at night on April 10, 1878. As the train eases to a halt, the gunmen swarm across the platform. Each man has a role. One puts the station agent at gunpoint. Another leaps on board and does the same to the engineer. A pair rob the passengers, car by car. Bass heads to the express car for the big haul. The staff there refuse to open the

---

19 Martin, *A Sketch of Sam Bass.*

20 Ibid.

door until Bass pours oil on the door and threatens to burn them alive. There is almost no money inside; it's mostly mail.[21]

Elsewhere in the train, things are getting bloody. Those robbing the passengers didn't factor in a conductor like Julius Alvord. He's a U.S. Army veteran who joined the Thirtieth Illinois Regiment as a private and mustered out as an officer's adjutant.[22] Seeing the robbery in progress, he puts out his lantern and picks up a pistol. Using that and a passenger's pocket derringer, he gets into a running gunfight with the robbers. His surprise attacks wound three, but he's outnumbered and retreats after being shot through the arm. Even then, he remains defiant and refuses calls to surrender. "He is a brave fellow," a nearby, cowering porter overhears a robber comment. "It would be too bad to kill him."[23]

Finally, the gang flees. "The whole amount of money secured made but twenty-three dollars apiece for the seven robbers," notes one account.[24]

Pipes, Underwood, and Barnes each have gunshot wounds, but none are life-threatening. Pipes is the worst off, with a small-caliber pistol ball in his side. He convalesces in Denton; the wanted outlaw Underwood stashes himself in a haystack on Billie Collins's land for two days.

While all this is happening, William Scott has gone off to inform on the gang. He has heard the plan, knows the participants, and can secure indictments against them all. "With young Scott in his camp yard for the night, he heard them plotting and planning," says J. A. Brooks,

---

21 *Life and Adventures of Sam Bass, the Notorious Union Pacific and Texas Train Robber*, W. L. Hall, Dallas, TX, 1878

22 Civil War Soldiers and Sailors Database, National Park Service, https://www.nps .gov/civilwar/soldiers-and-sailors-database.htm.

23 Hall, *Life and Adventures of Sam Bass.*

24 Ibid.

recalling his captain's version. "When he went home the next morning, he told his father, who at once notified Major Jones at Austin."[25]

Major John B. Jones, commander of the Frontier Battalion, is already embroiled in this latest train robbery; the governor himself ordered him to investigate. Jones has already been on the hunt for Bass for months, and his gang members are emerging as suspects in the Mesquite heist. Now he has both proof and intel about his main target, both delivered out of nowhere by the brave and entirely irresponsible William Scott. With his information, Jones already has the identity of the robbers and their supporters. The young informant is also a wild card that he can continue to play.[26]

Jones asks Scott to return to Bass's camp to check out what's going on there. If there are no train robbers there, he's to return. If there is anyone there worthy arresting, Scott is to sit in place and wait for the raid. Scott agrees and heads to the Collins house on April 22.

That night, Jones rallies a squad of Rangers, and they ride to the Collins home, wondering if his young informant is bunking with outlaws or buried in a ditch somewhere. They surround the home and aim Winchesters at every exit. The adjutant general strides to the front door and knocks. Henry Collins answers, holding a pistol. He considers the hopeless tactical situation and puts the gun down.

Jones finds Sam Pipes sleeping upstairs. His pleas of innocence fall flat considering the bullet wound in his side. He's seized, as are Henry Collins, an unidentified Black man working at the home, and the "outlaw" Billy Scott. Taken aside, Scott tells the men where they can find Herndon—lodged just a few miles away at the home of a sympathizer named Tom Jackson. Jones takes Pipes, releases the rest, and rides to roust the other robber from his sanctuary.

Sam Pipes's and Albert Herndon's brief and lousy careers as outlaws

25 J. A. Brooks's handwritten memoir, courtesy of Texas Ranger Hall of Fame and Museum.

26 Miller, *Texas Ranger John B. Jones.*

are over. The pair are hustled off to the Dallas County jail and eventually to prison, where they share a cell, for a time, with the infamous John Wesley Hardin. Later, they'll distinguish themselves during a prison disease outbreak and earn a pardon.[27]

Now the hunt for Sam Bass becomes a declared war. Jones begins to organize a twenty-man force of mounted Frontier Battalion rangers, with Lieutenant Junius Peak in command, just to crush his gang. "Well, to give young Scott full protection he was enlisted," Brooks writes in his memoirs. On May 1, Peak signs William Scott as a private in the Texas Rangers, Company B. The rest of the Rangers are sworn in on March 19.

His first orders may be Scott's last. Peak and Jones dispatch Scott to Denton County to reconnect with the gang. None of them have any idea if the gang suspects the informant, but he's willing to take the risk. Scott prowls Denton, tapping into their tavern courier contacts for an invite to another gang meeting. This one will be held at the home of supporter Green Hill. Scott rides alone to the home, six miles south of Denton, once again not knowing if there is a bullet or a bottle of whiskey waiting for him.[28]

Scott is relieved to see Sam Bass is there. Not only is he the chief target, he's also Scott's biggest benefactor. The bandit chief is no more bowed by the last robbery than he'd been swayed away from crime by earlier failures. He's exhibiting the crazed tempo of the spree criminal, careening from one escapade to the next with pathological fervor.

The next target, Bass declares to the assembled men, is the Gaston and Thomas Bank in Dallas.

Scott's hometown knowledge can come in handy; Bass dispatches him to the city to case the bank. The undercover operator happily leaves camp just in time to miss a fatal arrival: Denton saloonkeeper Scott Mayes, hold-

---

27 Robert J. Pipes, "Short Story About San Bass and Sam Pipes," Pipes Family Gene-alogy, http://www.pipesfamily.com/sambass.htm.

28 Hall, *Life and Adventures of Sam Bass.*

ing a letter from Billie Collins in Denton. He writes Bass convinced that Scott betrayed them, leading to the raid on his home and the arrests of Pipes and Herndon. Collins's advice: Hang Scott from the nearest tree.

Scott's cover is blown, and Sam Bass clearly sees that it's time to leave Denton. The gang hits the road heading south, Peak in pursuit.

As the "Bass War" continues that summer, Henry Underwood rides off and never returns. On June 12, Peak and his men, backed by a posse, gun down Arkansaw Johnson. Bass's band continues south, intending to rob a small bank in Round Rock. With that money in hand, Bass vows, they will return to Denton County to kill a couple of deputy sheriffs there—and the traitor, Will Scott.

But there is more than one turncoat for Bass to worry about. In Georgetown, while sending a telegram summoning fellow gang members, Jim Murphy also writes one to Jones. He describes a near miss:

> I wrote to Major Jones, at Austin, that we were at Georgetown, and on our way to Round Rock to rob the railroad bank, or to be killed, and to prevent it for God's sake. I just got that letter in as Bass came in. He asked me what I was doing in there so long. I said I was trying to talk this man out of his paper. The man took the hint, threw down the paper, and said he would loan but said he could not sell it.[29]

The telegram spurs Jones and Peak to quick action. The Texas Ranger force surges from Dallas County to Round Rock. Jones, personally invested, heads there as well.

No one is expecting the Bass War to come to a bloody head in downtown Red Rock on July 19. A pair of deputy sheriffs spot a few of the members as the gang assembles to hit the bank, and follow them after they duck into a store. "We walked across the street and went into the store," says Deputy Sheriff Maurice Moore, one of the two deputies.

---

29 Ibid.

"Not wishing to let them know I was watching them, I stood up inside the store door with my hands in my pockets, whistling. [Williamson County deputy Ahijah] Grimes approached them carelessly and asked one if he had not a six-shooter."[30]

He finds out the answer when they promptly draw and gun him down with six shots. Moore is also promptly felled with a ball through the lung, which he'll survive. The robbers take to the streets, their heist in ruins. They find the town has become a madcap shooting gallery.

A Ranger named Dick Ware, leaping from a barber's chair with a face full of shaving lather, hears the shots and dashes into the street. He runs into Johnson, Barnes, and Bass, and the gunfight truly begins.

Ware is immediately joined by two welcome but improbable allies. A one-armed man named Stubbs picks up the dead Grimes's gun and is opening fire on the bandits. The other is none other than Texas adjutant general Tom Jones, who rushes from the nearby International & Great Northern Telegraph office and finds himself trading gunshots with the Bass gang. They miss each other, but a bullet smacks into a stone wall just behind his head. Ware then shoots the famous outlaw; the bullet hits his belt buckle and cleaves in two pieces that tear through his groin and stomach.[31]

The thwarted bank robbers retreat to the alley, where their horses are waiting. So, too, are well-armed Rangers and townsfolk. Rifle fire cracks, and Barnes falls dead from a head shot. The gang gallops away to a chorus of rifles.

A search party finds Bass the next morning, lying alone and helpless in a pasture north of town. Over the next few days, he refuses to sup-

30 "The Story of Sam Bass," City of Round Rock, https://www.roundrocktexas.gov /departments/planning-and-development-services/historic-preservation/historic -round-rock-collection/sam-bass/.

31 "When Sam Bass, the Notorious Texas Bandit Was Killed, by Capt. Gillett," *El Paso Herald*, August 12, 1902. There is some debate over this, but Bass says he was shot by a man "with lather on his face."

ply Jones with any information. He dies in Round Rock on July 21, his twenty-seventh birthday.

Scott appears to play no direct role in Sam Bass's swan song, although he eventually receives a share of the reward. Instead of staying near Bass's base of support in North Texas, he's sent to the panhandle as a newly minted Texas Ranger. He will in time provide star witness testimony during Bass gang member trials, securing sentences and facing unfounded accusations that he participated in the Mesquite train robbery.[32]

Private William Scott's first paycheck as a Texas Ranger, issued at a bank south of Tyler on August 31, 1878, is docked forty-three dollars to pay the organization back for his gear. That includes a Winchester carbine for twenty-seven dollars and a Colt pistol for sixteen.[33] The amateur sleuth is now a professional outlaw hunter.

THE STOIC AND THE DEFIANT
August 3, 1886

These memories make Scott think of Sergeant Brooks and his favorite campfire story about his own run-in with Sam Bass.

In 1871 or so, when Brooks is living in Dallas County, he owns a horse that is fast enough to win races. These are seedy gambling contests that, like all such, attract adventurous locals and wandering rogues alike. Brooks enters one alongside a young, budding outlaw who is there with some rough friends. "Bass was the only one wearing a black hat, but he had the fastest pony and he carried off the dough," Brooks recalls. Later that night, as Brooks returns home, he spots a campfire in the darkness, usually a hospitable sight. "When I approached the camp, a lot of men grabbed their carbines and gave me the greatest scare of my life," he says.

---

32 Miller, *Texas Ranger John B. Jones.*

33 "Adjutant General Service Records," Texas State Library and Archives Commission, https://www.tsl.texas.gov/apps/arc/service/.

"Well, it was Sam Bass's camp. I had a fast horse myself and rode out of there."[34]

Brooks may be stoic and Putz petulantly defiant, but Scott is growing very concerned by the developments in Fort Smith. In the age of the telegram, bad news travels fast. District Attorney Montgomery "Monte" Sandels is pushing forward with the case in Arkansas—just yesterday, his two Rangers were indicted by a grand jury for the murder of Albert St. John, as was T. R. Knight. Scott knows it's just a matter of time before his men will have to leave for Arkansas to prepare for a trial.

The idea of losing them, especially his trusted sergeant, is painful to contemplate considering the foes Company F is currently facing here in Sabine County.

Scott is forming an opinion of the Conner family, and it's one of wary caution. "The women grow small patches of corn and raise peas, the men shoot wild turkeys and venison and occasionally kill a steer or hog— this being the extent of their depredations," Scott describes the family to a reporter. "They live like Indians, always on the alert, understand the country perfectly and will never be caught napping, their rifles are always in their hands sleeping or waking."[35]

What worked on Sam Bass won't work here. That outlaw band was recruiting new members and engaging in brazen crimes, leading to opportunities for lawmen to use spies like Scott and leverage turncoats like Murphy. In comparison, the Conner family doesn't travel, commits no flashy crimes, and isn't seeking new members. The locals who trade with the outlaws are too loyal, scared, or both to cross them.

Finding a turncoat among the locals who support them is not proving easy for Scott and his local proxies. They must have limited information, Scott determines. "The [Conner] band sees no one but their women folks,"

---

34 Brooks's handwritten memoirs, courtesy of the Texas Ranger Hall of Fame and Museum, Waco, TX.

35 "A Desperate Set," *Fort Worth Daily Gazette*, June 13, 1887.

he says. "They do not communicate with their friends, for these friends can take their freedom from them but cannot grant it, and all the men want is freedom. Seeing no one but their wives, they are in no danger of betrayal, for a woman will never sell a husband she has suffered privation with."[36]

The truth is that there are many friends and family who are actively helping the family. The Conners need supplies from civilization, things like flour, cornmeal, and shell primers. They also have families and property that they need to stay close to. Yet somehow, no information leaks that can snare them.

However, there is a prominent crack in the Conner gang, but the Rangers and Weatherred aren't privy to it. "[L. L. Loggins] had a correspondence going on between himself and Sheriff Spradley, of this county, in which he proposed to arrest the entire Conner clan, provided that he could secure his liberty by doing so," says one later newspaper report from San Augustine County. "But he could not perfect a compromise, so he left the bushes."[37]

Instead, Loggins abandons Sabine County, his fellow outlaws, wife, and children. The aspiring physician flees to Arkansas under a new identity, Rupert P. Wright. He arrives in Little Rock with an eye for opportunity. His profession of erudite newspaperman travels well, and his swagger and smooth tongue mesh well with actual trade experience.

By July 1886, Loggins has wooed the staff at *The Arkansas Democrat* and secured work as a columnist. "He came to this city in the spring of 1886 and made application for a position on the reportorial staff of the *Democrat*," the newspaper reports. "He was given a case in the composing rooms where he worked for a few days when he was given the position of city editor . . . He was a good writer and made a capable city editor, and while he was never considered altogether reliable by his employers, they had confidence in his ability."

---

36 Ibid.

37 *Sunday Gazetteer,* September 10, 1893.

Like any good liar, he weaves in some truth to create his new life. "He informed his employers that he had been married twice," details *The Arkansas Democrat*. "His first wife he represented to have died many years ago and when he wont to discourse of this—his early love—tears would trickle down his face."[38]

His other wife, he admits to coworkers, is still alive: "He declared that he had discovered she was untrue and had in consequence sought and obtained a divorce." That's a pretty shabby description of his wife, Mollie Loggins, very much alive and left behind.

Loggins uses his position to hobnob with the cream of Little Rock society. He gets a gushing review from former U.S. congressman and fellow newsman W. Jasper Blackburn that *The Democrat* proudly runs. It starts with one of the most fawning run-on sentences ever printed:

> For some weeks the *Democrat* has had on its local columns a fresh recruit In the person of an already well tried and well known and efficient newspaper writer—Dr. R.P. Wright, who is making the local columns of that already popular daily sparkle and scintillate with a freshness of wit and humor and general brilliance and aptness of thought heretofore comparatively unknown to the same medium.[39]

In Little Rock, Loggins's alter ego will rise in stature, and he plays the role to the hilt. He accepts the position as city editor knowing it will expose him to public scrutiny. Similarly, he appears as a character witness in a libel trial and scorches the plaintiff.[40] In October, he even judges

---

38 "A Bigamist," *Arkansas Democrat*, July 21, 1888.

39 "Our New City Editor," *Arkansas Democrat*, July 24, 1886.

40 "The Libel Suit," *Arkansas Democrat*, December 1886.

a "finest bouquet" contest. He's part of a three-person committee that awards Mrs. S. A. Dukes with the prize.[41]

Who Blackburn and the rest of Arkansas regard as "personally and socially the cordial and genial gentleman" is a wanted murderer, swindler, and jailbreaker who also deserted his wife and children to poverty. Loggins has successfully turned his back on East Texas, and he's never been happier. But Sabine County has not seen the last of him.

POSSES AND MANHUNTS
August 1886

Not every local is intimidated by the Conner family, and Scott has tapped one of them to select members of a small posse. The Ranger captain turns to former state senator William Wallace Weatherred, one of the voices that summoned him to this godforsaken patch of Texas, to select steady men to supply some extra manpower.

By now, Scott is not overly impressed with the veteran's field skills, calling him "an old-line officer" despite the former politician's forty-five-year age, just thirteen years older than Scott. Unlike the Ranger captain, he didn't have to seek criminals to find excitement and danger. He had the Civil War.

When the war erupts in 1861, Weatherred enthusiastically enlists. His response to volunteer fulfills a hereditary impulse; his father, Francis, was a soldier in the Creek Indian War and the Texas War for Independence. In 1861, the Texas-born Weatherred, working in the county clerk's office in Fort Worth, joins Company G of the Thirty-Second Cavalry Regiment. The regiment ditches the horses after the Battle of Pea Ridge in March 1862 and serves the remainder of the war as an infantry unit.

The Thirty-Second deploys thousands of miles from Texas to take part in the Battle of Richmond. On October 31, 1862, the Thirty-Second

---

41 "General Notes," *Arkansas Democrat,* October 16, 1886. The "premium" awarded is not listed, alas.

combines with Ninth Texas Infantry, and they fight the Tennessee campaign as part of Ector's Brigade.[42]

Weatherred experiences the destruction of the Confederate forces at the Battle of Nashville in mid-December. Ector's Brigade takes at least 2,073 losses during the war, with many of them occurring in 1864. A combat-weary W. W. Weatherred receives a furlough on January 26, 1865, and watches from Fort Worth as the Confederacy finally crumbles.

He heads to Sabine to rebuild his life. His family has roots there— the first United States Post Office was established in the town of Milam in May 1846, with relative M. Weatherred Jr. as its inaugural postmaster. He settles in and marries local Sarah Eliza Williams Oliphant (his first, her third, hence the lengthy name). Weatherred teaches school in Milam and serves as district clerk of Sabine County. Southern pride costs him the clerk job. According to the official Texas histories, he's removed from this office "as an impediment to Reconstruction."[43]

A legal career awaits. He's admitted to the bar on November 16, 1871, and practices law in Milam and Hemphill. In 1880, he's appointed district judge by Governor O. M. Roberts, who clearly has a sympathetic ear for former Civil War veterans. He's the guy who led the passage of the ordinance removing Texas from the Union in 1861 and served as chief justice for the Confederacy's supreme court.

Weatherred's political career is born. From 1881 to 1883, he represents the Second District in the senate of the Seventeenth Legislature. Most notably, he serves on the committee that drafted the bill for building a new, majestic state capitol building.

He returns to practicing law in Sabine County, just in time to be hired to defend the Conner family during their initial trial in 1884. He's

---

42 Tim Bell, "Ninth Texas Infantry," *Handbook of Texas Online*, Texas State Historical Association, https://www.tshaonline.org/handbook/entries/ninth-texas-infantry.

43 Jeanette H. Flachmeier, "William Wallace Weatherred," *Handbook of Texas Online*, https://www.tshaonline.org/handbook/entries/weatherred-william-wallace.

not sure what he and cocounsel James T. Polley could have done to help them, since they refused to speak in their own behalf. Now he's hearing they are upset with him—an unsettling idea given the violent charges against them.

In 1886, Weatherred would be content to be a well-connected lawyer plying his trade in isolated Sabine County. His family is extending its roots here. In early March, his eldest daughter, Mattie, marries Hugh Short, a bright district attorney. The new son-in-law, who as a child lost his appointment to West Point due to a crippling disease, is already planning to open a family-run practice in downtown Hemphill.

The promise of a quiet life in Sabine County isn't working out as planned, thanks to the Conners. When someone breaks into his home and leaves the imprint of a pistol on his pillow, he takes it as a declaration of war.

As a private citizen, veteran, and former public official, W. W. Weatherred is a logical front man for the effort in the field against Sabine County's outlaws. But he was also the attorney for the men he's now trying to hunt down. His cocounsel on the Conner case, Polley, is equally involved. If it seems unethical for the former defense team to turn into manhunters seeking their clients dead or alive, it's not ground for disbarment since he and Polley are both now deputized.

The name "Polley" has serious pedigree in Milam, where the attorney operates. His grandfather Robert, an immigrant from Ireland, moves his family to Sabine in 1810, and his father, John Polley, is elected as Representative in the Second District of the Texas state legislature in 1870 and 1871. James Polley is cut from the same cloth as these public men. He becomes a lawyer and wins a narrow election to earn a seat in the state legislature in 1879, elected over the Republican candidate by a seventy-five-vote margin. He serves in Austin until 1883, when he returns to Milam to practice and grow his family.[44]

The posse of Weatherred's picked men also includes his friend,

44 *Texas Legislative Manual, 1879–80,* 1879.

forty-two-year-old Milam businessman Henry Harris. He served with the Ninth Texas Infantry, part of Ector's Brigade, and is a fellow survivor of the Tennessee campaign. The ties between veterans are not quickly broken.

The small posse also contains Hemphill merchant James O. Toole, the search party member and witness for the prosecution in Charles and Fed's joint murder trial. He's too young to have served in the Civil War but has a CSA tie, nevertheless. His father-in-law, Hampton Pratt, served as a colonel with the First Texas Infantry, which shared the battlefields of the Tennessee with the Ninth Infantry and Thirty-Second Cavalry. Pratt and Weatherred are prominent members of the First Baptist Church in Hemphill.[45]

There's some family drama going on within the Toole household—Pratt and Toole ran competing general stores in Hemphill before they became in-laws and business partners.[46] The ambitious businessman's presence in the posse seems a way to stand eye to eye with his veteran father-in-law and ingratiate himself with political men.[47] More charitably, it could be that the sight of the men shot dead in Holly Bottom, witnessed as a member of the coroner's party, has stuck with Toole. He wouldn't be the first to be propelled to seek justice, or revenge, after seeing a corpse up close.

These are the added guns that Weatherred can offer to augment Captain William Scott's company of Rangers. The posse is made of men of town, not the backwoods. They can't supply what Scott really needs:

---

45 *Minutes 1858–1890 First Baptist Church, Hemphill, Texas* (Saint Louis, MO: Igmire Publications, 1982), distributed by Ericson Books, Nacogdoches, TX.

46 National Park Service, "Toole Building," National Register of Historic Places Registration Form, October 1990.

47 Ibid. J. O. Toole will soon serve in office as county treasurer and donates reliably to the Democratic Party.

the location of Willis, William, Alfie, Leander, John, and Fed Conner. The darkened recesses of southern Sabine County represent nearly as great a mystery to the Hemphill men as it does to the visiting Rangers.

LAKE CHARLES
August 10, 1886

A break comes with fresh news: Alfred Conner has been seen at a ferry station at the Sabine River, bound for Louisiana. It's a tactical mistake on which Captain Scott plans to fully capitalize.

Alfred Conner's leaving Texas is based on the mistaken belief that getting out of state guarantees safety. In reality, the Texas Rangers don't care much about state borders. And Alfred's now subject to a more conventional manhunt, the kind with which the Rangers are more familiar.

The Rangers head into Louisiana by train, but in an unconventional way that is clearly meant to stop their prey from getting spooked. "The company—men, horses and equipment—made the trip sealed up in a box car for purposes of disguise," recalls one Ranger who likely joined Company F just after the trip. "They were seeking a gang of bandits who had been deprading areas of East Texas."[48]

The only other media report of the interstate hunt comes from Henry Putz, and it's more detailed. He recalls the Rangers going due south to the boomtown of Lake Charles specifically to hunt an outlaw Conner wanted for jailbreaking.[49] During his account, Scott and a force of eight Rangers stop outside of Lake Charles and wire ahead in expectation of

---

48 "Blood Curdling Days of '80s Live in Memories of Abilenian," *Abilene Reporter-News,* June 12, 1938. F. P. Carmichael joined the company on September 1, 1886, and the Rangers are back from Louisiana by late August.

49 Carmichael says Company F's clandestine rail destination is Shreveport, due north of Hemphill, but also acknowledges his memory may be faulty.

local backup. "We were expecting the sheriff of the parish to meet us and make the arrest," Putz says.[50]

Lake Charles is an island of light and civilization amid the darkness. It's always been a quiet center for the lumber industry but is now enjoying a postwar boom that will last until the Great Depression and ultimately fell the majority of the great forests of East Texas. Emerging lumber tycoons like R. H. Nason, N. B. Bradley, and William Ramsey own vast tracts of land in the area and will soon consolidate their acreage under the control of massive companies.[51]

Lake Charles is going through a population explosion, one based on northeast lumber money, local rice paddies, intrepid cattle farms, and a clever advertising campaign to lure settlers. The town is starting on its path to becoming a city and will grow 400 percent between 1880 and 1900. The regional powers that be are investing to make the place livable. For example, in 1886, Lake Charles officials order six thousand feet of pipes to build firefighting infrastructure.[52]

Upon arrival in town on August 6, Scott seems to know where to look for his quarry—a logging camp near town—which is a reflection of the quality of Scott's intelligence. Someone seemingly knew where the Rangers should look, but that person (law enforcement, a private detective, or a citizen) is never identified. The Rangers find Alfie Conner "before the sheriff appeared and covered him with our guns," Putz says.

50 "Ranger 40 Years Ago Had No Easy Life," *Dallas Morning News,* February 27, 1927. Putz misidentifies the Conner as Leander.

51 "Logging in the Pineywoods," Beyond Texas History, https://texasbeyondhistory.net /aldridge/logging.html.

52 Stewart Alfred Ferguson, "A History of Lake Charles" (thesis submitted to the graduate school of Louisiana State University, March 1931).

At this point, Conner makes a fair point. "You have no authority to arrest me here," he says, one hand falling to a holstered pistol.

"Our officer told him that while we had no authority, we had Winchesters," Putz says. "He submitted. We simply kidnapped him."[53]

In Sabine, life as an outlaw has been tiring for Leander Conner—his daughter hangs a rag on a pole to alert him of the presence of Rangers or posse members, and he's rigged his plow for a quick release in case he's surprised while working his land.[54]

The outlaw life proves too tough; Leander turns himself in shortly after Bubba's arrest, and by late August, they are both sitting in jail in Hemphill, arrested on charges of breaking their kin from it. Their trials will be held in September.

THE ACCUSED AND THE CONVICTED
August 29, 1886

Captain William Scott watches Henry Putz and J. A. Brooks ride away, side by side, his teeth gritting with frustration. The pair are off to Fort Smith to answer for the shooting of Albert St. John. They'll rendezvous with a U.S. marshal—otherwise known as *surrendering*—for escort to Arkansas by train.

There's nothing Scott can do about it but watch. As if the Texas Ranger captain doesn't have enough to deal with here in Sabine County— Scott's now left two more men short, one of them his sergeant.

At least there is a recruit on the way, and he's an experienced hand. Private Frank Carmichael arrives to camp on September 1. Everyone calls him "FP," as befitting his cowboy pedigree. He's a stout Texan from Abilene with years of experience riding herds of cattle, perfecting many of the everyday horse and tracking skills needed by a Texas Ranger. And,

---

53 "Ranger 40 Years Ago Had No Easy Life," *Dallas Morning News,* February 27, 1927.

54 Mark Dugan, *Judge Not* (unpublished, 1982), quoting Conner descendants.

no offense to Sergeant Brooks, but there is something reliable about a man who swears off "all four poisons: alcohol, tobacco, tea and coffee."[55]

It takes extreme willpower for a Ranger to resist all of these vices. Riding the trail without the support of caffeine is unthinkable, and even the pious John Rogers enjoys an occasional cigar.

In Hemphill, the trial of the five jailbreakers goes quickly; the district court's session ends on September 6, and before it closes, the court delivers sentences to a host of Sabine County men. *The Galveston Daily News* calls it "the most exciting session ever held at that place or any other place in eastern Texas, the principal business being the trial of the jailbreakers."

Not surprisingly, among a mob of amateur criminals, the jailbreak gang doesn't keep a unified front. Dutch Watkins, convicted during the court's earlier session, is pardoned on August 24 (before he's shipped out) in exchange for informing on the others. As for turning state's evidence, "the rest refuse to do so." Testimony condemns Leander Conner, Alfie Conner, Sterling Eddings, and Jim Sanders to two years of prison. W. E. T. Ogletree, the teacher, inexplicably, gets four years. "These men were all respectable in their neighborhoods," *The Galveston Daily News* sniffs after listing their sentences.[56]

It's about 4:00 p.m. on September 6 when the town of Hemphill gathers to gawk as their fallen neighbors leave for Rusk Penitentiary. "Such a scene has never yet been known in our town—five men, all in irons and chains, leaving loving families at home and guarded by a cavalcade of Rangers loaded down with Winchester rifles and heavy revolvers, regularly equipped as warhorses," reads a dispatch filed from the town

---

55 Carmichael's personality is best detailed in "Blood Curdling Days of '80s," *Abilene Reporter-News*.

56 Rusk Prison Records, *Convict and Conduct Registers, 1875–1945*, Texas State Archives, Austin, TX.

in *The Galveston Daily News*. "And this," the correspondent adds, "all in civilized country."[57]

Scott is also grim. He doesn't feel for the convicts in his charge; he's seen the wretched sight of such "necked" prisoners plenty of times before. It's the idea that his two men could be the ones in chains that bothers him.

Their prison delivery duty ends at the walls of Rusk Penitentiary, and with it, Company F's 1886 search for the Conners. Adjutant General King has already officially ordered Company F out of Sabine and off to Brown County.[58] Their next foes will be a band of committed fence cutters, just the kind of enemy Scott is comfortable handling. The haul of jailbreakers will have to be enough of a victory for now. Scott will lobby his superiors to go back, but he never loses his distaste—and fear—of East Texas.

Reviews of Company F's performance at the time are mixed, since Willis, John, William, and Fed Conner remain at large. "The Rangers did good service in aiding the Sheriff to capture the fugitive jailbreakers and in restoring the feeling of security, long disturbed among citizens," summarizes the *Fort Worth Daily Gazette*. "But made a total failure in the chief object of their visit."[59]

THE BLACKENED CLOUD
September 18, 1886

Leander Conner eyes the twenty-foot-tall brick wall of Rusk Penitentiary looming overhead. He can't crane his neck enough to see the top as

---

57 *Galveston Daily News*, September 20, 1886.

58 This order is dated September 16, making the trip to Rusk (at Perkins's request) the company's last action before leaving the county.

59 "Futile Search of the Rangers for the Conners in Sabine County," *Fort Worth Daily Gazette*, October 7, 1886.

he gets close, since that would cause the metal collar around his neck to dig into his skin. The only comfort to be had here is that some of the prisoners he's chained to are his friends and family; there are five members of the Sabine County jailbreakers about to be encased within the steel gates embedded in the brick walls. Elsewhere in the connected line of necked men are Alfie Conner, Sterling Eddings, Jim Sanders, and disgraced schoolteacher W. E. T. Ogletree.[60]

The walls surround a seven-acre compound custom built to entomb incarcerated men. The buildings are sandstone and brick. A trio of large structures dominates the grounds: a tall administration building, a combined kitchen/dining hall/hospital library/chapel, and the three-story cell house holding 528 double-bunked cells.

Outside the walls are manufacturing shops, iron foundries, a sawmill, a brick kiln, and an ice factory, all staffed with weary inmate laborers. Gazing down over the other industries is the smokestack of "the Old Alcalde." The blast furnace, nicknamed for Governor Oran M. Roberts, first ignites in early 1884. This is where prisoners (white only) manufacture pig iron and finished fixtures to sell and use in state buildings. The captive ironworkers are even now sweating over all the cast-iron fixtures destined for the brand-new state capitol building. It's a bitter era for the Conner boys to do time, since the convict work being done is for a project brought into being by family foe W. W. Weatherred while he was in the legislature. Such an ornate building is expensive, and prison labor is being maximized to keep costs down.

Texas's prison industries are vertically integrated, with convict labor at every level. Prisoners fell lumber, dig ore, operate the furnaces, and create the finished goods. The Texas State Railroad is created just to bring hardwood to feed the smelter at the Rusk Penitentiary. Naturally, inmates hack out the route and lay the tracks. Hundreds of inmates are likewise breaking rocks in granite and limestone quarries for the domed structure's construction.

---

60 Rusk Prison Records, *Convict and Conduct Registers.*

Working here at Rusk means cruelly long hours spent at hard labor. But that's the best the inmates can hope for. Many are unlucky enough to be sent to remote camps, where life is much worse. Texas also leases convicts to private farm owners in sharecropping arrangements. These camps range from harsh to inhumanely horrific.

No matter where the jailbreakers end up, the experience will be grueling and dehumanizing. They trade the hated neck chain for striped clothes. Food is served in rusty tin plates, eaten in silence. Discipline is enforced with the Bat, a wooden rod with a leather strap. Men are stripped from the waist down and whipped in front of the others, or held down by friends. The allowable maximum is thirty-nine lashes.

"The convict lay down on the floor and all was silent: breathlessly I listened, and all at once there was a sudden, violent meeting of the strap and human flesh, and a scream," writes former inmate Charles Favor of the first strapping he witnesses at Rusk in 1892. "A wild scream for mercy, but another lick was the reply. I counted twenty-five. The man was told, like a dog, to go back to his bunk and to it he went."[61]

Favor served time years later, but his first-day emotional state likely matches that of the men from Sabine County. "I could not dispel the blackened cloud which hovered so closely about me," he writes. Another anecdote, this one from 1883 inmate Andrew Wallace, highlights the unreality and horror of the inmate's first night at Rusk:

> I could not sleep and I suppose it was about 11 o'clock when all at once someone in the cell adjoining ours commenced yelling at the top of his voice, and in a twinkling another one commenced and still another and so on until there was a chorus of the most unearthly yells mingled with oaths and moaning that a person could imagine. The noise awoke my companions and one of them, an Irishman, grabbed hold of me and said, "For

---

61 Quoted in Gary Brown, *Texas Gulag* (Plano, TX: Republic of Texas Press, 2002).

God's sake Andy wake up! They surely have made a mistake and brought us to a lunatic asylum instead of a state prison."[62]

Leander Conner's depression is only deepened by the thought of his family. Two years is a long time in the life of a young child, and he's leaving five behind: Jessie, the eldest at ten, Lizzie, Wiley Gilbert, Cornelia, and Rosa, the youngest at just five. They'll be so different when he's released, and the thought eats at him.

A newspaper describes the gloom among the families of the jailbreakers in Sabine County. Their homes "are occupied now only by their sorrowing wives and some twenty young and helpless children, which doubtless are sad examples of the effect of human passions run riot and even man's retributive justice."[63]

At least Leander and Alfie Conner can fix their minds on the day they'll get out. For poor brother Charley, dealing with twenty-five years for murder in the Huntsville work camp system, any promise of release is so distant that it must be swallowed by his immediate misery.

As for his other outlaw brothers, it's obvious that they've gained freedom at the expense of his and Alfie's. Leander made the trade consciously, and he only hopes it was worth it. He imagines a day when he'll visit his father and brothers, living free at one of their campsites, cooking the results of the day's hunt, weary dogs panting nearby.

His father, Fed, William, and John show no sign of surrender, and he suspects they never will. But Leander spent time in the company of the Rangers, too much time, and he finds that they are serious individuals who will risk death to get their quarry. Leander can only hope that the bands of dangerous men led by William Scott and Willis Conner never meet. If they do, people will die.

Alfie didn't pull his pistol when facing the Rangers in Lake Charles.

---

62 Ibid.

63 *Fort Worth Daily Gazette*, October 7, 1886.

The old man would never have hesitated. His father would rather live the hard life of a wilderness outlaw, sacrificing family members, losing the family's land, and risking violent death than face these hellish prisons. Hearing the hollow metallic boom of the gates of Rusk shutting behind the prisoners, it's hard to blame him.

OFFICIAL REPORT TO AUSTIN
December 1886

> For several years past a gang of outlaws, of dangerous and desperate character and conduct, have been troubling the good people of eastern Texas—particularly in Sabine and adjacent counties—and various efforts have been made by this department to aid in the capture, dispersal, or destruction of this band. Detectives have been sent into that section, and from time to time small detachments of Rangers have gone, but the densely wooded character of many parts of the country, and the immense swamps; the grouping of population at particular points and its scarcity at others; the bold, and yet cunning character of these desperadoes, with their half wild natures, and their skill in wood craft, seemed likely to render all efforts futile for their capture. Continued appeals from the good people of that region caused another effort to be made this summer and fall, and for this purpose Captain William Scott and his company were sent to Eastern Texas, and by good fortune, unflagging energy, and persistent, well managed efforts, he succeeded in capturing two brothers, Connor [sic] by name, who belonged to this band of outlaws, and though this was only a partial success its effect will go largely, it is believed, to ridding the country of the others.

—*Wilburn King*, Annual Report of the Adjutant-General of the State of Texas, 1885–86, *December 1886*

4

GUNFIRE AND MOONLIGHT

COMANCHERIA DAYS

September 5, 2020

The posse gathers at just after 7:00 a.m. on Saturday, each member bearing a personal arsenal of shotguns, pistols, and rifles. It's a cool but humid morning, the product of an impending cold front and a previous day of torrential rain.

Here at the Stieler Hill Ranch, nearly ten miles outside the Texas Hill Country town of Comfort, the weather doesn't dictate the wardrobe. Everyone here is dressed to the nines, as well as armed to the teeth.

Gunmen wear frock coats, dusters, western suits, garish shirts and vests, polished-but-muddy boots, and ubiquitous suspenders. Cowboy hats of every species—Derby, Reno, Gus, Cattlemen, Ringo, you name it—nestle on the men's heads. Brims are festooned with bands, feathers, buttons. The women come in either Belle Starr, bustle-skirt finery or Calamity Jane, saddle-seat-pant trail wear. Custom-made hats grow flowers, bunting, flags. Belts are decorated with beads, tassels, and endless loops of ammunition.

Many rifles here are similarly adorned with embroidered buttstocks, narrow leather straps wrapped around levers, and complex etchings swirling around metal barrels and receivers. Two pistols hang on each embellished belt. The quickest seventh shot, as the saying goes, comes from a different gun.

The weapons conveyances of choice here are three-wheeled baby carriages, installed with rifle racks and ammunition boxes. Some build their own wooden carts in the boxy, snake-oil-salesman style. The posse members push these mobile gun racks through the mud, heading for their first shooting platform. Soon, the air will be filled with the cracks and booms of gunfire, and clouds of smoke will cling thickly in the heavy air.

This is the third day of the 2020 Single Action Shooting Society (SASS) Texas State Championship, called Comancheria Days.[1] At first, this quirky niche pastime seems to have as much in common with the Texas Rangers of Company F as a Western-themed party on a cruise ship. But beyond the spectacle, there are some real lessons to be learned here.

The cowboy action shooting subculture exists at the intersection of cosplay, club competition, and gun worship. Participants in teams of "posses" use fully functional replica firearms from the 1800s during full-costume shooting matches. These weapons here include the tools of the Texas Rangers in 1886, and there's no better place to become acquainted with them than a SASS match.

The costumes are not optional; they're part of the sport. "Our members have developed and adopted an attitude toward their participation called 'The Spirit of the Game,'" reads the SASS website. "It is a code by which we live. Competing in The Spirit of the Game means you fully participate in what the competition asks. You try your best to dress the part, use the appropriate competition tools, and respect the traditions of the Old West. Some folks would call it nothing more than good sportsmanship."[2]

---

1 Comanchería is the region of New Mexico, West Texas, and nearby areas occupied by the Comanche before the 1860s. The area doesn't include Comfort, Texas.

2 "What Is Single Action Shooting?," SASS, https://sassnet.com/About-What-is -SASS-001A.php.

No one at a SASS meeting or match uses their real names; instead they use adopted nicknames that evoke the outlaws and lawmen of the Old West. These aliases hold, even during casual conversations and on-line exchanges.

Canyon St. Cloud is a heavyset San Antonian in his late twenties, dressed in a tan buckskin ensemble. He's loading his Winchester '76 replica, double-barreled shotgun, and pair of six-shooters at the on-deck table at stage 5, which is fashioned after a steam train. (There are metal buffalo silhouettes serving as targets, with shooters plunking the shapes from the mock train's windows.) St. Cloud's age is a bit of an outlier; the demographic at Comancheria Days skews about two decades older.

St. Cloud became involved a year and a half ago when a friend from church recommended he attend a local shooting match. "I like history, I like to shoot stuff," he says, immediately friendly when approached. "I thought I might like it." That day, organizers announced him as a shooter. Recruitment is not subtle at SASS events; new blood is welcome, especially if it's pumping through preretirement veins. That day, his cowboy alter ego was born.

"I'm not trying to be fast," he says before his turn to shoot. "My goal at these championships isn't to win but to shoot clean."

Shooting clean means a run through the shooting range without technical fouls. SASS shooting is about more than not missing. There are specific patterns to be followed at each platform: For example, shooters' bullets on stage 5 must strike the five pistol targets (numbered 1 to 5) in one of two orders: 1–1–2–3–4–2–3–4–5–5, or the reverse, 5–5–4–3–2–4–3–2–1–1.

St. Cloud takes his position, lever-action rifle in hand, hammer down on an empty chamber. He squints down the barrel at the steel targets from behind protective goggles, going through the pattern in his mind. The starter holds a buzzer to his ear and waits for the shooter to say the stage's catchphrase—every shooting platform has its own.

"He's riding with a secret, heading west," intones Canyon St. Cloud, and his run begins. The revolver is first, quick reports from the barrel immediately followed by the telltale ting of the lead ball smacking the steel. Bits of metal sometimes spit back at the shooter and spectators, stinging cheeks like bees. This happens often enough that it has a name, "splatter," requiring eye protection for anyone nearby.[3]

The Winchester is next. He works the lever as fluidly as possible, rhythmic biomechanics being the key. In previous runs, he's tended to go too fast, kicking out an unspent round and fouling his time. For him, like any young gunslinger, mastering the ability to shoot smoothly means calming his mind and letting his hands work on rote, learned instinct.

The speed of competition rifle shooters is not just determined by the physical action of jacking rounds into the chamber but the act of swiveling the barrel from target to target. These are tools made to produce high rates of fire. Being on the receiving end of a well-aimed barrage from multiple Ranger-aimed Winchesters means facing a terrifying swarm of projectiles.

After the rifle comes the pistol finale, featuring a nimble-fingered reload and sequence of close-range shots. The run of Canyon St. Cloud ends, and the timer announces the results immediately: "41.38 and clean." St. Cloud heads to the safety station to verify his empty chambers to a fellow posse. He holsters the pistols and brings the long guns to the baby carriage with a good-natured swagger.

A single, fairly inexperienced shooter has just put twenty-four rounds from four weapons downrange in short order. The match's overall winner, Whiskey Kid, does this run in just twenty seconds.

Most of the guns here, like St. Cloud's, crack sharply but aren't loaded with full charges of black powder as they would have been in 1886. The recoil and smoke would pretty much ruin the fun for a lot of shooters, especially older competitors. As always, anything worth doing is worth fighting over. There was a schism between hard-core black powder

---

3 This author got dinged in the cheek with splatter within the first five minutes of arriving but remained unscathed during the following two days of close observation. Several others got dinged in the face, and close examination of photos reveals bits of debris flying among the crowd. I have to admit, it was pretty cool.

shooter traditionalists and more open-access SASS members. Splinter groups now hold rival matches and trade harsh words about authenticity and exclusivity in niche cowboy-action-shooting magazines and websites.

Shooting full black powder charges is allowed but not required at the state championships. It's not hard to find those shooters at Comancheria Days—just follow the heavy explosions and blooms of gun smoke hanging in the air. Behind one such cloud you'll find Yuma Jack, just finishing a speedy round on stage 3, the Barn.

He's a competitor and a long-range match official, and he wears his custom-fit outfit well. There's a pin on his vest that says, "Black Powder Matters." Yuma Jack shoots full charges for one reason: "That's the way *they* did it."

Yuma Jack's weapon wagon is a rolling exhibit showing (among other things) the evolution of the Winchester rifle from the '73 to the '76. Shooting powder gives him a practitioner's perspective on the ammunition loaded into the later rifle, so ubiquitous among the Texas Rangers. "The .44–40 was more high-powered than the rimfires before it," he says. "They only had twenty-eight grains of gunpowder, but the .44–40 has forty grains."

One thing Yuma Jack appreciates as a black powder shooter is the way smoke would obliterate strategy during gunfights. "After that first or second shot, the air would be filled with thick smoke, ruining the aim of shots after that," he says. "No one would know what was going on." Realizing that every shoot-out witness, including those pulling the trigger, is recalling things through an opaque haze makes a difference while considering their testimony.

The steady noise of the match, too, is revealing. Its sound travels for miles across the scrub brush. The rattle of shooting competitions coming from Ranger camps outside of a town must have had a deterrent—or antagonistic—effect on the local population. Shooting contests honed Ranger skills but also announced that a well-armed band of lawmen was around. It was a form of psychological warfare.

With such devastating firepower at everyone's disposal, it's no wonder that the Rangers preferred to get the drop on their targets and could be tempted to shoot first. No matter the costume and nostalgia, these are not romantic weapons when aimed at humans. Those who could produce and endure such rapid violence must have had bravery and ruthlessness in equal measure.

Indeed, one tends to view the senior citizens of this crowd with a certain respect after seeing them scamper down a series of shooting platforms, coolly putting round after round into targets. They may dress outlandishly, but their sport can still be used to deadly purpose. Imagine the aura around a Texas Ranger like J. A. Brooks, practiced in his craft by continuous matches with peers and hardened by year after year of violent service. He must have struck as deliberately and deadly as a viper when he chose to pull.

Comancheria Days is free to attend but doesn't attract many spectators. As a result, those not wearing cowboy costumes and functional, holstered six-shooters are the obvious outsiders. Still, the participants are extremely friendly to unarmed gawkers, and conversations come easy. But ask the SASS members what draws them to cowboy action shooting, and the responses are not especially profound. One former police officer and pastor does claim it taught him how to de-stress and "saved his life." Otherwise, the SASS shooters claim an earnest love of history, firearms, and their local community of enthusiasts. The pin on Yuma Jack's lapel is as close as it gets to politics here.

No one ruminates on the academic, sociological reasons why such seemingly nice people choose to worship this violent era of U.S. history. There's no discussion of the current need for rural empowerment or the growing passion to preserve regional identity in an era of mass media. No presidential campaign signs or NRA booths stand on the ranch to mar the festive illusion.

It seems that the posses at Comancheria Days have embraced the Spirit of the Game not to change the modern world outside the Stieler Hill Ranch but to escape it.

THE BELLE OF FORT SMITH
September 29, 1886

J. A. Brooks watches the woman in black bring her massive charcoal steed to a halt before the federal courthouse in Fort Smith, Arkansas. It's impossible for him to take his eyes off Belle Starr, whom the newspapers call "the Bandit Queen." He's the first to admit that he's a sucker for a woman who knows how to handle a horse. It's too bad she's so often accused of stealing them.

Starr is clad in a velvet riding habit, a bent-brimmed hat festooned with a circular plume decoration, and a single-loop holster with a prominent but unloaded pearl-handled revolver resting inside. Her sharply defined face, for all the attention turned her way, remains calm. A deputy marshal rides with Starr, marking the woman as a defendant being escorted for a court appearance, as Brooks well knows, having been brought here with a marshal at his elbow as well.

This is a frontier town; across the river from Fort Smith are the Indian Territories. But over the years, Fort Smith has transformed from a military outpost to a transportation hub. The Arkansas River is alive with traffic, and Brooks knows some of it is illegal liquor bound for the Indian Territories or contraband equipment to set up illicit distilleries.

The courthouse sees plenty of action. This district court's jurisdiction covers more than any other in the nation—seventy-four-thousand square miles packed with murderers, smugglers, bandits, and drunks. Or so it would appear from reading the docket. With such a vast stretch of the frontier to administer, this river town is a hotbed for criminal justice, if not crime itself. Media-darling outlaws, grieving and vengeful kin, dogged lawmen, and fiendish criminals are all compelled to make appearances here, like acting troupes on a theater circuit.

Brooks hates being at Fort Smith, under house arrest in the abode of a U.S. marshal, but at least he can say that he's seen Belle Starr with his own eyes. Now he can know that what he has read about this famous woman is true: She's beautiful and she rides sidesaddle. Brooks can't help but admire her poise.[4]

Belle Starr is born Myra Maybelle Shirley; her father is a Missouri hotel owner and her mother a Hatfield, of the feuding Hatfields and McCoys. The teenage girl watches as her brother Bud joins Quantrill's Raiders, the infamous Confederate bushwhackers. Her family relocates to Texas in 1864. That same year, the young woman meets Quantrill veteran and family friend Cole Younger and starts to ride with his soon-to-be infamous gang. She accrues a nickname, husbands, and shooting skills. They accrue criminal charges and body counts.

By 1883, Starr's been linked to a series of crimes and convicted of horse theft. She makes the newspapers for this, and when release comes, she has a reputation. She poses for studio portraits and dresses the part of her frontier tabloid nickname, the Bandit Queen. But now Starr is considered a usual suspect in all Younger gang crimes. "Although summoned again and again, she was always acquitted by the juries that were composed of sympathizers," Brooks notes in his handwritten memoir.

Her last court case, a June 1886 trial for involvement in a string of robberies, is a good example. She arrived majestically, smiled through the trials as witnesses described only male bandits, and then rode back to her cowboy-gangster friends as a free woman. Now, three months later, Starr's back to Fort Smith to stand trial for horse theft.

Brooks watches her enter the one-story building, a converted army barracks, where Judge Isaac Parker presides over the U.S. Court for the Western District of Arkansas. His jurisdiction encompasses the Indian Territories.

Brooks idly wonders if the Bandit Queen is the correct match for

---

4 "I saw Belle Starr when she came riding to court on her big black horse. She was really a picturesque character in her black riding habit seated on an old-fashioned side saddle," Brooks wrote in his memoir. He also spoke of her to the *Corpus Christi Caller-Times* (October 24, 1937), saying, "I saw her once, riding into Ft. Smith." There is a photo of her in Fort Smith for this appearance in the insert of this book.

a Texas Ranger. She can ride, she can shoot, and she's obviously attracted to men who can handle firearms. But it's an idle thought—when
Brooks thinks about a mate, he's seeking stability and comfort. As he
once puts it: "I began to think of romance, and a housekeeper I began
to think I needed."[5]

Belle Starr's reputation doesn't hint that she'd be much of a home-
maker, and Brooks's sight of her doesn't change this opinion. She looks
like the proud outlaw the newspapers say she is.

The drive to marry has existed since before Brooks became a Texas
Ranger, as proven by his failed attempts as a young suitor. Ranger privates are required to be bachelors, but officers can marry. Now he's in a
quandary: He *can* wed but has adopted a lifestyle that makes it hard to
settle down. As a Texas Ranger, his pick of possible wives is wider and
more varied than a typical rancher or laborer, who usually must choose
among whomever is available locally. Many families of stature—those
who have the most to lose to lawlessness—see Rangers as good courtship
prospects. Many young women do, too, taken by their city clothes, trail-
hardened physiques, and dashing attitudes.

The sedate existence expected from a family doesn't seem to sit
well with the job. Captain Scott, a major influence on Brooks, remains
a bachelor. Texas Rangers are always moving, camping in areas that are
inherently dangerous. Where does a wife and child fit into all of that?
This predicament doesn't stop Brooks from courting women, scouting for
something to long for beyond the trail.

Now both his career and his family prospects are left in limbo by
the shooting of Albert St. John. It all unraveled quickly. Brooks, T. R.
Knight, and Henry Putz were indicted on August 2 and held in Fort
Smith by mid-September.

They are facing a formidable foe in District Attorney Montgom-

---

5 Paul Spellman, *Captain J. A. Brooks, Texas Ranger* (Denton: University of North Texas
   Press, 2007).

ery Hinds Sandels. Everyone in town knows to call him "Monte."[6] The Tennessee-born lawyer becomes Fort Smith mayor in 1877 but resigns during his second term, citing ill health. He returns to public service in November 1885 when he becomes the U.S. attorney for the Western District of Arkansas.[7] This case, then, is unfolding fairly early in his tenure.

There is pressure to prosecute coming from St. John's survivors and area cattlemen. "St. John came from a good family," notes U.S. Indian agent Robert Owen in his annual 1886 report. "His friends are wealthy and they are very active in prosecuting Knight."[8]

St. John's "friends" have done a good job of corrupting the attitude against Knight and the Rangers. They score an early public relations win with news coverage of the shooting when the *Fort Worth Daily Gazette* calls it a "Cowardly Assassination" in a headline. The article states Knight tried to buy St. John's pistol and put a hand on his leg. When St. John slapped his hand away, the Rangers opened fire. Knight then took the pistol he wanted from the corpse and rode out of town.

"At Alexander the affair is regarded as a deliberate, cowardly murder and steps will be taken by the friends of the dead man to have the guilty parties brought to justice," the newspaper says. "Albert St. John was well known in that section of the country, especially by cattlemen, with whom he had been much associated."[9]

The newspaper the next day runs "a different side of the story" as presented by Indian agent Robert Owen, Knight's boss. His version hews

---

6 Born August 13, 1851.

7 "Montie Sandels & Bettie Bliss Johnson Sandels-Oak Cemetery-Ft. Smith, AR," Waymarking, https://www.waymarking.com/waymarks/WMN8AP_Monti_Hines _Sandels_Bettie_Bliss_Johnson_Sandels_Oak_Cemetery_Ft_Smith_AR.

8 *Report of the Commissioner of Indian Affairs* (Washington, D.C.: United States Bureau of Indian Affairs, 1886).

9 *Fort Worth Daily Gazette*, May 28, 1886.

more closely to the events as described by later court witnesses, even those appearing for the prosecution: St. John had a gun, fought when asked to hand it over to authorities, and was shot while resisting but never shot at the lawmen. The second *Gazette* article makes it a point to identify the source of the previous article's information: Obadiah Love. Owen calls the letter Love sent "a malicious misrepresentation of the unfortunate occurrence . . . doubtless written to create bad feelings among the cattlemen."[10]

People's impression of the shoot-out at Fort Smith leaves a sour taste in Brooks's mouth. It's more than just pride. That first article is a good sample of what his enemies are telling people—including the prosecuting authorities—about the shooting.

Love has done more than poison the media with his version of events. He's also provided detailed testimony against Brooks, Knight, and Putz that goes beyond the testimony of a typical eyewitness. After all, he didn't actually *see* anything happen. But he writes a letter to the court documenting what he saw when the corpse was stripped in the storeroom and itemizes five wounds on the dead cowboy's body.

"One shot had struck him on the inner part of the thigh and ranged upwards and came out the buttocks about the hip pocket of his pants, one shot entered his breast just at the left of the middle of the shirt bosom," Love reports in his cleanly worded, handwritten official statement. "One shot had struck him in the back." He also discusses what he purports to be telltale powder burns on St. John's back, indicating it was an entrance wound.[11] These details, coupled with his role as employer and de facto character witness, make Love a formidable part of the prosecution's case.

The Rangers and Knight have a two-man defense team. Their presence has a backstory as well, one that makes Knight feel like the government that employs him doesn't fully have his back.

That spring, Robert Owen petitions his bosses at the Department of

---

10 *Fort Worth Daily Gazette*, May 29, 1886.

11 Trial transcript, Arkansas, Criminal Case Files, 1866–1900, NARA, via Ancestry.com.

the Interior to ask the U.S. attorney general to supply counsel for Knight. A June 26, 1886, memo to the Secretary of the Interior reveals Indian Affairs' internal version of events: "The Agent (Owen) states that St. John's reputation, as far as he can learn, was that of a desperado and cow thief . . . and that these parties seem to have filed proceedings against Knight in federal court for murder and have raised a purse to embarrass Knight or require him to employ lawyers—an expense which he cannot well bear out of the small salary allowed him, an attorney's fees in such cases being equivalent to about two years gross salary, or two hundred and fifty dollars."

The Department of the Interior punts the request to the Department of Justice, where it receives a chilly reception. On June 29, the Department of the Interior hears a rebuff: "The District Attorney will not be available to do this, it being his duty to prosecute."[12]

U.S. Attorney General Augustus Garland shuffles the whole mess out of Washington, D.C., and back to Judge Parker in a July 20 message: "I informed the Secretary (of the Interior) that there was no law authorizing the Attorney General to employ counsel for such defense, but that I was willing to submit the correspondence (from Owen asking for a lawyer) to the United States judge having jurisdiction in this case, with the suggestion that the court may designate counsel for the defense, the understanding being that such counsel shall look to Congress for compensation."[13]

Luckily for Knight and the two Rangers, a pair of prominent local lawyers are essentially donating their time to their case. The first is Thomas Barnes, a well-regarded attorney in Fort Smith. He's a local luminary that city officials trust to speak at public events. The lawmen also have the services of Elias Cornelius Boudinot, a famous litigator, newspaper publisher, and politician. "He was a full-blood Cherokee

12 Ibid.

13 Ibid.

Indian, but a good one," Brooks reminisces in his memoirs. "He offered his services to us without pay and we loved him for his magnanimity."[14]

Boudinot is in near exile from Indian Territory due to the backlash against his position advocating the allotment of Cherokee land to America. His position stems from his legal attempt to nullify the federal government seizure of a tobacco factory he co-owned in the Cherokee Nation. Boudinot argued that the excise taxes he owed violated treaty agreements made in 1866. The case made it to the U.S. Supreme Court, which ruled against him. Boudinot now argues loudly that Indians should become citizens and be protected by the Constitution, which he feels he wasn't. The position endears him to white politicians and business interests in Arkansas but doesn't go over so well in the territories themselves.[15]

His involvement in the Rangers' case fits Boudinot's support of the Cherokee Strip and need to maintain a high profile. He also likely feels for Knight, who isn't finding much help from the government that ordered him to disarm cowboys to begin with.

The defense duo sees the opportunity offered by St. John's reputation. In September, their attorneys ask for the court to call their anti-character witnesses, which include officials with the Cherokee Strip Live Stock Association, to testify. In a handwritten court filing, Barnes states that the defense can't continue with the input of witnesses who "were acquainted with the reputation he bore in the community where he resided on said Strip, as to being a dangerous, overbearing, brutal and vindictive man and that said character was bad."

Maybe Brooks's lawyers can learn something about how to beat charges from Belle Starr. On September 30, a jury hands her another

---

14 The Texas Hall of Fame and Museum in Waco has the memoir on display and has copies available in their research center and (very helpfully) offer a transcript online.

15 "Boudinot, Elias Cornelius," Encyclopedia of Oklahoma History and Culture, https://www.okhistory.org/publications/enc/entry.php?entry=BO026.

"not guilty" verdict, and she gallops from Fort Smith as a free woman. Brooks is chagrined; the outlaws ride out of courtrooms while the lawmen bringing them in have to worry about being hanged.

Brooks is eager to likewise ride away from his aggravations, sheltered safely back inside Company F. He'd rather face a horde of bandits than walk around here, past the gallows, meeting with lawyers, enduring accusatory stares in the streets, living with the deputy marshal, and drinking his nights away in boredom while his comrades hunt outlaws. The weeks crawl past.

On October 13, Brooks delivers an official statement to the court. His defense is in the details that put the dark-haired cowboy's actions at center stage—St. John defying Knight, drawing his gun, and grabbing at Brooks's pistol. The Rangers, in comparison, were supporting Knight in his lawful duties as an Indian agent. Brooks makes sure to note that no one shot anyone in the back.

Now there's nothing to do but wait for the defense witnesses to arrive and set a court date. Judge Parker releases Brooks, Knight, and Putz from house arrest at Fort Smith; they are all allowed to go back to their lives as they wait for the trial, which will be sometime in 1887.

Brooks sets out to meet up with Company F in Brownwood. He arrives during the first days of November, just in time for the shooting to start.

FENCE CUTTER CONFIDENTIAL
November 7, 1886

The ragged cowboy rides through the quiet night, fourteen miles north of Brownwood. Scraggly hair falls from under a dark hat. Ira Aten is used to nocturnal trips through Brown County, following the fence-lined trails that connect the sprawling cattle ranches. Not so long ago, he was on the other side of these fences, shooting other people's cattle and butchering the illicit meat by moonlight.

But tonight is about a cabal, not a crime. Torchlights at a gate indicate he's arrived at the ranch of W. M. Baugh. The ranch hands nod knowingly as he rides through the gate and direct him to where the others are waiting. This rendezvous, if discovered, could get him killed.

Intelligence is often more important than bullets. So before Adjutant General Wilburn King deploys Company F to Brown County, he taps Aten, a Texas Ranger sergeant, to scout out the situation. He's been working undercover for months, posing as a desperate cowboy while gathering information.

Brown County is filling up with farms, destined to go from 22 in 1870 to more than 1,300 by the late 1800s. Newcomers' livestock are overcrowding the herds of the larger cattlemen, who are fencing their lands to secure their holdings. Open-range ranchers find water sources are blocked and roads severed. The tensions boil over in 1883 when more than two hundred citizens gather in Brownwood and threaten to burn down the town if the fences blocking their cattle are not removed. This is not the profile of fringe activists, but of a popular resistance. In response, stockmen arm themselves and take to the town's roofs. Only Brown County Sheriff Will Adams's intervention—and his tacit approval of fence cutter activities—prevents a bloodbath.

A political organization called the Farmers' Alliance forms from this turmoil. The fence cutters act as the alliance's illicit, armed wing. They destroy about $1 million worth of fences in the county by fall 1883, all the while enjoying deep local support.[16]

W. M. Baugh and his brother Lev have taken a hard line against the Farmers' Alliance and earned their marauders' special attention. He is an original pioneer of the area who once killed a Comanche in hand-to-hand combat—in his kitchen.

Baugh has endured an extended campaign against his spindly property lines. After he takes some potshots at a band of fleeing cutters, they later leave him a note on a cedar fence post: "If one drop of cutter's blood

---

16 Wayne Gard, "Fence Cutting," *Handbook of Texas Online,* https://www.tshaonline
    .org/handbook/entries/fence-cutting.

is spilled, your life will be forfeit." They find one from him dangling in reply, calling them "cowardly curs."[17]

The state law may have changed after Brooks's report to the governor in 1884, frightening many "nippers" into retirement across the state, but Brown County remains fiery. Cutters still destroy fences, and the ranchers stubbornly rebuild them. Baugh goes to the local law for recourse. In March 1885, he delivers the names of the fence cutters that he and his men recognized during some scary nighttime encounters. The names include the most outspoken in the ranks of the Farmers' Alliance, including Brown County constable Jim Lovell, as well as suspected cattle thieves. Indictments are brought against Amos Roberts, Wood Runnels, Bob Parrock, John "Ace" Mathews, Frank Johnson and his two brothers, and, two times over, Jim Lovell.[18]

There's zero local desire for the cases to move forward. The indictments languish, postponed by continuances. Sheriff Adams remains toothless, and the fence cutting continues unabated. That's when Baugh and his fellow ranchers get the ear of the governor, who sends word to King: Dispatch the Rangers to Brown County.

This is when Ira Aten is tapped to go undercover to gain the fence cutters' trust and catch them in the act. He takes a train thirty miles from Brownwood, buys a cheap horse, and abandons the Rangers' typical city outfit for a vagabond cowboy's getup. He stops grooming his hair. The "ragged cowboy" is born.

He rides into Brown County as just another broken seeker, hanging around looking for work and sleeping in haystacks. Aten uses the list of indicted fence cutters to choose where to lurk, always offering his

---

17 Bob Alexander and James Alexander, *Rawhide Ranger, Ira Aten Enforcing Law on the Texas Frontier* (Denton: University of North Texas Press, 2011).

18 "Nate Perry," Brown County Museum, 2016, http://www.browncountymuseum.org /blog/category/all/3, and ibid.

services. Bob Parrock and his wife eventually pity-hire him to do menial chores.

Soon, he's seeing mysterious cuts of meat passing hands and overhearing discussions of fence cutting. The scene at the Parrock ranch is tense and suspicious, as he balances caution with spying. "When his friends would come to the place, I would not force myself into their company and seemed not to be interested in anything they said," Aten says. Still, the group is loath to see a new face: "Some of the man's friends said I was no good and should be run out of the county."[19]

Aten earns his stripes by aiding in common cowboy crimes. "I was invited to go on one of these night beef raids," he says. "When I showed them I was pretty handy with a rope and skinning knife, they put more confidence in me." He also accepts stolen horses and leaves the county for an alleged resale, instead bringing them to a pasture of a friend who knows his identity.[20]

This is a hair-raising stunt, since he's bringing the stolen animals through Bell County, where they often hang horse thieves on the spot. "I was frightened almost to death all the way that I would meet someone who might recognize the horses and have me arrested," he later recalls. The job finished, Aten waits a few days at the ranch before returning to Brownwood. Seemingly satisfied, Amos Roberts tells him he'll soon steal more.

Aten has achieved what any undercover officer craves: a position inside his quarry's criminal circle. But the deeper he gets, the higher the stakes rise. If discovered, he won't be run out of town. With what he knows, he'll be killed.

It's time for an end game. Aten hopes that's the topic of tonight's meeting with Baugh and William Scott, captain of Texas Ranger Company F.

---

19 Ira Aten, "Fence Cutting Days in Texas," *Frontier Times,* July 1939.

20 Ibid., "All the way that I would meet someone who might recognize the horses and have me arrested."

His hopes for definitive action rise when he sees Joe Copeland at the meeting. Baugh and his brother have hired this local rancher as an inside man. Copeland now rides with the cutters, gaining a level of access that Aten hasn't been granted. An itinerant cowboy is fine to include when it comes to petty crime, but only trusted locals are invited to a fence-cutting party.

Copeland tells Aten the cutters are striking on November 9. He knows because he'll be with them. It's the critical information their foes have been waiting for—a time and a place to aim the guns of Company F.

Scott and Aten plan the ambush carefully. First, the Rangers will have to get to the Baugh ranch without any weapons visible. Rangers can only go armed while on assignment, so this detail could throw off any unwanted observer. There are too many sympathetic eyes in Brown County to assume word of their movements won't spread.

Once in place at the fence, they'll wait in silence. When the cutters approach the ambush spot, the Rangers will reveal themselves, weapons at the ready, and hope for an immediate surrender. No one expects it to go down smoothly, least of all the informant who will be with the cutters. Aten has advice for the understandably nervous Copeland: "Stay in the back and I'll tell them not to fire that direction."[21]

There's no point tarrying, so Aten retreats into the night to ride back to his host family's homestead, back to his fake life to betray the people who took him in and offered him work.

Despite the promise of an end to the charade, Aten's jowly face is scowling under his mustache as he rides. He knows that catching a criminal in the act requires foreknowledge that only an undercover agent or an informer can provide. But it's an unsavory necessity. "In order to round up these fence cutters it was necessary to be deceitful, to lie, and even to steal, so as to win their confidence," Aten later says of his work in Brown County. "I wasn't raised that way and I just didn't like the

---

21 Ibid.

business. It was an insult to an old-time ranger to call him a 'detective' and this was too much like detective work."[22]

It's a loaded word, says author and Ranger researcher Doug Dukes. "This word was not liked by Ira Aten mostly because, at the time, judges and juries did not like the fact that Rangers were coming in and 'pretending' to being something or someone they were not," he says. "It was also a word used by the Pinkertons, and they were not people that were well liked in the South."[23]

Captain William Scott listens to Ira Etan's plan with grim satisfaction. He can imagine the governor's happy reaction when they strike a visible blow against the embarrassingly persistent fence cutters of Brown County. He is certainly not shy about the kind of "detective work" that got the Rangers to this point. Being an informer is what got him onto the Ranger roster all those years ago.

Two days after meeting Aten, Company F prepares to go into harm's way. Luckily, the captain again has his trusted sergeant back. Brooks's unwavering presence is very welcome as they set forth to their mission outside Brownwood.

All Rangers are marksmen; the shooting competitions rattle every camp. But Scott has never seen a smoother, faster man than Brooks pull a six-shooter or work a Winchester. His machinelike motions produce high volumes of on-target fire. None of that skill matters as much as willpower when a human is in the crosshairs. But after Alex, Scott now knows for sure that Brooks won't hesitate. He shot St. John twice, whereas the others fired just once. When he pulls, Brooks aims to put men down for good.

Aten joins the company at camp to provide directions and launch the operation. Before sunset, he and Scott lay out the plan to the gathered men. The orders are as grave as they are simple: Take hidden positions

---

22 Ibid.

23 Email to author.

near the fence line and do nothing but watch until Scott announces their presence. These fence cutters travel armed, so be on guard for violence in the moments that follow. But don't shoot the last rider; he's the informant.

Aten leaves to make his surreptitious way to the W. M. Baugh ranch. Scott and his men fill canteens and pack food for a stakeout, then stow their pistols and hide their rifles inside bedrolls.

The captain leads his men away from their camp after dark. Aten and the Baugh men will be waiting for them, ready to stash the horses in a hideaway and show them the ambush location. The Rangers will pick spots that offer concealment and divvy up their fields of fire.

And then they'll start the vigil.

THE INFORMANT RIDES LAST
November 9, 1886

There's something different about Brown County constable Jim Lovell's face. Joe Copeland can see the man's new addition in the pale light of a waxing gibbous moon. Lovell is wearing a fake mustache.

Copeland knows Lovell's face well, just as he knows the identity of the other half dozen fence cutters gathering for another overnight act of sabotage and intimidation in Brown County. Most are his fellow cattle ranchers or their hired hands. There are also a couple of cattle thieves present—he knows their criminal professions because he's accepted their stolen beef.

Tonight, however, is not about profit. The target is the fence of W. M. Baugh, the man who is dead set on literally blocking them from having a future in Texas. The state might now call them felons, but these band members of fence cutters see themselves as part of a righteous movement.

Once assembled, they travel as one to Baugh's farm, driving the horses through the darkness. Riding together, as if they were meeting at rallies, gives the men strength of purpose. It's just another night of risk-taking for those among them who steal meat and horses, but for those less criminally inclined, this is a risky, thrilling descent. Baugh could have men patrolling the fence tonight or be out there himself. His grit is not to be underestimated. The cutters travel in packs, armed with rifles and pistols for a reason.

Copeland makes sure to ride in the back. This isn't just another midnight expedition; he knows who's waiting for the nipping party tonight.

Baugh's fence stretches along Jim Ned Creek. The process of sabotaging it is well practiced; a few men dismount to cut the barbed wire as the others keep watch. Then, off to the next stretch between posts to repeat. The riders pull up to a nondescript section, and Lovell and Amos Roberts dismount and lead their horses to the fence. Roberts leaves his rifle in the saddle, but Lovell carries a Winchester.

Lovell leans his rifle against a post and goes to work with a pair of clippers. The noise of metal cords suddenly releasing tension signals his success. Roberts does the same on a nearby section. Copeland calls out, loudly enough so that the men he knows are lurking nearby can hear him, "Boys, you're not cutting that short enough. Let's do this well if we're going to do it."

He leaps down from his horse, as if to help them, secretly relieved to be on his feet and closer to the ground. That's when a voice calls out, "Texas Rangers!"

Copeland sees Lovell reach for his rifle. The informant dives to his belly just before peals of gunfire and billowing, moonlight-illuminated clouds of gun smoke fill the night air.

CUT DOWN
November 9, 1886

Scott blinks the gun-muzzle afterimages from his eyes. He sees what he expects to see through the dissipating smoke: two prone figures lying near the fence and two dead horses. There's no sign of the other cutters, who fled into the night.

It happened quickly. He and the other Rangers were squatting behind bushes, spaced out a few feet between them. They heard the riders approaching and halting, the telltale twangs of fences being snipped, and then more hoofbeats coming closer. The gang already cut one and a quarter mile of fencing when they reached the Rangers' position.

A wire sent to the *Austin American-Statesman* says that after Scott's hail, "the only reply was a pistol shot" from the cutters.[24] Ira Aten gives a similar account: "They were leading their horses and clipping the wires twice between each post. Suddenly a challenge from Captain Scott rang out on the midnight air, and, like a flash, this was answered by shots from the fence cutters. The Rangers returned the fire, and when the smoke of battle had cleared away, the horses being led by the fence cutters had been killed and two men lay dying on the fence line."[25]

Whether or not the Rangers had the fire discipline to wait for the surprised men to retrieve, aim, and fire their weapons is certainly debatable. It seems more likely that the first dismounted man reached for his rifle and maybe even began to aim at the Rangers, prompting a fusillade from the concealed men. The other man and the animal were then cut down as he pulled his rifle from the saddle holster. The other cutters rode off in an immediate panic.

The Rangers now approach the two writhing bodies. One stops moving as Scott approaches. He peers into the face of Jim Lovell, Brown County constable, shot dead next to a rifle and a pair of wire cutters, an absurd fake mustache knocked askew on his still face.

Scott breaks the spell with commands. He orders some of his men to fan out, both to scout the direction of those fleeing and to make sure they don't double back to attack the Rangers in retribution. Others tend to Amos Roberts, who is still alive despite gunshots under his left shoulder blade. The Rangers build a fire, carry the wounded man to it, and lay him down. He dies there. While he does, the men discuss the shooting.

24 "Bloody Fight Between Rangers and Fence Cutters in West Texas," *Austin American-Statesman,* November 11, 1886.

25 Aten, "Fence Cutting Days."

Copeland confirms Wood Runnels, Bob Parrock, and Ace Mathews as fence cutter accomplices. The informant stays alongside the Rangers, the only place he'll be safe from reprisal. Scott sends a contingent of Rangers to find Parrock, who submits without a fight.

The night's haul of evidence, arrests, and testimony should secure more indictments, but it's not safe to assume trials will ever happen given the state of local politics. More importantly, a pair of cutters has been lawfully killed by the State of Texas. That should serve as a more effective deterrent than any court case.

When the sun comes up, Company F is ready to head into town to report what happened, stow their suspect, and deliver the two corpses. They can expect backlash from Brown County's residents; Scott warns his men not to be provoked. They find Brownwood buzzing with indignation, the news having spread through the Farmers' Alliance's sympathizers, and crowds of unhappy citizens are milling around town.

Sheriff Adams is clearly alarmed at this disruption in his carefully maintained status quo and has deployed his deputies to clear the streets of anyone wearing a weapon. A downtown shoot-out with the Texas Rangers is the last thing he needs, but his orders unwittingly set the stage for one.

Scott leaves his men in the street as he wires his boss, Adjutant General King, detailing the night's events and the charges that the Rangers will be pursuing against Parrock, Johnson, and Mathews. As he does, Copeland is attracting glares outside.

One of Adams's deputies, Will Butler, tracks Copeland with narrow eyes. The now-reviled informant is still wearing a pistol on his belt. It's a clear reason for confrontation, given the rules of the day, and excuse enough to gun Copeland down if he resists. Butler's sympathies lie with the fallen fence cutters, and he's angered by the acknowledged turncoat strutting around with the out-of-town gunmen.

Butler stalks over to the men, ignoring the Rangers and stepping to Copeland. He has a simple, stark demand: Hand over the pistol. As Sheriff Adams walks over to the developing faceoff, his deputy's gun appears, leveled at the informer. Frank Carmichael attempts to help, in his own way, by drawing his pistol and training it on Butler. Adams pulls his own gun on the Ranger. Lev Baugh steps in, a double-barreled shotgun covering the sheriff.[26]

What we have here is an authentic Old West standoff.

Scott appears, pleading for everyone to lower their guns. There is, the unflappable Ranger captain says, a convenient explanation. The moment teeters on disaster before the firearms are stowed. Scott then tells Adams that Copeland has been deputized and as such can carry a weapon.

This only needs to be true enough to buy the informer time to skip town and head for home on a mule-pulled buckboard wagon. That's when the gunmen strike. The first shots miss their marks but spook the mule into a sudden gallop. The jerking motion topples Copeland into the wagon, just as more rifle balls crease the air where he just sat. Using some innate tactical sense, the mule doesn't slow until they're both safely outside of the ambushers' kill box.[27]

EXILE FROM RANGER HEAVEN
January 29, 1884 (two years, five months before William Treadwell joins the Texas Rangers)

It can be easily argued, especially as William Treadwell's finger curls around the trigger, that Richard Linney shouldn't have attended his brother's dance tonight.

The event itself is a bad idea, considering the tension in Goliad County, Texas. Last fall, Richard Linney was acquitted for killing Henry Welder, but it's hardly been forgotten. To stay safe, he's been living in Sarco with his brother Charles. "It is thought he anticipated still further trouble to grow out of the Welder affair and studiously avoided appearing

---

26 Mike Cox, *The Texas Rangers: Wearing the Cinco Peso, 1821–1900* (New York: Forge, 2008).

27 Alexander and Alexander, *Rawhide Ranger, Ira Aten.*

in localities where danger from this source seemed probable," reads an item from the *Victoria Advocate*.[28] He must have thought the dance a safe place.

And it is, until Treadwell arrives at Charles Linney's after midnight. He's clearly not there to show off his dance moves, which are known to be good. "After the dance was over [Richard] Linney went outside the house," reads the *Advocate*'s article, one of the first newspaper accounts. "Treadwell, whose horse was nearby, suddenly drew his pistol and fired."

Moments later, Linney is dead in his brother's yard, and outraged cowboys are firing bullets at Treadwell as he gallops away. His destination is his employer, a famous haven for rough-hewn Texas cowboys, the Pettus Ranch.

The *Advocate* has some harsh words about Treadwell, coming from the Linney camp. "Treadwell has always borne the character of a desperado and has before been involved in several serious affairs." That may be a nod to his violent past. As a young man, Treadwell left Tennessee after killing the two men involved with the murder of his brother.[29] In Texas, he becomes a well-liked cowboy on the Pettus Ranch, a bedrock institution of Texas history.

William Pettus arrived in Texas in 1822 as one of the original members of Austin's colony. His grandson, cattle drive veteran James Edward Pettus, now operates the ranch. The Frontier Battalion calls the Pettus Ranch "Ranger Heaven" for its embrace of the lawmen.

There are much more charitable accounts of Treadwell's reputation from his employers. T. Wheeler Pettus, who spent enough time with Rangers to earn a nickname from them ("Red"), describes Treadwell as "a loveable vagabond, loyal, trustworthy and a fightin' fool."[30]

---

28 Reprinted in *The Galveston Daily News,* January 30, 1884.

29 William Sterling, *Trails and Trials of a Texas Ranger* (Norman: University of Oklahoma Press, 1959); "When as a mere youth killed two men who had murdered his brother."

30 Ibid.

The Pettus ranch version of the Treadwell-Linney shooting makes it sound like a more two-sided exchange than the press coverage did. "In this fight, Billy was shot through both legs but managed to get on his horse," Sterling relates via Wheeler Pettus. "Badly wounded and bleeding profusely, he rode to the Pettus Ranch. Uncle Buck [William Albert Wheeler] put a bed in a light spring wagon and sent his cowboy to a secluded spot in a mesquite thicket on the San Antonio River. He then dispatched a rider to Goliad for Dr. Joseph Getzweller, a pioneer medico." The doctor returns to the hidden wagon three times a week until Treadwell is healed.

It takes until late 1885 for the trial to be held in Goliad. It must not have been as cold-blooded of a killing as the initial reports indicated, since Treadwell is acquitted of all charges. "Some of the old timers say that a fast horse, ready saddled and with a Winchester in the scabbard, had been tied in a convenient spot by Billy's friends," according to Sterling. "If the verdict had gone against him, he intended to burn the wind for Mexico."

Being cleared in court is only one problem solved. Treadwell still has enemies, and he's eager to leave the Pettus Ranch until the feud heat cools down. So instead of becoming an outlaw, he finds himself a Texas Ranger. The Pettus connection to the organization makes joining the service easy and logical, if a temperamental man with a violent past becoming a law enforcement professional can ever be considered such.

Treadwell joins the Frontier Battalion in May 1886, with Company C in Laredo. In November that year, he transfers to Company F and reports to his new captain, William Scott.

GLOOMY CHRISTMAS
December 1886

It takes months after the shooting for Company F to tie up the loose ends in Brownwood. The county is upset, but the deadly blow to the cutter network has weakened its resolve. The Rangers can now more easily work leads to find their wanted men.

They develop suspects for the bid to end Copeland's life; two weeks after the attempted shooting, Brooks ventures into Callahan County to bloodlessly arrest Wood Runnels for the assassination attempt and returns in early December to nab Frank Johnson for the same crime. The pair come peacefully, trusting the courts to bend in their direction once again.

Another slate of indictments from the night of the fence cutting rattle the county. This time, in addition to Runnels and Johnson, Bob Parrock, Ace Mathews, and a pair of Johnson's siblings are named accomplices. Local authorities will eventually drop all these charges.

For Scott, business as usual includes recruiting and indoctrinating new men, or in this case, adopting the Pettus problem child Billy Treadwell. Company F's November arrival is a study in contradictions. He's a goofball, easy to like, and livens up camp playing songs on his guitar. But he also has a temper lurking just beneath the façade. Scott knows he's killed men and won't hesitate to do so again. No matter how happy he is, he also always seems ready to fight.

He's not getting a chance in sleepy Brown County. Scott is more than ready to take Company F away to chase outlaws elsewhere. "I will leave here today to scout in Concho Co. for some of my Brown Co. fence cutters," he writes his boss, Adjutant General King, in mid-December. "Will be out 6 or 7 days; should I find them, maybe something will pop. Unless we can make another killing on fence cutters very soon the outlook for a gay Christmas with myself & boys is rather gloomy. Brownwood is rather a light night city for the average Ranger."[31] The town boasts a dozen saloons at the time, so maybe this last comment is sheer irony. Or maybe it indicates that Company F is not as welcome in town as the Rangers would want.

The winter months drone on. Pressure on the cutters is producing deterrent results, but also the boredom that comes with it. In January,

---

31 Scott to Sieker, December 12, 1886, reproduced from the Texas State Archives and found at the Texas Ranger Hall of Fame and Museum's research center in Waco.

Scott relays news to Austin that there has been absolutely no fence cutting activities to report the past thirty days.

There's not much action and the weather is unnaturally cold. Stationed in a key node of the cattle country, Company F has a front row seat to a cataclysm that will end the era of the open range for good.

THE GREAT DIE-UP
January 9, 1887

There's nothing beautiful about the snow blanketing North Texas today. It's been sixteen hours straight, and it won't stop falling, dropping about an inch an hour on a massive swath of United States cattle country. Residents besieged by the weather peer from their homes, emerging only to watch the drifts accumulate. Through the wind, muffled by the flakes in the air, is the bellowing sound of starving cattle.

This is the worst day of the "worst winter in the West." It will change the cattle industry forever, costing the lives of herd animals literally beyond measure.

The cattle industry was already a balloon ready to burst before the winter of 1886/87. Like all balloons, it initially inflates with a very real market demand. In this case, refrigerated train cars and cargo ships have opened new markets for beef across the country and the Atlantic.[32]

Streams of longhorns from the open ranges in Texas are driven north to graze on fields in the Dakotas, Wyoming, Montana, and even Canada. (Disease management and regional rivalry led to quarantines of Texas cattle in the Midwest.) Rail lines bring cattle that are destined to become Chicago steaks and English meat pies to slaughterhouses. Roundups organize drifting cattle, and the rest of the herd is driven to Texas to feed on grass.

Texas transforms as the industry creates powerful ranchers, rail line

---

32 David L. Wheeler, "The Blizzard of 1886 and Its Effect on the Range Cattle Industry in the Southern Plains," *Southwestern Historical Quarterly* 94, no. 3 (1991), htttp://www.jstor.org/stable/30238759.

boomtowns, and seasonal floods of cowboys who sweat the roundups and long cattle trails. The open ranges become chaotic, with massive herds wandering across state lines. Drift fences of once-unthinkable lengths appear to halt this migration; one stretches across the entire Texas Panhandle, two hundred miles from Higgins into New Mexico.

Entrepreneurial enterprise by individuals becomes corporatized. Local ranchers become major players by acquiring larger herds and forming cattle companies. International investors jump in with almost limitless, low-interest capital willingly supplied by banks. The wheeling and dealing gets so heated that many cattle traders stop counting heads of cattle, instead relying on breeding algorithms to estimate herd sizes. Massive deals for ghost cattle become common.

It spins out of control, but no one wants to see it. Baron Walter von Richthofen, who moves from Silesia to Denver in 1877, publishes a book called *Cattle-Raising on the Plains of North America* in 1885. In it, he proclaims a cattleman is guaranteed profits of 156 percent over five years. "There is not the slightest amount of uncertainty in cattle raising," he determines.

The flesh and blood result of the greed behind this statement is massive overcrowding on the ranges, north and south. Richthofen is blind to the beef glut that is undercutting the market. In November 1886, wholesale cattle prices in Chicago fall to $3.16 per hundredweight, half of what they had been in 1884.[33] The bubble is already bursting when winter comes.

The industry should see the risk that weather poses to the entire house of cards. The winter of 1885/86 was a harsh one, with snowstorms pummeling the herds grazing up north and causing large casualties at fence lines. Cattle bunch up and move together when it's cold, so when

---

33 Samuel Western, "The Wyoming Cattle Boom, 1868–1886," Wyoming History, November 8, 2014, https://www.wyohistory.org/encyclopedia/wyoming-cattle-boom-1868–1886.

one falls into a snowy creek bed, the rest will follow. The losses are ignored by the relentless industry, and it's business as usual.

The next winter is worse after a Texas drought murders the grass that the cattle depend on to fatten. When the lean animals are driven north, they're not ready for harsh weather. Conditions in their grazing lands are not any better than they are in Texas. In his annual report of 1886, the commander of Fort McKinney in the Wyoming Territory wrote that "the country is full of Texas cattle and there is not a blade of grass within 15 miles of the Post."

The starvation begins even before the snows. By the time the January blizzard blankets cattle country, the animals are already on the brink. In Montana, temperatures drop to sixty below zero. Storms from the north push the desperate cattle south.

They press up, mewling, against drift fences and perish by the thousands. Railroad men wander the lines to clear the snowy cuts of the heaps of dead cows that toppled inside. Passengers stare in horror out the windows at miles of scrawny animals pressed freezing against fences, tightly enough to smother them to death.

There's little that can be done. Some ranch hands venture south, clipping drift fences to try to rescue the trapped animals. Most ranchers just hunker down and wait to assess the damage later. When the storms abate in late January, the Texas Panhandle and Indian Territories are charnel houses. For many ranchers, the winter becomes a marathon of skinning frozen animals. One ranch employee reportedly skins 250 carcasses a mile for thirty-five miles along one section of drift fence.

Losses are massive, but greed obscures numbers as ghost cattle become ghost losses. But tens of thousands of animals certainly died miserable deaths during January. Bankruptcies and ranch ownership transfers follow, but the real aftermath is collectively felt by the cattle industry. It has been scared into ending the open range.

The idea of seasonally moving herds of cattle north so they can eat is clearly fraught with too much risk. Too many variables—especially the weather—can spell doom for a cattleman. It's time to keep the animals close and feed them hay in the winter. That means growing opportunity for local farmers to grow cattle feed and new life for cow towns on rail lines. But the cowboys who depended on roundup and long cattle drives find work lacking, and many of these eye theft and banditry as new careers. Others find their ways into law enforcement.

The winter of 1886/87 spells the end of longhorn steers. These were bred for the open range and the long trail, but such hardy animals aren't needed anymore. British-derived breeds of cattle, better suited to a more sedentary life, will now largely replace them.

These new animals serve as an apt metaphor for what will happen to Texas. The Wild West of the state's history, so vital to its identity and iconography, dies in January 1887. It doesn't happen at once—something so vast needs to gradually fade into obsolescence. There are many cattle drives to come after the storm, with all the Wild West mystique that comes with them. But this romantic, chaotic age is ending, replaced with something that is as calculated and cold as a railroad line.

NEW YEAR IN AUSTIN
January 11, 1887

Texas's new governor, Lawrence Sullivan Ross, stands in front of the assembled legislature to deliver his first speech in office. "Sul" Ross projects a personable, everyman aurora that balances an august résumé. "His bald head and friendly smile made him look like a good old farmer," describes Ira Aten, who will soon meet him to be tasked on missions personally.[34]

But today, his gravitas is on full dramatic display. "Probably no legislature was ever confronted by graver responsibilities," he tells the lawmakers within the first minutes. "Those who study the public affairs of our state and consider the lack of homogeneity in its population, its industrial pursuits business enterprises and social sympathies, are aware

---

34 Aten, "Fence Cutting Days."

of the fact that it presents questions vastly more complicated and embarrassing than any other state."[35]

Ross spent no money on his campaign other than traveling expenses, then cakewalked through the Democratic nomination and general election. He garnered 228,776 votes against 65,236 for the Republican candidate and 19,186 for the Prohibitionist. His steady base of support is Confederate veterans.

Ross is from Waco, a city his family founded, and he attends Baylor University (in the town of Independence at the time) and Florence Wesleyan University in Alabama. He returns to Texas on breaks, and on one such trip, he's wounded fighting Comanche. Education is no shield from violence—he seems to seek it. The new college graduate joins the Texas Rangers and is promoted to captain. In 1860, he gains fame by leading the Rangers in the Battle of Pease River, featuring the recapture of Cynthia Ann Parker, a child seized by Comanche in 1836.

This fame follows him into the Civil War, during which he's an ardent and capable Confederate leader. Ross participates in 135 battles in the Civil War (some skirmishes, but still impressive) and rises to become one of the youngest Confederate generals. Following the war, Ross serves as sheriff of McLennan County and serves as a two-year state senator, but he's really focused on his ranch. Still, his reputation makes the path to the governorship an easy one, and friends hardly have to twist his arm before he's campaigning.

His chief focus is to defuse the tensions in the state, especially sharing public property, ensuring access to water, and protecting valid grazing rights, by introducing land-use reform. This is the root cause of the majority of the "embarrassing" conflicts in the state. He also declares himself a foe of all illegal settlements.

While land use is the core of his platform, he makes room for talk

---

35 House of Representatives, Twentieth Legislature, State of Texas, January 11, 1887, https://lrl.texas.gov/scanned/govdocs/Lawrence%20Sullivan%20Ross/1887/IA _Ross_1.18.1887.pdf.

about law and order in his inauguration speech. When he does, it doesn't sound much like a hard line: "We neglect our duty so long as we fail to establish suitable industrial schools or reformatory institutions where they may be taught respect for law and order, the necessity for virtuous principle and to look forward to labor of some kind as their ultimate duty and privilege."

Ross also obliquely addresses fence cutters, steady foes of the Texas Rangers, almost as an apologist. "In any portion of the state, when laws relating to public lands are defied and set at naught, our first duty is to re-examine the laws, with the view of ascertaining what defects, if any, have produced this condition of society and, upon discovery of any defect, to apply a remedy," the new governor says in his speech. It doesn't sound very much like the approach taken by sending the Rangers to places like Brown County.

But then again, the fence cutters are stubbornly persisting. On February 5, a detachment of Company F will be ordered to McCulloch County after Rochelle postmaster Theodore Evans reports "fence cutting, houses burned down, horses stolen, etc . . ."[36]

Ross doesn't mention the Frontier Battalion specifically, but there may be a reference in the inaugural speech that's worrisome. "Where there are extraordinary combinations to violate the laws, there should he extraordinary legislation for its suppression," he tells the legislature before him. "If our present laws are defective in that respect, they should be promptly amended."

Talk of "amending laws" could be a threat to the Rangers. There is a legal loophole that is winding into a noose meant to strangle them to death. The source of the trouble is baked into the legislation that created the force, which grants "officers" the power to arrest. In law enforcement terms, that seems to encompass every Texas Ranger in service. But the Frontier Battalion, created during the Indian Wars, has a martial heri-

---

36 Requests for Rangers made directly to the Adjutant General's office, 1887, https://play.google.com/books/reader?id=hVoMAQAAIAAJ&hl=en&pg=GBS.PA49.

tage that leads to a different legal interpretation of "officer" that would limit arrests solely to Ranger sergeants and captains.

It's a word game that people take seriously. The governor's speech is read like tea leaves. Is Ross entertaining the idea of changing the laws to make things clearer? That process would lead to a reorganization that could spiral out of control and doom the organization. The Rangers can only wait and hope the governor, as a former lawman, has a sympathetic ear.

Ross finishes by exhorting the legislature to unleash the communal spirit of the people of Texas. In a land of deputized posses, freelance reward hunters, and self-appointed vigilantes, the words are ironic. "Give the people just and wholesome laws," he concludes, "and they will not only obey them but aid their enforcement and execution."[37]

---

37 House of Representatives, Twentieth Legislature.

5

SHOOT-OUT IN SABINE

THE TENDERFOOT

March 1, 1887

J. Allen Newton takes in the town of Brownwood from the train depot as he waits for his ride and for his new job to begin.

The town's size is impressive, considering the Atchison, Topeka & Santa Fe Railway opened here just a year before. Brownwood boasts a dozen saloons, a pair of hotels, two mills, and a public school. The place even has a waterworks. The depot is newer than many of the buildings, standing along wide, well-worn streets. In comparison, in the Texas town where Newton moved from, Jacksonville, the train is literally life. The population there actually uprooted the entire town, building by building, to locate near a newly built railhead.

Main street in Brownwood is wide for a reason. Cattle have been king here for a while, with about two thousand head in Brown County. The Chisholm Trail (opened in 1867) doesn't come directly through, but enough of it overspills onto the trail that the trail serves as a detour for water and grass. Cowboys would drive these herds right through Brownwood. These days, the future of cattle is increasingly tied to trains.

At age twenty-two, Newton has come to Brownwood to meet up with his new employers, the Texas Rangers. He's answered the call, via telegram, to become a private in Company F. All of Newton's belongings are in a trunk sitting on the Brownwood train depot. These include his most recent purchases: a Winchester rifle, six-shooter, two blankets, saddle, and bridle. He plans on buying a horse here in Brownwood, making his Ranger starter kit complete.

A rider gallops up to him; behind him is a wagon with a Black driver. The young Ranger sees a familiar face: his new commanding officer, Captain William Scott. The Rangers' makeshift camp is scratched out of the prairie a few miles outside of town, on the ranch of Lev Baugh on the Pecan Bayou, where they've been eating fresh beef from the grateful cattleman's herd. Scott has come to replenish his chuck wagon and fetch his new recruit.

"Hold on," Newton says. "I have to get my trunk."

The Ranger captain laughs in his face. "We move too fast to carry a trunk," he says. "You better express it back home. But take out your best suit first. We'll buy you duckins [coveralls] for camp as we pass through town."[1]

Newton hustles off, under his first orders as a Texas Ranger. He's a long way from his clerk's desk in East Texas. If not for a chance encounter in a train car and a fight with a woman, he wouldn't be here.

The young man has chosen wanderlust over his desire to settle down with Josie Gossett. She's a catch in more ways than one, being part of the family that donated the land to create the town of Crockett. There is opportunity there for a clever clerk, especially one courting someone from such a well-heeled family. But Newton feels more satisfied on the road, and he takes advantage of the rails to travel when he can.

On a trip home on a leg between Austin and Dallas, he sits in a train car with a group of county sheriffs. The lawmen are on the way to a convention in Dallas and feeling amiable. One of them introduces Newton to a well-dressed man, with a high brow, handlebar mustache, and slightly pinched eyes. It's Company F Captain William Scott.

---

1 Sarah Ellen Davidge, "Texas Rangers Were Rough and Ready Fighters," *Frontier Times,* November 1935.

Newton's mouth changes his life when he tells the man that it's been a dream to become a Ranger.

"You really mean that, kid?" comes the reply.

"Sure do," Newton says, meeting the older man's gaze.

"I'll be wanting a recruit soon," Scott says. "I'll let you know if I need you."

After that, Jacksonville and his desk job both seem even more deadening. His courtship also sours, and he and Josie get into a proper fight. The aftermath of the blowup is still stinging when the discontented man receives a telegram from Scott: If you want to become a Ranger, come to Brown County right away.

The culture at camp can be cruel to tenderfoots. As Henry Putz put it about his Company F hazing: "My initiation was rough enough to daunt anyone who was not filled to the brim with the wild west craze, for the unavoidable hardships incidental to Ranger life were aggravated by the practical jokes the men employed to test and season a new recruit."[2]

The first weeks as a Ranger are painful for Newton. He's kept on the road immediately and any downtime is spent shooting at camp. The Rangers have made a religion of firearms proficiency. "He finds that target practice is a favorite diversion among his comrades and that perfection in this branch of his calling is the best life insurance he can carry," Earl Mayo says of new Ranger recruits. "So he practices assiduously, shooting from over to protect his own body, shooting from the hip, shooting with his left hand as well as his right and from every position which the exigencies of frontier conflict might lead him to assume."[3]

Newton finds it easy to play what others in the company call "the

2 "Ranger Forty Years Ago Had No Easy Life; Henry Putz, Who Enlisted at 18, Tells of Their Exploits," *Dallas Morning News,* October 3, 1926.

3 Earl Mayo, "Texas Rangers: The Most Efficient Police Force in the World," *Frank Leslie's Popular Monthly,* October 1901.

clown of the outfit,"[4] but he's also getting the chance to prove himself as a lawman. He gets a solo case when Scott, eager for his men to find action elsewhere since Brown County is so sluggish, sends him thirty miles west through the snow to the town of Santa Anna to investigate a spate of cattle thefts. Arriving at the Walker House, the only hotel in town, the weary Ranger is invited to dinner with a local family. "I was almost speechless when I found one of the people at the table was Miss Della Parks of Ennis, who was my first sweetheart. She was visiting her sister, Mrs. Walker," he will later tell a reporter.[5]

"It took me quite a while to investigate the cattle business," he ends cryptically, not making clear if the snowy weather hampered his investigation, if his targets proved challenging, or if the presence of Della Parks was the cause of the delay.

Ever the romantic, Newton only writes about his personal details, but doesn't dwell on the results of the case.

BACK TO THE BIG THICKET
March 21, 1887

Company F breaks down their camp in Brownwood, and it transforms into a small caravan. It's time to go back to Sabine County.[6] Teamster James Johnson morphs from cook to logistician, and then to commander of the moving chuck wagon. All the supplies—tents, cooking gear, ammunition, extra clothes, water containers, food, shackles—are

---

4 Per fellow Ranger Frank Carmichael; "Blood Curdling Days of '80s Live in Memories of Abilenian," *Abilene Reporter-News,* June 12, 1938.

5 Davidge, "Texas Rangers Were Rough."

6 "March 20: Capt. Scott and Company F were sent to Sabine County at request of ex-senator W. W. Weatherred and District Judge Perkins, with other citizens and county officials, to arrest the Conner gang, who for years terrorized that county." From "Requests for Rangers Made Directly to the Adjutant General's Office 1887," Texas State Archives, Austin, TX.

stowed and secured for the trip. Another wagon carries necessities for the horses, under the charge of an unnamed hired driver or farrier. "Followed by two wagons driven by negroes who took care of the baggage, we drove across country to Cisco, where we took the train for Marshall," Newton recalls.[7]

They move on without Captain William Scott, who disembarks in Dallas. Scott has entrusted Brooks with getting Company F to Marshall while he visits his thirty-seven-year-old sister and her growing family. Emily Virginia (Scott) Bower gave birth to twins Jack and Robert in early February, adding to a family of boys of eleven, eight, and three, and a fifteen-year-old girl.

Seeing this brood makes Scott think about his own prospects for marriage. He's a thirty-three-year-old, trail-grizzled lawman with the smell of gunpowder on his hands. He's been riding for too long to just settle down like Bower has, but he also doesn't want to remain a lonely Texas Ranger forever. All he needs is a steady job with a sense of adventure and a mate who can tolerate it. No problem.

His father, Methodist minister James Edward Scott, moved from Richmond County to Georgia to Texas, and the easiest way to trace his path is by charting the birth of his children from two marriages. J. E. Scott marries Miley Hall in November 1833. Emily, Sam, Jack, and William Scott are all products of this marriage. In 1859, J. E. Scott remarries Mary Elmore, and the family have two girls, Lilea (in 1861) and Vernon Dalkeith Scott (in 1865). The family leaves Montgomery County for the big city where he serves as a "prominent Methodist divine of Dallas."[8] In 1870, he and the girls appear in census records living in Dallas County's Precinct One.

Jack, a war veteran, becomes a Texas Ranger, and he and the younger girls return to Montgomery County, Vernon Scott included.

---

7 Davidge, "Texas Rangers Were Rough."

8 *Dallas Morning News,* December 1, 1901.

That spirited twenty-two-year-old lives in Willis, fifty miles north of Houston, and seems to have inherited some of the Scott thirst for travel. Just this month, she was visiting friends—and breaking hearts—in Galveston.[9]

Emily Virginia's husband, E. G. Bower, is an attorney who's been elected judge of Dallas County. Scott's brother-in-law is acquainted with the violent, seamy side of life, which for Scott makes him easier to get along with.

E. G. Bower served in the Civil War with the Confederate bushwhackers, who eventually formed the James-Younger Gang, who robbed banks, trains, and stagecoaches in at least eleven states. (These are Belle Starr's people.) A Fort Worth paper mentions that Bower "remained a steadfast friend" to both Younger and James, "always contending that any desperate acts they may have been guilty of they were forced to because of persecutions during and immediately following the war."[10]

One thing to remember about notorious outlaws: To their friends, they are usually not quite as notorious.

Bower goes to Dallas to study law. In 1866, at a seasoned twenty-three years old, he marries Emily Virginia Scott, the reverend's daughter. His political star rises, and in 1872, he's elected county attorney, holding the office until winning the county judgeship in 1884.

When William Scott visits his sister and brother-in-law on his way to Sabine County in 1887, his family finds the Texas Ranger captain uncharacteristically nervous. "He expressed his knowledge of the danger of the trip, saying the outlaws had all the advantages, would fight, were on foot and acquainted with the country and would without a doubt ambush him," reads a dispatch from Dallas in *The Galveston Daily News*, later

9 *Galveston Daily News*, March 23, 1887.

10 *Fort Worth Morning Register*, December 1, 1901.

describing the visit.[11] He leaves them for the train station so that he can arrive in Marshall in the morning.

Scott's appearance leaves the Bower family disquieted. E. G. Bower, at this point, likely starts making plans to meet with his brother-in-law in Hemphill as a show of support. Since Vernon Scott lives (comparably) nearby, plans are also crafted for Bower to meet her there, as well. The young woman is no stranger to travel, having just returned from a jaunt to Galveston. The Scott family is coming to Sabine County.[12]

Company F's captain knows the danger ahead, but at least his Rangers are not going to aimlessly scour the Big Thicket for the Conners, not this time. Instead, they hope to launch more pinpoint operations based on new intelligence from the locals. He hopes changing tactics will even the odds.

On March 25, Scott rendezvouses with Company F outside Marshall. From there, he plans on slipping into Sabine County unnoticed. But when he arrives, a newspaper reporter is waiting to pry an exclusive from him. An item from that day in *The Galveston Daily News* reveals the result of the questioning:

> Yesterday a company of ten Rangers, in charge of Sgt Brooks, arrived here by rail and went into camp. Captain William Scott arrived this morning, and the company will take up the line of march. Nothing can be learned of their mission. They are hunting somebody, and some developments will be made in a few days.[13]

This last sentence proves to be prophetic.

---

11 This actually ran after the Conners and Rangers met in the woods, lest anyone think the article gave the family any warning.

12 *The Galveston Daily News* on March 23, 1887, notes that "Miss Vernon Scott today went back to her home in Willis."

13 *Galveston Daily News*, March 25, 1887.

Outside of Marshall, the reunited Rangers of Company F wait, hidden at camp, for W. W. Weatherred to come through with a location on the Conner camp. In the meantime, Scott leaves for Nacogdoches. He's been summoned by Sabine County's judge to follow his plan to ensnare the outlaws.

PERKINS'S GAMBIT

February 2, 1887 (eight weeks before Company F's second Sabine County deployment)

Judge J. I. Perkins hears the results he wants to hear from the senatorial election: John Reagan has been elected to the Senate. The seat of the Texas Second District in Congress will be open. The East Texas judge will see how far his preparations have reached, now that the race is on. *The Galveston Daily News* on February 3, 1887, calls him "the fitting successor."

Perkins's power base is within rural Anderson County and the town of Palestine, but he's facing four other contenders who are siphoning away those same votes. His foes include Rusk resident J. B. Long, who's trying to secure farmer support, and William "Howdy" Martin, district attorney of four counties, including Anderson. The DA in particular is dimming the luster of Perkins's own law-and-order credentials.[14]

There is nothing that flies in the face of the judge's image as an "implacable terror to evil-doers," as the Galveston paper puts it, more than the at-large Conner family. The prosecutions of the jailbreakers continues—farmer Lem Taylor is convicted for it and sent to Rusk Penitentiary for a three-year stretch this month—but the family at the center of the storm remains at large.

Perkins visits Sul Ross shortly after the governor takes office in 1887. It's an in-person plea for help in Sabine County, where Willis Conner and his boys are still lurking. "He got on a train, went to Austin and asked Governor L.S. Ross to send two special-picked Rangers to Sabine County and help make capture of the Conners," Nacogdoches sheriff A. J. Spradley puts it.

---

14 *Fort Worth Daily Gazette*, March 8, 1887.

It takes two months for the plan to bear fruit. Just before Scott deploys the full company to Sabine County in late March, he's drafted into Perkins's plan. He and a "hand-picked Ranger" head to Nacogdoches to meet the judge and Sheriff Spradley. It's hard to imagine he didn't take Brooks, his fastest gunman, but Spradley doesn't identify the man.

When the lawmen gather in Nacogdoches, the mission becomes a little clearer. Perkins has assembled a crew of well-known, manhunting lawmen. The Rangers' reputations speak for themselves. Sheriff Spradley has firsthand experience with the Conners and the terrain. Not only had he held them in his jail, but also he and his deputy, William Burrows, joined a Conner hunt in Sabine County in 1885.[15]

Perkins lays out the plan. He tells the lawmen that he has a guide that can show him where the Conners are camped. The small force here will move directly to the site in southern Sabine County, bypassing Hemphill and the spying Conner sycophants there.

"What's the plan if they show up?" asks Spradley.

"Shoot, and talk afterwards," says Scott.[16]

This is exactly what Spradley *doesn't* want to hear. He's already of the opinion that the Rangers are up to "a game of cold-blooded assassination." Spradley will never budge from his opinion that the Conners acted in self-defense and were unwise but not murderous. He silently decides to

---

15 *Galveston Daily News*, August 15, 1885. This small article produces large questions about the time line of events. The article reported the presence of two Rangers, but it couldn't refer to the same incident as Spradley's story. Spradley's prominent mention of Governor Ross fixes the excursion in 1887, the governor's first year in office. The oral version passed down through the Harper family, as related in *Gunsmoke in the Redlands*, describes a failed manhunt spoiled by dogs that occurred just "a couple of days" before Company F arrives in full, further backing Spradley's time line. Scott's report only says he left Weatherford on the twenty-second and arrived "in Sabine County" on the twenty-ninth.

16 Henry Fuller, *A Texas Sheriff: A. J. Spradley* (Whitefish, MT: Literary Licensing, 2011); originally published in 1931 by Baker Printing Co., Nacogdoches, TX.

go to Sabine County as an observer, fulfilling the Sabine County judge's wishes and remaining unhelpful at the same time.

The governor and his allies in Sabine are not Spradley's cup of tea. The Sheriff's Populist stances and equal treatment of African Americans will soon upset the Democratic Party, but, at this time, he is just a young, respected sheriff with experience with the manhunt's targets.[17] How was Perkins to know how attached he became to the Conners during their incarceration in his jail?

Anyway, Spradley tags along with the Texas Rangers to watch the manhunt unfold. The men delve into southern Sabine County, heading for the secret meeting spot and treading as softly as possible. As they close in, the din of barking dogs filters through the dense trees. They must be getting close. The Rangers muse that the pack is chasing a deer, but it soon becomes clear they are trailing something else.

When Spradley tells the story to his biographer, Henry Fuller, he makes it clear that he knows what those howls mean: "They would not see the Conners that day, he felt sure."

The dogs are the Conners' early alarm system, a pack that sweeps through the forest like a living trip wire. Spradley describes the woodman's mastery of the animals as they discover the raiding party: "On the dogs came, pell mell and presently the entire pack bayed the officers, changing their cry used in running entirely. For a minute they bayed and then the long, clear call of the horn, half a mile away, sounded through the woods. The dogs instantly left and disappeared in the woods in the direction of the horn, which repeated the call a moment later in another direction. Of course there were two horns to deceive the officers who hurried in the direction of the first one that sounded but never saw anybody."[18]

---

17 Worth Robert Miller, "Spradley, Andrew Jackson," *Handbook of Texas Online*, https://www.tshaonline.org/handbook/entries/spradley-andrew-jackson.

18 Spradley's respect for the Conners' dog handling is not surprising. He is enamored of tracking dogs and will be a major advocate and supplier of man-tracking bloodhounds.

Another reference to this manhunt comes via Edwin Harper, grandson of Elmer Harper, who has a foot in both Conner and Low camps and "handed down his version of the affair to their children and grandchildren," which was then relayed to author Joseph Combs. "After a time the dogs caught up with the men and a bedlam of barking and yelping took place," the account reads. "The Conners knew what that meant, so they sounded a horn, the customary way woodsmen called their dogs to them, and the dogs immediately left the men and returned to the Conners. In the meantime, the Conners sounded horns in other directions to confuse the searchers."[19]

The family and their canines slip away into the dark woods, now silent. There's no way Scott can get the drop on the family now that the element of surprise is gone. Perkins's assembled team has failed.

Spradley remains proud for his whole life that he didn't help the Rangers catch the Conners. The sheriff "did not like the tactics pursued by the Rangers."[20] The Conner apologist returns to Nacogdoches with his deputy alongside, unaware that he'll soon return.

Scott heads back to Marshall to collect his entire company for the next attempt. Scott will need to find another way to catch the Conners unaware. Success will depend on locals—people the family trusts too much—willing to help locate the outlaw family's nightly campsite.

The Spradley recollection indicates that the family is already being betrayed by an informer working with authorities. Spradley specifically mentions the presence of a "local guide who knew every foot of the ground was employed by the officers."

It may have failed, but the men of Hemphill are using a new weapon against the Conners—their fellow backwoodsmen neighbors. The betrayals have begun.

---

19 Fuller, *A Texas Sheriff*.

20 Ibid.

VANISHING SPIES
March 30, 1887

After five days of practicing shooting, hazing wisecracking tender-foots, drinking moonshine, listening to Treadwell play guitar, and hearing everyone's best stories from when they were apart, Company F is finally mustered for a nighttime raid from Marshall into Sabine County.[21]

The men engage in some subterfuge. "Capt. Scott ordered us to conceal our weapons and to pass through the country as cowboys looking for cattle," J. Allen Newton later recalls. "We put our Winchesters in the wagons and wore our other guns under cover. Polley had made arrangements with Capt. Scott to meet us in Milam."[22]

The plan is for nearly the entire company to head into the woods to meet an informant under cover of darkness, after he returns from a hunting trip with the Conner family. This way, he can lead the dismounted Rangers to where the outlaws are confirmed to have bedded down for the night. Surprising the Conners while asleep is the safest way to take them in—holding to the seldom-appreciated Ranger tradition to strike when least expected.

And if they do fight, Scott has Company F ready, except for a pair of Rangers he's sent to the houses of friends and family members "to guard and prevent them from rendering aid to the Conners during the raid."[23] To augment his forces in the field, Scott has Weatherred, Polley, James O. Toole, and Henry Harris embedded with his men.

There has been a schism in Sabine County, one the Rangers and men

---

21 "On the 30th I proceeded with my men and a few citizens of Sabine County southward for the purpose of scouting for the Conners."—Report of Captain William Scott, to the adjutant general, March 1887.

22 Davidge, "Texas Rangers Were Rough."

23 Scott, to the adjutant general.

of Hemphill are exploiting to the fullest. Men of the southern reaches of the county, neighbors who know the Conner Community and have the family's confidence, are now turning informant.

But which locals turned on the family—and when—is a little muddled. Ranger reports don't specify the sources and methods, and newspapers didn't report particulars. It comes down to the dueling accounts of the Rangers who were there versus accounts passed down from family members of those involved. This is the way of the criminal informant—acts done in the shadows, swept under the rug with vagaries, and never discussed beyond the whispers of those betrayed or the memories of old cops.

Still, one name rises to the surface in every account: Redden Alford.

Redden Alford is born in January 1858 in Saint Clair, Alabama.[24] There are Alfords all over Sabine County, which eventually draws him to Texas. He marries Delia Jennette Moore, a fellow twenty-two-year-old, in Sabine County, and by 1880, he's listed in census records as a literate but unschooled laborer in a tannery. By 1887, they have five children together, the latest born just this year.[25]

Alford somehow has choice cuts of pork and venison that he brings to town to trade. The meat comes from the Conners. He trades it for whatever can't be scrounged from the woods and delivers it to the family, often via dead drop.

James Polley sees an opportunity, and he braces Alford with a threat: When the Texas Rangers come back, he's directing them his way. Being on the Rangers' bad side has already led to the arrests of Alford's friends and neighbors, and who knows what could happen to a man they catch in the act of trading with the outlaws. "Polley had scared Alford, the man that always brought Conners' goods into town, by telling him the

---

24 1860 U.S. Federal Census.

25 1880 U.S. Federal Census.

Rangers were coming," Newton later tells a reporter. "Alford agreed to tell us where the Conners camped."[26]

The plan hinges on Alford's fresh information, but Newton says the man who shows up at the 11:00 p.m. rendezvous does not have it to share. Newton says Alford's "brother" arrives instead, saying the informant had sent him to say that the Conners intended to settle down for the night after the late-afternoon hunt, so he had gone hunting with them so as to locate their camp.[27]

Company F settles in for a long wait. Cigars are lit, smoked, extinguished. Stories are swapped—outlaws hunted, Civil War battles survived, frontier towns compared. There's a good chance moonshine is passed around to those willing.[28] The calendar day switches unceremoniously to March 31. The tense night stretches on, with only the steady hum of insects, frogs, and small game disturbing the still air.

All hopes are on the second informant's arrival. At around 3:00 a.m., he arrives. He points into the dark woods and says, "The new camp is down that way."

Local lore holds that the first man is Redden Alford and this second man is another Conner family confidant—Fed's brother-in-law twenty-year-old Milton Anthony. His name is not within any Ranger or newspaper records and is not in the detailed account given by Allen Newton, who clearly ascribes the role of second informant to "Alford's brother."[29]

There are other male Alfords around Sabine County, and one of

---

26 Sarah Ellen Davidge, "Texas Rangers Were Rough and Ready Fighters," *Frontier Times,* " November 1935

27 Ibid.

28 More on this later.

29 Author and feud investigator Mark Dugan theorizes that locals intentionally misled newspapers by saying Reddon Alford led the Rangers in order to protect Milton Anthony from reprisal. However, Dugan doesn't cite Newton's account, in which the

these may have arrived to be mistaken for a sibling. So why suppose Milton Anthony was involved, if newspaper and Ranger records, then and now, don't mention him? Elizabeth, Milton Anthony's daughter, is one who places him at the scene. She tells Ray Longron, her grandson, that her father said he went hunting with the Conners that day and met the Rangers afterward to tell them where the camp's location is.[30]

Alford is being squeezed by the local posse, but Milton Anthony has even more personal reasons to turn on the outlaw Conners. He has tension at home, mostly in the form of his wife Theodosia, Nancy Conner's sister.

By this point, Docia's already been involved in one Sabine County scandal, one that has nothing to do with the feud. It begins in 1879, when fourteen-year-old Theodosia Travis experiences salvation and, after being "received by experience," seeks to be baptized at the First Baptist Church of Hemphill.[31]

The church is familiar to her family, since the White-Travis families were founding members in 1858. These initial members first met in homes before moving into a school building near the Housen Bayou. Now, by the early 1880s, they are prosperous enough to consider building a new church in Hemphill.

James J. Roundtree's career as the leading spiritual guide of Sabine County grows with the Baptist community there. He's a South Carolina transplant, born there in 1824. He meets and marries his wife, Malinda, and they have two children. By 1860, he's in Nacogdoches, where his

---

former Ranger names "Alford" specifically, and has no reason to lie for the Anthony family, many years later.

30 Mark Dugan, *Judge Not* (unpublished, 1982). Dugan interviews Longron in 1982 and thereby preserves this oral history. If not for Dugan, these voices would have been lost.

31 *Minutes 1858–1890 First Baptist Church, Hemphill, Texas* (Saint Louis, MO: Igmire Publications, 1982), distributed by Ericson Books, Nacogdoches, TX.

speaking ability propels him to the role of elder, a congregation's designated speaker. He appears in the 1870 census there, but by 1875, he and Malinda have moved to Hemphill, and he's regarded as an elder of the First Baptist Church there.

There appears to be a bit of a leadership vacuum that Roundtree is ready to fill. According to the church's internal records, there is no meeting in September, and in October, the pastor doesn't show up. But Roundtree is there, and he does the preaching and runs the meeting. On May 28, 1876, Roundtree holds a candlelight service, after which he's selected to be the pastor. He baptizes new members, casts out several for irreligious behavior, and exhorts a public apology from a congregation member for dancing.[32]

The Baptists of Sabine County are gently splintering and setting up in other parts of the county. Pastor Roundtree is at the helm of this expansion. Just after New Year's in 1876, he and fellow elder J. S. Lambert organize the Antioch Church in the Gravel Hill community, seven miles north of Hemphill. With his involvement in both churches, Roundtree's influence seems to be heading in a steady upward trajectory.

Categorizing what happens next would be challenging in any era. All that remains are the First Baptist Church records, which detail a sex scandal in 1883 that rocks the county. Roundtree that April is investigated for "gross unchristian conduct" including "seduction and adultery." The name associated with this scandal in church records is Theodosia Travis.

Roundtree is fifty-nine and Docia is seventeen at the time he's investigated. Legally, he's in the clear since the age of consent in much of the United States, and the world at the time, is twelve.[33] Morally, her age and inexperience and his position and age make him a manipulative predator. The First Baptist Church doesn't see her as a victim, however.

32 Alabama, U.S., County Marriage Records, 1805–1967, and ibid.

33 Stephen Robertson, "Age of Consent Laws," Children and Youth in History, https://chnm.gmu.edu/cyh/items/show/230.

At the same meeting where they call for deliberations over their pastor's behavior, they resolve "that this Church withdraw fellowship from Theodosia Travis for gross unchristian conduct."

The emergency meeting ensues, with members from any churches where he serves as pastor, including Antioch, "invited to send delegates to said meeting to participate in the investigation and deliberations." Charges against Roundtree are sustained and "fellowship withdrawn" from him in June 1883. News of his removal will be published in statewide Baptist journals, the church records state.[34] Roundtree doesn't appear in any more Sabine County census records—or any other available records, for that matter.

Docia Travis can't flee. The investigation has included church members of several counties, ensuring word of the scandal spreads to Baptists across East Texas and beyond. It's the crowning public humiliation of a teenage girl in an unforgiving religious community.

If Milton Anthony knows about this painful history, it certainly doesn't hinder him from marrying Docia. They wed on March 24, 1886, one full year after the Conners break out of jail. Milton Anthony is now in the center of the feud, with a brother-in-law on the run, a sister-in-law still grieving, and a wife at home who's coping with a traumatic, demeaning experience.

"Adults who were victimized as children may find it difficult to trust others," notes the Texas Association Against Sexual Assault. "You may feel that if you trust and let people near, you will be vulnerable to being hurt and victimized again. This fear is understandable, especially if the person who abused you was someone who you knew and trusted."[35]

Docia doesn't appear to have confidence in her husband. Instead,

---

34 *Minutes 1858–1890.*

35 "Adults Molested as Children," Texas Association Against Sexual Assault, 2015, http:// taasa.org/wp-content/uploads/2015/05/TAASA0020_AdultsMolestedAsChildren _vFinal.pdf National Sexual Assault Hotline: 1–800–656-HOPE.

she's angry that he spends so much time with her sister. Being married to a wanted man has been hard for Nancy Conner, and she appeals to young Milton to help her when he can. This is too often for Docia, who it can safely be guessed doesn't have a support network prepared for her emotional needs. Milton Anthony's frustration at the situation is aimed at Fed, whom he feels brought about all this misery and should treat his wife better.[36]

His father, Thomas, is even more of an influence, upbraiding him for supporting outlaws and urging him to help bring them in and collect the reward. Any father can have an outsize influence on his son, and in this case, Thomas B. Anthony has stature beyond his profession as a farmer. He served with the CSA in Company H of the Thirty-Third Regiment Alabama Infantry, a quirk of fate that places him with East Texans at battles like Pea Ridge and Stone's River.[37] He sees real action, gets wounded, and is then captured, to be furloughed from a prison camp at the war's end. The elder Anthony takes his wife and children and follows his father, Middleton W. Anthony, to the town of Sabine, Texas. There they operate farms and make new generations of Anthonys.

The Conner quagmire is entangling Anthony's son, and he's ready to resolve the situation—no matter how uncomfortable that might make the young man. With the Rangers back and ready for action, Milton Anthony is under a lot of pressure to serve as an informant.

Despite conflicting names, there is a scenario that aligns everyone's stories about what happened on March 31: Milton Anthony, through Nancy, is asked to help the Conners during a hunt. His role is likely to carry any excess meat back to town to trade for goods the outlaws need. Redden Alford finds out about this and tells Thomas B. Anthony. The demand on Milton to inform on the Conners grows from without and

---

36 Ibid.

37 Per his grave, verified via "Alabama Civil War Muster Rolls, 1861–1865," https://archives.alabama.gov/civilwar/search.cfm.

within as the Rangers are brought in for a raid. Milton Anthony agrees to go hunting with the Conners, while Alford meets the Rangers to tell them that the young informer will soon be there with specific information on their location.

Milton Anthony comes to the Ranger camp, tells them where the night's camp is located—*and leaves it to Alford to guide the Rangers there.* Years later, Newton misidentifies this second man as Alford's brother. Since he never uses either Alford's first name, it becomes more likely he could have jumbled the identities. (He makes other mistakes, like calling Weatherred and Polley the Conners' prosecutors, not defense attorneys.)

Redden Alford, the citizen's posse, and Company F get ready to move out. They prepare accordingly, taking spurs from their boots, stripping their light-colored leggings, and securing anything that can cause noise. Retreating straps are loosed from pistols.

Their equipment is only somewhat standardized, and that includes their iconic rifles. Most Texas Rangers carry Winchesters, but which model is entirely up to them. The most popular is the Winchester Model 1873, produced in three variations: a twenty-four-inch barrel rifle, a twenty-inch carbine, and a seldom-seen version with a full-length stock strictly for military customers.

Besides the length, there are other ways to tell a Winchester '73 carbine from the full-length rifle version at a distance. Carbines have two metal bands, one near the receiver and the other at the barrel's tip, that secure the sights. The privates have carbines, which are lighter and thereby a little easier to use. Brooks has a rifle, distinguished by a crescent buttstock and brass cap holding the sights near the receiver in place.

A tenderfoot private, J. E. "Ed" Randall, showed up at camp in March with a newer rifle, a Colt Lightning. He thinks it's pretty slick, and in many ways it is. This is Colt's first-ever pump-action rifle, released just three years ago. Being a slide action, which means it keeps the trigger hand in place during reloading, it is inherently faster than any lever-action Winchester. But Randall's attempts to outpace Brooks and his honed biomechanics have proven the limits of hardware alone.

A shotgun-wielding competitor lets fly during the Single Action Shooting Society event called Comancheria Days. He's firing a fraction of the load of black powder the Conners would have used.

Joe Pappalardo

This statue welcomes visitors to the Texas Ranger Hall of Fame and Museum in Waco, Texas, which is the state-designated official historical center of the law enforcement agency.

Joe Pappalardo

Staples of a Ranger camp on very static display at the Texas Ranger Hall of Fame and Museum

Joe Pappalardo

Weldon McDaniel, head of the Sabine County Historical Commission, points to the location of Holly Bottom (now underwater), where the bodies of Kit Smith and Eli Low were discovered. *Joe Pappalardo*

Murder victim Kit Smith had to be relocated to a new cemetery close to the location of his death to escape the waters of the Toledo Bend Reservoir. The plaque details the story of the Oak Hill Baptist Church, which stood here when Smith was killed. Workers fixing its roof heard the gunshots, according to family lore.

Joe Pappalardo

The modern canopy of Sabine County is less dense than it would have been in the 1800s, when longleaf pines dominated the landscape.

Joe Pappalardo

Dams created the Toledo Bend Reservoir, which swallowed the land where the Conner family ran their hogs, as well as several displaced communities. Creeks on old maps have become channels deep enough for boating.

Joe Pappalardo

A bloodless depiction of a fence cutter arrest at the Texas Ranger Hall of Fame and Museum in Waco, Texas. The actual incident that inspired the designed-for-children display occurred during a night ambush and killed two men and two horses.

Joe Pappalardo

Belle Starr arriving under guard at Fort Smith in 1886, just as J. A. Brooks would have seen her

Public domain via Heritage Auctions

A drone's-eye view of the Sabine National Forest in 2021

Joe Pappalardo

Vernon Scott, who was in Hemphill on the day of the shoot-out that left her half brother near death. She rode to the scene and treated the wounded.

The Heritage Museum and Ranger Reading Room of Falfurrias

Texas Ranger James H. Moore, "killed by outlaws" in Sabine County and laid to rest there

Joe Pappalardo

Texas Ranger Company F, taken June 27, 1887, not long after the shoot-out with the Conner family. Note Brooks's damaged hand, the various Winchester loadouts, and the presence of a baby-faced Kid Rogers. *The Heritage Museum and Ranger Reading Room of Falfurrias*

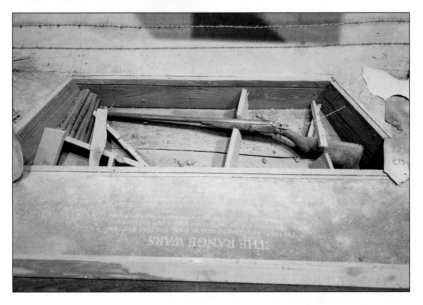

Ira Aten designed this improvised explosive device using a shotgun and sticks of dynamite to detonate when someone snipped a fence.   *Joe Pappalardo*

Decorations on the gate of the Conner Cemetery, placed by persons unknown, are reminders that children are buried here, as well as outlaws.

Joe Pappalardo

Frederick Conner's grave in Sabine County, alongside his father in death as he was in life

Joe Pappalardo

The muddy banks of the Conner Creek in Sabine County, the most visible family namesake in the county

Joe Pappalardo

Charles Conner in one of the few known photos of a Conner family member, taken well after the events of the feud and his prison sentence. The presence of dogs in the photo is fitting, given the family's masterful use of them to herd, hunt, and alert the Conners to intruders.

Sabine County Historical Commission

The Heritage Museum in Falfurrias doubles as a repository of J. A. Brooks artifacts and information. The small town is the seat of the county named for the Ranger captain and long-serving county judge.

Joe Pappalardo

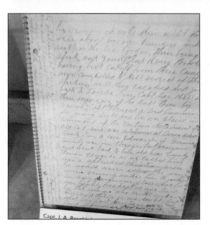

As an old man, J. A. Brooks wrote this journal, which chronicles some of his life's exploits in third person. It's on display at the Texas Ranger Hall of Fame and Museum.

Joe Pappalardo

James Brooks while a judge of the county he helped create and which still bears his name

The Heritage Museum and Ranger Reading Room of Falfurrias

The grave of J. A. Brooks in Falfurrias, Texas. Before the state marker was placed, the stone listed only his name and dates of birth and death.

Joe Pappalardo

It would take a Gatling gun to keep up with the company's sergeant. In any case, the slick Lightning is an acceptable Ranger weapon because it chambers the .44–40.[38]

Someone must guard the horses, per Ranger custom, and there's only one fair way to choose. "We were all anxious to go, so we drew straws," Newton says. "Ed Randall was the one who had to stay, and he was mighty disappointed."[39] It's quite a coincidence that the least experienced Ranger has been fated to stay, which leads any cynical, future observer to ponder if the drawing was rigged.

Scott quietly orders the party to move. Winchesters loaded and ready, Company F and their posse start their march into the piney woods. Their horses, wagon, beloved mule, and solitary, tenderfoot Ranger fade quickly from view. By sunrise, they hope to leave these claustrophobic surroundings for good, with the outlaws of Sabine County either in their custody or lying dead under the trees.

The night is alive with the croaks of frogs and crickets. The canopy blocks stars and breaks the moonlight into colorless columns. There is no sign of human passage, no telltale bell on a packhorse. Any hope of quick action fades, step by step. It becomes clear that Alford can't find the camp.

After tramping around this tortured land for two hours, the party is tired—and angry. Scott squares his broad shoulders to Alford and flatly accuses him of being a liar; the man maintains the Conner camp must be nearby.

Finally, Alford stops and won't move another step. He's pretty sure the family is camped at the crest of a humble hill, about three hundred yards away. Because five pines stand on its otherwise bald crest, Alford

---

38 Loadouts based on a photo of Company F taken June 27, 1887, at Falfurrias Heritage Center, Falfurrias, TX.

39 Davidge, "Texas Rangers Were Rough."

says the Conners call it Camp Handy. The lack of foliage means good lines of sight and a smart defensive position.

"They're right there," he says. "I don't want to go any further because if you don't kill or arrest them all, they'll kill me." This is actually a prescient thought; Milton Anthony is the last one to see the camp and will be the only one considered a traitor if the Conners get away.

"All right, you coward," Scott says to Alford, disgusted. "Lay down here."[40]

Scott divides the group into two. Scott, Rogers, Brooks, Treadwell, Moore, and Carmichael go to the right, while Newton, J. B. Harry, Weatherred, Toole, and Harris head to the left. It's a basic pincer maneuver, with two prongs meant to meet atop the knoll, surprising the Conners from two directions and overwhelming the wanted men with numbers.

Five minutes later, Scott and the Rangers step into a creek bed, facing the uphill climb to the outlaw's campsite.

Willis Conner watches them approach with a hunter's patience. In moments, the men will be totally exposed, whereas he, Fed, John, and William have found cover behind trees on the upslope of the creek. Willis himself has positioned the packhorse—bell removed—between him and the approaching men.

How could the Conners get the drop on the Rangers? "You will get several different thoughts on that," says Ranger researcher Doug Dukes. "Was the 'informer' the Rangers used playing both sides of the fence?"[41] This isn't just something that dawned on modern researchers. "It seems that the desperadoes were advised of their coming," says *The Galveston Daily News*.[42]

One explanation may be found in Milton Anthony. If he knew the

40 Ibid.

41 Interview with author.

42 "The East Texas War," *Galveston Daily News*, April 3, 1888.

Conner campsite's location, Alford and the Rangers should have found it sooner. Maybe the young informant gave Scott inaccurate or incomplete information to avoid bloodshed.

Maybe it was Redden Alford. This may not be the first time a local guide led the Rangers astray during the search for the Conners. If Alford is the same man who previously led Scott and Spradley into the woods, maybe the sheriff wasn't the only one harboring secret support for the Conners. Alford's refusal to walk with the Rangers is manifestly suspicious, as if he expected an ambush, but then again, he may have just been legitimately scared of getting near Camp Handy and being identified as a turncoat.

The Conners' reputation as master woodsmen remains a possible explanation for their ideal tactical placement. It's conceivable that they found the Rangers' trail as Alford led them around and doubled back to get ahead of their quarry. As in a wolf hunt, the idea is to surprise the approaching quarry with a surprise volley from an optimal position.

In the predawn hours, under a canopy of moonlit pines, Company F and the Conner family are about to meet.

BLOODY GULCH
March 31, 1887

The night explodes around the Texas Rangers as flashes erupt from the bank of the creek, all the sudden noise and smoke seeming like discharges from naval cannons. The bursts of light are immediately followed by the angry-insect sound of unseen bullets tearing the nearby air. Somewhere in Brooks's mind, he recognizes the shots as coming from Winchesters.

Jim Moore falls backward, rifle tumbling from his hands. The thirty-year-old man has been shot in the chest, a rifle ball tearing through his heart. He dies almost immediately. John Rogers also crumples to the ground, searing pain spearing his upper arm, above the elbow, and his side.[43]

---

43 Scott's official report to King, 1887. This is Newton and Scott's version of the fight; Sabine County memories recall it being very different, as we'll see.

The correct thing to do is to shoot back. Even if they miss, the smoke and threat of being hit will spoil the aim of their opponents. "Suppressing fire was the main tactic used to get out of the ambush," says researcher Doug Dukes. "The Rangers certainly did that."[44] As for helping the wounded, Company F instinctively knows what later gunmen will make into canon: Fire superiority is the best first aid.

The once-silent woodlands now erupt in two thin lines of bright bursts and smoky booms. Experienced Ranger hands rhythmically work rifle levers before any fear, strategy, or comprehension kicks in. The fusillade doesn't deter the Conners, who continue to shower the creek bed with shots from the high ground.

Muzzle flashes reveal a man-shaped silhouette moving behind a tree, and Scott and Brooks immediately take beads on the form. It's William Conner, aiming their way. The two Ranger officers fire just as William pulls the trigger, and the outlaw spins to the ground.[45]

But Brooks is also down, his rifle ripped from his hands. He raises them in a daze—his left hand is missing a finger, and two more dangle on strings of skin and cartilage; there is a rifle ball bloodily lodged in his right wrist, which burrowed through his first and middle fingers to get there.[46] The Winchester round dug a groove through Brooks's rifle, sheared off his fingers where they gripped the weapon, and continued along the length of the weapon to smash into his other hand. A mere inch closer and it would have found his chest.

Scott leans forward to scan for another target, seeking to aim at a shadow or barrel flash. A heavy Winchester ball rips into his shoulder

---

44 Email with author.

45 Davidge, "Texas Rangers Were Rough," and "A Desperate Fight," *Arkansas Democrat,* April 6, 1887.

46 "A Desperate Fight," *Arkansas Democrat.*

and plunges into his chest, breaking ribs and puncturing a lung.[47] He's prone and gasping before he starts to feel any pain.

This is about when Billy Treadwell's rifle stops working. Most jams are caused by shooter error, but one newspaper report, a "special to the *Dallas News*" from Sabine County, notes that the rifle's lever malfunctioned.[48] Treadwell throws himself down to hug the earth as the firefight continues.

Carmichael now stands alone. He continues to ply his Winchester carbine, peppering the trees. He knows that the remaining ambushers have only one upright target left—him—but he doesn't seek cover. He just keeps shooting.

A sudden pistol blast from the ground makes Carmichael jump. It's Brooks, firing while prone. Hands nearly disabled, he's working the Colt's hammer with his teeth and using his knees to help aim shots with his wounded right hand.[49] Scott, too, is back in the fight, now propped up against a small tree and emptying his pistol into the woods.[50] Each shot brings new pain to his punctured chest, but at least he's spreading it around. Bullets smash into the pack mule, dropping the creature and leaving Willis exposed.

Newton, Harry, and Weatherred's civilian posse hear the initial gunshots but don't race to the scene. This is not where the fight is supposed to happen, and the Civil War veteran isn't one to change up orders just because of some unexpected gunplay. Harry is especially desperate to move, but Weatherred fears racing heedlessly away from the knoll will

---

47 *Fort Worth Daily Gazette,* June 13, 1887.

48 "A Desperate Fight," *Arkansas Democrat.*

49 "Blood Curdling Days," *Abilene Reporter-News.*

50 "The Man Who Knows No Fear Retires," *El Paso Herald,* February 4, 1911. Rogers specifically recalls Scott fighting after being wounded.

enable the Conners to escape. In his memoirs, Brooks describes Weatherred as "an old line army man who had gotten orders on how to proceed, and when he heard shooting, after we stumbled on the outlaws in the brush unexpectedly, the army's training for obedience held. The citizens stood by and listened while the fireworks went off."[51] But the gunfire doesn't end—as it continues it becomes clear that this isn't a skirmish but the battle itself. Weatherred, his posse, and the eager Company F Rangers finally dash toward the peals of gunfire.

Back at the gulch, the Conners hear the sound of more men approaching. Willis, John, and Fed retreat, leaving William where he lies. As they break cover to speed away, Fed is staggered by the impact of a gunshot to the arm but stays on his feet to vanish into the dark woods.

Willis Conner will later say that the only reason he retreated was that he ran out of bullets, and had he not, "he would have killed all them sons of bitches."[52] Rangers, always ready for an extended shoot-out, didn't have that problem. Those bullet-lined belts are there for more than showmanship.

In Willis Conner's version of the shoot-out, related to friends and family, the Rangers open fire without warning and immediately wound William Conner. They don't see Willis Conner getting water from the creek at the time, so when he races back to camp, he's in a perfect position to pour accurate, unexpected rifle fire into the Rangers from a place of concealment. He claims to have killed and wounded all the Rangers that night, which conveniently exonerates his sons.[53]

Accepting this sub-rosa Sabine County version means Scott abandoned the pincer plan just as it was on the verge of working, which doesn't make sense. A more convincing argument for the official version

---

51 Brooks's memoir, courtesy of the Texas Ranger Hall of Fame and Museum, Waco, TX.

52 Dugan, *Judge Not*, quoting Norman Ener, son of Conner family confidant Bob Ener.

53 Ibid.

considers that only one Conner is killed during the shoot-out and one lightly wounded. Given that a similar ambush in Brown County killed two men and two horses within seconds—by sticking to the plan—it's hard to imagine that William, Fed, and the rest wouldn't have fared worse if they had been the ones attacked without warning. The cruel arithmetic of an ambush indicates that Company F is on the receiving end of a surprise attack.

When Newton reaches the scene of the shoot-out, he sees just one Ranger on his feet: "We found Carmichael standing alone. The other ranger had thrown himself on the ground, scared stiff. Carmichael had reloaded and was firing in the direction in which they had disappeared, cussing the Conners for being cowards."[54]

Treadwell now seems to overcompensate for his tepid showing during the shoot-out by snatching up Moore's rifle and running into the woods after the Conners. The Ranger and posse move into the Conners' former positions and find a hat and pair of spectacles near the dead pack mule, where Willis Conner was last seen retreating into the woods. Hard-won trophies, these.

The men push through the brush up the knoll, finally reaching the long-sought outlaw camp. The family is gone, leaving a cache of supplies and a handful of hunting dogs behind. News filters back to Scott, who is still lucid and giving orders while leaning against a tree. He tells them to set fire to the supplies and shoot the chained dogs, who remain eerily silent even while executed.[55]

---

54 Davidge, "Texas Rangers Were Rough."

55 "A Desperate Fight," *Arkansas Democrat*. This is a reprint of a "special to the *Dallas News* from Sabine County" that uses Scott as a source. Also, Newton is quoted in the *Frontier Times* article "Rangers Were Rough and Ready Fighters," saying, "The old man with Fed and Charley, their pack horse and four dogs were all in them trees. Their dogs were trained never to bark, and all during that fight they never uttered a yelp." Some versions include dogs attacking the Rangers during the firefight, but primary sources don't mention it, just the deaths of tied dogs.

Sabine County residents believe that there's more than one execution at the scene that morning. Willis's daughter Catherine will tell her great-nephews that Frank Carmichael walked up to where William Conner lay wounded in the arm and gasping for water. "Here's your water," the Ranger then says and shoots him in the mouth.[56]

By all accounts, Fed and Willis had fled the scene before this event would have occurred, so they didn't witness it. But the execution story comes complete with specifics, including a ghastly tagline, which argues against its plausibility. It would mean one of the posse who witnessed the shooting that day—Weatherred, Toole, or Harris—would have told her what happened, which is hard to imagine.

It's hard to square the sober cowboy Carmichael with the deed and harder still to imagine Rogers, Newton, Scott, and Brooks going out of their ways to praise his bravery that day (as they will) and bring attention to a potential scandal. Newton even disparages Treadwell's performance (if not by name) while extolling Carmichael's, something that only enhances his credibility as a source.

If the Sabine County memories didn't name Carmichael, the hero of the day, would the story of William's execution be more believable? What if Catherine Conner Williams told her family that *Billy Treadwell* killed a wounded man, the action of a known hothead who could have been overcompensating for a poor performance? That feels more correct, but it still leaves Scott and Weatherred to clean it up, masking the needless killing in falsified official reports and getting away with it except for lingering, whispered memories.

It may not be likely, but it's also impossible to disprove. The Conner family, and many others in Sabine County, will certainly hear these details and believe them. But all these questions and conspiracies must recede with the sunrise. Now it's a matter of survival.

Newton watches the sky brighten over a bloody scene. His captain and sergeant are both horribly wounded; Brooks's hands are mangled.

---

56 Dugan, *Judge Not.*

Rogers is in pain but is nevertheless lucky. The round that tore through his arm struck his memorandum book, sitting as always in his side pocket, and thereby lost much of its destructive energy before entering his side.

Newton is dumbstruck to see the extent of the damage done to these seemingly indestructible men. "When dawn came, we were in a serious fix," Newton recalls. "We were four miles from our horses and 14 miles from Hemphill, the nearest settlement. We had three wounded men in a pretty bad shape and one dead one."

Scott issues orders through bloody lips and painful coughs from his punctured lung. Newton is to rush to Hemphill to fetch Dr. J. W. Smith, and he's to tell Crowder to race to San Augustine to fetch Dr. Frank Tucker. Some of the remaining Rangers set up a perimeter in case the Conners return while others craft pine-bough litters for the dead and wounded.

Newton takes one last look at the remains of Company F before running back to the horses, wondering if this is his captain's last sunrise.

MISS VERNON SCOTT
March 31, 1887

Vernon Scott takes in the empty town square of Hemphill on a typical early morning. The young woman has seen enough of Texas to be unimpressed by the tiny town and awed by the forests that surround it. She has ventured on her own through an ocean of trees, the final leg by stagecoach, to reach this place. The whole way, she could imagine Conner villains skulking behind every pine. She doesn't understand how her half brother could even *walk* through that kind of growth, not to mention search for criminals.

"A woman taking a train or stagecoaches locally around Texas, big as it is, does not strike me as unusual," says Patricia Cohen, a historian who has studied travel records from the era. "A train with its fixed track has a built-in guarantee that you will wind up at your destination, and it has conductors and porters who might be kindly on the lookout to make sure you are not molested—and they would be lifting your valise or small trunk. A stage trip is a bit more unpredictable, and there are meal stops and overnights to contend with. In the early railroad days, some city railroad stations had ladies' waiting rooms to keep a female apart from the riffraff."[57]

Indeed, Vernon Scott traveled on her own and was already on a trip the week Company F arrived in Sabine County. A notice from Houston that ran in *The Galveston Daily News* on March 23, 1887, states that "Miss Vernon Scott" that day went "back to her home in Willis, much to the dismay of her many admirers."

That news item puts Vernon Scott on the road during the same week that her half brother and sister are meeting in Dallas. Willis is located between Huntsville and Houston, and not too far from Sabine County. Cohen consults the available maps to trace the route.[58] "It appears there was a short line road from Houston up through Nacogdoches and beyond, so your traveling sister could get off at that town and get a stage to Sabine," says Cohen.

The logistics of her trip fate Vernon Scott to be the first person in Hemphill to hear about the forest shoot-out between the Conners and Company F.

Hoofbeats announce a rider, coming in fast. Vernon Scott figures from his appearance and armaments that he's a Ranger under William Scott's command. The man quickly hitches his tired horse, and as she approaches, she can tell the young man is almost panicked with urgency. He identifies himself as Private Allen Newton, from Company F. One

---

57 Interview with author.

58 "Rare Promotional Map for the Houston & Texas Central Railroad," Barry Lawrence Ruderman Antique Maps, https://www.raremaps.com/gallery/detail/49764 /texas-and-mexico-showing-houston-and-texas-central-system-of-rand-mcnally -company.

Ranger is dead, and Captain Scott even now is lying in the woods fighting for his life.

This bombshell dropped, Newton then leaves her to race to the home of Dr. J. W. Smith. Like any frontier doctor, he wakes easily and immediately prepared to treat trauma victims. There's good money to be made in emergency medicine, administered at a rate of five dollars a day.[59]

Naturally, Smith has an emergency bag ready for immediate travel. Companies like Truax, Greene & Co. have entire catalogs of cases stocked with medical instruments for frontier physicians; many models come ready to attach to saddles. They contain all the equipment needed to treat trauma wounds in the field, performing anything from sealing a flesh wound to a limb amputation. The gear includes a large scalpel, a pair of saws, carbolic-soaked gauze, forceps, steel artery clamps, a long metal probe, a trephine, and silk sewing thread.[60] Bag in hand, Smith follows the desperate Ranger into the streets of Hemphill.

There, the pair of men see a cart and horse team already hooked up in the streets. Vernon Scott arranged the transport and is on board, eager to leave for the battle site.

The sun is hanging in the midmorning sky when they arrive, leaving the wagon with the Rangers' horses and heading for the battle site on foot. They find a scene from the Civil War—slain animals strewn on the ground, smoke in the air over the remains of the burned outlaw camp, and bloodied men lying untended in the grass and shade of trees. The captain's sister proves steel runs in the family—she immediately becomes a field nurse, carrying out whatever tasks Smith orders. Her presence

---

59 Taken from the impending bill. "J. W. Smith to Liam Sieker," May 19, 1889, Texas State Archives, Austin, TX.

60 Meg Langford, "Medicine on the Move: Kits, Cases and Carry-alls from the History of Healthcare," Oregon Health & Science University, 2018, https://www .ohsu.edu/historical-collections-archives/medicine-move-kits-cases-and-carry-alls -history-healthcare.

stiffens the resolve of the wounded, particularly a stunned and struggling Scott. "I found Capt. Scott in a faint and dying condition," the Hemphill doctor later says in a letter.[61]

Smith later tells his family that some of the Rangers have booze on their breath and are moving sluggishly, as if drunk or hungover. Smith is not the only one to report drinking during the Conner fight; Anthony descendants say Redden Alford was passing a bottle with the Rangers as they waited for the informer. It's entirely conceivable that the rattled men took to drinking after the shootout as they waited to see if Scott would die but less forgivable if they got soused before a dangerous raid. Two of the Rangers of the six in the shoot-out are teetotalers, and the long, Alford-led trek through the woods would have been sobering for those who aren't.[62]

Smith surveys the wounded Rangers and silently does what all trauma doctors do: clinically calculate each's chance of survival. Their captain has a lung wound. Smith triages him, thinking his chances are dim, and focuses on the others. Sergeant Brooks has gruesome damage to his hands, but he'll live. The private, Rogers, has ugly wounds in his arm and side, but overall, his chances are also good.

Infection is the real threat here. When placing Scott, Brooks, and Rogers on a time line including every gunshot victim in history, they land just on the preferred side of a massive divide. The schism happens when a young chemist named Louis Pasteur concludes in 1860 that the process that sours milk is initiated by microscopic organisms. It is wild, controversial, and entirely correct.

New medical procedures sweep Europe. By 1875, sterilization of instruments and the scrubbing hands is widely practiced there. Not so in

---

61 "J. W. Smith to Ranger Captain Liam Sieker."

62 Dugan, *Judge Not,* quoting Sadie Nelson, daughter of Dr. Frank Smith and granddaughter of J. W. Smith. She told the author that her grandfather informed her father that the Rangers were either hungover or drunk from the night before and cited moonshine as the beverage.

the United States, where physicians' first course of action remains probing wounds with unsterilized fingers to locate the paths of bullets.

This lack of acceptance is not from a lack of trying. In a little-known but vital chapter in American medical history, British surgeon Joseph Lister tours the United States in 1876 to convince physicians that they should accept his ideas about surgical antisepsis. His two-month-long visit includes a transcontinental railroad trip across North America that leaves controversy and converts in his wake. Some doctors just can't visualize the mysterious "bacteria" responsible for their patients' deaths. The best example of this are the sixteen men who attended to President James Garfield after he was shot by an assassin in 1881. Exploring his wound with dirty hands and instruments caused the agonizing infection that killed him.

For those doctors that listened to Lister—including many frontier physicians—understanding hygiene enables more intrepid trauma treatments. In Tombstone in 1881, around the same time Garfield is dying, Dr. George Goodfellow performs the first laparotomy to treat an abdominal gunshot wound. Common sense finally prevails by the mid-1880s, and carbolic spray becomes the ubiquitous trauma antiseptic (replacing a slew of others) in the United States by 1885.

Even better, nothing needs to happen without some pain treatment. Smith's medical bag includes laudanum, which is opium mixed with alcohol. Rogers will be tasting booze today. The frontier doctor also has chloroform on hand for more serious field surgeries.[63] He's not dismayed by the outdoor surroundings—frontier doctors typically perform any complicated procedures outdoors where the light is better, even in town.

Brooks's treatment is brutally easy: Snip the two dangling fingers from his left hand, douse the three stumps with carbolic spray to

---

63 I'm playing the odds here in terms of anesthesia. Dr. George Cupples's 1887 report for the Texas State Medical Association's Committee on Surgery showed a thirty-five-to-one preference for chloroform over ether. Cited in the Bexar County Medical Society's monthly magazine, *San Antonio Medicine*, December 31, 2015.

chemically cauterize the wounds, and apply a clean dressing to stop the bleeding. The other arm has left his fingers intact, but there is still a Winchester ball lodged in his wrist. This is exactly why medical bags contain forceps and long metal probes. Smith inserts the freshly wiped slender probe into the wound, and when it clicks, he knows he's found the intruding object. He cleans the forceps with carbolic wash and fishes out the sphere.

The next patient, Rogers, is a lucky man. The Winchester ball that struck him passed through his left arm and struck a notebook in his breast pocket before entering his torso. The book slowed the bullet, so it never struck any organs. Smith cleans and dresses these wounds as Rogers writhes through an unaccustomed chemical haze. The injuries will heal, but nerve damage leaves his thumb and two fingers permanently numb.[64]

Dr. Frank Tucker, roused from his bed in San Augustine, finally arrives. He finds Scott is propped up against a tree so he won't drown in his own blood, Vernon Scott fretting over him. The ball remains stuck in his back. Smith hasn't even dressed the wounds, busy with the rest and fearing the worst for the captain.

Tucker doesn't give up on him. His first move is to dress the wound. Not doing so earlier is a more dangerous lapse than they realize. As Major Douglas Jolly, who fought in the Spanish Civil War, will one day note: "The most useful pre-hospital treatment of the thoracic wounded casualty is the application of a large, occlusive dressing to the open pneumothorax."[65]

Tucker keeps a sharp eye on Scott's breathing, and it's not the torn lung he's worried about. If the patient's body cavity fills up with enough blood to restrict the lungs, he'll need to puncture it and drain the fluid.

64 "The Man Who Knows No Fear Retires," *El Paso Herald.*

65 Douglas W. Jolly, *Field Surgery in Total War* (London: Hamish Hamilton Medical Books, 1940).

Called *paracentesis thoracis,* it was first recommended by Crimean War doctor Patrick Fraser in 1859.[66] This is as dangerous a proposition as it sounds.

The wounded man needs to be stronger to take the bullet and debris from his body. The doctors carry what they think they need to rouse wounded patients, what Smith calls "restoratives." This label covers a swath of possible tonics; some recipes have stuff like quinine (treats chills), strychnine (gives a boost like caffeine in low doses), and ethanol (a stimulant for a lagging patient.)

Scott may welcome the booze, typically the basis of most restoratives, but the most relevant ingredient to him is likely ferrous sulfate.[67] Anyone who's lost as much blood as Scott needs to replenish the iron in the bloodstream, which in turn creates the red blood cells that carry oxygen. The problem here is that ferrous sulfate is most effective over long periods of time, taken as a supplement. Taking too much at once can cause an ugly overdose.

So it may be easier to credit a clean dressing and Scott's hardy constitution, rather than "restoratives" as Smith does, for his recovery the first day after being shot. He also has Vernon Scott's company to help keep him alive, in a clinical way. Talking is a way to gauge symptoms. A lack of awareness is the best indicator of cerebral anoxia—if his brain doesn't get enough oxygen, with a wounded left lung, he may act irrationally or pass out. So far, despite the bloody coughs, his body and brain both remain functional.

With Scott gaining some strength, it's time for surgery. Again, the odds of survival are pretty good, even in these crude settings. One 1886 report for the Texas State Medical Association's Committee on Surgery

---

66 Clifford C. Cloonan, *Immediate Care of the Wounded* (Bethesda, MD: Uniformed Services University of the Health Sciences, 2016).

67 Wayne Bethard, *Lotions, Potions and Deadly Elixirs* (Lanham, MD: Roberts Rinehart, 2004).

describes 4,293 operations performed by 138 doctors, and an overall mortality rate of 8 percent. Nearly half of the operations were described as major, and the mortality rate for those was 15.9 percent.[68]

At noon, Smith and Tucker, with Vernon Scott attending as OR nurse, lay Scott down and clean their hands with carbolic wash. The captain huffs ether. The doctors use a clean probe to trace the path of the bullet. It's lodged just under Scott's shoulder blade. With a crosshatching of scalpel cuts, the doctors carve a path to the ball. Forceps fold back skin; others serve as pliers to grip the rifle ball and firmly yank it from its resting place.

After making sure every extraneous bit of debris is gone, the docs seal the wound and stitch it closed. "I extracted the ball about noon which relieved the difficulty of breathing to some extent," Smith reports. "I was very doubtful as to his reacting."

The next day, they see Scott is strong enough to travel. It's time for the moment they've been dreading—the ride back to town. Rogers and Brooks lie in the wagon, tended by Vernon Scott and Dr. Smith, while the privates carry Scott on a homemade litter.

Brooks and Rogers exchange an agonized look as the wheels lurch ahead, rolling across the open plain. It's literally a torturous trip. Each bump makes their wounds radiate with fresh pain. It's no better for Scott, languishing in the litter and feeling every step. The privates take turns as bearers to stay fresh over the miles, first over open terrain and then along the county's roads. "Captain Brooks told me many years later that this trip was the most painful of his life," writes fellow Ranger, William Sterling.[69]

---

68 Mike Cox, "Frontier Medicine: Texas Doctors Overcome Disease and Despair," Texas Medical Association, 2003, https://www.texmed.org/Template.aspx?id=2012. The stats come from an 1887 report compiled by Dr. George Cupples.

69 William Sterling, *Trails and Trials of a Texas Ranger* (Norman: University of Oklahoma Press, 1959).

After an eternity, the procession reaches Hemphill. Dr. Smith hustles Scott inside to a bed, and Brooks pulls Newton aside: "Brooks took charge and ordered me to go to Nacogdoches, the nearest railroad station [and therefore telegraph office], to wire the dead and wounded men's relatives and to get some dogs to track the Conners with from Rusk."[70]

His sergeant wants him to ride hard before the trail goes cold. "He gave me his horse, which I was to change for a fresh one at San Augustine," Newton later says. He leaves Hemphill, with Dr. Tucker alongside, not knowing if his captain will live or die. "Scott was so bad off we thought we were going to lose him too," Newton adds.[71] He turns his attention to his orders and the vengeance he hopes the dogs will bring for the night's losses, and drives his spurs into Brooks's horse.

Newton rides to San Augustine, pauses to switch horses as instructed, and immediately starts the forty-mile trip to Nacogdoches. It takes the better part of the day. There, he crafts a telegram seeking tracking dogs from Rusk Penitentiary. Newton can't avoid his next sad duty: sending the next telegram to Sheriff Frank Moore to tell him his nephew is dead. As he waits for the dogs, newspapermen find him and get reports of the shoot-out that run in *The Galveston Daily News*.[72]

Naturally, the sheriff in Nacogdoches hears of the shoot-out. A. J. Spradley immediately gets ready to head back to Sabine County, ostensibly to join the manhunt. The opportunity to work with the tracking dogs of Rusk Penitentiary may be an additional draw, considering his preoccupation with bloodhounds. But he undoubtably wants his own vantage to see what happens to the Conners now that Sabine County is in a complete uproar.

---

70 Davidge, "Texas Rangers Were Rough."

71 Ibid.

72 *Galveston Daily News*, April 3, 1887 (with an April 2 dateline).

"PROCEEDINGS WERE HAD AND MEASURES ADOPTED"
April 2, 1887

The town of Hemphill has turned out in droves to see Texas Ranger private Jim Moore buried in the local cemetery. There is no permanent marker yet placed; his grave is just a raised hump of rust-colored earth adorned with a temporary cross.

The large crowd is a symptom of the furor sweeping the county. This is the biggest thing to happen here since John Wesley Hardin shot a deputy in downtown Hemphill. No one wants to miss the spectacle or the chance to join in.

After the funeral, a "committee of citizens" meets in Hemphill. It's a public meeting that draws an estimated two hundred people. The committee is led by familiar faces William Weatherred (its chairman) and James Polley, both of whom deliver speeches. The purpose of the committee is to organize the expanding hunt for the Conners. "Every proper and expedient measure, notwithstanding it may not come within the bounds of the law, must be resorted to in order to accomplish our object and restore order, peace and quietude within our county," the committee declares.

Like a good military officer, Weatherred creates an organization to coordinate the response (i.e., organize a vast posse to assist the Rangers in the coming manhunt). There are eight geographic beats established, each with a designated leader. It's predictably stocked with known Conner foes like J. O. Toole, Henry Harris, and Ed Smith, Kit Smith's brother. George Williams heads two beats.

"Proceedings were had and measures adopted to prosecute the search for the Conners to the end," reads *The Galveston Daily News*, pretty much making it sound like elected officials had gathered.[73] A close read of those measures shows the county's leading men sanctioning a crackdown on Conner supporters: "We endorse and heartily approve every act done by

---

73 "The East Texas War," *Galveston Daily News*, April 3, 1887.

our officers and State Rangers in making arrests and hailing and otherwise preventing the free movement of all those persons whom they may suspect as aiding, abetting or otherwise rendering sustenance to the noted outlaws, the Conners, or any other outlaws."

Throngs of volunteers stand ready to scout the deep woods and swamps, where it's now understood the Conners have fled. "Two hundred men are on the ground, waiting for the dogs to arrive," reads an April 2 dispatch in the *Fort Worth Daily Gazette*. "Lively times are expected by all."[74]

The goal of the meeting is to harness support for the Rangers by putting vetted posse members under some sort of chain of command. In reality, it sanctions a vigilante mindset that will grow out of Weatherred's control. Reward money, personal vendettas, and backwoods ambushes will belie any civic attempt to organize the mobs of Sabine County.

With no other targets, the heat falls on the Conner sympathizers. The Rangers and Sheriff Oliphint, backed by the posse, descend on the Conner supporters and family members, hustling some into jails and subjecting others to intense surveillance and scrutiny.

On April 2, Bob Ener is eating dinner with his family when Carmichael and posse members storm into his house. What is considered a prudent Ranger operation surprising their quarry at odd hours to minimize the chance of resistance, is of course also extremely invasive. When Carmichael begins to fix handcuffs on Ener, he starts to resist. His wife quickly intervenes, asking the Rangers for a chance to speak with her husband. She calms him down, fearing worse violence, and says he has nothing to worry about.

Ener will tell his family that he never aided the Conners, despite their lifelong friendship. He saw Willis Conner after the shoot-out, but only when the outlaw rode up to his fence to explain his version of the

---

74 "A Bloody Battle," *Fort Worth Daily Gazette*, April 2, 1887.

shoot-out with Company F. He tells his family that he was so nervous around Willis that he wouldn't even stand next to him.[75]

Now he's being rounded up like a criminal. He's not alone—he steps outside to see Wiley Smith (Leander Conner's brother-in-law), mounted on a horse and shackled to a saddle horn. The next day, the Rangers raid Nancy Conner Harper's home, hauling off her husband, Elmore Harper.

The arrests will continue all week. "Twelve men, sympathizers of the Conners, have already been placed in jail, and many others under surveillance, and the probability is that many more arrests will follow," *The Galveston Daily News* reports later that week. "These men [the Conners], notwithstanding their dark and bloodcurdling deeds and promiscuous and general foraying, have many sympathizers—some by relationship, some by kindred feeling in crime and a feeling of fellowship and not a few from a feeling of awe and terror."[76]

The Ener family say the intervention of defense attorney Steve Blount checked these aggressive detentions. After meeting with Ener in the Hemphill jail, he made it clear that he planned to challenge the legality of these arrests in court—a good tactic, since the resolutions passed by the citizens' committee aren't legal in any sense and the detentions are of dubious legal merit. Any charges of harboring fugitives that are filed against Ener and the others are dropped and they are released.[77]

The roundups are not meant to produce arrests, per se, but are coordinated to keep the Conners isolated and alone during the shoot-out's aftermath. It doesn't help catch them. The outlaw family is fleeing farther into the southern wilds instead of seeking shelter amid the hornet's nest that used to be the Conner Community.

Feelings are running high among the public men across Texas. Dal-

---

75 Dugan, *Judge Not.*

76 "East Texas Outlaws," *Galveston Daily News*, April 7, 1887.

77 Dugan, *Judge Not.*

las County Judge Bower, Scott's brother-in-law, shows up in Hemphill on April 2 to visit his brother, collect his sister, and throw his weight around. Judge Perkins wires Adjutant General King an update from the scene, and in it mentions that "Judge Bower in Sabine says Conners can be easily captured if you will come now."

The prevailing attitude is that the Conners are doomed. "All of Sabine County is thoroughly aroused," proclaims *The Galveston Daily News* on April 3. "There is no doubt but that all the Conners will be captured or killed in a few days."[78]

---

78 "The East Texas War," *Galveston Daily News*.

6

SCENT TRAILS

BLOODHOUND PSYCHOLOGY

April 4, 1887

Private J. Allen Newton arrives with the bloodhounds from Rusk in Nacogdoches. There are five of the animals, all panting and eager. Nacogdoches Sheriff J. A. Spradley is with them.[1]

Although man-tracking dogs have been around for a long time, humanity's relationship with them is deepening in the late 1800s.[2] George Romanes's book *Animal Intelligence*, published in 1882, chronicles evidence of mind in creatures other than man. Romanes, a close acquain-

---

1 Based on details in a newspaper account of *The Galveston Daily News* with a May 13 dateline. Interestingly, he doesn't mention his return to Sabine County during this manhunt to his entirely sympathetic biographer Henry Fuller in *A Texas Sheriff, A. J. Spradley* (Whitefish, MT: Literary Licensing, 2011); originally published in 1931 by Baker Printing Co., Nacogdoches, TX. In fact, he says he's proud not to have taken part in any manhunts after his and Scott's adventure. One can guess that he came along to observe the animals from Rusk as much as to monitor the manhunt, especially since he was keenly interested in tracking dogs and will later famously use and breed them.

2 Hunting dogs are ancient, but Robert Boyle in 1627 described how a bloodhound tracked a man seven miles and found him in an upstairs room of a house, the first recorded description of canine man tracking.

tance of Charles Darwin, compiled stories from which he built a theory of the evolution of intelligence. The psychologist's writings mark the beginning of the field of comparative psychology.

But that's not what we care about. We care about his dog.

Romanes conducted a series of tracking experiments with his setter Bango and published the results in the *Journal of the Linnean Society* in December 1886. This is the first scientific study of canine tracking, and it catapults it to a new popularity. Following Romanes's report, also widely seen in the January 1887 journal *Nature,* police scent dogs are gaining fresh acceptance around the world.

But in the United States, the stigma of slavery still clouds their use. The stain begins when slave owners seek dogs that could not only track slaves (any hunting dog can do that) but bite them into submission when cornered. For this, they turn to a breed corrupted to hunt humans in bondage: the Cuban bloodhound.

The Spanish first bred the dogs for use during their New World slave trade. They don't look at all like a family-friendly hound. These are athletes. They are a stout 150 pounds, three feet tall at the shoulder, with keen eyes shining under clipped ears. A judge named John McWhorter in 1920 wrote a defense of the breed that gave this disturbing yet telling description: "The common hound was then crossed with the Great Dane, or the Cuban Mastiff, both savage and vicious breeds of dogs, and a new strain produced called the Cuban Bloodhound, and later and more appropriately called the Nigger Hound."[3]

The Spanish used the dogs for a hundred years, until Cuba abolished slavery in 1886. But by then, they proliferated beyond the island. They first arrived in the United States in 1835, used on the fringes of the Second Seminole War. American slavers saw their real-world subjugation advantages and bought them as is or just bred common hounds with mastiffs for homegrown versions. "They thus unite the unerring scent of the deer hound, the savage bloodthirstiness of the mastiff and the

---

3 J. C. McWhorter, "Bloodhound as Witness," *American Law Review* 54, no. 109 (1920).

fleetness of the greyhound," says one newspaper of Cuban bloodhounds in 1888.[4] "They will track a fugitive, and, having 'bayed' him, will tear him in pieces."

Luckily for the Conners (and everyone else), these terrifying beasts had fallen out of favor after the Civil War. Two Cuban bloodhounds were used to guard prisoners at Andersonville, much to the shock of the Union inmates. But their fall from grace took the name *bloodhound* with them. For example, in 1886, the state of Massachusetts banned all bloodhounds, a law aimed at the Cuban breed. It would take six years for the language to be amended to exclude other bloodhounds from the prohibition.

However, that doesn't mean that Rusk prison uses actual English bloodhounds, with their floppy ears, friendly dispositions unflagging devotion, and all. These have been working in Europe for centuries but are not common in North America until after 1888, when English breeder Edwin Brough brought three hounds to exhibit at the Westminster kennel show in New York City. American Kennel Club records (the "Stud Books") in 1889 show only fourteen English bloodhounds registered. These animals are rare commodities, not frontline trackers.[5]

The bloodhounds that arrive from Rusk are not English, nor are they Cuban. They are Texas bloodhounds, which is a nebulous term for a foxhound crossbred with other dogs with useful traits.

The Texas bloodhound is not just uniquely Texan, it's also uniquely American, mostly because the fox hound stands as one of the nation's first registered breeds. Fittingly, George Washington owned thirty-six of them. Their calls can be heard for miles, which is suitable for the expanses of the New World wilderness, a hallmark baying shared by the

---

4 *Yellowstone Journal* (Miles City, MT), June 21, 1888.

5 *The American Kennel Club Stud Book,* vol. VI, cited in "Scapegoats: Part 1-The Bloodhound," September 5, 2010, The Truth About Pit Bulls, http://thetruthaboutpitbulls .blogspot.com/2010/08/scapegoats-part-1-bloodhound.html.

Texas bloodhound. These bloodhounds do have drooping ears that help waft odors toward the dogs' nostrils.

Unlike the Cubans, trained to bite what they track, Texas bloodhounds' strong noses and voices are more useful than their teeth. "Far different from this terrible animal is the genuine Texas bloodhound. The name 'blood' hound is, in fact, in a certain sense, a misnomer," says an 1888 newspaper essay called "The True Bloodhound" that ran in many American newspapers, trying to correct the misperceptions. "The Texas hound is not a savage animal, save when wounded, or when resistance is made. They are true descendants of the splendid animals which made such royal sport for the Norman kings and nobles."[6]

That's a bit much—that original royal breed went extinct—but the Texas bloodhound is the spiritual heir of those animals, which never bit their prey no matter how lively the chase. Discipline and stamina are their hallmarks, not ferocity.

In contrast to Massachusetts, Texas embraces the bloodhound. In 1887, there is already a law being considered in Austin to require every county to maintain bloodhounds. It fails, but the difference in attitude between states is pronounced.

Human reinforcements have also arrived in Sabine County in the form of a single, large man: Texas Ranger Company B sergeant John McNelly. His unit's records on April 3 record that he left Quanah "to Capt. Scotts company to see what is needed."

He's a solidly built man, if only five foot nine, and with a pedigree to match his physical stature. His uncle is a famous Ranger captain, Leander McNelly, whose Special Force state troops fought in South Texas and along the border. With his nephew in his ranks, the famous captain waged some of the bloody Native American battles that would later prove so contentious in Texas Ranger history.

John McNelly continues his career with the Frontier Battalion and

6 "The True Bloodhound," *Buchanan Record,* October 25, 1888; *Yellowstone Journal,* June 21, 1888.

rises to become a battle-hardened sergeant. He cuts his teeth with Company F, protecting the Texas & Pacific Railway as it's being built across the Great Plains, before being brought into Company B to stamp some professionalism on that reorganized unit. There's one familiar face among Scott's privates—T. S. Crowder served with him in Company B in 1885 before rejoining the Rangers with Company F a year later.

His presence is needed, in the estimation of the nameless correspondent for *The Galveston Daily News:* "Captain Scott being shot disorganizes their forces, and they need a new commander."[7]

McNelly takes charge of the Company F privates, Weatherred's citizens' posse, and the dogs. The hunt starts at the scene of the shoot-out. There, the bloodhounds run the show. The dogs inhale Willis's items, taking on his unique mix of sweat and skin particles. The animal's brain, more specifically its olfactory bulb, creates an "odor image" from the chemical mélange that the dog then uses to identify a trail.

G. L. Potts is a retired police officer living in Crowley, Texas, who volunteers his and his dogs' time tracking missing people. He describes scent in a very physical way. "As we walk throughout the world, it's sort of like we've got a can of spray paint on the top of our head," he says. "I'm red, you're blue, your wife is yellow, and my wife is green, and so forth. Everybody has a different color. As we walk along, this spray paint is coming out, and the wind blows it over to the corner of the house here, and it blows it down the street. So, you'll have heavy spots of scent, and you'll have lighter spots of scent. And it isn't necessarily where we stand, walk, our exact path, because atmospheric conditions will change, that the wind will blow it off one direction or another and so forth."[8]

---

7 "East Texas Outlaws," *Galveston Daily News,* April 7, 1887. The dispatch has an April 3 dateline.

8 Interview with author, August 2020. His origin story as a volunteer tracker is interesting: "I had adopted a dog that was a hound, and a kid turned up missing close to us here. It turned out he just wandered off from home. But I was like, 'What could

There are some choice items at the shoot-out scene to form this odor image, including any items not destroyed in the camp, most of all Old Man Conner's hat. These scents form distinct odor trails for the dogs to follow.

The recent light rains should help the dogs track the Conners. "It's going to kind of release the scent that might be trapped in the ground and make it much better," says Potts. "The whole *Cool Hand Luke* kind of thing, where they're running through the creeks, that's just a Hollywood thing. It actually helps the dog."

But this is where the trackers' advantage begins to fade. The fact that the scent trail—the shoot-out spot—starts on well-trodden Conner turf confuses the dogs with overlapping layers of the same scent. The whole area is crisscrossed with the same trails that the dogs are seeking, and the rain sharpens all these older scents. It's a recipe for canine confusion.

"My hardest works are usually *Grandmama wandered off from the house*, when grandma walks from the house every single day," Potts says. "The easy ones are, *Someone stole this car, wrecked it, jumped out, and ran off*. That's an easy one to work with because it's a fresh trail, and also because he's never been there before."

If there is one thing Willis Conner knows, it's dogs. There's little doubt that the experienced woodsman who raised trained pups would know some tricks to defeat them. In the end, they just need to wear out the dogs. That's easy to do in Sabine County. Fallen logs, messy bogs, and steep creek inclines sap the energy of dogs and handlers alike.

As a hunter, the Conners know to move with the wind whenever possible, knowing that to do otherwise is like waving a banner. Making

---

Maggie have done?' I started researching, and I just kind of got lucky to get with some of the better handlers throughout the U.S. Turns out, Maggie couldn't have ever found that kid; she was terrible. But I ended up getting a puppy and working with him. It turns out that a bank probably a third of a mile from my house got robbed, and they knew that I had him. One of them called me in, and my dog was able to track down and find the guy."

sharp, illogical turns could make the handlers doubt the dog is following an actual scent and is confusing them with the Conners' earlier scents.[9]

"I would probably try to go down into a ravine or a gully area and climb up the side," says Potts, thinking through the scenario as a Conner. "That scent is just falling down into that low area, and the dog is just going to get trapped down in there, because that is where the scent is." There are plenty of creeks and inclines for them to choose from during their flight, now on foot.

The Conners have the space and expertise to get the distance they need, even without horses. "The best thing you can do initially is get as far away as possible as quickly as possible, traveling through harsh terrain and then keep on moving, hoping to tire out both dogs and handlers so they give up the search," advises one modern survivalist website.[10]

This is what happens in Sabine County during the fruitless manhunt for the Conners after the shoot-out. As the days stretch and the hounds go in circles, the truth becomes painfully obvious: The outlaw family has again melted away, hidden in the endless backwoods. "They are certainly the most desperate set of men that ever infested this section," *The Dallas Morning News* says. "And the officers are powerless to enforce the laws."[11] The day that runs, Governor Ross issues new rewards for the Conners: $500 for Willis and Fed Conner, and $300 for John Conner.[12] In terms of 2021 purchasing power, that equals a total of $37,000.

---

9 Connor O'Malley, "Wilderness Evasion," Alderleaf Wilderness College, https://www .wildernesscollege.com/wilderness-evasion.html.

10 Mark Lawrence, "How to Evade and Escape Tracking Dogs," Secrets of Survival, August 20, 2020, via https://secretsofsurvival.com/how-to-evade-and-escape -tracking-dogs/.

11 *The Dallas Morning News*'s article reruns in *The Arkansas Democrat* on April 6, 1887, where L. L. Loggins likely reads it with interest.

12 John, for some reason, is identified as "Berber Conner."

"The excitement in the neighborhood continues unabated and nearly all citizens are under arms and searching for the desperadoes," *The Galveston Daily News* reports.[13]

This is when the Conner family starts leaking misleading information that makes it to the newspapers. "Old Willis Conner went to a house in the neighborhood and stated that Fred was badly wounded and would die, and since that time news came to Hemphill that he was dead," reads one April 7 newspaper report.[14]

Fed is hurt but very much alive. This won't be the last article the family plants in local media to throw off their pursuers. However, it must be said that local newspapers are vicious in describing the family during 1887. They may win these small information skirmishes, but the Conners lose the overall media war miserably.

Sheriff Spradley is not impressed with the search. Nancy Conner, Fed's wife, recalls to her relatives that the lawman stopped for friendly conversation and coffee on her porch while others searched the grounds for her husband. In time, the family will pass along their version of the shoot-out to him, that there was no ambush at all and the Rangers opened fire without warning. Scott's quip to Spradley about "shooting first and asking questions later" will take on a new, sinister meaning.[15]

Spradley in his biography, published in 1920, says the Rangers lied about being ambushed and says, "The Conner raids were unfair, cowardly and inhuman." However, he does not accuse the Rangers of killing a wounded man. In the end, despite trashing the Rangers, the sheriff's sympathies seem to remain divided. "The Conners were as brave men

13 *Galveston Daily News,* April 8, 1887.

14 "East Texas Outlaws," *Galveston Daily News.*

15 Mark Dugan, *Judge Not* (unpublished, 1982), and Henry Fuller, *A Texas Sheriff: A. J. Spradley* (Whitefish, MT: Literary Licensing, 2011), originally published in 1931 by Baker Printing Co., Nacogdoches, TX.

as ever lived," Spradley opines. "So were the Rangers. It was a fight in which men faced death and met it with gun in hand."[16]

MOURNFUL TRAVELERS
April 16, 1887

F. M. Moore, the sheriff of Kerr County, feels more than the weight of travel as he arrives in San Augustine. He's stopped here for a somber night before moving on to Sabine County, where the body of his nephew is buried.

The sudden loss of Jim Moore has shaken the veteran lawman, who knows full well that his example prompted the young man to become a Ranger. But he's not heading to Hemphill to join a vengeful posse. His primary destination will be the graveyard, where he needs to arrange a suitable marker.

He crosses paths in San Augustine with Jack and Vernon Scott, returning home from Sabine County. "Mr. Scott reports his brother Captain Scott, and Messrs Rogers and Brooks are convalescent, and doing as well as could be expected," *The Galveston Daily News* notes from San Augustine.[17]

Moore crosses into Sabine County the next day and immediately sees the manhunt roiling the population. "Residents living near the line of San Augustine and Sabine counties spy a large posse of citizens and Rangers moving through the area, chasing leads," notes *The Galveston Daily News.* "They discovered two fresh camp fires on the northeast side of a large hill called Iron Mountain, nine miles from town. A large posse was organized at Sexton to join in the search . . . Sabine County is in the worst state of excitement ever known there."[18]

---

16 Fuller, *A Texas Sheriff.*

17 "Citizens Still Vigorously Searching for the Conners—A Hot Trail," *Galveston Daily News,* April 18, 1887 (April 17 dateline).

18 Ibid.

This area is in northern reaches of the county, close to the Conners' original homestead on Bull Bay Creek. This lead will fizzle like all the rest.

In Hemphill, Frank Moore decides to keep his nephew where he lies and arranges for a tombstone. It reads: "James H. Moore, Texas Ranger, Killed by Outlaws." Moore leaves Sabine County with the slain Ranger's horse in tow. The animal is to be retired to pasture with his brother's grieving family, a gentle coda to the violent death.[19]

As much as the posse has swelled in numbers, the Conners are nowhere to be found. Frustration and condemnation, delivered via the newspapers, lands on the citizens who are supposed to be supporting them. "Were if not for the sympathizers of these terrible outlaws they could be easily hunted down," *The Galveston Daily News* sniffs on April 19. "Strange to say, among them are many men heretofore considered respectable."

The hunt for the outlaw family again stagnates. Eventually, everyone seems to recognize that the Conners have vanished. The Rangers have heard that Willis and his sons are hiding near the fork of the Angelina and Attoyac Rivers and scout the area in response. This is as close as they will get to catching the Conners, who are indeed there, lurking near the home of Alexander Lewis Conner. Alex brings food to the men and leaves it for them in the brush. The Rangers leave empty-handed.[20]

McNelly returns to Company B on April 22. Brooks is now solely in charge of Company F.

His hands are healing as well as can be expected. There's been no sign of infection, so the wounds won't be crippling. That's a testament to the two doctors' skills. But staring at his bandaged left hand, and the stumps of his fingers wrapped within, he ponders his future as a gunman.

---

19 *Gonzales Inquirer,* March 16, 1909; family memories of the horse posted on "Francis M. 'Frank or FM' Moore," Find a Grave, https://www.findagrave.com/memorial /39912336/francis-m_-moore.

20 Dugan, *Judge Not,* quoting a 1981 letter to the author from Hazel Stevens, granddaughter of Alexander Lewis Conner.

True athletes adapt to new physical realities, and so too must Brooks. One of the best known and least popular methods of shooting a six-shooter is "fanning" the hammer, using the palm of the left hand to repeatedly cock the pistol. It offers no advantages that a two-handed grip can't provide, and drawbacks in terms of aim and reliability—that is to say, if both hands are whole.

Brooks's aren't, and the optimal two-handed grip is impossible. Using his left hand to fan the hammer of the pistol in his right is the best way to produce a high rate of fire. Making sure it doesn't spoil his aim will just be a matter of practice.

Brooks has a chance to demonstrate his mastery of the method later in life. "He fanned the hammer of an old .45 so fast it sounded like an automatic," says William Sterling. From ten paces, four of five of these shots he fires hits the oak tree knot he's aiming at, and the fifth is just a little wide.[21]

Brooks doesn't need specialized hardware, but there are options if he wants. "He likely had the hammer extended to accommodate his palm," surmises John Rooney, an avid SASS shooter and period gun collector who lives outside of Corpus Christi. "People customized their firearms all the time, and that would make sense for that shooting style."[22]

Lingering in Sabine County, Brooks is also functioning without his metaphorical right hand, John Rogers. The pious Ranger has spent two weeks with doctors in San Augustine before heading to a ranch in Kingsbury, Texas, to rest with his family.

There is a sign of tension between Company F and the locals of Hemphill. George H. Schmitt, who is busy spreading critiques of Scott's tactics in letters to his superiors, makes sure to spotlight an incident of

---

21 William Sterling, *Trails and Trials of a Texas Ranger* (Norman: University of Oklahoma Press, 1959).

22 Interview with author.

Company F men getting drunk and yelling at locals. One of those mentioned specifically is Billy Treadwell.[23]

But in Sabine County, the Rangers find that much of the town's attitude has shifted in their favor. That includes the very important demographic of young, unmarried females. "The people around there couldn't do enough for us, they thought we were real important," says J. Allen Newton. "They would feed us all the fried chicken we wanted and just begged us to stay longer with them. The girls, who had never seen anybody but the country boys in their homespun clothes, thought 'we were it' in our city clothes."[24]

Brooks is certainly not immune to this change of heart. He fixes his eye on twenty-one-year-old Martha Peddy, the daughter of First Baptist Church minister A. J. Peddy.

Scott stays with the Peddy family as he recovers, giving Brooks the opportunity to chat her up. This isn't some clandestine seduction. It's so aboveboard that even Rogers would approve, were he around to pass judgment; Brooks invites her to accompany him to church.

The Ranger sergeant arrives at her home in his best outfit, vest and long-sleeved shirt, hatless, mangled hands freshly bandaged. Martha pops out of her house in her Sunday best, but Sabine girl that she is, she's wearing no shoes.

She makes the walk with her suitor barefoot, sitting on a stone in front of the First Baptist Church to slip them on before heading

---

23 Paul Spellman, *Captain John H. Rogers, Texas Ranger* (Denton: University of North Texas Press, 2003). Schmitt complains to Sieker that the diminished Company F is "drawing full rations & supplies—having picnic times—even though only half of the men were in camp," quoted in Spellman; originals unavailable due to COVID-19 closures.

24 Sarah Ellen Davidge, "Texas Rangers Were Rough and Ready Fighters," *Frontier Times*, November 1935.

inside. Prominent members of the congregation include Dr. J. W. Smith, Hampton Pratt, and W. W. Weatherred.[25]

Brooks is taken with her, but the Rangers are merciless. "We sure did tease [Brooks] about his girl," says Newton, ever the joker.[26]

THE SLOW SUMMER
May 3, 1887

William Scott is one tough son of a bitch. One month after being shot through the lung, he's riding on horseback from Hemphill into San Augustine. He's not alone: Dr. Tucker attends him during the trip, and Private Ed Randall joins them as a well-armed orderly. They'll head on to Nacogdoches to catch the next train to Dallas, where Rangers' families are eager to see them.

A *Galveston Daily News* correspondent calls on Scott and finds him tired but spirited:

> Captain Scott was lying down, being a little fatigued from riding. He seems rapidly improving and thinks it will be but a short time until he will be able to be at his post of duty again. He does not seem to be tired of the Ranger life; talks of the fight with the Conners like a frolic, but a right serious one, and seems very anxious to try it over.[27]

Scott also seems to defend his performance: "He regrets very much that he had not been furnished a pack of dogs; thinks his men could have been successful in following them up." One thing he also does, not for the

---

25 *Minutes 1858–1890 First Baptist Church, Hemphill Texas* (Saint Louis, MO: Igmire Publications, 1982), distributed by Ericson Books, Nacogdoches, TX.

26 Davidge, "Texas Rangers Were Rough."

27 *Fort Worth Daily Gazette*, June 13, 1887.

last time, is praise his Rangers. "Captain Scott speaks in glowing terms of how manfully his five men he had with him at the time of the fight acted."

The news of the shoot-out has been covered in newspapers across the nation, but those in Dallas show more interest than most. They have two of their prized sons—William Scott and Ed Randall—in the line of fire. Randall's appearance in Dallas will be a relief, since "much uneasiness has been manifested in regard to him" as word of the shoot-out spread.[28] By now, everyone knows he's safe, but there's nothing like putting eyes on the young Ranger to really understand he's unharmed.

By the time they get to Dallas, backlash has already been aimed at Scott from within the Frontier Battalion. Fellow Ranger George Schmitt is less than sympathetic with the entire incident, blaming Scott for the failed assault in a letter to Captain Liam Sieker: "It looks like Capt. Scott and his men got the worse of it, and three of the criminals got away. It seems to me that Capt. Scott had not men enough with him or else he could have captured the whole gang. This is a very unfortunate affair and I feel sorry for them."[29]

Scott writes in his official report of the fight that the plan basically worked in that they used the informer Alford to successfully find the Conner clan. He does not present the ambush as a failure; instead, he lays blame on the posse. "The citizens being more accustomed to hunting deer than desperadoes, held their stand, not being more than eighty yards distant from the fight and [did] not even come to our assistance for minutes after the fight was over," he writes. "Had the squad come we would have captured the entire Conner gang."[30]

---

28 "The East Texas War," *Galveston Daily News,* April 3, 1887.

29 Paul Spellman, *Captain J. A. Brooks, Texas Ranger* (Denton: University of North Texas Press, 2007).

30 "Scott to Sieker, July 31, 1887, Adjutant General Official Correspondence," *Frontier Battalion Monthly Reports,* March 1887.

The respite in Dallas is all too short. After three weeks, Scott and Randall get back on the trail. They reach Sabine County just in time to see an article from Jasper County, to the south of Sabine. "We understand that Old Man Conner says he thought he was fighting citizens, that had he known it was the damn Rangers he would have made a better fight," *The Jasper Weekly Newsboy* runs on May 25, 1887. "If reports are true, the old fellow talks recklessly."[31]

Scott also hears unwelcome news that his medical treatment is the cause of a dispute between the local doctors and the Texas Rangers organization. On May 19, 1887, Dr. J. W. Smith, representing them, writes quartermaster Sieker: "I received voucher for services rendered Capt. Scott and men today, which you return for curtailment. I must contend that I think the services rendered are worth $495. However I will give you facts of the case as to what services were rendered. Then you can allow such renumeration as your conscience dictates." He goes on to describe the work he and two other doctors performed over more than twenty days of attendance, each at five dollars a day, plus more for the surgical fieldwork. "Now I leave the case with you," he finishes.

There's a new tenderfoot to break in, Carlton Hines, who joined Company F in May.[32] What he thought of his new job, seeing the freshly dug grave and bullet-scarred bodies of Company F's members, is not recorded. But at the end of May, Company F also loses a Ranger.

Since he joined Company C in May 1886, William Treadwell's year of service is up. He's had enough of law enforcement and aims to bring his skill with horses, guitars, and dance steps back to the Pettus Ranch, where he figures the heat has cooled off from the Linney killing. Besides, he's a former Ranger now and the survivor of an infamous gun battle, and there-

---

31 *The Jasper Weekly Newsboy*, May 25, 1887. This item first ran in *The Hemphill Reporter*.

32 Sometimes spelled *Charlton* in Ranger records. "Adjutant General Service Records," Texas State Library and Archives Commission, https://www.tsl.texas.gov/apps/arc/service/.

fore a much more intimidating target. The Pettus Ranch embraces the "loveable vagabond" and "fighting fool." T. Wheeler Pettus himself later says Treadwell's tumultuous life "enumerates more virtues than vices."[33]

A welcome return lifts the Company's spirits when a repaired and rested John Rogers reappears in early June. If that isn't good enough news, he's come with his own personal reinforcement. Curren Rogers, his younger brother, is the newest private of Company F. He just turned eighteen years old. They immediately dub the baby-faced Ranger "Kid Rogers." His positive energy and devotion to his brother become a salve to the lingering wound left by Moore's death.

On June 10, Adjutant General King orders Company F away from Sabine to the town of Weatherford to chase train robbers. They pack up their camp with the bitter knowledge that the remaining Conners are still at large. And so much for the free fried chicken and available, small-town daughters.

It doesn't take long for a *Fort Worth Daily Gazette* reporter to notice Company F's arrival in Weatherford. Scott tells a reporter that he doesn't know what his mission is or how long he'll stay. In reality, he's there to chase John Barber's gang, fresh off a train caper, and everyone knows it.

Once again, the reception from locals is chilly. "Some of our citizens say this is a peaceable city and the people are law abiding, and fail to see the object in the Governor ordering the Rangers here," says the *Fort Worth Daily Gazette*, relaying a report from town. "They say this is no resort for train robbers."[34] Indeed, Barber is arrested elsewhere, and the Rangers get their new assignment on July 5, 1887: a request to head to San Angelo. The endless trail continues.

But not for J. A. Brooks. Word comes to Scott in the form of a

---

33 Sterling, *Trails and Trials.*

34 "Captain Scott Awaiting Orders, Some Citizens Upset," *Fort Worth Daily Gazette,* June 14, 1887.

telegram from deputy U.S. marshal Ben Cabell: his sergeant is finally being put on trial for murder.

Scott summons Brooks and grimly tells him the details. He is to meet Cabell in Dallas, collect the former Ranger Henry Putz (who's living there), and the three would then head to Fort Smith, Arkansas, where the gallows are used so often that one is a permanent fixture next to the courthouse.

Brooks isn't to be treated like any other criminal; Scott has seen to that. A wealthy rancher named Bill Butler, of Karnes County, "wired the marshal at Fort Smith to have my bail bond fixed and that he and other friends in Texas would sign for the money," Brooks says in his handwritten memoirs. He doesn't plan on taking advantage of this gesture and decides to bunk with the accommodating marshal the entire time he's at Fort Smith and thereby spare his allies of posting the bond.

Brooks boards the train wondering if he'll ever ride with his comrades as a Ranger again. His life has centered around this profession for so long he can't imagine giving it up. Now his fate is in the hands of strangers who will convene in a courtroom in Fort Smith. He arrives there, with Putz and Cabell at his side, on July 1, 1887.

"PRETTY GOOD CIDER, WAS IT?"
July 15, 1887

District Attorney M. H. Sandels faces his witness, the cowboy Price Fulton, and asks him what he hopes is a damning question. "Did you see St. John at any time draw his pistol?"

"No, sir," he responds.

"Did you see it out?" Sandels persists, wanting to reinforce the point.

"No, sir," Fulton says. "The last time I saw of St. John's hand was when he pushed his hand on the pistol and said, 'Let it be' or something like that."

Sitting in a defendant's chair, J. A. Brooks peers past the DA at the sunlight streaming through the three windows behind Judge Isaac Charles Parker's cherry-paneled desk. The view isn't much, but the fresh air is needed to dilute the smell.

The stench of urine is wafting from the floorboards of the federal courtroom here at Fort Smith. Brooks tries not to imagine what's underfoot: dozens of filthy whiskey peddlers, bruisers, thieves, and chronic drunks crammed into a pair of rooms, each just under 1,600 square feet. There are urinal tubs stuffed into unused fireplaces, under the assumption the reek will travel up through the flues. Instead, it permeates into the first-floor courtroom.

"This dark, crowded underground hole is noisome with odors of every description," writes crusading reformer Anna Dawes of the jail in the summer of 1885. "A veritable hell upon earth."[35]

The U.S. Court for the Western District of Arkansas moved into the army's former barracks building in 1872. The courthouse is on the first floor. The jail, once a mess hall, sits belowground. It stores male prisoners waiting for trial, shipment to prison, or the end of their brief sentences. There is no segregation between the petty and violent criminals.

Change is coming. Dawes's report has reached the U.S. Congress, and money has been dedicated for a new facility. Construction is even now underway, the new jailhouse budding from the current courthouse. Its heart will be a three-tier cellblock ringed by an iron cage. Each tier will hold twenty-four cells. The current, wretched basement is to become a consulting room for lawyers, a guard bunkhouse, and a kitchen. But for now, the federal prison at Fort Smith remains, in the words of the Arkansas state attorney general, the "most miserable prison, probably, in the whole country."[36]

With that smell in his nostrils, it's hard for Brooks to forget that

---

35 Juliet L. Galonska, "Reforming the Hell on the Border Jail," National Parks Service, https://www.nps.gov/fosm/learn/historyculture/reforming-the-hell-on-the-border-jail.htm.

36 "Congressman John Rogers of Arkansas reading from the Attorney General's report on the jail at Fort Smith, Arkansas," S. 610, 49th Cong., 1st sess., Congressional Record March 1, 1886, National Park Service, https://www.nps.gov/fosm/learn/historyculture/reforming-the-hell-on-the-border-jail.htm.

his enemies were eager to see him thrown down there before the trial started. "There was a lot of grumbling around the courtroom that Knight and I were not being held in the Federal Jail," Brooks recalls. "But Judge Parker remarked, 'If there were more like them in this land of blood, it would be a better country.'"[37]

It's good to hear the judge speaking on his behalf. Those who are on the wrong side of that man have a hard time in his courtrooms, and he has no soft spot for those accused of murder. Parker has not earned the nickname "the Hanging Judge" when Brooks stands before him, but this reputation is already established.

The jury determines guilt, but Parker alone lays out the punishment. The judge is the final legal word; there's no higher court for appeal since his court has both circuit and district court powers. He's not shy about pressing juries for sentences he'll agree with, and those are usually convictions. Parker presides over about six hundred cases a year; the heavy foot traffic literally wears out the straw carpeting, which must be replaced about every two years.[38]

His court is so busy that the number of death sentences keeps piling up. Parker has his own executioner, deputy U.S. marshal George Maledon, who during his career up to 1887 has hanged dozens from the nearby gallows. Several have ridden the "Fort Smith elevator" this year, but none while Brooks is there.

The judge's reach extends well beyond the courthouse. He commands a cadre of seven deputy U.S. marshals, plus a kennel of tracking and guard dogs, working at the court's behest. They usually ride throughout western Arkansas and Indian Territory to bring prisoners to trial, but also work cases, gather evidence, request warrants, and hunt down suspects.

---

37 Brooks's handwritten memoirs, courtesy of Texas Ranger Hall of Fame and Museum, Waco, TX.

38 John Demer, "Furnishing Report, the Fort Smith Courtroom," National Park vice, https://www.nps.gov/parkhistory/online_books/fosm/courtroom_hfr.pdf.

Parker's marshal and deputies provide security for the courtroom while court's in session. They come and go from offices adjoining the courtroom. One stands near the doorway while another stands behind the judge, protecting him and blocking the three open windows in case a prisoner takes the opportunity to leap out. Between the stench rising from the floor and the simmering July heat, closing them is not an option.

The courtroom is laid out strategically, according to an article in the ghoulishly named newspaper the *Fort Smith Elevator*. The arrangement ensures that the witnesses and defendants are in proximity, making testy exchanges on the stand seem even more personal:

> The witness sat on a low chair on the same level as the attorneys and spoke in a low voice (as witnesses generally do); but the witness must "take the stand." A dais has been erected opposite the District Attorney's position, upon which there is a chair for the witness. This places the witness to the left of the jury and to the right of the Judge, in fair view of counsel. It is an excellent thought on the part of the Court, for the witness can answer direct questions touching the case without embarrassment or the misunderstanding of attorneys in cross examination.[39]

The cowboy Price Fulton is one of a series of witnesses from in or around Alexander's store that day. They come in two categories—those who were inside Red's Store during the killing and those who saw the body afterward.

Sandels is trying to weave a clear narrative with every question. Indeed, all the witnesses will tell a common story, but only up until the struggle between Knight and St. John ensues. For example, the defense witnesses seem to think Brooks shot first, while prosecution witnesses say Putz was the first to use deadly force.

H. M. Long says that he saw Putz shoot first and low. "I saw Mr.

---

[39] *Fort Smith Elevator,* August 5, 1881.

Putz draw his pistol with his right hand and fire," Long tells the jury. "St. John was then on the counter. I didn't see St. John have a pistol or doing anything."

Sandels also asks Long, "Did you notice what part of the body the shot was directed?"

"It seemed to me, very low," says Long. After the first shot, gun smoke immediately blocked his view.

A similar version comes from Fulton, who says he saw Knight reach for St. John's pistol with his left hand, kicking off the fatal sequence of events. "St. John said, let it be and pushed [Knight's] hand off with his right and laid his open hand on the pistol handle," he says. "Just at that time I seen Putz draw his pistol and St. John throwed his eyes on Putz when he drew it . . . I could tell it was Putz that fired."

Fulton tells the jury of the moment that the Rangers realized that the man they shot hadn't pulled the trigger. "Knight was looking at St. John's pistol and someone remarked, 'Thought he shot you.'"

According to these witnesses, Brooks appears to think St. John shot his gun. A later witness, cowboy Henry Witt, in his testimony gives a detailed account: "One of the crowd argued that St. John shot, I don't know which one though. Brooks remarked to them to 'examine the pistol and they could tell by that.' It was examined and had five charges in it, and the hammer was resting on an empty barrel."

The scenario that this testimony creates is plausible: St. John starts to struggle with Knight, fending off the Indian agent's grasp for his pistol. He sees the Rangers' drawn guns, tries to pull his own, and lunges at Brooks's gun. Putz shoots, prompting Brooks and Knight to think St. John has pulled the trigger, and they fire, as well.

Defense attorney Thomas Barnes handles the cross-examinations as Elias Cornelius Boudinot listens in, tossing in occasional queries. Barnes spends a good amount of time showcasing the fact that each witness had a limited and narrow view of the fatal encounter. His treatment of witness Thomas Burke showcases this tactic.

"Who fired the first shot?"

"I don't know who fired the first shot."

"Who fired the second shot?"

"I don't know."

"Who fired the third shot?"

"I don't know."

Barnes's cross-examination of Burke also reveals his tendency to belittle witnesses, in this case accusing Burke of being drunk. "I saw the cider barrel and got a drink of cider when I went in," Burke says, when asked about his presence inside the store.

"Pretty good cider, was it?" asks Barnes.

Burke just laughs. "It tasted pretty well to me."

"Spiked." Not a question.

"Well, it was pretty good cider," Burke says, then laughs again before trying to move to testimony along. "I suppose it was 10 or 15 minutes that I took the cider until they came in."

Barnes doesn't let it go. "Ain't it a fact that that cider crossed your eyes a little bit?"

There's no laugh this time. "No sir."

The defense attorney uses a drawl that either reveals a poor command of the English language or a clumsy attempt to appeal to the everyman ranchers in the jury. A newspaper dispatch from Arkansas that runs in 1889 describes Barnes as "a prominent orator in the city,"[40] which speaks either to his use of courtroom theatrics or the lamentable state of public speakers in nineteenth-century Fort Smith.

Of all the information that comes out of the cross-examinations, some of the most beneficial to Brooks, Putz, and Knight are details about the dark-haired cowboy's reputation. "I ask you if you didn't say to Knight that he had better get away from there and that St. John belonged to a bad crowd," Barnes presses Witt.

"I said his crowd was above there and he had better get away from there," the cowboy responds.

---

40 "Unknown but Severe," *Cincinnati Enquirer*, May 31, 1889.

"How long had you known St. John?" Barnes then asks Witt, not for the first time during his testimony, knowing the answer is, "Since the spring of '84." He wants the point to stick home—someone who knew the deceased pretty well is telling the Rangers to flee from the man's dangerous friends. It's the first of several blows the defense team will aim at St. John's reputation.

After Witt sits down, the trial then features a showdown between one of the initial architects of the smear campaign that led to the murder charges, Obadiah Love. He should be a key witness for the government, able to testify to St. John's character as his employer and doubling as a medical examiner, with vivid descriptions of the cowboy's injuries given from the stand.

"He had five wounds on him. One shot was on the inside of his thigh, above the knee. And came out back here." He points to his hip. "Another struck him in the breast here and another struck him in the breast, here, he was shot in the lower arm, and one struck him in the back."

Sandels uses macabre props to illustrate the dark-haired man's violent end. "Are these the clothes," he asks, gesturing at the bloodstained vest, shirt, and pants on the evidence table.

"Yes, sir." The pair then examine the holes and make sure the jury can see the bloody results of the shooting.

"When you undressed him, you examined the body?" Sandels persists. "Could you tell where the bullets entered and came out?"

"Yes, sir, they tore more where they came out than where they entered."

The district attorney ends his questions, and it's Barnes's turn to cross. He quickly makes his first thrust, this time highlighting the fact that Love himself carries weapons into town. "Were you carrying firearms down there?"

"Yes, sir," Love replies warily, probably now regretting the way he and his men rode into Alex after the shooting, armed to the teeth. "Sometimes I would lay them aside."

"Did you know this order of the Indian Agent [Knight] in regard to carrying firearms?"

"I didn't then," dissembles Love.

"You talked to St. John about it," Barnes points out.

"Yes, sir," the trail boss says, then adds defensively, "I was about 12 or 15 miles from there [Alex]."

For the defense, it's a chance to expose Love as a hypocrite and a liar. The problem is that his statements to the court are not as slanted as what he told the newspapers and the St. John family. Nowhere are the musings about Indian agents stealing firearms by gunpoint and shooting an innocent cowboy in the back while he was shopping. Instead, the details in his statement that exhibit the most overreach are his descriptions of the corpse's wounds.

"I don't think you have been asked [by the prosecution] whether that man had powder burns on his back, have you?"

"No sir."

"You have heretofore stated he was," Barnes says, referring to the detailed letter Love sent to authorities describing wounds consistent with a close-range shooting from behind. For a trail boss, Love writes well and reveals the ability to make some keen observations on paper. But he's no medical examiner, and Barnes does his best to remind the jury of this during the cross-examination.

"Yes sir."

Barnes raises the vest. "You don't see signs of powder burns on that vest, do you?"

"No sir."

Now Barnes raises the shirt. "And you don't see any on that shirt?"

"No sir."

"Are you familiar with gunshot wounds?" the defense attorney asks.

"No sir, not very."

"Don't you know that after a man has been shot for some hours, whether he is powder burned or not, the wound where the ball went in or out, there would be a dark appearance around it."

"There might be."

"And unless a man made a careful examination, he couldn't tell."

"No sir, I guess not."

This line of questioning moves onto sparring over details of the holes in the clothes, particularly their sizes and possible causes. Clouding the forensics, such as they are, should work to the defense's favor. But a strange thing happens as the cross continues. The importance of *how* the wounds were made fades before a larger question of *why* the Rangers chose to shoot to begin with.

Only they know the answer, and they'll take the stand next for the defense.

"I WASN'T IN LOVE WITH HIM"
July 19, 1887

U.S. Indian Police agent Thomas Knight has a story to tell the jury about the day he and Albert St. John met, ten days before the shooting.

For Knight, this entire trial is particularly galling considering the treatment that District Attorney Monte Sandels gave the two men who gunned down his father-in-law. Sam Sixkiller, deputy marshal and formerly the first captain of the United States Indian Police, was killed last Christmas Eve.

It was a revenge killing for an encounter in September 1886, when Sixkiller shot Jess Nicholson, who eventually died from his wounds. His pal Dick Vann already hated Sixkiller, having been arrested by him and allegedly kicked gratuitously during the encounter. On December 24, 1886, Van and Alf Cunningham spied Sixkiller, sick and unarmed, in downtown Muskogee to pick up some medicine. The pair shot him down and fled town on horseback.

It hardly took any time at all for the legal apparatus in Fort Smith to pass the buck on dispensing justice for the killing. "It has been decided that the Federal Court here has no jurisdiction over the murderers of Capt. Sam Sixkiller of Muskogee, all parties being Cherokees," reads a newspaper item dated December 30, 1886. "This being the case, the murderers could come right into this city and remain without fear of molestation, as there is no extradition law between the Indian Country and Arkansas, and the United States authorities here could not handle them."[41] The only thing to take the sting away is that on March 2, 1887, President Grover Cleveland signed a bill that made assault against an Indian policeman a federal offense.

District Attorney Sandels has obviously decided that Albert St. John, being a white man, is accorded different justice from Sam Sixkiller—different enough so that a half–Native American lawman can stand trial for his supposed murder.

There's no upside to letting this bitterness show while on the stand. Knight has his own future to worry about. With little prompting or interruption, the Indian agent tells the jury about the first fateful encounter at Red's Store in Alex. He makes sure to inform them that he didn't have a firearm when the dark-haired cowboy entered the store, six-shooter on his belt:

> Mr. St. John and this man Robinson came in, walked to the counter and ate a lunch. I waited til they got done eating and I beckoned to Mr. St. John and he came to me. And I says, "Are you an officer?" He says, "no sir." I says, "I am an officer of the Agent and it is in violation to his order to carry your arms." He says, "I don't know as the Agent has anything to do with me, carrying arms."
>
> I says, "Who are you working for?" "A man by the name of Love." I says, "You had better lay that pistol off or it will get you into trouble." He says, "I bought it and he will buy it off of me if he wants it," and then he walked off, got on his horse and rode off. I was not armed at the time. He was a very large man. I didn't feel like I could contend with him.

This account is backed by the earlier testimony of J. M. Robinson, who was there, who provides a neutral, bloodless account with scant

41 *Saint Louis Globe Democrat*, December 30, 1886.

details. He describes Knight's demeanor during the encounter as "pleasant enough. He didn't show any ill feeling."

The other critical part of Knight's testimony involves the moments before the shooting of Albert St. John:

> I walked up to him and said, "young man I have come to buy your pistol." He says, what? "I have told you to lay off your pistol and you have not done it," and just as I said that I run my hand at it. He said, "Let it be" and put his own hand back. Well, I said, I reckon not and reached the second time and he then drew his pistol. I grabbed it and Sergeant Brooks pulled down on him and he reached out and grabbed Brooks' pistol and said, "let them pop." He presented the pistol and stuck it in my side and grabbed Brooks' at the same time. I fired one shot in the middle of the shooting, as well as I could tell. It was all done in a flash.

He can't see Putz, but he thinks Brooks shot first, hitting St. John's leg, because the cowboy was pushing Brooks's pistol down with his hand. He surmises that Putz and Knight fired, thinking St. John had pulled the trigger, and then Brooks fired again, this time center mass. The Indian agent believes his own shot landed near the shoulder, the likely source of the collarbone wound.

He testifies that St. John's pistol had cleared its holster when the lawmen killed him, as evidenced by the fact that Knight ended up with the gun in his hand immediately after the shooting. "He was falling when he let go of the pistol," Knight says. "He staggered back some four or five feet from that counter, fell on his side and turned on his back."

Knight's move to seize the Winchester from St. John's saddle leads to much misinterpretation. This is his chance to explain himself. "About the first thing I thought of was to get to the gun. I knew he had a Winchester on his saddle," Knight says on the stand. "I thought his friends might get it and try to kill us."

"Why did you tell him when you went to him that day that you wanted to buy his pistol?" asks Sandels.

"Only because of the remark he made," Knight replies candidly. So much for an absence of ill feelings over their earlier, disrespectful encounter.

The district attorney tries to paint a picture of lawmen who ignored nonlethal options. Knight's honest reply is effective because it lacks machismo.

"Couldn't you have struck him with the pistol?" Sandels asks.

"No sir, I couldn't have reached him."

"Couldn't you have struck him across the hand?"

"I didn't try it," Knight says.

"Why didn't you put your right hand on that pistol and twist it out of his hand?" Sandels continues.

"He was stronger than me and he was a large man," Knight admits. "I caught hold of that pistol and held it right up."

"Why didn't you grab it with your right hand?" Sandels persists, in essence asking why he pulled a gun instead of grappling.

"I was afraid to fight him. When I caught hold of the pistol and Mr. Brooks presented his, I thought he would let go. Instead of that, he caught hold of Mr. Brooks' pistol."

When Sandels asks him to re-create the moments after the shooting, Knight describes a state of shock. "I don't remember having any particular conversation with anybody," he says. "Only I regretted that it had to be done." He will be the only one of the three lawmen to express remorse on the stand.

Knight has done well, explaining the events of the day and humanizing himself at the same time. He's become more than "an Indian trying to take my pistol," as St. John described after their initial confrontation. This is a lawman following orders.

Furthermore, instead of showing the jury how the three officers neglected to consider the tactical options, as Sandels surely wants, Knight's account doggedly centers on the risk St. John posed, and the way the dark-haired cowboy escalated the encounter. He could have survived the day by simply not struggling, which literally triggered Knight's Texas Ranger companions to protect him.

Still, Sandels sees a weak point in each of the lawmen's testimonies. None of their written statements, made just after the shooting, include the detail that St. John's pistol was pressed into Knight's side. But Sandels saves this line of attack for the less sympathetic Texas Rangers instead of when Knight first raises this very visceral detail.

Former Ranger Henry Putz next takes the stand. His testimony neatly mirrors Knight's, but any sympathy the Indian agent earned from the jury by lacking bombast is now jeopardized by the glib Dallas native. He responds with "I should say he did" instead of a simple "yes, sir." He's giving the performance of a young, reckless Ranger that Sandels wants to see.

Putz testifies that St. John's gun cleared its holster. "I seen [St. John] had his pistol, I didn't have much time to think," Putz says. "I thought it was time to shoot to get the pistol away from him."

Putz denies shooting first and says he acted when he thought St. John pulled the trigger, but Sandels won't have it and uses pantomime to walk the jury through the moment the bullets flew. "If Brooks fired from this side of you, how come you supposed St. John fired?"

"Well, I was looking for him to shoot the whole time." Such Ranger bravado, stemming from a professional need to always be ready for violence, can easily be interpreted as bloodthirst.

Sandels gestures around the courtroom for the benefit of the jury. "Say of us there and St. John out here, I grab his pistol with my left hand, Brooks fires from over this side and you suppose the pistol *here* has fired?" he asks skeptically.

"I couldn't tell, I thought it was," Putz says. "I have been after a good many men, I don't want to be last." (By this he probably means, *I didn't want this one to be my last.*)

"And so your plan was to shoot without knowing the necessity to shoot at the time?" Sandels pushes.

"I knew it was a necessity to shoot at the time."

Sandels gestures at Knight. "Did you hear him testify? Did you hear him testify that he had hold of the pistol?"

"Yes sir."

"When one shot was fired, without knowing whose pistol it was, you just commenced to shoot St. John?"

"Yes sir. I knew he made an awful attempt to shoot."

The cross-examination of Putz gets more heated than that of Knight. Sandels takes a blunt approach with the young man, an apparent attempt to get a rise from the former Ranger private. "Which one of you shot him in the back?" the DA asks abruptly.

"There was no man shot in the back at all, no sir," Putz says.

"How do you know he wasn't?"

"Well, I know he wasn't shot when he had his back toward us."

"Where did *you* shoot him?" Sandels responds.

"I don't know where I shot him," Putz admits.

The cross-examination contains some lowbrow statements of Sandels accusing the Ranger of "travelling on his pistol," and proposing that wrestling armed suspects is a viable law enforcement tactic. But instead of arguing the obvious perils of that approach, Putz cracks wise.

"When St. John jerked Knight up against the counter, that left St. John free to you," Sandels says. "Why didn't you throw your arms around him?"

"Well," Putz says. "I wasn't in love with him."

Barnes and Boudinot have higher hopes for Brooks. His steely demeanor could be a salve to Putz's seeming rashness. However, the Ranger sergeant doesn't make a very personable witness.

It starts awkwardly, with Barnes playing a sympathy card that only makes Brooks more uncomfortable on the stand. "Your hand seems to be disfigured there," Barnes notes.

"Yes, sir," says Brooks. "That was done the 31st of last March, after the killing." And he leaves it at that.

After that, his testimony echoes the other defendants', albeit with key details from Brooks's point of view:

I got my pistol near the same time as he did, and as I drew my pistol I said, "hold up." Knight made a grab for the pistol and [St. John] grabbed my pistol. I threw myself back and put both hands on my pistol. At the same time I jerked my pistol from him, he said "let 'er pop." He fell off the counter at the same time and was jobbing Knight in the side with his own pistol. My pistol went off at the same time, they all went off at the same time . . . I thought St. John fired at about the same time I did, another pistol fired about the time.

That "other pistol" would have been Putz's. Brooks is not saying his shot was in response to his private's; he's hinting at just the opposite. The sergeant makes a pragmatic argument: "I did it to keep the man from killing me or Knight. He was a powerful man. I was satisfied he could kill either one or all of us. I was satisfied the man would shoot. I only fired to save myself and these other men. I didn't kill him to disarm him."

By now, Barnes knows the prosecutors are attacking the Rangers' credibility by highlighting the missing details from their statements, most notably the recollection of St. John's pistol poking Knight's side. Barnes tries to inoculate Brooks from what's coming by asking questions about his mindset while reporting the shooting to the Indian agent Owen.

"I made it under oath," Brooks says of his statement. "There were some little things I explained to him as we went along. He asked me very few questions, I think. I made a brief statement of it."

"You may not have made a full—" Barnes begins.

"Please don't lead the witness," Sandels scolds.

"I only stated what I thought, to show in which way it was done," Brooks answers.

This sparring, made even more personal by the intimate courtroom layout, continues during Sandels's cross-examination of Brooks. The argument over the statement continues, with the prosecutor all but accusing the lawmen of lying to the jury.

Sandels starts with an attack. "It was not your object in making the statement to Owen to tell him the whole truth."

"There were some little things I didn't explain to him fully," Brooks responds.

"This 'little thing' of St. John sticking his pistol into Knight's side," says Sandels, savoring the categorization of the most compelling reason to use deadly force. "Can you explain why it is that all three of you failed to make that statement before [Owen] and yet all three of you make that statement here?"

Brooks hesitates long enough for the court stenographer to type "(Witness hesitates)" before an answer comes. "My object in telling what I did to Mr. Owen[42] was to tell him what happened in as few words as possible." This is classic stoic Brooks on display.

"Well, can you tell me or explain to me why that happened?"

Barnes objects. "He cannot answer for anybody, only himself."

"I think it's better to put that to the Court and not argue about it," Sandels responds.

"I don't need any lectures about it from you," Barnes retorts.

"I don't need any from you neither," snaps Sandels. "I understand my position exactly."

Judge Parker's eye roll can almost be seen in the transcript as he interrupts with an order: "Let the question go."

Sandels turns to Brooks. "Can you explain to me why that is?"

For all the furor, Brooks answer is flat and unsatisfactory. "I can in only this way, that I can't remember everything that happened at the time and I judge that's the reason I did not do it."

Brooks fares better when Sandels starts to discuss other ways to disarm a resisting man without resorting to gunplay. Brooks delivers a

---

42 Spelled *Ownes* in the transcript. I include this footnote only to reinforce that the stenographer is pressed for time and makes many mistakes but was able to type "Witness hesitates" before Brooks answered.

lesson on realities of law enforcement fieldwork. "After a man gets his pistol out there ain't no time to take it from him," he explains.

Sandels grills him over the exact time when Knight took St. John's gun—hinting but never saying that the Ranger put one in the man as he staggered away, disarmed and dying. Brooks repeatedly tries to explain why the cowboy was a threat.

"I know well enough to know that when a man has a pistol in his hands—"

"And so you concluded to kill him," Sandels interrupts.

"I expect my pistol was the first to fire," Brooks intones unnecessarily. He did shoot twice, to the other men's single shots. It doesn't take special skill to shoot a six-shooter a second time that quickly. But that second shot does speak to a deadly purpose. Always known as a hard officer, Brooks is now also publicly regarded as a quick and lethal gunman.

The defense has two gambits to play besides hearing from the lawmen. The first is the testimony of U.S. Indian Agent Robert Owen, Knight's boss. His presence, including a live reading of his order to disarm cowboys, should help bolster the case that Knight was fulfilling his duties literally to the letter. But his testimony also hints at some of the regional political overtones of the case—namely, the conflict between Strip landowners and intruding herds from Oklahoma. The witness stand becomes a platform to describe the open-range chaos challenging the sovereignty of the Indian Territories.

The order to disarm cowboys was part of Owen's efforts to keep the territories calm when cowboys from Texas swept through the area chasing wayward cattle. Confusing the issue are those who cross into the Indian lands intentionally and illegally. "There was a distinction between those drifted from Texas. Some drifted 'cross the bottoms, some drifted from the Chickasaw Strip, and they drifted there by accident," Owen testifies. "There was cattle from Oklahoma that was intentional. Some large herds would be driven in and would go back."

Owen says he was trying to avoid problems by issuing the order Knight carried into Red's Store the day St. John was killed. And he reminds everyone that he has a larger stick to employ, if needed. "I didn't want to have any conflict among the cow men and the Indian Police," he tells the courtroom. "I had two troops of cavalry in case I had any conflict . . . I was desirous of getting along without any trouble."

This information enables Sandels, during Owen's cross-examination, to highlight the fact that St. John was working for a legitimate roundup of Texas cattle when he was killed. The prosecutor does this in a patronizing way meant to convey that Owen has no idea what cowboys do, even as he tries to police them. "Don't you know it to be a fact in driving a large herd of cattle that some drop out and some will stray?"

"Yes, sir."

"Cow men sometimes gather up those that strayed from the herd in transit that are not illegally held," Sandels lectures. "Your order was to expel cattle *illegally* held."

"Yes, sir."

If Owen's appearance is a partial win for the defense, or at least a draw, the second gambit with a witness doesn't go as well. One cornerstone of the defense is Albert St. John's label as a suspected cattle thief, as bestowed on him by the Cherokee Strip Live Stock Association. To hammer this home, the defense calls John Blair, the association's treasurer. Like many mundane professions on the frontier, this includes more action than the title implies. Part of his job description includes being sent into the field to investigate illegal cattle intrusions and thefts.[43]

Blair just begins his testimony when he admits that he never knew St. John directly, but can speak to his reputation. The prosecuting team, which today includes W. H. Clayton, the U.S. attorney in Parker's court since 1874, use the admission to quickly derail the proceedings. Sandels

---

43 William Savage, *The Cherokee Strip Live Stock Association* (Norman: University of Oklahoma Press, 1979).

insists that Blair state where Albert St. John lived, to confirm he was speaking of the same man. He can't.

Sandels then objects to the man testifying at all, leading to a long legal argument before the judge. Parker agrees that "the weakness of the proposition lies in the fact of his being unable to show that it is the same man." When the defense team tries to work around this—"Did you know of any other St. John in that country?"—Parker shoots them down.

"If you have any other evidence, you had better produce it first," the judge says, and the defense team sits down. The cross-examination is brief and devastating:

"You say he was working down there on the Strip?"

"Yes, sir."

"How did you know it?"

"Responsible parties told me."

"Well, you don't know it."

"No sir, just what the cow men told me."

"You have no knowledge at all."

"No, sir. I never saw the man, of my knowledge, in my life."

It will be up to James McCormack, a Cherokee Strip cattleman who worked in Big Cottonwood, Oklahoma, before moving to Indian Territories in 1885. This witness knew St. John personally; he fired him from a job in April 1884. As it turns out, the cattle boss also released Obadiah Love "some time after I discharged St. John."

"State whether or not his reputation in the Oklahoma country and this Cherokee Strip was regarded as being dangerous, lawless and overbearing," Barnes begins.

"He was considered that all over the country," McCormack says. "That is what I discharged him for. That and other reasons. Good parties came to me and told me about it."

Details of the St. John/McCormack relationship don't emerge until the cross-examination, which again gut-punches the defense. "Did you ever know in your life of his being behind any trouble?" Sandels asks.

"No sir, nothing serious, but I hadn't seen him for six months before he was killed," McCormack says.

The U.S. attorney then presses him on the reports that prompted St. John's dismissal, made by two men whom the court reporter can't quite catch ("Havort and Gilroy"). The exchange becomes ugly. "You discharged him because these men told you he was a dangerous man to have about, that he was branding cattle."

"Yes sir."

"And upon the strength of *that* you come upon the stand and swear that he was a desperate and dangerous man, that's it, ain't it?" McCormack just sits there, as if stunned. "You are getting now like your old mules up there, you are getting the studs.[44] I wish you'd answer my question."

"I don't think he can ask the same question three or four times," Barnes butts in.

"This is not the question," says Parker, and Clayton continues. "And upon the strength of that you come to the stand and swear he was a dangerous and desperate man?"

"That and what I have seen myself," the affronted cattleman says.

"Now, Your Honor, I would like to exclude the whole of this man's evidence," Clayton proclaims.

Barnes leaps in with a couple of questions reminding the court that McCormack has already said that other parties, not just the pair that Clayton is going on about, had complained about St. John. "Do you consider that competent?" the U.S. attorney sneers at Barnes.

"Yes, sir."

"No, you don't," Clayton snaps.

The argument bounces like a three-way tennis match, with both sides questioning McCormack over how he knew St. John was a bad apple. "I have heard different ones speak about it," he says at one point. "That he would shoot anyone that took his cattle."

---

44 Slang for when mules stubbornly refuse to plow any further. Who can blame them?

Barnes soon loses the battle over the "dangerous and desperate" label when Judge Parker finally declares that the witness "doesn't seem to have any knowledge of that trait of character at all." McCormack's testimony ends with an admission that "I didn't hear them speak about him killing anyone." After that, Clayton again asks for the testimony to be excluded. "I will qualify it when I get to the jury," Parker says.

The character assassination gambit has backfired on the defense team. The prosecutors have managed to throw doubt over the sanctity of the association's cow-thief label. It's a tough way to end the trial. The taste of this courtroom defeat lingers as the three defendants wait for the verdict. It's not long coming.

On July 26, 1887, the jury emerges from their side room and sits solemnly in the courtroom. Dave Blair, the foreman, stands. The room is silent as he reads the decision: "On the charge of murder in the first degree: Not guilty. On the charge of manslaughter, we find all three guilty."

Parker has the three prisoners locked up in the Fort Smith jail until he can figure out what to do with them.

SUMMER IN SABINE
July 27, 1887

The summer of 1887 is a scorcher for most of Texas, but Sabine County, like the coastal counties along the Gulf, are spared unusual highs. It's just the usual steamy, muggy season.

The Rangers are gone, and the Conner family remain in their Sabine County refuge. The outlaw family has taken losses and remains hunted, but they have faced Texas's best and survived. They aren't going anywhere; at least, most of them aren't.

Anyone who doesn't know this from word of mouth can pick up *The Jasper Weekly Newsboy* newspaper and read the latest dispatch: "The old man and Fed Conner have been seen recently but John was not with them. When asked where John was the old man said he was away on business. Old Mrs. Conner and her daughter say John is dead. There are some circumstances connected with that report that he is dead that make some believe it. One is that he is well known to have been sick a few weeks ago . . . Another report is that John was wounded in the fight with the Rangers from which wound he died."[45]

John isn't dead, but he *is* gone. He flees Sabine County with his father's blessing, heading down the Sabine River to southern Newton County, to the inhospitable barrens Texans and Louisianans call the Devil's Pocket. He builds lean-tos, stalks fish and deer for food, and keeps his Winchester rifle close at hand. It's the start of a long, hard life as a fugitive.[46]

Confirmation of the time of John's flight directly from the family is interesting enough to appreciate *The Newsboy*'s untitled item, but the role of his mother and sister lying about his death is also instructive. The Conners will use any tactic to survive the onslaught against them, and public misinformation has certainly become part of the tool kit.

They use media, but when it comes to public perception, the Conners consistently get the worst of it. The newspapers are still railing against the family, painting them in consistently dastardly terms. *The Newsboy* sums up the local media's hopeful opinion in late July: "Perhaps they will all die this summer."[47]

---

45 *Jasper Newsboy,* July 27, 1887.

46 Dugan, *Judge Not,* quoting a letter sent to author Joe Combs from the Reverend Murray Burr, who lived in the Big Thicket and whose grandfather knew John Conner, albeit under an assumed name. More on that later.

47 *Jasper Newsboy,* July 27, 1887.

7

DESPERATE DEEDS

ROGERS IN CHARGE
July 1887

Company F has been in San Angelo since early July, protecting a controversial state's witness from mobs, chasing area criminals, and enduring
this summer's unusually high temperatures. Its captain, William Scott,
needs breaks for his health, but his Rangers can't slow their pace just for
him. Without Brooks available, someone else has to step up. That man
is Private John Rogers.

He's a very different person from both his superiors, being a more
pious and restrained Presbyterian, and a teetotaler on top of that, one
who is coming to believe the root of most crimes is alcohol. But the
"Praying Ranger" shares Scott's and Brooks's lack of swagger and the
implicit belief that truly tough men don't have to advertise. They just act
when needed. "He has never courted the reputation of being a 'dangerous man,' rather preferring to be recognized as an efficient officer and a
Christian gentleman," the *El Paso Herald* describes him.[1]

It'll be his task to keep Company F moving forward. Performance is
a matter of survival, with budget cuts already imposed and more coming,
so this is not the time for any Ranger company to go idle. When orders

---

1 "The Man who Knows No Fear Retires," *El Paso Herald,* February 4, 1911.

come to tamp down potential violence surrounding an impending election in Cisco, Rogers oversees the move. He has the benefit of Scott's reliable teamster, James Johnson, to help coordinate the logistics. Company F rides out for a new home outside the Cisco city limits. The vote proceeds peacefully, but just afterward, Callahan County cattle rancher John Wilson reports eight head stolen, so Rogers takes Newton and Kid Rogers on a search.

On August 4, just after they get back from that fruitless manhunt, news arrives from Brown County of fresh grand jury indictments for the attempted murder of their informant, Joe Copeland. The mule-thwarted assassination is still winding through the courts. So, it's back to Brownwood, where Rogers's depleted Company F rounds up men and crosses their names off the indictment list. They bring in familiar faces like Bob Parrock, Ace Mathews, and Wood Runnels. None put up a fight.

By the time Scott returns later in August, Rogers has run Company F as its de facto captain for months. He's handled some tricky logistics, ordered men into harm's way, performed in the field, handled local diplomacy, and gotten everyone paid. And he writes out Ranger pay records much neater than his captain or lieutenant.

Rogers is proving that he can lead.

PARDON POLITICS
July 28, 1887

It takes some willpower for J. A. Brooks to walk casually as he steps out of the jail underneath the courthouse at Fort Smith. What he wants to do is run screaming from that dank, disgusting hole and drink until he forgets he was ever inside. It's taken two sweltering days for Judge Isaac Parker to release him, Knight, and Putz. The time stretched for an eternity.

Until the court imprisoned him, Brooks couldn't accept the idea of himself as guilty. Now he's been locked up among criminals. Is that what he is, after all these years of hard service, just a drunk and a killer? It's a nadir for the proud, stoic man.

J. A. Brooks isn't a Texas Ranger anymore. That sickening fact settles on him like a hangover. Resigning from the Frontier Battalion is necessary upon the court's conviction. He thinks of Henry Putz and clenches his jaw; the former Ranger already quit and doesn't have to suffer the humiliation of being drummed out.

Brooks finds little solace in his Company F companion. In fact, he blames Putz for antagonizing the district attorney and jury. "Brooks says that their conviction was due to the impudent talk and actions at Ft. Smith of ex-Ranger Putz," Scott writes in a letter to fellow captain and Frontier Battalion quartermaster Liam Sieker.[2] But if Putz shot first and landed them all in this mess, as witnesses testified, Brooks never says so—on the stand or afterward.

Parker is holding three hot potatoes with this verdict. His instinct, based on his comments in court and overall disposition, is to favor the lawmen and suspend the sentence, but that holds obvious political risk from Arkansas. Until he knows how to help, the judge can at least rescue them from the ignominy of his wretched jail. He stashes them back at the marshal's home for another term of house arrest.

The defense team isn't done fighting. Their tactic now focuses on the White House. Defense Attorney Barnes immediately begins work on an application for the presidential pardon of Knight, Brooks, and Putz. Kentucky is the first to rise in defense of their native son. Kentucky representative W. C. Breckinridge vouches for Brooks in a letter to Washington, D.C., on August 8, and Kentucky Democrat John Carlisle follows the day after.

Captain William Scott isn't content to sit back as his man languishes. By August 6, he's asking Sieker "to assist me in getting up a document in Brooks' behalf to be sent to the president asking a pardon . . . the Judge will not sentence the boys until they can hear from the President on their case." Scott's determination comes with a plea and a character reference:

---

2 "William Scott to Liam Sieker," August 6, 1887, official correspondence.

"Please do all you can for Brooks. He is a perfect gentleman and has always made a first class soldier."[3]

The Frontier Battalion as an organization backs their man, as does the governor shortly after. On August 12, Ross writes the White House: "I respectfully recommend the pardon of the two Texas Rangers Brooks and Putz."

That day, Texas congressman Joseph Sayers goes one step further and sends a telegram from a train station to President Cleveland directly, urging the immediate pardon of Brooks: "I personally know him to be an honest, sober and law abiding citizen and a faithful and fearless official." Richard Coke, former Texas governor and U.S. senator, chimes in from Waco on August 27: "Great sympathy is felt in Texas for these young men. They are excellent men and fine officers. They could have refused to have come to Lt. Knight's assistance."[4]

The pressure campaign snowballs. The telegraph and rail-sped mail service spreads word of Brooks's plight across the state and into the Indian Territories. The groundswell effort generates two dozen petitions from Indian Territory and Texas townships, garnering more than seven hundred signatures.

The application, letters, and telegrams land on the desk of none other than Attorney General Augustus Garland, the man who refused to pay for Knight's defense. He's the gatekeeper for any pardons that reach the president and takes a personal interest in such cases; President

---

3 Ibid.

4 "Request for Pardon of J. A. Brooks," August 8, 1887. The details and time line are courtesy of Paul Spellman's tracking of the pardon process in *Captain J. A. Brooks, Texas Ranger* (Denton: University of North Texas Press, 2007). COVID-19 closed NARA offices in Fort Worth, so the documents were unobtainable in time for publication.

Andrew Johnson famously pardoned him for his role in the Confederate Congress.[5]

"Every application for pardon addressed to the President is referred to the Attorney General and by him to the clerk of pardons for his prompt and appropriate attention," clerk of pardons Alexander Boteler reports to Congress in 1887. The clerk of pardons then solicits views from U.S. attorneys and judges, seeking any information that can sway the case, and returns "an impartial representation" to the attorney general, who then decides whether or not to send it to Cleveland with a recommendation.

Boteler receives seemingly new information that was not presented in court. Indian agent Owen transmits the affidavit of Ridge Whitlock, the storekeeper eyewitness to the St. John killing who didn't appear at the trial. "It is my opinion and belief that Knight was in danger before he ever fired a shot," Whitlock says.[6]

When Garland sees the letters and affidavit, he decides the case bears presidential scrutiny and passes the bundle to his boss, President Grover Cleveland. About three hundred such pardon petitions are sent to Cleveland each year, but getting past his attorney general is no guarantee that he will sign one.[7]

Put on a scale with all other presidents, Cleveland is on the higher end of total pardons issued, with more than one thousand during his tenure. They include purely political examples, like forgiving Mormons for bigamy charges to help secure Utah as a state, and more personal ones, like commuting a sentence because of the pain caused to the in-

---

5 The Republicans, contrary to Lincoln's policy, intended to prevent political activity of ex-Confederates by requiring all voters and officials to swear they had never supported the Confederacy. Garland challenged these "Ironclad Oaths" in court and prevailed.

6 "Request for Pardon of J. A. Brooks," August 8, 1887.

7 Margaret Colgate Love, "The Twilight of the Pardon Power," *Journal of Criminal Law & Criminology* 100, no. 3 (2010).

mate's wife and children. He has a keen eye for commuting sentences of murders that were not done with premeditation—federal murder charges didn't have degrees, leading to some painfully unjust sentences that could have been ruled more lenient.

Cleveland first eyes the St. John case through a lens of fairness. It does appear to him that Brooks and the others were doing their duty and defending themselves when they shot St. John. The new affidavit seems to buttress that argument.

Then there is the political lens. This is only six months into his first-term as president of the United States, and he's being presented an easy way to curry favor with two states' congressional delegations and a wildly popular Democratic governor, as well. He's the first Democratic president since the Civil War, and party support is paramount. But the move also must jibe with the message of his administration when it comes to the Indian Territories.

There, things are a little more complex. He favors integration over reservations for what he considers humane reasons, but his moves will destroy the sovereignty of the Native Americans he aims to assimilate. That February, he signs the Dawes Act, which authorizes the division of some land into allotments for individual Indians. Those who accept acreage and live separately from their tribes for twenty-five years will be granted U.S. citizenship. The remaining land is declared "surplus" and sold to white settlers. It's the first step in a process that will by 1934 consume ninety million acres of Indian land, two-thirds of what Indians control in 1887.[8]

Cleveland is also an ardent opponent of illegal settlement, which puts him in alliance with the efforts of tribal officials—and the Cherokee Strip Live Stock Association—to safeguard their lands against incursion.

8 Alysa Landry, "Grover Cleveland: Pushed Land Ownership as a Way to 'Civilize' Indians," *Indian Country Today,* May 31, 2016, https://indiancountrytoday.com /archive/grover-cleveland-pushed-land-ownership-as-a-way-to-civilize-indians-J _a0BOFmy0ipa6C1jAmsMA.

Nine days after he takes office, Cleveland issues a proclamation specifically prohibiting non-Indian settlement of Indian territory. He needs law
and order to prevail there if his assimilation plans are to unfold smoothly.
Backing the Texas Rangers in this shooting seems a risk-free way to
send that message to intruding cattlemen and unwelcome settlers in the
Indian Territories.

By late August, Judge Parker now sees which way the political winds
are blowing and can safely make his move. He calls the men back into his
court and announces his suspension of all sentences, effective immediately.

The three men shake hands and go their separate ways. Lieutenant
Thomas Knight returns to Fort Sill, Henry Putz goes home to Dallas,
and Brooks goes to Cisco to visit his recuperating captain before rejoining his surrogate family in Company F.

The three men's fates have been linked together, for better or worse,
for nearly two years. They've ridden the trail, shot a man, endured house
arrest, faced a trial, and shared incarceration in the grim jailhouse, all
together. Yet they are not destined to be friends or even acquaintances
later in life. The closest thing to nostalgia comes from T. R. Knight, who
keeps two photos of the Rangers in his personal collection. The photos
are taken in a studio in Brownwood; the Rangers must have given the
Indian agent the photos as mementos after the trial.[9]

On September 13, while they're on the road, Cleveland signs the
pardons of the three men. Brooks's reads:

> Whereas, at the May term, 1887, of the United States District
> Court for the Western District of Arkansas, J. A. Brooks was
> convicted of manslaughter, his sentence being suspended; And
> whereas, it appears that the homicide of which he was convicted,
> was the result of rashness while assisting an officer in the dis-
> charge of his duty, rather than of malice or criminal intent; And

---

9 Thomas Rogers Knight dies on December 6, 1895, and is buried in Fairview Cemetery, Vinita, OK.

whereas, his pardon is asked for by a number of the most respectable citizens of the region where the killing occurred, and also by influential gentlemen in other parts of the country. Now, therefore, be it known, that I, Grover Cleveland, President of the United States of America, in consideration of the premises, divers other good and sufficient reasons thereunto moving, do hereby grant to the said J. A. Brooks, a full and unconditional pardon.

It's not really official until the paperwork is filed. The attorney general prepares a pardon warrant, which is copied at the State Department, signed by the president, and forwarded to the pardon clerk for delivery to the three men.

Brooks finds his pardon waiting when he arrives in Runnels County to reunite with Company F on September 15. J. A. Brooks reenlists in the Frontier Battalion five days later. His world has settled back on its axis. He's a Texas Ranger again.

LOGGINS'S NEW LIFE
September 23, 1887

It's another happy walk down the aisle for L. L. Loggins. Under the guise of R. P. Wright, this time he's marrying Alice White, a farmer's daughter, at the ritzy Gill House in Searcy, Arkansas.[10]

"This is quite a surprise to the doctor's many Little Rock friends as they had no idea of his intentions regarding matrimony," notes *The Arkansas Democrat* on September 26, 1887. "However, they wish for him and his bride a happy voyage through life."[11] It's a biting if politely veiled comment. Wright has apparently forgotten about the Little Rock woman to whom he's already engaged.

---

10 The Arkansas Historic Preservation Program states Gill House was built in 1882. It was replaced on the same spot by the more famous Mayfair Hotel in 1924.

11 "Married," *Arkansas Democrat*, September 26, 1887.

There have been quite a few life changes for "Wright," enough so that someone familiar with his true identity might be suspicious.

It began the year before, when a woman arrives in Little Rock "claiming to be his ex-wife in from Texas," as he explains to friends. This is no ex-wife; it's current wife Mollie Loggins. He takes her in and charms her as best as he's able, somehow convincing her to leave town without ratting him out. It's not clear how she found him.

Rumors in Little Rock circulate about the woman who moved in with him and then vanished. "Whispers of the strange circumstance went out, but he confronted all with a plausible story and the circumstance was soon forgotten," says *The Arkansas Democrat* in a later profile of their employee.[12]

But her visit is enough to prompt him to start planning to leave Little Rock and the unnamed fiancée there that he's courting. Loggins sells his property—news of the real estate deal appear days after his new marriage, recording that he sold a $740 piece of property to someone named W. Coleman. Just before the surprise wedding, he also leaves his newspaper job at *The Democrat*.

News of the unexpected nuptials reaches Little Rock from Searcy, which is close to Jacksonville, as the couple honeymoons. "After the wedding they returned to the home of the bride for a few days," adds *The Arkansas Democrat*.

What his friends thought was a courtship in Searcy becomes more permanent. "He purchased a horse, some drugs and general equipment and accordingly moved to a settlement five miles beyond Jacksonville and began practice of his profession," *The Democrat* will write two years later. "He had told several friends in the city that he intended to run for the legislature from that section of the county."[13]

Damage from the chaos he helped inspire in Sabine County continues to mount. The same day Loggins is married, jailbreaker Sam Swan

---

12 *Arkansas Democrat*, July 21, 1888.

13 Ibid.

is sent to Rusk Penitentiary, having been sentenced to two years. His relative and jailbreaking accomplice Jim Sanders is languishing in Rusk prison. He dies there on August 10, 1887, only thirty-three years old.[14]

Loggins seems to have pulled out of harm's way yet again. But things in Little Rock may be unraveling for him; he's been recognized and doesn't know it. "A gentleman of this city who became acquainted with Wright in 1882, recognized him in this city last fall," reads the *Daily Arkansas Gazette*. "And being aware that he was wanted in Texas, began an investigation of the case, Sheriff Worthen lending his assistance."[15]

Now there are two guillotine blades over R. P. Wright, one in the shape of Mollie, whom he naively thinks is under control, and the other being this investigation in Little Rock that he doesn't even know about.

He's busy with his medical practice and political ambitions, but Loggins can't leave rabble-rousing column writing alone. He pens a notable item for the *Arkansas Methodist* newspaper that accuses Christians of "unwittingly spreading the doctrines of spiritualism" in Sunday school books. Spiritualism, the bigamist concludes, is equated with the scourge of "free love."[16]

BALLINGER BLUES
September 29, 1887

When word comes that a stagecoach has been robbed by the Lone Highwayman outside San Angelo, less than thirty miles away from Cisco, Company F are the logical Rangers to respond.

Scott decides someone will travel to Ballinger in advance of the

---

14 Texas Inmate Records, Texas State Archives, Austin, TX.

15 "The Journalistic Bigamist," *Arkansas Gazette*, July 21, 1888.

16 Allie Lindsay Lynch, "Letter from the People," *Daily Arkansas Gazette*, February 3, 1888. In it, Searcy resident Lynch rebukes Wright for hypocrisy when his bigamy becomes exposed.

rest as a scout and a spy. He selects Carmichael to go undercover as a cowboy—no big stretch there—to see if he can dig up any information on the serial thief. He rides out alone, heading on an undercover mission in true Ira Aten style.

Ever since the shoot-out with the Conners, Scott's respect for Carmichael has deepened. He relies on him during tough assignments in a similar way he does Rogers and Brooks and seems to appreciate having him close by during any potentially dangerous situation.[17]

Ballinger, according to the state of Texas historians, attracts "a crowd of drifters, fugitives, gamblers, and ruffians to the town's nine saloons and gambling halls." The Gulf, Colorado and Santa Fe Railway town, named after one of the railroad company's trustees, is barely a year old. New towns like this one are springing up as the rails move west, repeating a cycle of lawlessness, conflict, and settlement. For now, it's a mess.

One thing the Runnels County boomtown doesn't have is a train connection. In fact, the railroad company is the one selling lots in Ballinger and running ads in big Texas city newspapers to entice people to live there. They want to create a population center so they can run a profitable rail line to service it.

It's working—the rail line is scheduled to open next year. Until then, Ballinger is reliant on stagecoaches to connect it with the nearest city, San Angelo. And these small vehicles make tasty targets for thieves. A rash of robberies there in 1884 ended with shootings, arrests, and army escorts. Now a lone thief has the county in a new uproar.

Company F leaves Cisco for Ballinger. Toward the end of the thirty-mile ride, the Rangers pass a posse led by the Sheriff John Formwalt on the road. They've been hunting the stagecoach robber and even have a prisoner in tow. When Scott scans the man's face, he sees it's his private, Frank Carmichael. The sheriff had arrested Carmichael for being a sus-

---

17 Ibid. "On another occasion [Scott] and Carmichael—who for some reason was his right-hand man—were instructed to pick up a man wanted for murder."

piciously well-armed cowboy with no legitimate business in the county—
just the profile of the Lone Highwayman.

Scott plays it cool. If his private isn't revealing his identity, neither
will he. It's true that nothing would get him closer to the actual criminals
than being treated like one, but Carmichael is in real danger here. "The
Rangers paid no attention to Carmichael until Scott casually asked the
sheriff about the prisoner, then asked to be allowed to talk to him," reads
one newspaper account. "They drew to one side, pretended that neither
had ever seen the other. Then Scott went back to the sheriff and told him
that he doubted if the prisoner has anything to do with the robberies."[18]

Carmichael is released without breaking cover. Scott can't help but admire his dedication. Nevertheless, he frees him from his undercover assignment and orders him to scout closer to San Angelo and seek signs or sightings
of the robber along the Concho River. Carmichael finds and follows a trail
before a rendezvous with Company F in San Angelo on October 5.

Three days later, the highwayman strikes again. The MO is the same:
passengers lined up, blindfolded, and mail satchels rifled. Company F is
alerted to the robbery at first light on October 9 and is eager to pounce.

But in what direction? Carmichael is advising Scott to head to the
mouth of the Concho River, south of San Angelo, where the trail he
followed ended at a ranch. Scott hedges his bets and divides his forces.
Brooks is to head north with local law, while Rogers and Carmichael
look to the south.

Rogers and Carmichael are heading out of town when locals tell
them that a horse thief named George Bright is lurking nearby. It's too
great an opportunity to pass up, and the pair change course to check out
the report. They see a solitary man lounging under a copse of trees along
the Concho River.

The man stands as Rogers approaches, and the Ranger sees a pistol
on his belt. Time slows, and his perceptions narrow. *God, give me strength*

---

18 "Blood Curdling Days of '80s as Ranger Live in Memories of Abelian," *Abilene
Reporter-News*, June 12, 1938.

for what comes next. Rogers announces his identity, knowing this will be the moment of decision.

Bright pulls his pistol, but by the time it clears the holster, Rogers has already fired a single shot that drops Bright into the dirt. Rogers approaches cautiously, ears ringing. The man writhes, wounded but alive. After getting a quick field dressing, Bright makes the uncomfortable trip to the Tom Green County jail in Ranger custody.[19]

While this unexpected confrontation is underway, Brooks meets up with Formwalt, Carmichael's former captor, and the pair look up local contacts. "Well, the robber, Jim Newsom, made the mistake of his life when he flashed a $100 bill in front of a friend of mine the night after the robbery," Brooks recalls. "John M. Formwalt, the sheriff of Runnels County, and I were soon on the trail of the marked $100 bill."[20]

Now they have a suspect. Newsom is from a place called Vingaroon, as wild as its name. The place only exists because the Southern Pacific Railroad is laying track along a nearby stretch of the Devil's River and they need a place to serve as a headquarters. Naturally, a tent city has sprung up to fleece those whom the *Fort Worth Daily Gazette* call "the riff raff of blacklegs and railroad men" working on the line. "The gamblers and the lawless coyotes of the frontier were the only ones besides the saloon men who has any money a week after the monthly pay day," the newspaper notes. "There was more shouting lawlessness to the square inch in that town than anywhere else in the country."[21]

Vingaroon's largest tent belongs to Newsom, who operates a saloon and dance house. What attracts local admiration is his role as judge of a

---

19 "Man Who Knows No Fear Retires," *El Paso Herald.*

20 From Brooks's handwritten journal, available at the Texas Ranger Hall of Fame and Museum. Mention of a "marked" bill is not included in any available court document or news report.

21 *Fort Worth Daily Gazette,* April 22 ,1888.

kangaroo court that not only collects fines from transgressors (tab skippers, sellers of bad liquor, violent drunks) but also orders them chained to stakes. Judgments are enforced by his hulking bartender and his own notoriety as a good shot. Both he and his unofficial deputy earn respect when it's their turn to be chained to the stake for public drunkenness.

The tent city's experiment in self-governance ends when the county tax collector arrives with a squad of Rangers to collect the money he's gathered in fines. When they get there, Newsom has fled Vingaroon with friends to find their futures elsewhere.

Formwalt soon learns Newsom and a partner recently bought a herd of horses. That's an easy trail to follow, and the two lawmen set out after the suspects. "We located the horses about 35 miles south of Ballinger," Brooks says. "Newsom and his partner were at Coleman, Texas, waiting for Newsom's partner to go to trial for horse theft."

They arrive in the dead of night and head to the only hotel. They ask the manager to set down a pallet in the same room as Newsom. The manager obliges, only to watch the two men pull pistols on his guests when the door opens.

But the case against Jim Newsom is not as ironclad as Brooks makes out when he later says in his memoirs that "the final result was a 99-year sentence in the federal penitentiary." Newsom has left many supporters in his wake, and they don't think he's the Lone Highwayman type. Newspapers soon report that a dozen witnesses place him at a rodeo forty-five miles away during one of the robberies. "Not one out of fifty of our citizens ever believed that Jim Newsom was the guilty party," says a dispatch from Ballinger in the *Fort Worth Daily Gazette*.[22]

Newsom, who maintains his innocence in a Waco federal courtroom despite Brooks's later comment that he confessed, is shipped to a New York prison for the rest of his life. But his story doesn't end there.

---

22 Ibid.

SETTLING DOWN WITH JOSIE
October 13, 1887

It's official—things are out of control in Callahan County. Today, Judge
W. E. Bentley is asking for Frontier Battalion protection as mobs throng
his courthouse. Adjutant General Wilburn King dispatches Company F.

Just after they arrive in the town of Baird, a telegram arrives for Private J. Allen Newton. It's an offer from T. L. Jones, an agent for Leon &
H. Blum Co. This is a sprawling firm (with offices in Paris and London,
even) that happens to be Galveston's leading importer and wholesale
dealer of dry goods. Jones is looking for someone to buy out a business
in Jacksonville and run it for a salary of one hundred dollars a month.

Now Newton is in a bind. He's already enlisted for a second year of
duty with the Rangers that hasn't ended, so he'll need Scott's permission
to quit early. Any sign of disappointment from his tough, loyal captain
would be too painful to bear. Deep down, he knows that the effects of
the shoot-out have not left him; seeing Moore and the others mowed
down has left him "scared." He admits this, years later, summing up his
feelings after the shooting: "I wanted to go home."[23]

The offer tempts him beyond the promise of safety. "I hated to leave
the boys, but it was about time I thought of making some money for
myself," he'll explain. "Besides, I had missed Josie."[24]

Newton's childhood love is still on his mind. The violence and chaos
of Ranger life stands in stark contrast to his dreams of living sedately
as Josie Gossett's husband—and the torture he imagines if she were to
marry someone else.

Newton's conversation with Scott goes better than he expects. Only

---

23 "One Ranger Admits Truth: He Was Scared," *Coleman Democrat-Voice*, June 23,
    1938. In the article, he claims he stayed with the Rangers despite his feelings, but
    his service records don't support this. After a lifetime, he's still guilty about leaving
    Company F early.

24 "Coleman Host to Ex-Rangers," *Fort Worth Star Telegram*, June 16, 1938.

fully committed Rangers can be counted on, so it's safer and easier to allow quitters to leave. "He said if I really wanted to go, he'd let me," Newton says. "And he would even sell my outfit to the next recruit."

As it turns out, Scott may have a soft spot for lovelorn men seeking to leave the Frontier Battalion. His quietest thoughts are not too dissimilar. The fresh scars on his chest and back drive home the risks, and his private's choice to leave is a reminder of the rewards of the life beyond manhunting.

Newton returns to Jacksonville with epic stories of midnight shootouts and hair-raising rides on the trail. He also has a solid job and enough reputation to woo one of Jacksonville's most eligible women. His courtship of Josie resumes, their quarrel long forgotten. They'll marry within a year and a half.

NANCY, FED, AND MILTON
October 1887

Nancy Conner, Fed's wife, thought things would get easier once the Rangers left Sabine County. And they have—leaving the county means an end to the midnight rousts by lawmen and returned most of the men of Hemphill to their homes, instead of traipsing around southern Sabine with rifles. But the Conner family is still wanted, with state rewards on their heads.

Her fugitive husband is unable to work his land without donning ridiculous disguises. She's seen him going so far as to wear her clothes in order to labor outside in the daylight, but he simply cannot provide and stay safe at the same time. It's the other way around—she had to save money to buy Fed and Willis a mule to replace the one the Rangers killed.[25]

As Nancy's desperation grows, she finds Milton Anthony is still willing to help her. The young man can't help but respond to a woman in distress. And this still angers Nancy's sister Docia. There is jealousy

---

25 Mark Dugan, *Judge Not* (unpublished, 1982), quoting an interview with Nancy Conner's grandson.

here that could hint at a growing attachment between the two or simply be based on claims on Milton's time.

Having Docia mad at her is bad. What's worse for Nancy is the way Fed is showing his displeasure. He holds Milton Anthony responsible for the raid on the Conner camp that killed William and drove John from the county. After all, he alone knew where the family was camped, since he had been hunting with them that night. No newspapers place him at the scene, but the Conners certainly regard the young man as a traitor—and one who has a habit of hanging around Fed's home to spend time with his wife.

Milton Anthony is working with Nancy in a field on the Conner homestead when movement catches her eye: two figures on the edge of the field, aiming rifles in the young man's direction. She can recognize her husband and father-in-law. Nancy Conner quickly hustles Milton Anthony away, not telling him what she saw until he's outside of her husband's gunsight.

Fed visits her soon after and delivers an ultimatum to pass along to his brother-in-law: Leave Sabine County. The younger man's inclination is to flee, but his father pressures him to hold fast. And when the old soldier speaks, Milton listens.

One day after Fed's threat, Milton Anthony's daughter catches ill. This is when the location of Hemphill comes in handy—it's only eleven miles to Toole's store to buy medicine, instead of sixteen miles to Milam. He's riding through the woods near his house when a sudden crack splits the air. At the same time, something snatches the hat from his head with a violent tug. It takes a moment for him to realize that he's been shot at. He spurs the horse forward and flees for town.[26]

Hearing this later, his father is infuriated and scared, two things the vet can't abide. Thomas Anthony knows the importance of initiative, and they need to regain it. It's time for the men of southern Sabine County to do what the Rangers, the local law, and the Weatherred's "council of

---

26 Ibid., quoting Anthony descendants.

citizens" could not. They mean to put an end to the Conners and collect the state's reward while they're at it.

Instead of an extension of the law, this posse represents the law's absolute inability to put an end to the Conner-Smith feud. As ugly as it has been so far, the misshapen face of real frontier justice is about to show itself. The backwoodsmen, motivated by state reward money and emboldened by local edicts decreed on April 2 after the Ranger shoot-out, will now run their own manhunt. Neighbors and in-laws are turning into assassins.

Of all the family's foes in Hemphill and beyond, these men of southern Sabine pose the greatest threat. They know each trail and hummock nearly as well as the Conners, and they have the locals' knowledge of how the family and their supporters operate.

Some bring geographic knowledge. Dan McNaughten, a leader of a Citizen's Council bloc, has had it in for Fed and Willis Conner since finding the bodies at Holly Bottom. He has three children, part of an ever-growing family, and has close ties to the Low family. Their future may depend on ending the Conners right now.

Milton Anthony and Thomas B. Anthony are both armed and ready. They know the terrain and are very motivated hunters. Given the hole in young Milton's hat, it makes sense that they are out for blood.

The elder Anthony's age and combat experience make him the logical head of this South Sabine posse, but another name is publicly associated with driving events in the fall of 1887. The enigma here is a man named R. C. Turner.

Newspaper accounts of the events of late 1887 never divulge his first name beyond initials but call him the "leader" of the extrajudicial manhunt, or designate it "Turner's posse." Yet biographical information on the man is impossible to pin down. It's not clear if he's a private detective or an East Texas resident drawn to Sabine County over a personal connection or for the reward.

It seems unlikely that an outsider could come into deep East Texas and become a posse leader over men like Thomas B. Anthony. It's better to regard him as the *acknowledged* leader of the posse. The designation is not an honor. As the feud comes to a bloody climax, the locals who are involved will divorce their names from the media coverage, and Turner will take the heat for what happens. The real story is one Sabine County residents know but won't easily talk about.

Turner spends his fall in Sabine County, hunting for the Conners while in disguise. He coordinates with Thomas Anthony so a posse of gunmen can be ready if he uncovers any information. "For the past three months a man named Turner has been in the Conner neighborhood pretending to be a cattleman, but in reality spotting the Conners," one newspaper notes.[27] Spradley disparagingly calls him a "cow buyer sleuth who came into the locality . . . pussyfooting around."[28] Newton says he poses as "a sewing machine agent" to gain access to the Conner Community. He's clearly an outsider, able to engage in such subterfuge.

In the meantime, the men of southern Sabine have a plan of their own. There is a location they know of to spring a trap: a four-walled, wooden shelter owned by Isaac "Little Ike" Low.

Low's new life as a married man with Melissa is being upended by the feud. Like many in the county, he has changed his stance on the Conner family. He's been more than sympathetic, later in life admitting to supplying them with food after they broke out of jail.[29] Now he feels he must kill his brother-in-law, if only to save another brother-in-law.

---

27 "Another Bloody Fight," *Times-Picayune*, November 24, 1887.

28 Henry Fuller, *A Texas Sheriff: A. J. Spradley* (Whitefish, MT: Literary Licensing), originally published in 1931 by Baker Printing Co., Nacogdoches, TX. In *Judge Not*, author Mark Dugan's unpublished book about the feud, R. C. Turner is identified as Robert Turner from Jasper, but this man was born in 1902.

29 Ed Wetterman, "Ike Low and Melissa Travis," East Texas Generations, July 31, 2010, http://easttexasgenerations.blogspot.com/2010/07/ike-low-and-melissa-travis -122-and-123.html. "Jack Lowe stated that he remembered Ike, his grandfather, telling him about the feud, and that Ike had, despite his feelings toward the Conners, 'fed them some' while they were running from the law."

The Conners are showing up on the Lows' property, but the question is why. "For several days one Low has been cutting cane in a bottom field and camping in an old crib that stood on the corner of the field," according to an article in the *Times-Picayune*. "Since they have been at work there, two of the Conners, the old man and Fed, have been in the habit of coming up to the fence and talking to Low and often passed the house during the night."[30]

This can mean two things to a modern reader: The Conners are being threatening or friendly. Either way, by taking the same route and stopping to exchange words, the outlaws are lowering their guard.

In the words of Sabine County historian Weldon McDaniel, Fed and Willis Conner were "lured" to the scene by his neighbors. With Ike Low's admission that he's previously helped the outlaws, it makes sense that the Conners could feel safe around him. On the opposite end of the spectrum, a self-described Low descendent on a message board relates some oral history from the family, saying her grandfather maintained "the Conners did want to kill Little Ike."[31]

Yet the end result is the same—Low allows the posse to use his remote crib as the spot to ambush the Conners. Or, as the *Times-Picayune* will put it: "Turner decided to attack them as they passed the house."[32]

MAKE IT MY RULE
November 7, 1887

The Sabine County posse huddles quietly in the log-walled structure, cradling their shotguns and Winchesters, and has something to eat while they wait.

---

30 "Another Bloody Fight," *Times-Picayune*.

31 Shonnastinsonashley, "Anyone Familiar with Conner Feud in Sabine County?," City -Data.com, http://www.city-data.com/forum/texas/513955-anyone-familiar-conner -feud-sabine-county.html.

32 "Another Bloody Fight," *Times-Picayune*.

Just after sunset, just after the men are finishing supper, two shadows approach the cabin. The ambush party shifts inside the log house for a better vantage, peering through slats in the walls. Fed and Willis are approaching from the opposite direction they expect. The air inside the shack thickens with tension.

When the pair of wanted men cross in front of the log house, a dozen or so feet away, the posse springs the trap. Newspaper accounts say Turner called "Halt!" but if he did, the demand came from an unknown person hidden inside a building. Fed and Willis Conner are holding Winchesters, which promptly rise to their shoulders in surprise. Inside the hut, the booms of shotguns and rattling of lever-action rifles drown out the world.

Fed responds to the ambush the same way the Rangers did—by pouring return fire at the source of the shots. He must figure the closer he can get, the better the chance he can slip a rifle bullet through the log slats. "Fed replied with his Winchester, advancing and firing with every step," the *Times-Picayune* reports.[33]

Other reports at the time, which place the Conners closer to the house when the gunfire erupts, state Fed Conner is injured immediately. "At the first fire Fed Conner fell, not being more than 10 feet from the door of the little house. Being only wounded, he drew his pistol—a Colt Frontier—and continued to shoot until a bullet from a Winchester ended his life," reports *The Galveston Daily News*.[34]

Willis finds cover behind a stump, which saves his life, and begins to fire at the house with his own rifle. But he can also see Fed lying dead on the ground. "You've killed my boy!" he cries. Some reports say he also screams, "Stop shooting!" but he keeps peppering the wooden hut.

Thomas Anthony feels a burn across his scalp as a bullet creases it.

---

33 Ibid.

34 *Galveston Daily News*, November 11, 1887.

Blood flows, but it's a superficial injury. He jams his shotgun through the slats, pulls the trigger, and feels some of his own buckshot ricochet off the wood and rebound into his hand, clipping off the tip of one finger.

When the shooting pauses, Willis Conner dashes from the stump to the shelter of a pine tree. The posse's concentrated fire follows him, and a bullet smashes into his arm.[35] He lopes awkwardly off into the woods, followed by errant Winchester balls. "It is estimated that at least 50 shots were fired," says *The Galveston Daily News* of both sides' tally, a likely inflated number.[36]

Alone and seemingly injured, the self-appointed manhunters still fear the senior woodsman. "Our reporter says that at this junction the attacking party became frightened and ran off to the woods in an opposite direction from Old Man Conner," notes the *Times-Picayune*.[37]

The fight's over and Fed Conner has been vanquished, but the article's tone, likely mirroring the mood of Sabine County, is not celebratory. "The condition of old man Willis Conner is indeed desperate," the report ends. "Bowed down with the seventy-odd years, outlawed, three sons in the penitentiary, Bill and Fred shot down by his side, and John, it is said, left him. Pitiable indeed is the condition of this misguided but brave old man. What the end of this doomed old man may be or how bloody he may make the sequel to the already harrowing and bloody drama remains for time to reveal."[38]

It won't be long.

---

35 *Evening Star* (Washington, D.C.), November 14, 1887. "It is supposed his arm was broken, but he made good his escape."

36 Ibid.

37 "Another Bloody Fight," *Times-Picayune*.

38 Ibid.

"AN AFFAIR THAT WOULD BEAR HARSHER CRITICISM"
November 13, 1887

Willis Conner sits in the woods behind the home of John Williams, his son-in-law, and takes in the pine trees as he waits for dinner.

These deep, wet woods have always been home to him, from his youth in Georgia through the wild Florida years, and now here in East Texas. After all that's happened, he's still nestled within the Conner range, just a handful of miles from his sons' graves. One of them is fresh. The wound from the ambush throbs, but not as much as the memory of Fed, shot down in the night.

The Ener family, custodians of the Conner family memories, maintain Fed Conner was killed by Dan McNaughten immediately, having been caught completely unaware while standing in the doorway. Willis Conner says he then fled without firing a shot; the posse must have shot up the cabin to make it look like a two-way fight happened there.[39]

He's a bitter and haunted man, in pain that's deeper than just the gunshot through his arm. Willis Conner made a mark on this land, but it's been erased. They've taken his permanence away by destroying his sons. It's not his sins but his virtues that passed to his boys, and they paid for their fierce, passionate loyalty. Some offered their lives, others their freedom. How could they suffer such a steep price for defending their land and their family? What kind of state is Texas becoming?

The thoughts make the appearance of Thomas Williams, basket swinging in one hand, even more welcome. Willis Conner knows he's an added burden to his already struggling daughter, especially now that her husband's has been carted away, as the old man haunts the woods behind her home to receive these clandestine meals.

Thomas's appearance is a good reminder that his blood remains in Sabine County. Even if this particular youth has a different last name,

---

39 Dugan, *Judge Not*. Catherine is a more likely initial source of this version, since she had contact with her father after the ambush at Eli Low's.

he'll grow up remembering meeting his grandfather, cheerful and defiant, sheltered in the woodlands where the family belongs.

Old Man Conner raises his good hand in greeting and smiles. Then he sees the men approaching behind the boy. They're carrying guns. The posse has not given up on the remaining at-large Conner, pitiable though he may be. The quarry is wounded, winded, and alone. And still worth a $500 state reward.

We only have the "Turner posse" account of what happens next—at least publicly. No reporter lists the names of the posse members. Most newspaper accounts have Turner telling Willis Conner to surrender and yelling at the boy to clear off before the old man reaches for his rifle.[40]

Bullets may have a brief life, as measured from the time they leave the barrel, but during that fleeting time, they make some fateful choices. These are based on barely perceptible variations of geometry, physics, and environmental conditions. No adequate explanation can change the end result of the posse's volley on November 13—Willis Conner lies wounded and twelve-year-old Thomas lies shot dead beside him.

The posse advances cautiously. "The Turner party, advancing until within 15 feet, ordered old Willis to surrender," *The Galveston Daily News* reports. "He, continuing to try to shoot, was shot to death."[41]

J. Allen Newton offers another version that casts the posse in a more reckless light: "The old man was sitting up against a tree with his gun resting across his knees. Turner got so excited that he killed both the old man and the little boy. The old man's body remained upright leaning against the tree. The citizens were so afraid of him that they thought he was playing possum and wouldn't go near him."[42]

---

40 "The Conners Again," *Fort Worth Daily Gazette*, November 15, 1887.

41 "Fought to the Death," *Galveston Daily News*, November 15, 1887.

42 Sarah Ellen Davidge, "Texas Rangers Were Rough and Ready Fighters," *Frontier Times*, November 1935.

There are even darker versions bandied around deep East Texas. Sabine County historian Weldon McDaniel adds a specific name to the shooter of Thomas Williams—Dan McNaughten. His version features McNaughten gunning down Thomas Williams intentionally, after Willis was dead. "Still tongues don't talk," McNaughten is reputed to have said before pulling the shotgun's trigger. Whether this is apocrypha is subject to conjecture, but in the future, McNaughton will identify himself as the shooter of Thomas Williams at least two times, once to Dr. J. W. Smith.[43]

The death of Thomas Williams breaks the spell in Sabine County. The minute the boy's body hits the ground, the pendulum of public opinion begins to universally swing toward the outlaw family.

This is obvious to the posse members; the Sabine County residents don't want to be associated with these two shootings. In newspaper accounts, only one name is connected to the death of Willis Conner and his grandson—Turner.

Turner posse is a good pseudonym for media coverage, but when it comes to collecting the reward, the real leader emerges. Nine days after Willis's death, the State of Texas pays a $1,000 reward to "Thomas Anthony et al." through the receivership of attorney James Polley. It includes a bloodless line: "Consideration: Arrest (dead) Willis & Fred Connor."[44] This clearly puts Thomas Anthony as a member of the Turner posse that day, with son Milton Anthony likely there as well. Polley this time is just a middleman for the transaction, acting as an attorney instead of a shooter or plotter.

Willis Conner is buried in the family plot, close to Fed, William,

---

43 Weldon McDaniel, interview with author, and Dugan, *Judge Not*, which also cites Norman Ener (recalling what his father, Bob Ener, told him) as the source that identifies McNaughten as a child killer.

44 General Warrant Register 1887–1889, Comptroller's Record Group, p. 69, warrant number 2917, Texas State Archives, Austin, TX. Thanks to archive staff for the research assistance.

and the dead children. "This breaks up the desperate gang of outlaws,"
The Galveston Daily News eulogizes. "Except John Conner, who deserted
them and fled the country last spring."[45] With him gone, there are no
remaining adult Conner males in Sabine County. But that won't be the
case for very long.

For a citizenry that was once dubbed "powerless" to stop the Conner
family, there is no rejoicing now that they are gone. In fact, it appears
the opposite is true. That's the case in Jasper, where R. C. Turner shows
up in early December "soliciting contributions to pay him for services in
exterminating that notorious family of outlaws."[46]

If Turner expects to be a hero, he's mistaken. Not only do people
fail to pony up, he feels insulted by the overall ungrateful attitude. "He
proceeded to give the place a general 'cussin' out', so we are informed,"
The Jasper Newsboy reports. "The people of Jasper County are ever ready
and willing to aid in bringing criminals to justice, but a large number,
if not a majority of our people are opposed to such heroic remedies for
ridding the country of even the most vicious criminals. It savors too
much of Judge Lynch and besides there was an innocent child killed in
this melee."

The article's coda damns all those involved: "When the county officers, who know the parties and all the facts, decline to take the responsibility of desperate measures, and outsiders with the hope of reward or the love
of glory proceed to execute the law in the woods, it is only natural for the
sober-minded people to be slow about paying for their desperate deeds."[47]

The Galveston Daily News reruns the *Newsboy* article. It's quite a
choice considering their years of steady, anti-Conner coverage. The

---

45 "Fought to the Death," *Galveston Daily News.*

46 *Galveston Daily News,* December 3, 1887. The earlier *Jasper Newsboy* article runs in
   full in this issue, with comments from local editors.

47 Ibid.

editors even start the reprint with an editorial note of their own: "The *Jasper Newsboy* deals gently with an affair that would bear harsher criticism."

With the outlaws gone, normalcy now becomes an immediate priority for Sabine County, as if the residents have a sudden hangover. No newspaperman digs too deeply into the details of Fed's and Willis's deaths. The whispers inside homesteads are swelling resident memories with details, and probable exaggerations, of the clashes. Government officials and public men are quietly voicing reservations after hearing how the backwoodsmen settled the Conner score and questioning if those in prison, like Charles Conner, should be there. Sheriff A. J. Spradley complains that the cordial family that he hosted in his jail were "simply hunted down like wild beasts."[48]

The groundswell in support of the Conners doesn't appear in many newspaper articles, but it grows nonetheless. This backpedaling reaches Austin, forwarded by Ross's men in Sabine County like William Weatherred, who are undoubtably encountering backlash for the ruthless way the Conners have finally been exterminated.

On November 22, a new missive comes from the governor's office. "Some considerable time ago rewards of $500 each were offered for Willis, Fred and John Conner, the Sabine County desperadoes," the *Austin American-Statesman* reports (even though John's reward was $300). "Since then, Willis and Fred have left this world, and John has reformed from his bad habits, though still a fugitive. Governor Ross, therefore, yesterday issued a proclamation reducing John's reward to $200."[49]

The bodies have all been buried, but the aftermath of the Conner feud in Sabine County is far from over.

---

48 Fuller, *A Texas Sheriff.*

49 *Austin American-Statesman,* November 23, 1887.

8

THE NEW SKYLINE

VOWS

December 13, 1887

Captain William Scott is dressed in his best duds as he heads to the station at Waelder, southeast of Austin in Gonzales County, arriving in time to meet the 2:00 p.m. train to San Antonio. The whistle signals the start of his new life with Georgia Lynch, who for several hours now has been his wife. Their wedding-day morning was marred by heavy rain, so they must avoid mud while heading into the depot.

Lynch, "the acknowledged belle of this place" according to the *Fort Worth Daily Gazette*'s unnamed correspondent in Waelder, turned nineteen years old last week. Now she's on the arm of the battle-scarred, thirty-five-year-old Ranger captain.[1]

Scott's brother, Jack, friend C. M. Smith, and bridesmaids Edie Hill and Minnie Miller board the train. They will ride with the newlyweds as far as San Antonio. After that, the rails will take the couple to Houston, Willis, and Dallas on a "wedding tour."[2]

---

1 Birthdays. His: June 17, 1854. Hers: December 6, 1869.

2 "Captain Scott Married," *Fort Worth Daily Gazette,* December 14, 1887. The article
  includes the weather and couple's travel itinerary.

Scott is eyeing his future, and Georgia Lynch is just one part of it. He's looking to start a family, and that will mean a better-paying job that's immune to budget cuts and incoming bullets. But he's been living a rootless lifestyle for so long that he can't imagine settling down as a rancher or a local lawman. Instead, Scott's been talking to railroad engineers who are finishing the long line work in Texas and hope to continue the state-spanning projects in Mexico. The question will then become: What will happen to his Texas Ranger family after he leaves it to start his own?

Company F welcomes their captain back after his honeymoon ends. They're in Edwards County after a busy fall and spring spent under Sergeant Brooks's command.

The sergeant turned thirty-two in November; he celebrated during a move from Ballinger to Tom Green County, to a new camp just outside San Angelo. Brooks spent much of that month on his own, scouting and sleuthing—and probably drinking—through Edwards County, home to many cattle thieves. He returns to Tom Green in December to fill in for Scott during his wedding. There, he, Rogers, and Crowder arrest a trio of livestock bandits.[3]

Brooks celebrates New Year's Day in Edwards County. Business brings him east in mid-February, when he takes a train to Crockett County to arrest R. T. Bailey on a warrant for assault. He returns to camp after stashing the man in jail at Runnels County, where he's wanted.

The company is kept moving as winter turns to spring. At the end of February, they're ordered to make another scout of Edwards County "on account of cattle thieves." On March 26, 1888, Company F relocates their camp back to Ballinger. That month, Private J. E. Randall leaves the Rangers and goes home to Dallas, his eventful year of service fulfilled.

One month later, Captain William Scott hands Brooks a letter to be delivered to Austin. The seemingly indestructible Ranger captain is quitting as well.

---

3 Paul Spellman, *Captain J. A. Brooks, Texas Ranger* (Denton: University of North Texas Press, 2007).

DYNAMITE ON THE FENCES
April 1888

Lieutenant Ira Aten watches the skin of Governor Lawrence Sullivan "Sul" Ross change to a deep shade of red. Ross's disbelief and anger seem to be growing the more the Ranger speaks, if the blood rushing to his bare scalp is any indication.

This is not their first meeting. Last fall, Aten stood in this very room and received orders to Navarro County straight from Ross's lips: "Stop that fence cutting at all costs." The personal attention Ross pays to the cuttings is due to Navarro's location just east of Waco. "The Governors always had a way of jumping into action when anything happened near their hometown," Aten says in a published memoir.[4]

For Aten, the assignment meant being sentenced to long months of mimicry, long hair, menial work, straight-faced lies, and personal risk. Now, many long months later, the fruits of his efforts have brought him back to the governor's office, this time with his job on the line. Aten expects to be fired by the end of the meeting. He doesn't care.

Aten first tells Ross about the steps taken to build their cover. He wants the governor to know how hard the job is.

He and fellow undercover Ranger Jim King first take a train to Waco and buy a one-eyed mule and rickety wagon. Ungroomed and dressed in tattered road clothes, the pair roll into Navarro County as what Aten calls "wagon hobos." They lurk near crossroad stores, King playing fiddle to attract a crowd. The goal is to be noticed by as many casual observers as possible.

With this backstory established, they next rattle into the neighborhood of Richland, a fence cutter hotbed, and fake a breakdown. "We accidentally on purpose turned a rear wagon wheel," he says. "We then placed a fence rail under the hind axle and pulled to a blacksmith shop. Saying we had no money to pay for having it fixed, and of course it wasn't

---

4 Ira Aten, "Fence Cutting Days in Texas," *Frontier Times*, July 1939.

fixed and we camped right there. King got out his fiddle. He soon drew a crowd and before long we got a job picking cotton."

Ross can hear the indignation rising in the Ranger's voice. It's bad enough to be reduced to work as a field hand, but even worse, the case has stalled. They are gathering plenty of intelligence, but there are no crimes being committed. "We were with the fence cutter bunch all right, as they would tell us all about the fences that has been cut and who was in their gang," he later says. "They were too busy picking cotton to cut fences at that time, but when the picking was over, they would lay the fences low."[5]

That meant at least two more months for Aten and King in the fields. This grinding, exhausting work is a fate worse than facing armed bandits—or angry politicians. "I wanted to do all my work on horseback," Aten says. "I had been in the Ranger service too long to spend my time in a cotton field."

This, Aten says, is when he starts thinking of new ways to discourage fence cutters. He comes up with a novel approach: placing bombs on random fences, rigged to explode when the metal line between posts is severed. No fence cutter would feel safe, and the landowners men could end their costly patrols.

"Bombs?" Ross asks, his cheeks beginning to flush with color.

The first move, Aten relates cheerfully, was to use the proceeds from the fields to fix their wagon, which they promptly drove to Corsicana for sale. King headed back to Ranger camp to Uvalde and left Aten to plant the bombs on his own. "I went to Dallas and bought 50 pounds of dynamite and two dozen dynamite caps," he says. "I carried the caps in my vest pocket and the dynamite in my luggage. Any one of the caps would have blown me to pieces had it exploded, but I know a little about handling dynamite and its dangers and was taking chances. As Rangers always do."

"You took dynamite on the train back to Richland?" Ross asks incredulously, his head by now glowing crimson.

---

5 Ibid.

"I did not know at the time that was against federal law," Aten says reasonably.

He continues the saga for the governor's benefit. Aten snuck back into the fence cutter neighborhood and hid at a friend's house, wary of fence cutters who knew him from the cotton fields. Placing the bombs just takes a shovel to bury a box with the shotgun and dynamite. When the fence was snipped, the shotgun would trigger the explosion, killing those above.

"That bald head of his got redder and when I had finished my story it was on fire," Aten later recalls. "I thought he was going to have me court martialed and shot. However, I had grown to be a man by that time and was not very much afraid of even the Governor, after the training they had given me."

Aten isn't repentant. Why would he be? The whole purpose of his stunt is to end fence cutting or get fired, or at least transferred off the beat. His fence bombs are part of a plea for attention from his bosses as much as a blow against fence cutters. Trapped in a never-ending cycle of duplicity, he's upping the stakes with his superiors and his Navarro targets alike.

Ira Aten knows it's easier to shoot people than lie to them. In July 1887, Aten and fellow Ranger John Hughes ended their pursuit of the murderer and jailbreaker Judd Roberts by cornering him and killing him in a gunfight.

The governor is angry but sympathetic. There is no punishment, but he orders him back to Navarro County to defuse the bombs before someone gets killed. "Instead, I exploded the bombs and they were heard for miles around," Aten recalls. "The next day people gathered about the little store to see what it all meant and the word was passed through the crowd that there were bombs planted on all the fences and these people were ready to believe it. That settled the fence cutting activities in Navarro county."[6]

---

6 Ibid.

For Aten, the fence bomb scheme achieves its central purpose. "I was never again ordered to catch any more fence cutters, after my bomb experience," Aten says. "Which pleased me mightily."

The last skirmishes of the Texas fence cutter wars are winding down, finally. After the events of the winter of 1887 and 1888, with the inhumane and economically crippling die-up, the dream of the open range is obviously over. The politics don't match the economics, and Texas technically remains an open-range state, leaving the question of regulating it in local hands.[7]

The Rangers of Company F are still cleaning up the mess in Brown County, but the courts remain disinterested. In early 1888, Rogers leads a detachment from Company F to arrest Bob Parrock, Ace Mathews, Wood Runnels, and a man named Bill Green for the attempted murder of Joe Copeland. By June, those charges are dropped, like all the previous charges against the fence cutters.

But even in Brown County, business as usual is coming to an end. In 1888, Nate Perry, a former deputy sheriff with a righteous reputation, is elected sheriff of Brown County. The days of acquiescent law enforcement in Brown County is over. It's another sign that local police are establishing better control over their cities, a trend that argues against the existence of the Texas Rangers.

Aten will prove his personal worth to Ross during his second term. In August 1889, the governor sends him and three other Texas Rangers to Fort Bend County, where white supremacist Democrats known as Jaybirds are rebelling against newly elected Black political leaders. The new power structure is backed by white supporters called Woodpeckers. Four people die, including Sheriff Jim Garvey, and six are injured during the ensuing gunfights.

---

7 In 1999, the Texas Supreme Court decided in *Gibbs v. Jackson* that a livestock owner has no duty to fence livestock unless dictated by city or county statute. See Susan Wagner, "Is Texas Still an Open Range State?," *Cattleman*, April 2004. The subhead answers the question: "Not really, and assuming it is could cost you a bundle!"

Ross calls in the Houston Light Guard, institutes martial law, and arrives on the scene himself, flanked by an assistant attorney general and a militia company. Ross then brokers a deal between both sides during a tense sit-down. The two groups agree to jointly choose the next sheriff, but can't come up with a name. Ross supplies one that they agree on—Ira Aten. The Ranger gets his next job, and the Jaybird-Woodpecker War in Fort Bend ends without another shot.[8]

TWO LETTERS
May 1, 1888

The capitol is buzzing with excitement. In just one month, Austin will be gripped with a patriotic Texas fever when the new capitol building is dedicated. Hundreds of thousands of visitors are expected, and some are already arriving.

Brooks doesn't have a mind for parties and state pride, or the sentiments of the crowd. He only cares about the thoughts of one person here—Governor Ross. He's here to meet the man face-to-face with two resignation letters in his pockets.

One belongs to Captain William Scott, dreaming of building railroads in Mexico. The other is his own. He's still expecting punishment for stirring up trouble in Indian Territory where his "enemies [were] making a howl about it."[9]

Adjutant General Wilburn King is also at the meeting, Brooks sees grimly. His dismissal will be done on the spot, it seems. Ross and King

---

8 In 1893, Aten was appointed sheriff in Castro County. In 1904, Aten moved his family to the Imperial Valley of California and was elected to the Imperial Valley District Board, which helped push legislation to build the Boulder Dam and the All-American Canal. Ira Aten died of pneumonia at ninety-one in August 1953. "Ira Aten, 1862–1953," Texas Ranger Hall of Fame, https://www.texasranger.org/texas -ranger-museum/hall-of-fame/ira-aten/.

9 Brooks's journal, courtesy of the Texas Ranger Hall of Fame and Museum.

are amused by the Ranger's stiff body language as he enters the room. The governor has a surprise in store.

Ross is in a banner mood, on the verge of a historic celebration during an election year. He's popular enough on both sides of the aisle that, later in 1888, he'll be running virtually unopposed for a second term. It's hardly a political risk for him to support Brooks.

These calculations are lost on the embattled Ranger, who has killed three men, gotten shot, been arrested, been put on trial, been found guilty, and received a presidential pardon, all in the past twenty-four months. "When Sergeant Brooks was expecting a discharge, that great and noble Governor of Texas had his Adjutant General King to place an envelope in his hand," Brooks recalls, using his handwritten memoir's customary third person.

Inside the envelope is a letter: J. A. Brooks is promoted to lieutenant and is now sole commander of Company F.

Brooks exits the city right away, not needing any pomp or parades. He came to Austin ready to quit the Texas Rangers; he's departing the city as his company's acting commander. The new leader has a natural second in mind; John Rogers is to become his sergeant. And for steady privates, he has J. B. Harry, who signed for another tour in January, and Kid Rogers. However, he is losing James Johnson. He began his career as a Ranger teamster when Scott took over Company F as a lieutenant in 1885 and ends it when it's clear Scott is leaving in February.[10]

Brooks's and Rogers's careers are rising during a time of budget cuts. "The last legislature reduced the appropriation for the pay and subsistence of the mounted force known as the Rangers, or Frontier Battalion, from $60,000 to $30,000 yearly and this necessitated a prompt reduction in the number of men employed in this service," laments Adjutant General King in a report describing 1888. "Five companies were then in the field, and were stationed at various points on the border where the public

10 "Adjutant General Service Records," Texas State Library and Archives Commission, https://www.tsl.texas.gov/apps/arc/service/.

safety and interests seemed most to need them; and as the companies were numerically small, the reduction made necessary by the limited appropriation could not be judiciously effected by individual discharges, but had to be done by company disbandment."[11]

The report describes a sad process: "Company E . . . was first disbanded. Capt. L. P. Sieker, quartermaster, having been sent out with orders from this office to perform this duty, and to take charge of the public property in the hands of said company. This property consisted of wagons and teams, harness, pack mules, pack saddles, tents and other articles which were disposed of by sale or by issuing it to other companies retained."

Survival depends on performance. During spring, Brooks keeps his new company on the move. (During all of 1888, he will drive Company F 47,781 miles and arrest 249 alleged criminals.)[12] They change camps from Ballinger to Kerrville to Laredo, and on May 18, the Rangers are ordered back to Kerrville, this time to thwart fence cutters targeting their own.[13]

The Coldwells are a family of Texas Rangers. Cornelius "Neal" Coldwell was a highly regarded captain of Company F in 1874 and Company A in 1876, when he retired. His son and nephew also joined the Rangers. Now fence cutters are striking the Coldwell family farm outside the unincorporated trade hub town of Center Point, Texas.

Brooks finds more than a criminal case at the ranch; Virginia Willborn lives there. She's a friend of the family, so close that she calls Neal Coldwell her "half uncle." Her grandmother in Center Point raised Virginia and her brothers, Thomas and Neal, after their parents died. She

11 *Report of the Adjutant-General of the State of Texas*, vol. 2, 1889. Texas State Archives, Austin, TX

12 Spellman, *Captain J. A. Brooks*.

13 Wilbur King, *Report of the Adjutant-General of the State of Texas, 1886–88*. Texas State Archives, Austin, TX

still lives there with her siblings, although one is a Texas Ranger and isn't around much. She's cut from the same cloth, raised to ride and shoot from the saddle.

It's too much for Brooks to handle. He's immediately smitten. By the time he leaves the ranch, soon to be deployed to Rio Grande City, he's formulating a courtship campaign to win her over.

DOME OVER AUSTIN
May 16, 1888

Governor Lawrence Sullivan Ross looks out at the sea of faces gathered outside the new capitol in Austin, spread across the stone steps, along Congress Avenue and the capitol grounds. The building isn't yet open for business, but the massive metal dome and Goddess of Liberty statue are installed, so the dedication and attendant party can begin.

It's truly the best of times for Texas, and Ross presides over a celebration of a state awash with pride. He stands to address the crowd, and that's when the clouds open up. Ross continues the program, undaunted. If you don't like Texas weather, just wait fifteen minutes. The sky clears as others take the stage. Later, this rain will reveal for the first time that the roof leaks, leading to investigations.

The Texas capitol takes up about 18 acres of floor space, with 392 rooms, 18 vaults, 924 windows, and 404 doors. The star on top of the dome reaches nearly 15 feet higher than the Capitol in Washington, D.C. Senator Temple Houston, the youngest son of legendary Sam Houston, stands before the crowd to accept the already iconic capitol on behalf of the entire state. "This building fires the heart and excites reflections in the minds of all," he says. "The architecture of a civilization is its most enduring feature, and by this structure shall Texas transmit herself to posterity."

There's a lot more to the festivities than just a couple of speeches from state politicians. This is a celebration of everything it means to be Texan. That means a weeklong party of cattle-roping competitions, baseball games, German choral performances, drill team exhibitions, band concerts, military displays, and fireworks. Austin builds a special street-car line just to ferry crowds from a visitor's camp a mile outside of town.

"A grand military parade," in the words of the *American-Statesman*, begins just after the dedication ends. "The flowers of the military of the great state of Texas were there. These, with their fair partners, beautiful faces that rival the chosen ones of the world; costumes rich and elegant, marvels of art and loveliness, all mingling in one grand assemblage within the walls of the building which, of its kind, in grandeur and magnificence of ornamentation, stands alone, presented a scene that language fails to adequately describe."[14]

Much of that "ornamentation" inside the capitol is made of metal, forged by inmates at Rusk Penitentiary. The stone supporting the zinc Goddess of Liberty statue atop the dome is likewise the product of prison labor. There's no mention of this in 1888, but there is a lot of discussion about how the pink hues of the rock evoke the grandeur of Versailles.

Mounted police may have led the parade, but the truth is that Austin still does not know what to do with the Frontier Battalion. The legislative sentiment is to continue to cut the overall number of Rangers despite their years of hunting outlaws to the limits of their endurance.

It's another symptom of the settlement of Texas: As frontier towns become small cities, their law enforcement agencies become both more effective and territorial, making the Rangers less necessary. They remain on the margins, a talented crop of lawmen with a shrinking mandate. More people in Austin are asking: Can the Rangers find a new purpose in the modernizing world?

Hunting outlaws and sleuthing fence cutters also adds unexpected costs, as Adjutant General King notes in his annual report of 1888:

> The sending of Capt. Scott's company twice to eastern Texas, keeping it there for months, and paying heavy medical bills for services given to him and Sergeant Brooks and private Rogers,

---

14 *Austin American-Statesman*, May 17, 1888.

all severely wounded in the performance of duty in that section; the services of detachments in Wharton and Waller counties and other places, and the costs of "special secret service" by individual rangers in Brown, McCulloch, Kerr, Lampasas, Navarro, and others, have all made heavy drafts upon the frontier appropriation, and yet we have enough to carry the present force safely to the end of the appropriation year, February 28, 1889, without deficiency, unless some extraordinary trouble should arise.[15]

The existential risk to the Frontier Battalion remains the legal language over the term *officer*. Ross won't change the status quo, but it's still an issue in Austin. It will take until 1901 for that question to be answered, and it will spell the end of the Frontier Battalion.

THE BALLINGER EXONERATION
April 21, 1888

The robber and his horse are draped in black as the two-car stagecoach trundles past, fifteen miles outside of Ballinger. With a kick of his spurs, he sidles alongside the coach, and the driver has a six-shooter pointed at him before he even registers a threat.

There are thirteen passengers in two coaches, and the robber forces all of them to line up on the roadside. The highwayman is familiar with this route and prepared for such numbers—he brings hooded masks for each of them.

After robbing the passengers, he keeps them in place for four hours, waiting for the stage from San Angelo to come up the road so he can rob it, too. Recent rains make that schedule impossible, and the robber calls it a night. "He then gave to each of them money enough to pay for their dinner at the stage station," one newspaper account reads.

---

15 Wilburn King, *Annual Report of the Adjutant General of Texas, 1888*, Texas State Archives, Austin, TX.

"Say," he adds. "What ever happened to that smooth-faced driver I met last winter?"

It would appear that the Lone Highwayman is back in business, even though Jim Newsom—tracked and arrested by J. A. Brooks—is even now languishing in an upstate New York jail. "Yesterday's development conclusively proves his innocence," declares the *Fort Worth Gazette Daily*, once a reliable place to read about Newsom's life as an arch-criminal.

It's natural to wonder if those incidents actually exonerate Newsom. A friend, motivated by what he thinks is a miscarriage of justice, could have committed the robberies and made sure to make comments that link them to Newsom's prior crimes. The behavior of the "facetiously exultant" robber raises some reasonable skepticism in the April 24, 1888, *Austin American-Statesman*, which notes: "It was a shrewd game for him to play the role of the former robber but it by no means proves he was such."

But an arrest is made in June. One of the Ballinger victims identifies John Gray, a twenty-five-year-old gambler from McGregor County, as the Lone Highwayman. The witness recognizes the six-foot-one man from the Legal Tender Saloon in San Angelo. That's the same place Gray borrowed a six-shooter from another gambler, before he left by train to nearby Sweetwater. That's enough for the authorities, and he's arrested shortly after he arrives in Colorado, Texas. By mid-July, Gray is in custody in Waco, jailed as he waits for trial.[16]

His escape in October is dramatic. He and a fellow prisoner jump a deputy, and they wrestle the guard to the ground as he enters the cell. Gray suggests throttling the man unconscious, which his companion does, after which the pair and five other prisoners steal a handcar and make their escape. However limitless the rails may seem, they are actually well-traveled lanes that don't accommodate unplanned traffic easily.

---

16 "Robber Captured," *Austin American-Statesman*, June 29, 1888, and untitled item in the *Waco Morning News*, July 16, 1888: "Marshall J.H. Bull is back in the city from a trip to the west. He brought back with him John H Gray, the alleged lone stage robber. Marshall Bull generally brings company with him when he goes on a trip."

They're forced off the tracks by a passenger train, only to be rounded up by a posse as they cower in a field. The prisoners' run lasts about four hundred yards.[17]

Cries of Newsom's innocence become louder. The *Daily Gazette* waxes poetical. It's worth reading, not just for its description of how the locals set about dismantling the case but also to experience the florid prose it inspired in the nameless writer:

> The last stage robbery between San Angelo and Ballinger gives a Victor Durand tinge of romance to the case of Jim Newsom, the alleged "lone highwayman" of last year's exploits . . . Now, Jim Newsom is a typical West Texas cowboy, who is utterly lacking the intelligence and polish that characterized Victor Durand. Newsom never studied grammar or anything else but roping cattle and horses and the mysteries of poker and seven-ups, but it begins to look very much like this wild, untutored Texan, who is wearing felon's stripes and working a life's sentence as a US prisoner in the penitentiary at Albany, New York, is innocent of the charge upon which he was consigned to this fate.
>
> Now, when the stage was robbed last week it was again by a "lone highwayman" who seemed facetiously exultant over his exploit and informed the passengers that he was the bold robber of last year—the perpetrator of the two offenses for which Newsom is imprisoned. The driver of the stage last week happened to be engaged in the same duty on one of the stages robbed last year, and he believes the robber then and now is the same man. It is an interesting muddle and gives Newsom's case national prominence. The attorneys for Newsom will no doubt at with renewed vigor on his behalf and in the light of recent

17 "Waco Excited," *Austin American-Statesman,* October 9, 1888.

developments this latest robbery ought to prove his innocence. The capture of the robber last week might throw new light on the case but in any event it seems very probable that Newsom must benefit by this latest exploit.[18]

Things don't go well for John Gray. In June 1888, he's brought before a judge in San Angelo, who discharges him. His freedom is short-lived as deputies from Tom Green County immediately arrest him on two charges of robbery of the stagecoach passengers.[19] On April 24, John Gray is convicted on two counts of robbery in Tom Green County and sentenced to thirteen years in Rusk Penitentiary. On November 8, 1889, he and several other prisoners try to escape, according to his official prison record. Guards shoot twenty-eight-year-old John Gray dead after "having scaled the walls with others."[20]

It takes another year for Newsom to receive a new trial. Witness testimony on the scene of the robberies supply crucial details about the robber's build that argue for Newsom's innocence. There is no mention of marked bills or confessions, as Brooks describes later in life. A December 1890 newspaper account summarizes the Waco jury's decision: "It was proven that the same man who held up the stage between San Angelo and Ballinger and for which Jim Newsom was convicted, robbed the same stage near the same place after Newsom was convicted and sent to prison."

---

18 "Jim Newsome's Romance," *Fort Worth Daily Gazette*, April 27, 1888. Believe it or not, the article is much longer.

19 *Galveston Daily News*, April 17, 1889.

20 Texas State Library and Archives Commission, Convict Record Ledgers, Convict Number Range: 0001–4622, Volume Number: 1998/038–148.

No longer wearing the mantle of "the Lone Highwayman," Newsom is a free man.[21]

Brooks writes of the Ballinger case in his handwritten memoirs, but never mentions the exoneration. His tone while writing about the case is not at all defensive. It seems he was either sure of Newsom's guilt no matter what the courts say or too embarrassed to bring up the exoneration. Knowing his character, it's more likely the former.

There is an anecdote that will be passed around Austin that sums up the Rangers' overall frustration at what they saw as a turnstile justice system. It involves J. A. Brooks in a courtroom, watching a cattle thief that he captured being sentenced to hang. Newspaper correspondent Kitty Barry quotes an unnamed colleague's version of the tale:

> Rising up out of his chair and hitching up his breeches with a quick motion, subconscious to the Western riders about to mount, [Brooks] reached into his coat, drew out a paper and passed it over to the judge, remarking hurriedly, "Here, judge, take this puncher's pardon. I got to go catch the rest of the gang." And in three minutes Brooks was a small cloud of dust on the prairie.[22]

It's quite an anecdote to attribute to a man once pardoned for killing a man, an incident that Barry doesn't mention.

While the courts untangle its recent past, Texas forges ahead into the future. The train station connecting San Angelo and Ballinger opens in spring of 1888. The Ballinger–San Angelo stagecoach closes by the end of the year as mail and passengers migrate to the trains. Thus ends the infamous era of roadside crime in Runnels County.

Mile by mile, Texas is being tamed not by lawmen but tech-

---

21 *Fort Worth Daily Gazette*, December 14, 1890.

22 Kitty Barry, "Brooks Is a Peaceful Man," *Daily Express*, January 12, 1911.

nology. But boom and bust economics are far from over in the Lone Star State and will produce chaos that brings the Rangers back into prominence.

LEFT FOR PARTS UNKNOWN
July 20, 1888

The crowd murmurs when L. L. Loggins walks into the federal courtroom in Little Rock. "The prisoner presented a pitiful sight," the *Arkansas Gazette* describes. "With a beard of several months and a suit of disheveled hair, Wright resembled a wild man and such a change had come over him in the past 6 months that those acquainted with him hardly recognized him."[23]

A half year ago, his latest transformation seemed to be going fine. The *Daily Arkansas Gazette* summarizes Loggins's new life: "Wright gave out that he would give up journalism and remove to Bayou Mato township and devote himself to medicine and to running for the legislature."[24]

But in January 1887, his doom appears in Little Rock. This time, Mollie Loggins is here for blood. "Wright's wife . . . came here and began talking about prosecuting him," says the *Arkansas Gazette*. "She says she has evidence to prove her marriage to the doctor and will also prove she lived with him in this city." For proof, she shows authorities a marriage certificate.[25]

Loggins, in his remote haven, catches wind of her arrival when a Little Rock businessman shows up to warn him. He lent "Wright" some money and is worried he won't collect from a prisoner. Loggins pays him off and, now warned that the walls are closing in, splits.

---

23 "Guilty as Charged," *Arkansas Democrat*, July 20, 1888.

24 "The Journalistic Bigamist," *Daily Arkansas Gazette*, July 21, 1888.

25 "A Bigamist," *Arkansas Democrat*, January 21, 1888. Her name is printed as M. N. Wright.

"Dr. R.P. Wright has left for parts unknown," *The Arkansas Democrat* reports. "Wright turned over his horse to settle the debt and left that night for new fields, leaving Mrs. Wright to look out for herself."[26]

The outraged father of young Mrs. White-Wright arrives in Little Rock in January, denouncing the doctor for his double identity and asking for a reward for his capture. On February 11, Mollie Loggins meets with Governor Simon Hughes, marriage certificate and tale of woe at the ready. *The Democrat* calls her "a plucky, determined woman and speaks as though she meant exactly what she said."[27] The Arkansas governor imposes a $200 bounty. Now even Loggins's fake identity is wanted.

The fugitive keeps moving frantically, a roulette ball seeking to rattle into place. Loggins hits New Orleans first, then tries Macon, Georgia, before scouting Tennessee, stopping in Chattanooga and Murfreesboro. He finally finds an opportunity in Nashville, where he begins work at the Southern Methodist Publishing House.

That's where Hadley Clack, Little Rock's chief of police, finds him in February 1888. It's unclear how he's tipped off. The nature of his crimes and reward money certainly help motivate people to look.

Loggins can't raise the money to meet a steep bond, and so he's stuck in the White County jail. "An effort is being made here to make a $1,000 bond to secure Wright's release," the *Arkansas Gazette* says in February. "Mr. Z.T. Hedges, who has gone away, promises to make the bond as soon as he returns."[28]

But Wright's Little Rock supporters will soon melt away with his unmasking as L. L. Loggins. The investigation into his secret life, started by a chance encounter with that Howard County acquaintance,

---

26 Ibid.

27 *Daily Arkansas Gazette,* February 12, 1888. The newspaper doesn't mention her name out of presumed courtesy.

28 Ibid.

now comes to full fruition. L. L. Loggins is revealed in headlines as "the Journalistic Bigamist" to a shocked Little Rock community. There's no more talk of passing the hat for bail; he's left to rot in jail until trial.

His alleged Texas crimes make him a target for extradition, but that doesn't go as planned. "When he was brought back to this city, the Texas authorities were notified and [Shelby County sheriff] B.S. Sims and a deputy came to Little Rock to get possession of the prisoner." The Arkansas officials are happy to see Loggins leave—after someone from Texas supplies his bail money. They only have $500, and the court won't reduce the amount. The Texans leave empty-handed. They will be back when Loggins doesn't come with a price tag.

As the spring months pass, Loggins seemingly suffers a mental collapse inside his jail cell. He reportedly tries to kill himself twice. He also maims himself by sticking a needle into his eye. By the time his trial begins in July, he's an obvious wreck, although there may be some showmanship in his appearance. "Wright entered the courtroom leaning on the arm of the deputy sheriff, and almost completely broken down with weakness he took a seat near his attorney," the *Arkansas Gazette* relates. "With an unclean rag tied around his eyes he seemed to be suffering considerable pain and it was some time before he could stand the light."

His case is causing quite a public stir. *The Arkansas Democrat* cites "unusual interest manifested at the court house when the case of Dr. R.P. Wright, charged with bigamy, was called . . . It was generally believed that the trial would be characterized with developments of a very sensational nature."

Neither wife is there, but the courtroom is crowded with "all classes of people anxious to get a glimpse of the man who had won such unenviable notoriety and to know what course he would pursue if found guilty."[29]

So there's an audience for L. L. Loggins, the professional attention-seeker. That makes a cynic wonder if his court appearance is crafted to

---

generate sympathy. Injuring his own eye could be the action of a mentally ill person, a doctor operating on himself—or a schemer seeking to create an even more pathetic figure in court. (One article mentions he "pricked his eye with a needle," which doesn't sound severe.)

The trial hardly begins when Loggins throws a curveball. He wants to speak to one of the state witnesses, Professor James Mitchell, in a separate room. Judge M. T. Sanders allows this, maybe sensing an easy way out of a sensational scene. Loggins returns "with trembling limbs" to plead to the court.

And oh, what a plea it is. He staggers to the rostrum and falls to his knees before the judge and "in tones just barely above a whisper pleaded guilty to the charge, claiming he was not guilty but that his attorneys who previously represented his case had failed to procure certain evidence."

This display doesn't move Judge Sanders, who intones a sentence: "Knowing but little of his past life, I believe at one time the prisoner bore a reputable character in this state and a man of his intelligence should have known better. The court fixes the punishment at five years in the penitentiary at hard labor."

Loggins makes his move on the trip to prison. "L.L. Loggins of Sabine County fame, who was sentenced to the Arkansas penitentiary for bigamy, has made his escape," reads *The Galveston Daily News* on July 2, 1889.[30] Maybe the man has some hidden reserves, or maybe the pathetic act has been a deliberate ruse in anticipation of a moment like this. Either way, his run is short-lived. There are no details chronicling his recapture, but he serves his time in the penitentiary in Little Rock.

On July 27, 1892, he's released into the waiting handcuffs of Texas lawmen, again Sherriff B. S. Sims and a man named R. J. Sinclair. They take possession of L. L. Loggins on charges of murder and set forth to return him to Texas. Newspapers note their arrival at Center Point "with the celebrated Dr. Pete Loggins, who is wanted in Sabine

---

30 "Notes from Nacogdoches," *Galveston Daily News*, July 2, 1889.

County for a murder committed several years ago and who has just completed a term in the penitentiary at Little Rock. Loggins appears very cheerful."[31]

Not mentioned, until months later, is a scam Loggins pulls on Sheriff Sims along the way. Loggins hands his cash to Sims for safekeeping but later steals the money. He makes such a show of disappointment over its disappearance that the lawman pays the prisoner back out of his own pocket. Loggins uses the proceeds to help make bail.

The court appearances in Hemphill become events. On the morning of September 15, "the streets were crowded awaiting the trial of Dr. L.L. Loggins on the case of forgery," reads *The Galveston Daily News*. "He has been acquitted. He will not be tried for breaking jail until the next term of court."[32]

His winning streak is about to come to an end. As Loggins struts around Sabine County, he brags about "how easy he worked Sims" during the trip from Arkansas. This loose talk blows back on him, and he's indicted for swindling and placed back in jail, awaiting his other trials. On November 29, 1892, Loggins is convicted of first-degree murder and sentenced to one hundred years in prison, and given two extra years for the jailbreak.[33]

The Sunday Gazetteer newspaper receives a postcard from Loggins from Rusk in 1893, saying he's seeking an appeal for his murder charge and "believes he will be granted a new trial. He says he is not guilty, but the victim of circumstantial evidence and local prejudice."[34]

---

31 "Brought from Arkansas," *Galveston Daily News,* July 29, 1892.

32 *Galveston Daily News,* September 18, 1892.

33 *Sunday Gazetteer* (Denison, TX), September 10, 1893. His prison records, however, list "DEATH" as his release date. Maybe 1994 seemed too far off to bother writing down.

34 Ibid.

He's wrong—the appeal falls on deaf ears. It turns out his attempt is based on linguistics. "The appellant complains that the court erred in his charge upon circumstantial evidence in stating it would produce 'in effect' instead 'the effect' of a reasonable and moral certainty," reads a summary of the case that ran in *The Galveston Daily News* on October 25, 1893. "It may be satisfactory to a metaphysical mind to weigh the difference between these two propositions and fail to see how any such determination can be of any practical value to the ordinary juror."

Judge James Simkins ends the appeal with a shot at Loggins. "The inculpatory facts while mostly circumstantial are positive and leaves no doubt of the appellant's guilt," says the judge. "He stands convicted of one of the most cowardly assassinations in the criminal records."[35]

In 1900, a census taker appears at the door of Mollie Loggins's rented house in Montgomery, Texas. She lives there with sons Lewis and John, both twentysomethings who work as farm laborers, and her fourteen-year-old daughter, Myrtle. Mary Elizabeth lists herself as the head of the household and notes her occupation as a housekeeper. Asked her marital status, she responds: "Widower."[36]

For all the barbarity, and perhaps partly because of it, the Texas prison system is susceptible to political appeal. Rusk prison records show one final legal magic act of the wily L. L. Loggins. The last entry in his prison file, where his final disposition is listed, says: "Pardoned December 22, 1901."[37]

A free man, he immediately writes a letter to the *Texas Medical Journal*. "Dr. L.L. Loggins requests us to say that he is permanently located

35 *Galveston Daily News*, October 25, 1893.

36 1900; Census Place: Justice Precinct 1, Montgomery, Texas; p. 7.

37 Texas Department of Criminal Justice, Archives and Information Services Division, Texas State Library and Archives Commission, Austin, TX, Convict Registers.

to practice medicine at Willis, Montgomery County, Texas."[38] This is where his sons and wife are living, but beyond that, signs of a family reconciliation are lacking.[39]

Loggins does become what he's always wanted to be: a practicing physician with office and everything. But the good life doesn't last long. On April 2, 1905, he has a disagreement with the wrong guy, a younger man named D. A. Hooks. At age thirty-seven, Hooks works as night watchman for a lumberyard and mill. He's been married since November 1889 and has five children at home, the youngest at two.

"The peace and quiet here was rudely broken," reads an item in *The Arlington Journal.* "Some trouble had been pending of a personal nature between Dr. L.L. Loggins, a practicing physician at this place for several years past, and D.A. Hooks, long a resident and a former Deputy Sheriff and Constable of this precinct, in which Dr. Loggins was shot and almost instantly killed. Mr. Hooks gave himself up to Constable Davis."[40]

The Galveston Daily News runs more details about the killing. Hooks was inside the Crescent Drug Building, where the doctor kept his office, and "Loggins was in the act of entering the same armed with a double-barreled shotgun when Hooks met him at the door entrance and shot him with a revolver. Apparently the first shot took effect in the breast of Loggins and so paralyzed him that he was unable to handle his gun and made no shot." Loggins staggers into the building, chased by more misplaced pistol shots. He makes it to his office, but Lewis Loggins,

---

38 *Texas Medical Journal,* vol. 17, 1901.

39 Mary "Mollie" Loggins dies in Houston in April 1934, her death certificate and tombstone at Brookside Memorial Park cemetery still bearing the Loggins name. Source: Texas Department of State Health Services, Austin, TX.

40 *Arlington Journal,* April 7, 1905.

a.k.a. Pete Loggins, a.k.a. R. P. Wright, a.k.a. Dr. Hemphill, bleeds out within minutes.[41]

As for the cause of the fatal encounter, the newspapers choose the euphemism most commonly used to describe a romantic entanglement: "Trouble of a personal nature." There's no telling what this refers to, but it would be true to form for L. L. Loggins to lose his life fighting over a woman.

SABINE COUNTY CODA
July 14, 1888

Leander and Alfie Conner embrace outside of Rusk Penitentiary as free men, having served nearly their full sentences. Due to be released in September, they have instead been released a few months early for good behavior. The sooner, the better. Every day at Rusk, they risk ending up like poor Jim Sanders, who died last August after eleven months inside.

Had he lived, he would be released the next day, along with fellow jailbreakers, Sterling Eddings and W. E. T. Ogletree. The former school-teacher has won clemency from the governor, who trimmed his four-year sentence to match the others' twenty-four months. Sam Swan and Lem Taylor are still locked up.[42]

The Conner family holocaust scythed three generations in Sabine County, but Leander does his best to restock it. The convicted jailbreaker lives his days on a plot of land outside Hemphill and stays out of all re-corded trouble. Starlin is born there in 1892, Ada in 1889, and Artie in 1898. That brings his total to eight children who survive to adulthood.

A look at Leander's lineage shows more signs that life in Sabine County continues, even after horrific violence. Leander's daughter Rosa marries into none other than the Smith family; she weds Ben Smith, the

---

41 "L.L. Loggins Killed," *Galveston Daily News*, April 3, 1905.

42 Rusk Prison Records, *Convict and Conduct Registers, 1875–1945*, Texas State Archives, Austin, TX.

grandson of Obadiah Smith, whose sister is married to none other than Jack Low.

Nella Conner, another of Leander's daughters, marries into the McNaughten family by wedding Daniel Edward McNaughten, who incidentally is part of the Smith family, since his grandfather Allen married a daughter of Obadiah Smith. And yes, Daniel's uncle is Daniel McNaughten, who hunted the Conner outlaws in the "Turner posse."[43]

Silence keeps the peace among county residents. "They just wouldn't talk about it, because they were all mixed up," noted the late Sabine County historian Blanche Toole. "In order to live, they had no choice but to drop the whole thing."[44]

Like everything else in the world, the obscure Conner feud in Sabine County has been discussed on modern internet message boards. Most of those looking into the feud are descendants, and some offer insights into the community's collective shame over the violence. "William Christopher (Kit) Smith was my great-great grandfather," writes one forum poster. "The feud was never spoken of. My grandmother's sister later married Gilbert Conner [Leander Conner's son], who was very helpful to my grandmother in raising her three sons, after my grandfather William Christopher Smith died at an early age. The Smith and Conner families were then connected by marriage and no one wanted to disturb this peaceful situation."[45]

---

43 "Daniel Webster McNaughten," Find a Grave, https://www.findagrave.com /memorial/13666607/george-washington-mcnaughten. In 1920, Dan McNaughten was buried in Oak Hill Cemetery in Yellowpine, Sabine County.

44 Ed Wetterman, "1990 Interview with Blanch Toole, Sabine County Historian," East Texas Generations, August 1, 2010, http://easttexasgenerations.blogspot.com/2010 /08/1990-interview-with-blanch-toole-sabine.html.

45 "Anyone Familiar with Conner Feud in Sabine County?," City-Data.com, December 2008, http://www.city-data.com/forum/texas/513955-anyone-familiar-conner-feud -sabine-county.html.

The benevolent spirit of Sabine community, best exemplified by the care of orphans or otherwise needy people, clearly remains undiminished in the feud's aftermath.

The conciliatory attitude of Sabine County is also reflected in Austin, in the form of pardons. One of the leading voices seeking clemency, interestingly, is Judge James I. Perkins. In January 1889, he writes Governor Ross: "Being convinced that it is the universal wish of the people of Sabine County that Charley Conner should be pardoned and that serious doubt of his guilt of participation in the murder for which he was convicted—most all of the people of Sabine Co. and especially those in a position to be best informed of the truth of this matter, as seen in the light of developments since the trial, I do now recommend that said Conner be pardoned."[46]

W. W. Weatherred writes his own letter that month. The former Conner defense attorney turned posse leader has now become a leading voice for releasing the only family member still in prison. "Can safely say 99 percent of the citizens of said county would be glad to have the said convict pardoned," he writes, saying a petition has been circulating around Sabine County for his release. "I can truly say myself that, being acquainted with all of the facts in the case (having been leading counsel in the *habeas corpus* and two trials in District Court), I do not believe or ever have believed Charles Conner was guilty."

And here comes the best part: "A much stronger appeal could have been made asking for pardon, but the facts necessary to be stated in such a petition would have been unknown to the people; and hence it was deemed best to present just what they could endorse, and no more."[47]

The statement is vague but possibly damning. It forces a new, hard look at the case against Charles Conner in 1884, one built on witness

---

46 Executive Clemency Records, "Charles Conner," Number 125563, Records of the
   Secretary of State, Texas State Archives, Austin, TX.

47 Ibid.

testimony. Octavine Cooper doesn't place him on the way to the scene of the crime with his codefendant, Fed Conner. But Joe Ford and John Marshall sure do. If they are exposed as perjurers whose testimony led to the destruction of a white family, it could unleash a backlash against African Americans in the area.

This is not an idle fear in the racial powder keg that is Sabine County; in just a handful of years, just such an eruption of violence will occur. In 1908, nine African Americans are murdered—five seized from the Hemphill jail and lynched from the same tree—after two white men are shot after a bootlegging dispute. It causes a mass exodus of African Americans from the county.[48]

Weatherred's cryptic comment about "facts . . . unknown to the people" leaves more questions than answers. If Joe Ford lied about Charles Conner, how much of his testimony should be considered as unreliable? Was his testimony accurate but sweetened just enough to ensure both brothers would be found guilty? Was John Marshall also involved? Did George Williams really confess to his family, as his descendants say, that he used the men to set up the Conners? Just how much hidden history is resting forever in Sabine County's graveyards?

The records from Huntsville Penitentiary, at least, are definitive. Whether for political expediency or long-denied justice, Charles Conner is pardoned and released on March 18, 1889, twenty years before his quarter-century murder sentence is finished.[49]

This is one part of what, if not a cover-up, at least is a concerted effort to address what most in the area consider a miscarriage of justice. Between 1889 and 1891, the governor issues a slate of pardons for nearly every jailbreaker, including Leander Conner. All pardons are political gestures, but these are especially toothless because those pardoned are

---

48 "Slaughter of Negroes," *Arizona Republican,* June 23, 1908, and "Negroes in Flight," *New York Times,* June 24, 1908.

49 Rusk Prison Records, *Convict and Conduct Registers.*

already released. (Sam Swan gets his one day after he's released from Rusk.) Still, a pardon reinstates a convict's full citizenship rights, which is more than a token to those involved.

This is a local play, not one made in Austin. Perkins, Weatherred, and the others are holding the pen, even if the governor is doing the signing. There is nothing strange about politicians bending with the prevailing political winds, especially when they are actions that cost nothing. The public men of Sabine County seemingly want to keep those citizens who were involved to be satisfied—and quiet.

Alfred Conner, who lives elsewhere, is not included in the pardons.[50] After his release, he moves to nearby Angelina County with his spouse and three sons; Sallie, his wife, dies there at age thirty-six. There are census records of Alfred Conner in Angelina County in 1900 with a new wife, Josephine Sterling, from Cherokee County, and they have daughters Myrtie and Dollie. His profession is listed as "logger," still at work in the disappearing forests where his family once felled trees to float down the river.[51]

Alfred Conner's life with his new wife is peaceful but not easy. Myrtie dies at age two, but five of Alfie's children have families of their own, all of them outside of Sabine County. Alfred "Bubba" Conner dies December 3, 1924; he's buried at Arnold Cemetery in the town of Forest, in Cherokee County, twenty miles from both Rusk and Nacogdoches. An effort from descendants leads to his pardon from the state of Texas on January 1, 1983.

After prison, Charles Conner moves to Nacogdoches County, just across the county line and not too far from brothers Alfie and Leander. He plans to raise his family away from Sabine County, in a new cabin

---

50 Executive Clemency Records, Records of the Secretary of State, Texas State Archives, and Pardon Proclamations, Executive Record Book, Texas State Archives, Austin, TX.

51 1900 Census, Texas, Angelina County, Precinct 4, June 11, 1900.

near the Angelina River, but he doesn't have long to enjoy it. He dies on March 1, 1895, at age forty-seven. Charles Conner is buried at the Old Smyrna Cemetery in Nacogdoches County, twenty miles from his homestead in Sabine County.

Catherine Conner Williams—father and brothers shot down, husband committed to an insane asylum, and young son murdered—has been left staggered in Sabine County. She and fellow widow Piercy Conner form an alliance to help raise the children and stay solvent. Life goes on. Catherine marries a Louisiana farmer named William Cain in 1889, after which she and Piercy move from Sabine County to stay with him.

Piercy Conner never returns to Sabine County alive. When she dies in October 1898, she is laid to rest in the Conner Cemetery. It takes Catherine Conner Williams Cain a lot longer to return, but she's living with one of Leander's sons in Sabine County as a widower (since 1912) when she dies in 1932. She's buried in the Oak Hill Cemetery.

Nancy Conner, Fed's widow, never remarries and never leaves. She lives the rest of a hardscrabble life with her children in Sabine County, by 1910 staying with her son William and daughter-in-law Emma and, ten years later, with son Willis and his wife, Nora. Her bitterness remains, lingering like an old war wound. She is sure to tell her neighbors and kin about slights from Little Ike Low, like the time he pawns low-grade corn off to her son during a routine deal. She dies on June 15, 1915.[52]

The mystery of John Conner's fate lingers over Sabine County. It would have never been solved if not for the efforts of two authors, Joe Combs and Mark Dugan, who unearth the story but never have the chance to publish it anywhere. In 1969, the year after his book *Gunsmoke in the Redlands* is published, Combs receives a letter in response to his chapter discussing the Conner feud. Combs sends the letter to Dugan in 1982, as he's researching his manuscript *Judge Not.* The letter is written by Rev. Murray Burr, whose grandfather knew John Conner when he lived

---

52 "Nancy Pauline Travis," McLemore Strong Genealogy, http://strongfamilytree.org /getperson.php?personID=17216&tree=STR06, and Dugan, *Judge Not.*

under an assumed name near the town of Starks, Louisiana. The area is called the Devil's Pocket for its isolated geography and shady reputation.

"Only a gentle and kind Deity would ever know the loneliness of this poor hunted man's heart," Burr writes. "Out of fear no doubt of being ambushed like his father, he constantly moved about in the river bottoms, not spending but a few nights in any one place." Over time, John Conner gets more comfortable and even loses the fake name, but he is never seen without a rifle, even when the Burr family invites him to dinner at the table. His network of lean-tos will one day become multiple still sites when he starts moonshining. A notorious alcoholic in the town of Deweyville, Texas, he runs afoul of authorities for being a public nuisance and is shipped off to insane asylums. He dies in an overcrowded state-run facility in Jackson, Louisiana, on July 26, 1910.[53]

If only he had come back. Authorities quietly drop the murder case against him on August 18, 1898, another quiet act of clemency from Sabine County. He wasn't a wanted man after all.

On November 24, 1923, seventy-seven-year-old Leander Conner, still spry enough to travel on horseback, rides out of Hemphill toward his home. At his age, he's still "healthy and active" despite being "one of the oldest citizens of Sabine County," notes *The Galveston Daily News*. But on November 26, he's found lying dead on the trail, thrown from his horse. He's buried at Oak Grove Cemetery two days later. The newspaper covering his passing doesn't mention the jailbreak or infamous feud, of which he's the last Conner who's a direct participant.[54]

LONESOME GRAVEYARD
February 28, 2021

There's a large dog chained to a tree near the trailhead that leads to the Conner Cemetery. The lean, healthy pit bull / boxer mix stays silent, but

---

53 Dugan, *Judge Not*.

54 *Galveston Daily News*, November 26, 1923.

watches intruders keenly as they pass by. Only when interlopers are out of sight does the dog bark, a pair of deep booms that echo hauntingly through the Sabine National Forest. It's a sound that the Conners, buried close by, would appreciate.

The cemetery trail is a dirt road, just wide enough for a four-by-four truck, blanketed with pine needles. Bright sunlight filters between the towering trees that flank both sides of the path, which leads steadily upward to a bald hilltop ringed by trees.

A forty-five-foot by forty-five-foot, chest-high metal fence forms a rectangle marking the Conner Cemetery. This is where the family buried its own, before and after Willis and the boys went rogue. It doesn't feel like outlaws are buried here. The fence has a "Welcome" sign that faces those walking up the trail, with a blue metal flower, ladybug decoration, and several glass baubles dangling from it. A metal chain, but no lock, secures a light cattle gate. Unraveling it to enter the cemetery means braving a thorny vine that has woven itself through the links.

The graveyard is overgrown with several seasons' worth of weeds and shoots of young trees. Aggressive vines creep along the ground and reach up to grab feet and ankles like B-movie zombies. White and granite headstones, too few for such a large plot, stand among the growth. Sabine County historian Weldon McDaniel, using mainstream methods backed by his trusty dowsing rod, counts twenty-three bodies in this plot. There are six unidentified stone markers.

Based on the overgrowth, the old but still visible scars of truck tracks, and the new headstones, it's clear that this cemetery is tended but not meticulously. McDaniel has six old cemeteries, including this one, to care for, with no budget. He did put the fence around the Conner Cemetery in 2010 "to keep hogs from rooting around" but admits he hasn't been to the plot in quite a while. "These old cemeteries have fallen on hard times," he says. "It's tough to find help keeping them up."

The decorations outside make more sense when it becomes apparent that this is a children's graveyard. There are nine children buried here for certain, including poor Thomas Williams. Fed's children are here and have their own, new grave markers: Millie Conner (1873–1877), Monroe Conner (1876–1877), and Fannie Conner (1886–1888). It's painful to imagine the haunting specter of Nancy Conner burying Fannie here a just a few months after her husband was killed.

McDaniel says he doesn't know who placed the modern gravestones. Thomas Williams received no such attention. His is one of the many obscured graves in the Conner Cemetery, covered by weeds and overgrowth. Even from the air (via quadcopter drone), only a handful of headstones are even visible amid the scrub and emerging tree saplings.

The Conner outlaws are buried in a tight cluster, just as they lived, fought, and died. Willis Conner's headstone is tall and flat, standing as straight and firm as a pylon planted in concrete. It reads, "CSA: Texas Infantry," in deference to his three months as a Confederate private in 1863. Piercy, the mother and wife of the Conner outlaws, is somewhere in here, laid to rest here in October 1898. William Conner has a flat marker lying among the leaves, the date of March 31, 1887, stamped on its face, mottled by the shadows of nearby tree limbs.

Frederick Conner is buried next to his children. His stone is a thick wedge with a tapered face reading, "Father, let thy grace be given, that we may meet in heaven." It's very hard not to think that the inscription has a more literal meaning than just a plea to God, or maybe that's just because the man who enabled Fed's downfall, and vice versa, is buried just a few feet away. No matter what, he lived and died his father's son.[55]

Charles Conner's homestead is a short drive away. Weldon McDaniel knows the place well. "In 1948, my father bought the Charley Conner place, and we moved from down on the creek up to that place. That's where I partially grew up," he says. "We actually moved *into* the old Charley Conner house and lived in it until my daddy built a newer, more

---

55 The grave misstates his death date.

modern house. Now, it's gone. After my daddy built a new house on the creek, we tore it down."[56]

At over eighty, McDaniel has a steady stride and firm handshake. Everyone ignores his first name, Ernest, including his mother. He's a one-man repository for area arcana. The county court bestowed the title of "Historical Commission President" on him in 2016, but his volunteer position gets little financial help from the local government. Sabine County does donate an office near the jail, but only budgets $150 a year for the commission. McDaniel does his best to solicit funds and promote historic preservation. No one in East Texas can wield a grave-finding dowsing rod like he can.

Weldon McDaniel has a personal interest in the "Conner troubles" that erupted in Sabine County eight decades before the reservoir filled. "The first person killed in the feud was my great-grandmother's brother, William Christopher Smith. They called him 'Kit'," he says. "This feud is really not a whole lot different than the Hatfields and McCoys, but it's nowhere near as famous."

Today, there is a family living in a modern, single-story wooden home where Charles Conner and Weldon McDaniel each lived. It's in decent shape and has people living there—not always the case in Sabine County, home to so much abandoned property. A tractor stands out front, covered in a blue tarp, and a couple of long, tin-roofed sheds extend across the receded yard.

McDaniel points at a log cabin–style water well, standing alone under its own awning, close to the fenced entrance. "That well is in the same place it was when Charles Conner lived here," he says.

The Conner home and Hemphill are separated by a ten-minute car ride on State Road 87. Logging trucks and pickup trucks thunder along hilly stretches of the tree-lined road. Along the way, a driver is bound to see the remains of a feral pig. Red-tailed hawks and the occasional bald

---

56 Interview with author.

eagle can be spotted feasting on the roadkill. Along the way, a traveler will pass over the Conner Creek.

There is no sign or marker, but the moniker appears on most official maps, including official USGS documents and even Google Earth. The locals call it "the Charlie Conner," and it can be seen passing under State Road 87. Charles Conner is buried in Nacogdoches, but his most permanent marker in Sabine County is the stream that bears his name.

There is no great place to park a car to visit the Conner Creek; just pull onto the shoulder enough to avoid the lumber trucks, staying clear of the soft mud. The creek itself is pretty, winding serenely through thick brush and under the signature, shadowy Sabine canopy. The water moves quickly with recently melted snow and produces clean, melodic gurgles.

But walking the Charlie Conner's slick banks is a mess. The thick mud obscures gaps in tree root systems, creating deep and potentially ankle-snapping pits. Nearly every vine seems designed to trip passersby, and most come equipped with thorns. Downed trees crisscross the banks, making both bridges and obstacles. The ticks that plagued the Rangers are still in these woods, too.

It doesn't take too much time hiking to want to return to the road. The route back to Hemphill showcases the sparseness of Sabine County, just 10,800 or so people spread across 577 square miles. The population has shrunk by 3.65 percent since 2010. The county peaked at 12,300 residents in the early 1920s, a number that would decline as the lumber companies thinned out the timber and began to move on.

A map of public and private land in today's Sabine County looks like a patchwork quilt, but it explains the long stretches of undeveloped woodlands interrupted by an occasional ranch or trailer park. There are no traffic lights in the county. Locals have rejected the advances of big-box stores and food franchises, none of which can be found anywhere in Sabine County. (Well, there is a single Dairy Queen. This is *still* Texas.) Clusters of fishing supply shops, trailers, churches, and the occasional antique store populate intersections and roadsides near boat ramps.

The forests that insulated Sabine County from outsiders is what brought in the modern world. The so-called bonanza era of Texas lumbering began about 1880, but it only came to isolated Sabine County in the early 1900s. East Texas was estimated to have had almost 3 million acres of longleaf pine, which has since been cut to fewer than 44,000 acres. In 1907 alone, 2.1 million board feet of longleaf was cut from East Texas forests.[57]

After harvesting virtually every tree in Sabine County, leaving denuded forests surrounding camps locals call "stump towns," the lumber companies turned their backs and moved on. What to do with such ill-used land?

In 1934, the Texas legislature passed a resolution advocating its federal purchase to create national forests in Texas. The Texas Forest Service and the USDA Forest Service worked together to acquire land in what's now the Davy Crockett, Sam Houston, Angelina, and Sabine National Forests. The feds planted trees where natural reseeding hadn't started, but the longleaf pines were replaced with imported slash pine (sown in large numbers by the Civilian Conservation Corps) and shortleaf pine trees. Over the ensuing decades, disease and fungus ripped through Sabine County's trees, including the few original longleaf pines that had been spared the saw.

What remains is a different forest. Longleaf pines have a higher, thicker canopy, so there was less undergrowth when they dominated the area. That means the line of sight of a hunter, outlaw, or lawman in these woods during the 1880s would have stretched much farther than it would today.

Louisiana and Texas took a different route in the 1960s when it came to using the land; they combined efforts to dam the Sabine River and create a massive lake. The Toledo Bend Reservoir began rising in 1964 and filled up quicker than expected, leading to entire homes being unexpectedly drowned instead of being torn down. The watery state line now roughly traces the Sabine River's original route.

Toledo Bend is now a world-class bass lake, with uncounted miles of shallow inlets, bays, and tributaries. The reservoir is also home to bald eagles, alligators, otters, and red-tailed hawks. Homes and boat

---

57 "Restoring Longleaf Pine in East Texas," Texas A&M Forest Service, February 3, 2016.

ramps dot the shoreline, and starting at dawn every day, the surface is crisscrossed by shallow-draft boats. The remains of the forest still claim victims on the reservoir, as many a fiberglass hull has been shattered on a stump lurking just below the water.

Weldon McDaniel strides to the edge of a small bluff on the Toledo Bend Reservoir and points to a spot in the water, just off the shoreline. "Holly Bottom," he announces with an uncharacteristic flourish.

The patch of Sabine County where the Conner and Smith families ran their hogs in the 1880s is now under the water of the fifth-largest man-made lake in the United States. The old Housen Bayou Creek is now just a winding channel that cleaves the muddy bottom of "Housen Bay."

Even after nearly 140 years, Sabine County's interred history can quickly claw to the surface. Oak Hill Baptist Church is just a handful of miles from the submerged Holly Bottom crime scene. A handful of graves were moved here from Fairmount, a nearby town and center of gravity for the Smith family, to escape the man-made lake. Those relocated include Kit Smith. His simple, flat stone now sits a few feet from the base of flagpoles flying the U.S. and Texas standards.

McDaniel stands by the marker solemnly as the wind flaps and twists the flags overhead. The grave site jogs memories. He recalls when his grandfather told him that, on the day Kit was killed, workers putting a roof on an earlier church building here heard the gunshots echoing through the trees.

McDaniel shares the sympathy for the Conner family that persists in Sabine County. Most of all, he regards them as a frontier family that moved to one of the most isolated places in the state to set down roots and live on their own terms. It's no coincidence that this desire is consistently shared by most current residents, including him. "Most of the people who lived here then were like I am now," McDaniel says. "They wanted to be left alone."[58]

Even with all these versions of events at his disposal, Weldon Mc-

---

[58] Interview with author.

Daniel knows which side he's on. "Of course, there's an emotional connection," he says, two hands gripping the cemetery's fence as he looks fixedly at Kit Smith's grave. "He was my great-uncle. He was my kin."

The Sabine County feud is not like the Hatfields versus the McCoys, mythologized to the point of romance. One reason for this feud's obscurity is the unique, insular nature of Sabine County. "For years, no one wanted to discuss what had occurred as it was simply too divisive and the families too intermingled to be considered a worthy subject of conversation," noted Ed Wetterman, a late, local amateur historian.[59]

Suppression worked, but only up to a point. "There are still a lot of hard feelings," McDaniel says. "The name *Conner* still sets some people off."

This can be seen in sporadic internet discussions about the feud. "It should be called the Lowe and Smith rustling feud," rails self-identified descendent Beverley Conner on a genealogy board. "It depends on just who was in with the law officers and what connections they had, back then. The Conners did not have a chance, so they choose to defend their rights."[60]

Descendants describe the veil of secrecy maintained by their elders. "My grandfather, son of Charles Wilson Conner, was William A.H. Conner. He was about 13 years old during these gun battles," reads one such post. "William would never speak to us children about the feud, so it was a mystery to me until I became an adult and began to research the story."[61]

It's a communal amnesia, as befitting the enduringly proud, insular

---

59 Ed Wetterman, "Ike Low and Melissa Travis," East Texas Generations, July 31, 2010, http://easttexasgenerations.blogspot.com/2010/07/ike-low-and-melissa-travis-122-and-123.html.

60 Beverly Conner, "Re: CONNER FEUD in SABINE TEXAS," Genealogy.com, July 8, 2011, https://www.genealogy.com/forum/surnames/topics/conner/4119/.

61 "Texas Anyone Familiar with Conner Feud in Sabine County?," City-Data.com.

streak running through the spine of Sabine County. "The secret here of getting along is to mind your business and ride the fence rail and don't take either side," Dr. Grover Winslow, drawing on four decades as the county doctor, tells *Texas Monthly* in 1986. "People here are a different breed of people from any place you've ever been."[62]

Twenty-five years later, this remains true. This is not the land of big sky, oil money, and Whataburger. In Sabine County, even lifelong Texans can hear the familiar, damning phrase leveled by a local: "You're not from around here, are you." One sign posted near a trailer sums it up: "We are too poor to buy anything. We know who we are voting for. We have found Jesus. NOW LEAVE US ALONE!"

Visitors are not the only ones who experience the insular nature of Sabine County. Captain Steve Scobie is a Toledo Bend Reservoir fishing guide who brings out clients in a custom-made, steel-hulled bass boat virtually invulnerable to subsurface stumps and other debris. He's a well-known transplant to Sabine County, moving here from Houston fifteen years ago to be a full-time resident. Captain Scobie, as he's nearly universally called, used to fish other Texas lakes, like Sam Rayburn, but found the access too restrictive. Here on the Toledo Bend, he can use any number of public boat ramps whenever he chooses. The reason he's in Sabine County is also why his shallow-draft boat is ruggedized to reach the lake's most inaccessible tributaries—to be left alone.

Scobie also sells and repairs rods, making him a popular figure among locals, as well as a small business employer. Grizzled men in boats hail him by name on the water, inquiring about his wares. Given this, it's surprising to hear that Captain Scobie is still regarded as a foreigner. "They're sweet people, they know who you are," he says. "They also know you're not from around here, and they don't forget it."

---

62 Keith Kachtick, "Hanging in Hemphill," *Texas Monthly,* July 1996. The article makes no mention of the Conners or the feud. Kachtick notices that people in passing trucks in Sabine County don't return the customary wave he offers from behind the wheel of his rental car, something that is common courtesy elsewhere in Texas.

It would be easy to point out that the only reason people come here is to kill living things, but hunting and fishing are not de facto blood-thirsty activities. However, not all people prowling the outdoor here deserve the label of "sportsman" as Scobie does. He catches plenty of gar, for example, but releases them. He won't fish out a school—it's both cruel and bad for business—and he doesn't tell anyone where he sees alligators because they will shoot them for no reason.

Along the banks of a tributary of Six Mile Bay, he spots a limb line set illegally to catch a gator but leaves it so the game warden can investigate. "Some people," he laments in disgust, "just want to kill *everything.*"[63]

On land, the national forests are very active hunting areas. The woods are alive with so much seasonal gunfire that No Shooting Zone signs are posted around boat ramps. There are deer and varmints in good numbers, but the preferred game here is pig.

Leaving the paved roads and exploring the backwoods means finding massacred wild hogs, like the clutch of corpses alongside the old Civilian Conservation Corps road near the Conner Cemetery. At least six tattered pig bodies are strewn at a trailhead here, tusks and rib cages gleaming against torn hide and mud-matted fur.

If only there was a way to DNA test these grisly remains and somehow match them against the Conners' free-range herds of the 1800s. There were plenty of feral hogs living in the area before Willis and Piercy Conner moved to Texas—and a whole lot of hogs escaped or were released during the war for Texas independence—but having such a large, open-range herd must have helped infuse the feral swine of the area with new genes.

If the pigs are somehow the genetic heirs of Willis Conner's herd, then it suits that they, like he, are being hunted for money. The Sabine

---

63 Interview with author. Captain Scobie mentions that he's seen a possible swamp ape track before. If he saw one in the flesh, would he report it? "No way," he says immediately. "It would draw every kind of idiot to my fishing spots."

County Agricultural Committee and the Texas A&M AgriLife Extension Service have established Operation Pork Chop to wipe out as many as possible.

"Wild hogs continue to grow in numbers in Sabine County," the program's announcement states. "Because of their destructive feeding habits and potential to spread disease, wild hogs are a substantial liability to agriculture, native wildlife, property owners and the general public." They are invasive and often diseased, but the porcine carnage is still jarring. Feral pigs can be legally killed by snaring, trapping, aerial gunning, hunting with dogs, and sniping them with rifles equipped with thermal scopes. You don't need a hunting license in Texas to kill them, either.

Operation Pork Chop opens annually between January 20 and May 1. Collecting a bounty means cleaning the severed snouts and stashing them in a transparent, sealed freezer bag, but no more than five snouts per baggie. These can be turned in at designated drop-off spots sprinkled throughout Sabine County. Anyone who turns in a hog nose has a chance of winning cash during weekly drawings. The program awarded more than $3,000 in previous seasons. Note: "Decomposing (rotting) snouts will not be accepted."

Most of the dead pigs on CCC road near the Conner Cemetery have their snouts in place. With ribs and hindquarters likewise intact, they don't appear to have been butchered for meat. These feral hogs met their ends following a dark, unspoken tradition of Sabine County; they were shot dead in the woods and left by the roadside to molder.

9

GOODBYE TO THE PASSING THRONG

BACKBONE AND FRIED CHICKEN
September 16, 1890

This summer has been about the chase—not for an outlaw but for the hand of Virginia Willborn. J. A. Brooks, captain of Company F since May, takes a monthlong leave of absence in Center Point to court her. Today, the chase ends.

He and Wilborn's marriage ceremony is held at Coldwell family ranch and attended by current and former Rangers, cowboys, and cattlemen. The newlyweds move to none other than Cotulla, where Brooks, Lieutenant Rogers, and Company F are recently stationed. The pair of lawmen, who split the company to cover more ground, are reuniting in the rowdy town where they first met. The lifelong drinker and teetotaler are unlikely but close friends. They run a well-regarded company. Among other things, Company F is known to have the best food; they eat backbone and fried chicken instead of beans and goat meat.[1]

Cotulla is still a rough town, but it's been lurching toward civilization for long enough to be habitable for a young family. There are only about one thousand folks living there when J. A. and Virginia Brooks

---

1 William Sterling, *Trails and Trials of a Texas Ranger* (Norman: University of Oklahoma Press, 1957).

settle there in 1890. There are two weekly newspapers, a pair of churches, and a bank. There's a single saloon. Two years later, the town shows more signs of progress, with a hotel, four general stores, two more saloons, a pair of grocery stores, and daily stage service. And there are schools, which for Brooks is becoming a priority.

Shortly after they relocate, Company F loses another seasoned private, T. S. Crowder. During his service, he appears in virtually no public documents beyond his Ranger pay receipts. There is one newspaper account of Crowder chasing mule thieves through South Texas. The correspondent captures a snapshot of an ongoing chase: "Mr. Julian Palacios . . . reported to the sheriff that thieves had stolen at his ranch five of his mules while he was away from his ranch, and two Rangers stationed here, Messrs. W. T. Shely and T. S. Crowder, went in pursuit of the thieves guided by Mr. Palacios. It is thought that the thieves are making for the Rio Grande."[2]

Crowder retires from the Rangers after seven years of riding the endless trail. His final service record on file is dated early 1891; ever since joining Company F, he's only ridden with J. A. Brooks. Now he leaves his captain for his new wife. He heads for Martin County, where he has family, to find his own way.

In June 1894, Virginia gives birth to Mary Vernon. Brooks misses the birth, being on a scout, but ventures home soon after to visit his firstborn. However, the infant dies two weeks before Christmas. It will be four years before they have another.

They're still in Cotulla for the births of Corrinne on December 7, 1898, and John Morgan on August 17, 1899. While he clearly favors him to his daughter, Brooks ultimately proves to be an absentee father to both and is often lost on the trail and inside the bottle.

As a professional lawman, his accomplishments only grow. His burgeoning stature as one of Texas's best oil boomtown pacifiers, trusted by the state's most powerful politicians, comes at the price of his wife, who

---

2 "In Hot Pursuit of Horse Thieves," *Galveston Daily News*, July 26, 1890.

is left on her own in a rambunctious city but for the occasional company of a distant husband.[3]

SCOTT'S ROUGH RETIREMENT
November 2, 1893

William Scott doesn't mean for the gun to go off. It just explodes in his hand as he's pistol-whipping the rich cattleman.

The Ranger captain's retirement should be spent divided between his exotic, lucrative work and family in Texas. Things are good on both those fronts; he's a contractor supervising the construction of major road projects in Mexico, and his young wife has given him two sons: George in 1890 and William just this year. He's got money, stature, and a job that satisfies his need for open spaces, rough men, and loaded firearms.

Yet the old rage is still inside him. Or maybe it's a case where the man left the Rangers, but the Rangers didn't fully leave him. Whatever the source, anger surfaces when Scott sees an old foe in San Antonio this early November.

"In a personal affray, William Scott, ex-captain of the rangers, beat James Taylor, a wealthy stockman, over the head with a pistol and severely wounded him," says the *Fort Worth Daily Gazette*. "In this fray Scott's pistol was accidently discharged, but the ball did not take effect. An old feud was the cause of the trouble."[4] No charges are filed.

Scott's life since leaving the Rangers has been a series of blessings

---

3 Paul Spellman, *Captain J. A. Brooks, Texas Ranger* (Denton: University of North Texas Press). The author interviewed family members, who provided a pretty grim view of Brooks at home.

4 There is a good chance this is James Creed Taylor II, who is related to those involved in the Sutton-Taylor feud, the deadliest in Texas history, of the mid-1870s. If so, his father and John Wesley Hardin killed Jack Helm in a blacksmith shop in Wilson County, and Taylor Sr. himself was later shot down. Captains Leander H. McNelly and Lee Hall were both brought in over the years to tamp down the feud in the mid-1870s, ample opportunity for ending a lingering Ranger feud. C. L. Sonnichsen,

and tragedies proportionate to his dramatic life. In 1891, the Scott family suffers a deep blow. Vernon Scott, twenty-five, is on the road in mid-August, this time visiting Galveston. She catches ill, and within days, the intrepid young woman is gone.

William Scott is far from alone in his grief. "She was a most beautiful, popular and accomplished young lady," *The Galveston Daily News* laments. "Numerous friends and relatives bemoan her untimely demise." The news spread to Huntsville "and has cast a gloom over the community. Miss Vernon was a very attractive young lady and quite popular among a large circle of acquaintances over the state."[5]

Two years after the public pistol-whipping, violence again finds William Scott. On February 3, 1895, Scott's in the mountainous wilds forty miles south of Puebla, working at a lumber camp that's clearing land for a road.[6] The ex-Ranger, his brother John, "and a man named Franklin . . . were eating supper when a band of about 80 bandits rushed in upon them," according to *The Brownsville Herald*, quoting a letter from survivors of the attack. "The Americans were cut off from their guns and could only defend themselves with their hands and were shot, cut and clubbed into insensibility."[7]

An earlier account adds that a woman was with the Scotts at the camp, and the bandits "abused her shamelessly." No identity is given and no subsequent account mentions her, either because it's erroneous or because they are shielding the victim. "When the news was received the Americans and English to a man started in pursuit," the *Fort Worth*

"Sutton-Taylor Feud," Texas State Historical Association, https://www.tshaonline .org/handbook/entries/sutton-taylor-feud.

5 *Galveston Daily News*, August 20, 1891.

6 Probably near Tehuitzingo, along modern Highway 190.

7 "The Scotts Saved," *Brownsville Herald*, February 26, 1895.

Daily Gazette, the source of the woman's abuse, reports in February. "It is reported that a number of them have been captured or killed. The governor of the state of Puebla called out the *rurales* and ordered them to bring in the bandits dead or alive."[8]

Scott, as has been mentioned, is a tough son of a bitch. He not only survives the deadly encounter but he also does interviews about the incident within weeks of his return to the United States. "The scars of that battle will be with him all through life and when he is laid in his grave, but they nowise mar the looks of the man who could ever look death squarely in the face without fear or tremor," reads an article from *San Antonio Express*.[9]

Undaunted, Scott returns to work on megaprojects like the Monterrey-Matamoros extension of the National rail line in 1903. That project alone employs 1,200 men and nearly as many mules. He has until 1904 to complete the extension; he finishes it early. Instead of working Mexico, in May 1904, he's taking an extended trip to Saint Louis with his family.[10]

The Scott family relocates to San Antonio, and by 1910, William Scott lives there with them. In late 1912, he falls while strolling in downtown San Antonio. This injury, of all things, sidelines the legendarily tough man, and he dies on November 12, 1913. William Scott is buried in the Masonic Cemetery in Waelder. Georgia Lynch Scott moves back to Waelder, never remarries, and eventually dies a resident in a Dallas County convalescent home in 1952.

In many ways, Scott is a forgotten Texas Ranger captain. After an epic term of service, perhaps his most lasting influence on the organization is the mark he made on John Rogers and J. A. Brooks. When the Rangers will need to be guided through future reorganizations, these two men will persevere by using their old captain as a steady role model.

---

8 "Mexican Bandits," *Fort Worth Daily Gazette*, February 14, 1895.

9 *Brownsville Herald*, May 3, 1904, printing an article from *San Antonio Express*.

10 Ibid.

"I owe much of my success to him, not only as a Texas Ranger but in other vocations while passing through this long life," says Brooks.[11]

By imprinting Rogers and Brooks with his law enforcement ethos—the relentless chase, judicious hand, deliberate violence, unyielding fraternity—Scott helped set the mold for generations of Rangers to come.

THE LAST ARREST
June 21, 1901

Captain John Rogers leaves the posse, with two riders at his side, just outside of the village of Palafox. He, deputy U.S. marshal William Hanson, and U.S. Customs mounted inspector William Merriman are content to hunt Texas's most wanted man on their own.

Gregorio Cortez has been on the run all month, ever since he and his brother's shoot-out with Karnes County sheriff (and former Texas Ranger) W. T. "Brack" Morris. Cortez's brother and Morris lie dead, and the twenty-five-year-old suspected horse thief is now running a gauntlet of posses and lawmen to reach Mexico.

Rogers is a man on the rise, in his personal and professional life. He married Hattie Burwell, of Cotulla, in the spring of 1892 and was promoted to captain at the end of that year. Rogers assumed command of the revived Company E on January 1, 1893, moving to new headquarters in Alice.

Rogers cradles a unique Winchester, its stock crooked at an odd angle. This is a custom-made firearm crafted for Rogers, to compensate for a gunshot he sustained two years ago. In 1889, Rogers and his Company E are ordered to help keep the agitated citizenry in line as patients are isolated and mandatory immunizations distributed. Widespread distrust between the Mexican community and public health officials feeds fears and unrest. As Rogers and his men respond as riots grip the city, a rifleman shoots him through the upper arm. He staggers from the field as his men continue the fight.

---

11 Transcript of Brooks's handwritten memoirs, Texas Ranger Hall of Fame and Museum, Waco, TX.

Rogers is horribly wounded, and this time, there is more permanent damage. Surgeons remove a length of bone from his arm, leaving it inches shorter. Gunsmiths have customized his Winchester's stock with a bend to offset the imbalance between limbs; Rogers is still regarded as a crack shot.

On June 22, 1901, he may get another chance to prove it. That's when a vaquero named El Teco approaches him and the trio of lawmen with news that a road-weary cowboy just arrived to sneak into a shack on his goat farm. The man, El Teco says, could be the fugitive Cortez.

It's not blind luck that brings Rogers here. He knows the area from previous scouts, and the river crossing west of Don Abran de la Garza's ranch. The wanted man will need some food and shelter, and probably a horse, and that means stealing from the border ranches. The hunch, it seems, is paying off.

He and Merriman follow El Teco to the goat farm and rein in their horses well shy of the small shack where the vaquero last saw the man in hiding. The customs inspector aims his Winchester at the back door of the shack as Rogers slowly approaches the front. Pushing the door open, Rogers scans the dim room. A man lies prone on the floor.

He doesn't move until Rogers prods him awake. Gregorio Cortez gives up without any struggle. The Ranger escorts the prisoner to Laredo and hops on a coal train with him to Karnes County, where he hands off the prisoner to the waiting sheriff.[12]

This arrest is the last for the Frontier Battalion. The Texas legislature is shelving the organization and replacing it with the Texas Ranger Force "for the purpose of protecting the frontier against marauding or thieving Parties, and for the suppression of lawlessness and crime throughout the State."

The Rangers hear the news in April, when the adjutant general sends a telegram to his Ranger captains, notifying them that the bill had

---

12 Paul Spellman, *Captain John H. Rogers, Texas Ranger* (Denton: University of North Texas Press, 2003). Cortez would endure several trials, a lynch mob, prison, and an eventual pardon. He's the subject of popular *corridos* in Mexico.

been passed in Austin. The law takes effect July 1, making the seizure of Cortez the Frontier Battalion's last official action.

The new law rectifies one lingering sticking point, at least. Each Ranger is now explicitly considered an officer with the right to perform arrests. For monthly pay, captains get one hundred dollars, sergeants fifty dollars, and privates forty dollars.

But, as expected, the new service will be reshuffled. It could be much worse. The law divides the Texas Rangers into four companies, each with twenty men. That means four captains will guide the new force into the twentieth century. The Rangers tap notably old-school lawmen to helm the companies—longstanding captains John Hughes and Bill McDonald, and the Company F veterans J. H. Rogers and J. A. Brooks.

The activities of the new service, according to a Texas Department of Public Safety website, is to be "similar to those of the Frontier Battalion after 1880" (i.e., focused on domestic law enforcement work).[13] It's a role that, for all its problems, seems to fit the Texas Rangers best. It will be up to captains like Rogers and Brooks to show how their bold, headstrong style can apply to the new, systemic lawlessness roiling Texas.

WIDE-OPEN OIL TOWNS
January 20, 1904

Ranger Captain J. A. Brooks disembarks at the Liberty train depot, with Sergeant Winfred Bates and Privates Lott Tumlinson and Clyde McDowell behind him. It's an eighteen-mile trip by hack from here to Batson, the notorious oil town.

Most of the ride from Liberty is a smooth journey across flat prairie land, but the last five miles into town is not so smooth. "Imagine a drive over five miles over a corduroy road," says a *Galveston Daily News* reporter who took the same ride between Liberty and Batson in 1904. "That is

---

13 "History of the Texas Ranger," Department of Public Safety, https://www.dps.texas .gov/TexasRangers/texasrangershistory.htm.

over a road built by laying thousands of fence rails across the road to prevent the heavily-loaded wagons from sinking to the hubs in soft mud. Your teeth either rattle together as you lean forward in the cloud of dust or spray of soft mud."[14]

Texas may have left its Wild West trappings behind, but the state is hosting plenty of chaos and corruption of a more modern variety. The oil bonanza has brought a new dynamic, new people, and new power brokers. Awash with money and transitory men, boomtowns become havens for corrupt deputies, organized crime, and all manner of petty predators who specialize in parting grimy workers from their wages. Drunks, whores, and gamblers make the oil towns festive, profitable, and dangerous, depending on your point of view.

Just such a place is Batson. In 1903, wildcatters open a handful of lucrative wells northwest of Beaumont, causing an economic wave that sweeps over the village of Otto, which relocates and renames itself Batson. The town's population has waned in the months since the first boom, but at least four thousand workers are still here, most of whom live in tent cities and makeshift shacks in three distinct camps they call "groves."

Downtown is a single north-south street, lined with hotels, saloons, stores, and two banks. The town's ramshackle growth is evidenced by the uneven, surreal appearance of Main Street. "The street is straight in a general direction, but the houses twist and squirm in and out in a bewildering manner," according to *The Galveston Daily News*. There are no cross streets. No one who built these homes owns the land they sit on, and it's uncertain who should get the rent. Clashing surveys have prompted 1904 locals to call Main Street "the disputed Strip."

The street, of course, leads to the oil fields, the reason Batson exists, just north of town. From anywhere on Main Street, the reporter notes, "you can hear the threatening rumble of the hundreds of oil burners and pumps at work getting the greasy fluid to be pumped away to Beaumont and Port Arthur."

---

14 "Calves Laid Out Batson," *Galveston Daily News,* September 25, 1904.

Brooks and his Rangers check into a hotel constructed of "cheap, un-seasoned pine lumber with resin still oozing out of the unpainted boards," recounts William Sterling, Brooks's friend and author. "After spending one miserable day in the so-called hotel, the Rangers procured a tent, borrowed some cooking utensils and pitched camp in a grove on the edge of town."[15] The antiquated pleasure of a chuck wagon campsite is not forgotten.

Law and order in oil towns like these is understandably lacking. There is an understanding here—gambling, prostitution, and wanton drinking are tolerated twenty-four hours a day, including Sundays. "Public sentiment seems to have been favorable to a wide-open town," *The Galveston Daily News* says. In the same way, the idea of a jury trial in Batson is absurd. Hell, the town doesn't have a jail. Any given morning, a half dozen hookers and drunks could end up chained to a tree at the end of Main Street, glumly sitting in the mud.

This is clearly not an environment for conventional law enforcement. It will take both grit and flexibility to bring any sense of order to Batson. The Rangers are not here to clean up the town, per se, but to tamp down the worst of the violence and excesses. Their approach is imminently re-alistic, the kind of compromise between the demands of their duty and the limitations of circumstances.

There are too many oil towns and too few Rangers to police them all. So they rove, doing what they can. As Ethel Stivers, wife of an oil field worker, once told Texas historians: "The Rangers would come into Batson and they'd clean it up and it would be decent for a while. Then the gamblers would come back and start up again. The Rangers would return, the judge would fine everybody $10 and they'd pay it and go back to what they'd been doing."[16]

---

15 Sterling, *Trails and Trials.*

16 "Mr. and Mrs. Bert Stivers Interview," August 26, 1953, Texas Pioneers of Oil Collection, Center for American History, Austin, TX, reels 143 and 144. Hat tip, as they did in the 1800s and say on social media in 2021, to author Paul Spellman's research.

One thing that the Texas Rangers do bring to oil towns is a focus not on the citizenry, which can be expected to be wicked, but the corrupt local police who abuse their positions. There is more long-term good that can be done by pushing back against crooked deputies than dealing with drunks, pimps, and brawlers.

Punishing crooked local law becomes part of the formula adopted by Brooks and the other captains. This deployment to Batson will soon give the Rangers an anecdotal story that sums up the coming years of work inside oil boomtowns.

The villain is a hulking, 220-pound deputy who made his reputation by shooting down a drunk man. He had spent the weeks preceding the Rangers' arrival boasting about how he planned to set them straight, and Brooks tells his sergeant that he expects that they'll end up shooting the man.

When Bates hears that the lawman is beating a dancing girl, he expects trouble. Indeed, the deputy reaches for his pistol when Bates intervenes, but the diminutive Ranger pistol-whips him into unconsciousness. The large man wakes chained to the tree outside of town. The local constable and justice of the peace soon end up in the mud with the deputy after trying to free him.[17]

In February, Brooks heads to Austin to brief the bosses. He first meets with Adjutant General John Hulen,[18] and then the two men attend a strategy session. "They had a conference with the governor, during which the

---

17 The Bates anecdote comes from William Sterling, who was in a good position to pick up Ranger lore from their sources. Independent corroboration is difficult, however. For example, he mentions Beaumont and Houston newspapers running stories about the Bates fight under an ace headline: 120 POUND RANGER WHIPS 220 POUND DEPUTY. However, Newspapers.com and the Texas State historical newspaper archives have no articles about the incident.

18 Wilburn King retires as adjutant general on January 23, 1891; he started the job in July 1881. King dies in Sulphur Springs, Texas, on October 12, 1910. "His body was taken by train to Corsicana and was met at the depot by a contingent of Confederate veterans from Camp Winkler and a large group of Masons." David S.

situation was gone over in detail. Captain Brooks will return to Batson, as his presence there will not complicate matters in the slightest."[19]

THE ESCORT
September 1904

Captain J. A. Brooks has been a Texas Ranger for twenty-one years. He bears the scars and bearing of a man who has seen action and a hard-won wisdom when it comes to leading and persuading tough men. He's becoming a legend in Texas, and it's this stature that now brings him to Fort Sill in Indian Territory. It's impossible not to remember riding into here with Knight and Putz, the relief of reaching safety from any pursuing posses. He won't linger; this is just a stop on the way to Missouri.

The Louisiana Purchase Exposition—better known as the St. Louis World's Fair—has been open since the end of April 30. It's a celebration of the American frontier, reveling in the centennial of President Thomas Jefferson's $15 million real estate deal for six hundred million acres of French territory. Of course, the president and Napoleon Bonaparte inked the Louisiana Purchase in 1803, but it took until 1804 for the word of it to reach Saint Louis. Later that year, Meriwether Lewis and William Clark departed Missouri to map the new lands, opening the West to American manifest destiny. It's reason enough to have a party.

Brooks won't be traveling to the Fair alone. He's here to escort another living legend to Saint Louis.

The Apache chief Geronimo has been living under a loose house arrest at the Fort Sill reservation for more than a decade but has accepted an invitation to attend the World's Fair. "I didn't wish to go," Geronimo later writes in an autobiography. "Later, when I was told I would receive good attention and protection, and that the President of

---

Walkup, "King, Wilburn Hill," *Handbook of Texas Online,* https://www.tshaonline.org/handbook/entries/king-wilburn-hill.

19 "Report on Batson," *Houston Post,* February 16, 1904.

the United States [Theodore Roosevelt] said that I would be all right, I consented."

Part of his protective detail is the famous Texas Ranger captain J. A. Brooks. The men don't know each other, but their reputations precede them. The Apache chief and grizzled lawmen hop a train to join the thousands of Texans streaming north to celebrate Texas Day on September 12.

Brooks and Geronimo are an unlikely duo on this road trip, especially considering a near miss that would have pitted the two men on opposite sides of a Winchester. It's not known if Brooks mentions it to Geronimo, but the pair almost crossed paths decades ago under very different circumstances.

The tale comes down from Frank Carmichael, who told a reporter in Abilene that the governor of New Mexico (when it was a territory) wrote Captain William Scott with an offer. He'd pay handsomely if Company F could travel west and hunt down Geronimo.

"Capt. Scott consulted his men, all of whom were eager to go," the article relates Carmichael's tale. "Then he asked permission of Governor Ross, who refused permission but promised that if Geronimo came into Texas, Company F would have the honor of taking him."[20]

In spite of this averted clash—or possibly because of it—the two veteran warriors get along during their time together. The Apache leader even whittles a child's bow and arrow as a gift for Brooks's five-year-old son, John Morgan.[21]

The 1904 World's Fair is the largest in history, with more than 1,500 buildings spread over two square miles. There are canals and lagoons, dotted with festive mariners in gondolas and boats. The world's largest pipe organ plays inside the opulent Festival Hall. Saint Louis Art Museum, the only permanent exhibition facility, houses masterpieces and ancient artifacts from around the world. The Smithsonian Institution sets up a 228-feet-

---

20 *Abilene Reporter-News*, June 12, 1938.

21 On display at the Ranger Heritage Museum, Falfurrias, TX.

long, fifty-feet-high Flight Cage, the largest walk-through aviary ever built. There are eleven "palaces" built as temples to such concepts as Electricity, Fine Arts, Horticulture, Agriculture, and Machinery. Sixty-two countries and forty-two American states represent themselves in freestanding halls.[22]

Brooks squires Geronimo to Texas's hall, a star-shaped building with five long, pointed wings radiating from the circular rotunda, which sits on a hill overlooking the other state buildings. The dome on top of the central rotunda is adorned with a bronze statue of the goddess Liberty.

They pass under a welcoming banner that says: WISE MEN OF THE EAST, BEHOLD THE STAR OF TEXAS. They stroll past exhibits showcasing oil, cattle and rail lines, paintings of battlefields, and portraits. Statues of Texas figures both old and new—like Steve Austin, Sam Houston, Governors Sayers and Ross—stare down from pedestals.[23]

There are also flesh and blood Texas luminaries everywhere. The Texas House is the premier hospitality center for the Lone Star State at the fair. A small army of hostesses, all prominent Texas ladies, are on hand to schmooze and coordinate a slate of social activities. On top of the fair itself are club gatherings, society parties, and political meetings. Fraternal orders hold national meetings.

This makes it a logical place for power broker hobnobbing and scheming. Brooks's journey to the World's Fair comes during the early part of his transition from lawman to politician. He plans on making his stake in South Texas, and this is a fateful time for both himself and the political map of the state.

For the past two years, Company F has been engaged in a campaign to tamp down horse theft in South Texas, rounding up more than three hundred stolen horses during the process. It's given him plenty of opportunity to see the power politics at work south of Corpus Christi.

---

22 Edward H. Phillips, "Texas and the World Fairs, 1851–1935," *East Texas Historical Journal* 23, no. 2 (1985).

23 Ibid.

While on the job there, Brooks meets a man who will become his guide to a post-Ranger life, Edward Cunningham Lasater. He owns more than three hundred thousand acres in the northern part of the unreasonably large Starr County and has a sprawling ranch he calls Falfurrias. He has become the center of gravity of a movement of dissident farmers and businessmen who are chafing under the rule of Manuel Guerra, the undisputed political boss of Starr County.

Guerra headquarters the organization in Roma, the seat of his mercantile business and near his own sizable ranch. He's a self-made businessman but operates under the umbrella of the local Democratic Party, which in turn is held by Cameron County power broker James B. Wells.

Lasater needs an independent power base, so he decides to build one from scratch. In 1904, he forms a company to spark a new settlement. The Falfurrias Immigration Company offers tracts of land in the soon-to-be incorporated town of Falfurrias. He wants the town to be the seat of a new county and needs a face in Austin to push the idea.

Brooks is already signed on. In June, he puts a $240 down payment on a modest eighty acres eight miles south of Falfurrias. He'll pay the remaining $960 at 7 percent interest over the next four years. The move officially pits him against the Guerra machine. Even as he continues as a Ranger, the political battles that await his retirement are forming like clouds on the horizon.

The Brooks family moves to the Falfurrias homestead in 1905. A photo of the family shows a ranch home on short stilts, with a humble steeple roof and small porch. There are two girls in dresses on the lawn and a child in a crib. Brooks himself stands near the doorway, wearing very high-waisted pants and a long-sleeve shirt. Hatless, it's clear he's now fully bald, making his bulging brow even more pronounced. The overall impression of his head is that it's shaped like a peanut.

Like all photos and paintings of him since 1887, Brooks holds his maimed hand behind his leg, out of view. He never loses his self-consciousness about the injury, but on occasion uses it as a prop for gallows humor among Rangers. One time, hearing his sergeant bragging about the "picnic" he expects to find during an impending assignment to East Texas, Captain Brooks holds up his mangled hand. "It may not be much of a picnic, boys," he intones. "This is what I got over there."[24]

Virginia is seated on the porch, staring at the camera. The details of her face, blurred and inscrutable, hide the hardship of life with a dissociated, alcoholic spouse.

Increasingly over the years, Brooks's service record becomes dotted with unexplained breaks. A few of these trips are family visits, and more are made to promote his South Texas machinations. But these trips are also opportunities—or excuses—to indulge. "Some of those protracted absences—and even times at home—were alcohol-related binges," says Brooks biographer Paul Spellman, basing the assessment on family interviews.[25]

When he turns fifty-one in 1906, he's ready to pivot his entire attention to South Texas. He works up until his last days. On November 9, Brooks joins Captain Bill McDonald in the aftermath of the assassination of a judge; three days later, he asks the adjutant general John Augustus Hulen[26] for permission to go to Falfurrias. A day after he arrives on November 13, he sends a telegram to Austin:

> "I desire to tender my resignation as captain of Company A of the Texas Rangers, said resignation to take effect on Nov. 15, 1906, which action on my part is due to pressing private business which demands my personal attention and which renders my further service in such position detrimental to my best interests. Trusting this will meet with your kind attention and acceptance, I beg to remain, Yours very truly, J. A. Brooks."

24 Sterling, *Trails and Trials.*

25 Ibid.

26 Adjutant general from 1902 to 1907.

Hulen sends a telegram in return: "You have made an enviable record, and the loss of your experience to the State cannot be estimated. You have always most faithfully and excellently performed your duties, and you can and doubtless will, look back upon your long service as an officer of the State with pride and satisfaction."

It's the end of a contentious life for Brooks but the start of another struggle, this one fought with legislation, ballots, and cartographer's pen.

"THEIR OWN CONSCIENCE WAS A SELF-RESTRAINT AND LAW"
February 12, 1919

It's a tough day in the capitol building in Austin for U.S. marshal John Rogers. He's surrounded by friends, but right now, they're all acting like the politicians and lawyers that they are. Both sides are badgering him to score points—that is, when they are not fighting each other—as he tries to testify before the Joint Commission Investigating the Texas State Ranger Force.

He's not being accused of any wrongdoing; he's not even a Ranger anymore, being retired since 1911. But the commission needs a lawman of impeccable reputation to speak for the embattled Texas Rangers, accused of mass murder by Texas state representative José Tomás Canales. He may be a U.S. marshal, but the commission feels Rogers's nineteen-year legacy in the Rangers makes him a legend worth hearing from.

The famed lawman is also an ideal witness because he won't be savaged by Canales. The marshal and representative have been friends since Rogers's and Brooks's Company F was stationed around the South Texas town of Alice when Canales was just a boy. In these very proceedings, he has called Rogers and other Ranger captains of the previous generation "the noblest and best men that I know . . . At that time they gave us protection. They were a capable set of men, and did not need any restriction because their own conscience was a self-restraint and law."

That stands in stark contrast to the Special Rangers that Canales is investigating. And that is the point.

When Rogers retired in 1911, the *El Paso Herald* declared him "the Man Who Knows No Fear" and predicted he'd settle down. "He prefers a dove colored fedora hat to the broad brimmed Stetson so common among the men of the plains, and a hard-bled shirt and standing collar appeal to him more strongly than the heavy brown flannel shirt of the cow regions," the article describes. "He has long discarded the high heel, long boots for patent leather laced shoes, and the buckskin leggings and khaki coat have given way to the tailored suit."

The article all but says, once Texas is fully tamed, the Rangers will be consigned to history: "It is not likely his equal will be developed during the remaining few years these hardy, daring 'cowboy police' are destined to enforce the law in the sparsely settled districts which are being so rapidly developed and populated."

But chaos is coming to Texas. Rogers leaves the organization on the eve of the Mexican Revolution, and a dark era in Ranger history.

In 1915, incursions of raiding bandits from Mexico, coupled with wartime intelligence battles between the U.S. and German governments, put the entire Rio Grande Valley in Texas up in a panic. It's not all phantom threats and racism: Trains are derailed, ranches pillaged, and, in a particularly inflammatory incident, ten Mexican raiders are killed during a pitched assault on the King Ranch. The instinct in Austin to use Texas Rangers like mounted soldiers flares once again.[27]

Ethnic tension dovetails with fears of sedition. To face the crisis, Governor James Ferguson sends hundreds of newly drafted Special Texas Rangers to the border to curb violence between Anglos and ethnic Mexicans. Instead, they wage a campaign against the population and summarily execute at least three hundred "suspected" Mexicans. Many of these are identified by Special Rangers who work as local state-sanctioned informants. The response of the Mexican American population of the Rio

---

27 This lesson is nearly lost during the U.S. war with Spain. On April 19, 1898, Rogers and Brooks are ordered to "immediately recruit your company to twelve men and make preparations to move at a moment's notice." They are being called to secure the border against retaliatory strikes from Mexico. They see no action, but the episode is a premonition of things to come.

Grande Valley is exodus; hundreds of families flee into Mexico by September.[28]

Rogers doesn't return to the Rangers during the panic; he's been appointed U.S. Marshal over the Western District of Texas in 1913. But Winfred Bates does go back. After leaving the Company F, the young man has wandered the fringes in search of opportunity, working as an oil operator in Houston, for the government in the Panama Canal construction zone, and on rail projects in Brazil. By 1912, he's the transportation superintendent for a Mexican subsidiary of Standard Oil. He rejoins the Rangers on March 29, 1915, as a thirty-two-year-old private in Company C. With his qualifications, Bates would have been a rare, seasoned recruit.[29]

But he doesn't last long. It's not certain why, but he resigns on June 15, 1915. Maybe he saw just how different the Rangers had become. In 1916, magazine writer George Marvin says of them: "Twenty-five or thirty years ago they were a fine body of men, but degenerated into a roving body of mankillers."[30]

The 1919 hearings are part of the reckoning. Representative Canales's demands for an investigation before a joint committee have finally been heard, but he finds a hostile commission that sabotages his attempts to demand accountability.

The flavor of the exchanges is best captured when the chairman of the committee, W. H. Bledsoe, accuses Canales of fabricating outrage during Rogers's appearance. "I will ask you to state whether or not such information, surreptitiously conveyed over there, would not have a tendency to re-intensify the smoldering hatred in the breasts of those bandits against the people on this side of the river?"

---

28 Proceedings of the Joint Committee of the Senate and the House in the Investigation of the State Texas Rangers, Thirty-Sixth Legislature, regular session, 1919.

29 "Bates" (obituary), *San Antonio Express*, October 29, 1969.

30 George Marvin, "Bandits and the Borderland," *World's Work*, vol. 32, October 1916.

"That kind of an examination of the witness is argumentative and absolutely improper in this case," Canales snaps.

Rogers may be the commission's witness, but that doesn't mean he plays along. For example, he demurs when Robert E. Lee Knight, the Dallas attorney retained by the adjutant general's office, asks him for his opinion of current Rangers.

"Do you consider the general average of the men engaged in the service now up to the standard of former years?"

"Well, I will tell you," Rogers says. "I haven't kept in very close touch with them for the last six years since I have been in the Marshal's office."

Rogers is more evasive when Knight asks for his opinion of Captain William Hanson, the head of the Loyalty Rangers:

> I would rather leave that out; of course, if you absolutely force me I would tell the truth. That does not mean that I know anything definite against Captain Hanson but I would rather not enter into personalities for different reasons, but one is this: I have a riverfront here of six or seven hundred miles and these boys help and cooperate with me. They are my personal friends, and even if they were not my personal friends they cooperate with me and I want to be friendly with the Rangers. I don't want this Committee to consider this against Captain Hanson, but I would rather not go into it unless you have me to do it.

They let the matter drop. So does Canales, when he faces his friend and now witness.

Canales first invokes the already hallowed names of the Rangers of an earlier era to amplify his charge that the organization has lost its way. "Now, at that time that you were in the service, Captain Hughes was also a captain. And Captain Brooks."

"Yes sir."

"Did you ever hear of any Captain then, or any of the other men, taking a man out of jail or in their possession, and after having them in their possession shooting them?"

"Absolutely not," Rogers says. "Such conduct is a blot on the history of this State, such a thing as that."[31]

There is a revealing exchange between the two men, who are discussing the need for principled and sober law enforcement officers, whom Canales refers to as "God fearing men."

Rogers takes exception: "What do you mean by God fearing men? You mean that every man on the force should be a Christian man?"

"No," the politician says, now being questioned by the witness. "I mean that every man should be of good character, of good moral character and good habits."

Rogers nods. "Yes, that is all right."

Canales goes back to an earlier discussion Rogers had with the commission lawyers about the frequency of "mistaken killings" at the hands of Texas Rangers. "You say it occurs maybe once in twenty years," Canales says. "Now, when these things happen once or twice a month, don't you think it is time to undertake to regulate it?"

"Yes, I certainly think so," Rogers responds. "And if it can't be done any other way, why, to abolish the force."

"I thank you very much, Captain," Canales then closes.

The committee unsurprisingly absolves the Texas Rangers of all legal wrongdoing, but the public exercise documents abuses in ways that cannot be ignored. The legislature soon adopts many of the reforms Canales champions, including reducing the overall number of Rangers by twenty men, to sixty, and establishing protocols for citizen complaints. The state also makes two changes that Rogers and Canales agree on: giving the Rangers a pay raise and, for the first time, listing "high moral character" as an enlistment requirement.

Canales's stamp of approval of Rogers and the other four captains

---

31 It's hard to reconcile Rogers's piousness with the bloody execution of William Conner alleged by family members after the 1887 fight.

resonates through the years. He is the historic face of Ranger accountability, after all.

The Rangers of this era earned their good reputations and are usually credited with stopping racial violence, if anything. For example,
in 1902, J. A. Brooks arrested six Latinos suspected of killing a Texas
Ranger near the King Ranch. Brooks paid a visit to the gathering lynch
mob in Brownsville, where the suspects were jailed, and told the mob
they would have to kill him and all his Rangers to get to the prisoners.
The mob backed down.[32]

The nostalgia for the leaders with roots in the Frontier Battalion
men becomes more important in the wake of the Rangers' disgraces.
The names and images of the late 1880s conjure days not of suppression
of minorities but the establishment of law and order to create the modern
state of Texas.

Rogers and Brooks are the faces of their outlaw-hunting era, and
their records are free of the atrocities that besmirch the service after
they retire. In a review of the scathing book *Cult of Glory*, reviewer
Paul Spellman notes author Doug Swanson's lack of attention paid to
Brooks and Rogers:

> Even within the framework of the notes there are tells as to the
> bias of his theme. For example, in the period from the 1880s
> into the early 1900s, three Ranger captains—John Harris Rog-
> ers, John R. Hughes, and J. A. Brooks—embodied the very
> characteristics of responsible leadership and physical courage
> under fire that any enforcer of the law would want to emulate,
> inheriting similar capabilities of former Rangers such as Lean-
> der McNelly and John B. Jones, promulgating the bright aura

---

32 Garth Jones, "One Mob, One Ranger Tradition Is Still True with Great Law
   Agency," Associated Press, September 9, 1956.

of what it meant to be a Ranger and thereby extending the prototype another generation forward.[33]

The absence of William Scott from the list of influences notwithstanding, what stands out is the importance these famous captains have to the modern view of Ranger heritage. Rogers and Brooks did indeed put their Old West stamp on the modernizing organization, something unique in law enforcement and a hallmark that remains intact today. Their careers as captains were exemplary and should not be ignored while examining the sweeping history of the Texas Rangers.

In the culture wars of the twenty-first century, these men are also supposed to be "bright aura" avatars, not overworked cops working a vast, challenging beat. This heroic shroud obscures the realities of their lives as Texas Rangers and is nearly as unfair and dehumanizing as branding them racists by association.

LEGENDS ON THE WALL
October 7, 2020

It's a slow Wednesday for the Texas Ranger Hall of Fame and Museum in Waco. Until this year, weekdays hosted hordes of tourists and students unloaded by the busload. But in the age of COVID-19, there are only a handful of sightseers wandering the exhibits. Masks are required for entry; even the statue of Ranger and prospector George Erath outside wears a bandana across his face. The virus is a disaster for the museum, but a boon to visitors who can enjoy each room privately.

Painted portraits of famous Rangers stand vigil around the Hall of Fame rotunda, which circles a movie theater with seats scattered per CDC guidelines. Some familiar faces leap from the gently curved walls—J. H. Rogers, J. A. Brooks, and Ira Aten.

---

33 Paul Spellman, "Criminal Law and Criminal Justice Books," February 2021 (a book review project run by the Rutgers Law School and Rutgers School of Criminal Justice).

"By the late 19th century and after the Civil War, Texas Rangers were concerned with feuds, mobs, fence cutting, bank and stagecoach robberies and general lawlessness," reads one exhibit. "Rangers pursued criminals using new methods and tools."

The most extreme example of this—Aten's fence cutter bomb—has earned its own life-size diorama in the museum. The scene depicts the Ranger burying a long box, shotgun, and dynamite beneath a fence festooned with a death threat from fence cutters. The Aten mannequin, leaning over a shovel to admire his improvised explosive device, has a mustachioed face frozen in a suitably inscrutable look.

Other tableaux are familiar from Company F's turn-of-the-century outlaw hunting. Most striking is the children's exhibit of two mannequins, one a fence cutter caught in the act in broad daylight, the other a ranger drawing down on the man. Old fashion wooden ponies circle the scene, each with a child's seat facing the dramatic moment. Missing are the dead, bleeding horses and men, gunned down in a surprise moonlight ambush.

The museum gift shop has the usual array of key chains, shot glasses, T-shirts, and posters. There are plenty of books on the stands: biographies of famous Rangers, Bonnie and Clyde retrospectives, children's books about Texas's past, encyclopedic tomes on the firearms the Rangers carried. *Cult of Glory* is notably absent.

Leather belts and diary covers have tags saying, "Handmade in prison." Some things never change.

Brooks and Rogers are joined in the Four Great Captains exhibit by their contemporaries, William MacDonald and John Hughes. These leaders did more than steer their men through budget cuts and political resistance: They defied predictions that the Rangers style would become irrelevant once Texas lost its frontier wildness. Instead, they became the state's elite lawmen.

The four captains' display case is Rogers-heavy. There's a photo of him and his brother propped upright in a wooden mount; John Rogers is standing, his maimed arm extended to rest a hand on the shoulder of Kid Rogers, who's sitting. Both men wear light hats; John wears a six-shooter, vest, and tie. His frame is solid and stocky. Next to it stands a signed catechism that he gave to fellow Ranger J. L. Dibrell.

The information card below is titled "A Man of God" and reads: "Captain Rogers is referred to as one of the 'Christian Rangers' for he was said to 'carry a bible in one hand and a six shooter in the other' and was ready to use both. He was an active member of the church throughout his lifetime and did not drink, smoke or swear. He was also a mentor to his men and had a hand in appointing a chaplain for the Rangers."

Rogers serves as a U.S. marshal until 1921 and dies in Temple, Texas, on November 11, 1930. "He was the friend of many of the leading sheriffs of this state, and they will miss and mourn him for a long time," reads a full-page article acknowledging his passing in the *Sheriff's Association of Texas Magazine*. "He did every duty that was ever assigned him, whether as a Ranger, city marshal or deputy sheriff. When death called and his commission was returned, it was clean and brilliant. He had never left a stain on it."[34]

The museum artifact on display that truly showcases the captain's imprint during the Rangers' transition to modernity is a photo of Rogers and Frank Hamer, famed for a long career capped with the bloody ambush of the machine-gun-toting celebrity outlaws Bonnie Parker and Clyde Barrow. Rogers recruited and mentored Hamer, ensuring the lessons of William Scott passed to a new generation of legends. The trap that snared Bonnie and Clyde would be familiar to Scott, even if the weapons and vehicles of 1934 would not.

Near the museum's entrance, Henry Putz stares handsomely from a black-and-white photo mounted behind glass. T. R. Knight kept studio photos of Brooks and Putz, taken in Brownwood well after the shooting, in a personal collection that has been acquired and donated to the museum. Knight scrawled on the bottom of the photo cards that the men

---

34 "Many Brilliant Exploits Manifest Courage of Captain Rogers," *Sheriff's Association of Texas Magazine*, March 1931.

were involved "with the death of Albert St. John in the Territories." There is no further information presented with the photo.

This is more recognition than most of Company F is given, in the museum and in general. Brooks, Rogers, Aten, and even Kid Rogers achieved some fame, but history has largely overlooked the rest. They stare mutely from colorless photos of Company F, dressed in their city outfits and clutching rifles. They exist in biographies only to fight and die alongside their more famous fellows. Very few have biographic files in the Ranger museum's research center that go beyond their service records.

For most of the Company F men, their time as Texas Rangers is brief but significant. Their lives are not defined by their service. Still, they build on those experiences and embrace them in unexpected ways.

PUTZ'S PICTURE SHOW
July 1898

Henry Putz unfurls the bedsheet like a banner, hanging it on one end of the storeroom above the Bumpas and Kirby drugstore.[35] He's on the second floor, and the heat is rising from the floorboards under the empty seats, making the room feel like a kiln.

This upstairs storeroom is Dallas's first movie theater. The selections are not that compelling, in terms of plot. There are, in Putz's words, "a railway train in motion, a few rounds of a prize fight and some rough comedy stuff."[36] Nevertheless, in his gut, he knows people will show up to be enthralled by the technology.

Putz has always been interested in engineering, and this is cutting-edge machinery. It could also be profitable, in time. But first, he has to start humbly, showing the films above this hot drugstore on Main and Lamar Streets. His trust in the populace's wonderment for new things

35 D. Troy Sherrod, *Historic Dallas Theatres* (Mount Pleasant, SC: Arcadia Publishing, 2014).

36 "Corsicanan First Movie Operator," *Corsicana Daily Sun*, September 15, 1921.

and his skill at marketing is well founded. Flush from small-scale successes, he arranges an outdoor viewing downtown, with images projected across Main Street onto a wall, and "the exhibition drew such large crowds that the street was entirely blocked."[37]

Such progressive, future-embracing displays are exactly what Dallas—shedding its cow town image for a more cosmopolitan mask—is eager to embrace. By 1909, Putz's picture shows appear in the iconic grounds of Fair Park, free of charge. Putz cleverly sees the potential for profit from his monopoly on concessions. Of course, the city gets a kickback from sales.

"The concessionaire made his income by selling advertisement time to local merchants and then showing these 'commercials' to the audiences between movies, much in the fashion of a modern television commercial," reads one official Dallas history of Fair Park. "Also, in some parks the concessionaire sold cold drinks with a fifteen percent commission going to the park board. In 1911 this park attraction expanded to Oak Lawn and then later to all the playground parks."[38]

This is Texas, and anything worth having is going to be fought over. Putz fends off competitors for the lucrative concessions, one of the biggest threats being J. Waddy Tate, who will become both mayor and park board president.

Putz isn't easily cowed and retains control against all contenders. He shows his resolve again when he screens "wet propaganda" advertising and earns the ire of the State Prohibition Committee. This son of German immigrants doesn't have much patience for proponents of abstinence and continues to show what he wants.

His theater empire expands to Wichita Falls. Putz opens and manages

---

37 Ibid.

38 Dr. Harry Jebsen Jr. et al, "Centennial History of the Dallas Texas Park System 1876–1976," 1976, City of Dallas, https://dallascityhall.com/government/citysecretary/archives/DCH%20Documents/Dallas_Park_Rec_Centennial_History.pdf.

a theater there, but still lives in Dallas and keeps control of the free movies there well into the 1920s. "The 1922 season has been the most successful in the history of free moving pictures in the Dallas parks, Henry Putz, in charge, reports," reads the *Austin American-Statesman*. "More than one million persons have viewed the pictures during the summer, according to Mr. Putz, who estimated an average of 2000 persons at each performance.[39]

While there's no evidence extant that *indisputably* links Putz the movie operator with Putz the former Texas Ranger, clues are there.

When Putz opens his movie house in Wichita Falls, a news item mentions that Putz worked in that town as a gunsmith in 1884. That fits perfectly with his service in the Frontier Battalion, which started in 1885. The young man's knowledge of firearms could only add to his appeal as a recruit.

There is another tantalizing item, published in *Frontier Times* magazine in 1926. Henry Putz, the former Ranger, is meeting a sheriff who worked with Company F to break up a rustling ring in 1885. The former lawman sits in his Ford as he's interviewed. The venue: the Texas State Fair, located in Fair Park where the movie operator Henry Putz operates his movie concessions. It all adds up, but it's circumstantial.

Only one known Dallas grave bears the name Henry Putz, in Highland Park Cemetery. He dies on June 30, 1930. The birth date on the stone reads May 24, 1866, which matches the age given for Henry Putz, Texas Ranger, during the 1886 shooting.

Similarly, tracing the seasoned private T. S. "Bob" Crowder after his retirement from the Texas Rangers in 1891 yields no concrete results. A "T.S. Crowder" appears in Martin County, Texas, as the constable of Precinct No. 1 in 1906.[40] By 1913, he's serving as a county commissioner. He's also a rancher in the county, shipping significant amounts of livestock into the county with a business partner.

There's scant evidence, beyond the accommodating time line and

---

39 *Austin American-Statesman*, September 8, 1922.

40 Ogden K. Shannon, *Biennial Report of the Secretary of State of Texas*, 1906.

choice of law enforcement as a profession, that proves this is Company F's stalwart private. One teasing bit of information surfaces when Crowder and his business partner, Flanagan, get embroiled in a lawsuit with the Texas & Pacific Railway after dozens of sick mules arrive in Stanton from Fort Worth, where the Martin County men purchased them. During the case, Crowder testifies: "I know the reasonable market value of mules."

Indeed so, if this is the man who once chased mule thieves across South Texas. But he and his partner lose the suit in appeals over the testimony, which the appeals court says should have been excluded.[41] This T. S. Crowder dies in late March 1926.[42]

Luckily, the fates of other Company F men are better known.

"THE TRAIL THAT ADVENTURE BLAZES"
August 1938

Frank Carmichael stands before the plaque, eight miles outside of Fort Concho, lost in memories. He's in good shape for a man in his midseventies. One reporter at the time describes him as "a brisk, healthy man . . . short, ruddy-faced, gray-haired and the red-blood showing in the tiny veins of his face mark him as a man of the north."

The gray granite marker looks like a gravestone. It reads: "The United States Military Telegraph Line Established in 1874–1875 from Fort Griffin to Fort Concho, crossed here."

The former Ranger smiles. He, too, crossed here in May 1888, after he quit the Frontier Battalion. That summer, he followed the old military telegraph line from Fort Griffin, north of Abilene, to Fort Concho to start his trek away from Texas.

Two years ago, in 1936, the Texas Historical Commission asked Carmichael to locate where the Bankhead Highway crossed the telegraph

---

41 *T. P. Railroad Co. v. Crowder et al.*, Court of Appeals of Texas, April 10, 1913.

42 *Cooper Review* 47, no. 13 (1926).

line, and he planted this marker at the spot he identified.[43] It's a small piece of permanency marking his life of wanderlust, close brushes with death, and fortune hunting.

Fort Concho, near San Angelo, was only a limbo for soldiers awaiting reassignment when he passed through in 1888, just a year before the army abandoned the fort. The installation only had value when Texas was a frontier. The same could be said of F. P. Carmichael.

He left his native state behind, finding it "too thickly settled" for his taste, and followed the edge of the frontier to Washington State. There, he put his cowboy's skills to good use as a team driver and horse wrangler. Census records also record an American named F. P. Carmichael, married and living in the Blackrock area of King County, renowned for its coal mining operations.[44] His job is mine foreman.

The entire Pacific Northwest is swept by gold fever after the Klondike strike of 1897, and Carmichael catches a case. In 1898, Carmichael sets out north for Alaska to make his fortune. It takes him three years to fail. "Gold," he quips, "was where I did not find it." He heads back to Washington State and eventually settles in Seattle.

But the need to revisit those earlier times, and draw strength from that person he was, grows steadily. In 1935, Frank Carmichael heads back to Texas for the first time since leaving forty-seven years before. "I decided that I'd rather be in Texas with my back against a hill than in some of the centers of population with my back against the wall," he says of the move.

"The people of Texas," Carmichael adds, "are thoroughbreds."

---

43 "Blood Curdling Days of '80s as Ranger Live in Memories of Abelian," *Abilene Reporter-News*, June 12, 1938. The marker is still there. From Baird, take U.S. 80 east to Finely exit and take Finley Road east about 3.2 miles. See "The United States Military Telegraph Line," Texas Historical Markers, https://texashistoricalmarkers .weebly.com/military-telegraph-line.html.

44 *Washington Territorial Census Rolls, 1857–1892* (Olympia: Washington State Archives, n.d.), microfilm. Another F. P. Carmichael, annoyingly, lives in Seattle at the time. His family is from Maryland.

That final comment is at least partly a projection of himself. In Texas, he's a somebody. The local media interview him and laud him as a "double pioneer" of Texas and the northwest. "He has followed the trail that adventure blazes from the Louisiana swamps and West Texas plains to the barrens 250 miles north of the Arctic circle," waxes the 1938 article.

The newspaper notes that Carmichael lost touch with his Company F friends, but as an old man is eager to look them up. "Recently, however, he made connections with J. Allen Newton, who lives at 1912 Avenue P, Galveston," the article states. "Carmichael recalls Newton as the comic of the company, and also as a real man and a true friend. Of Carmichael, Newton wrote the *Abilene Reporter-News* that he was 'One of the most courageous, fearless men that ever wore pants!'"[45]

Since Brooks and Rogers are now legendary captains, Carmichael's clutch role in the Sabine County shoot-out has extra panache. Being the last man standing over those bloodied Texas Ranger legends is the centerpiece of his adventurous legacy.

There's a convention of the Texas Ex-Ranger Association in Coleman coming in July 1938, and Carmichael has every intention of attending. "No doubt he'll be the most spry old-timer at the reunion," *The Abilene Reporter-News* predicts.

The reunion seems designed to summon ghosts from a dead era. The two-day gathering is held within a replica of a Texas Ranger camp, specifically Camp Colorado in Mills County. That was the place where, during the 1850s, Indian-fighting luminaries like Sul Ross and John Bell Hood passed through on their way to bigger Confederate glories. But the camp equipment, blankets, saddles, and tents all evoke his own rides as a young man.

Carmichael is one of just eighteen Rangers in attendance. He's happy to once again see J. Allen Newton, in from Galveston. His has not been what newspapermen would call "a life of adventure." He marries Josie Gossett Newton on January 22, 1889, in the Houston County town her family founded, Crockett. They have a single child.

---

45 "Blood Curdling Days," *Abilene Reporter-News*.

The passionate young woman he dreamed of is now a force for the temperance movement, not just in the Houston area but statewide. And she brings this loud work right home with her: "The Loyal Temperance Legion met yesterday afternoon at the home of Mrs. J. Allen Newton," reads *The Galveston Daily News*, September 24, 1930. "During the session the children rehearsed songs, rally cries and yells for Loyal Temperance Day at the national convention of the WCTU in Houston in November."[46]

Newton's happy to report to his Ranger colleague that his son, Andrew Jameson, has a child of his own, Josie Elsie. Young Andrew served in the Great War, an experience that traumatizes the elder Josie, who has developed an anti-war fervor as Europe teeters closer to the brink. In the 1930s, Josie Newton founds a new group called War Mothers, trying to keep America out of foreign conflicts.[47]

So that's life for "the clown of the outfit," J. Allen Newton. Aside from him, the rest of the faces at the Ranger reunion are unfamiliar to Carmichael. The meeting begins with a welcome address by the secretary of the chamber of commerce and a toast by the school superintendent.

The focus seems to be on celebrating the fort and its august Indian-fighting history, and not so much a celebration of the kind of outlaw hunting that Carmichael and Newton experienced. They have to endure a lengthy presentation on the history of the fort and the two times Robert E. Lee visited there.[48]

Major George Black, a Comanche former Ranger, presides over the meeting. In time, he announces committee appointments. The Company F veterans both find positions: Newton on the nominations committee and Carmichael on the resolutions committee.

Newton takes time during the gathering to speak to a local reporter

---

46 "Loyal Temperance Legion," *Galveston Daily News*, September 24, 1930.

47 Ibid.

48 "Coleman Host to Ex-Rangers," *Fort Worth Star Telegram*, June 16, 1938.

about his post-ambush departure from Company F that generates the unflattering if accurate headline: ONE RANGER ADMITS TRUTH: HE WAS SCARED.[49] The now aged Company F tenderfoot doesn't have much time left. J. Allen Newton dies in Galveston later that year, on October 9, 1938. Josie follows in October 1952, at age eighty-nine, old enough to see the United States win World War II and wade into the bloodbath of Korea.[50]

After connecting with fellow Rangers, and seemingly short of money, Carmichael writes the former Ranger and author William Sterling in 1939. "He had been out of state since 1888 and on his return to Texas had heard of my efforts to get pensions for old time Rangers," Sterling recalls. "When I told him in my answer that Capt. Brooks has given his courage in the Conner fight full credit, the gratitude of the veteran over his comrade's praise was unbounded."[51] After 1939, Sterling loses touch with the former Ranger, and Carmichael after that slips unheralded into history.

In his declining years, Carmichael found his surrogate Ranger family still had a spot for him around the campfire, even after more than five decades. Clearly, the ties that bound the Frontier Battalion ran deep as any military veterans', woven with memories of terror and beauty that, like the prints on a saddle blanket, faded but never truly vanished.

THE COUNTY
January 10, 1911

It's a new session for the Texas legislature, and with it a new governor, Oscar B. Colquitt, and a new Speaker, Sam Rayburn. J. A. Brooks is starting his second term as representative for District Ninety-Five. Succession, of a kind, is his mandate. He holds in his hands a petition signed

---

49 "One Ranger Admits Truth: He Was Scared," *Coleman Democrat-Voice,* June 23, 1938.

50 Per her grave and obit. "Margaret Josephine 'Josie' Gossett Newton," Find a Grave, https://www.findagrave.com/memorial/50334139/margaret-josephine-newton.

51 Sterling, *Trails and Trials.*

by sixty-five citizens from northern Starr County "vitally interested in the creation of a new county in order to secure relief from the almost intolerable conditions under which we suffer."

This is a political declaration of independence from Guerra-dominated Starr County. Brooks has been elected for one purpose: to separate Falfurrias from Starr County, making the city and surrounding area a new county. His stake in South Texas is rising; he now owns 1,400 acres in the area.

The struggle between Lasater and Guerra has reached a fever pitch. This empty, hardscrabble land must be worth something, because Texans are fighting and dying over it. Gregorio Duffy, a Republican appointee as Roma's customs inspector, is shot down in Rio Grande City during a 1907 street scuffle with Starr County sheriff Deodoro Guerra (the boss's cousin) and his men.[52] Now both sides retain armed followers who are ready to spill blood during every election season.

This, then, is Brooks's kind of fight.

In the fall 1908, he announces his run to represent District Ninety-Five—as a Democrat. He's a candidate with crossover appeal, picked to dispel fear of an emerging, Republican-controlled enclave. After long weeks campaigning far from home, he's elected.

Kitty Barry, *The Daily Express*'s first female correspondent in the House, writes a small profile of the new member from Falfurrias. "He sidles from notoriety with a distrustful glance," she writes. "While his enthusiastic admirers tell look-who's-here stories . . . he pulls meditatively at the projections of his Long Horn mustache and takes good advantage of the good places to deny his glory."

The former Ranger shows an absolute lack of flash. "There is nothing spectacular in spirit or truth about Captain Brooks," she notes. "His

---

52 "Guerra, Manuel (1856–1915)," Texas State Historical Association, https://www .tshaonline.org/handbook/entries/guerra-manuel. A federal grand jury indicted Manuel and Deodoro Guerra, two deputies, and a Texas Ranger for conspiring to murder a federal official, but all the defendants eventually won acquittals.

clothes are just plain everyday raiment and even on gala occasions he taboos the frontier costume."

Still, Brooks's luster as a gunman follows him through life. Barry closes the article by saying: "Yes, Captain Brooks loves peace. But it is said of him that he used less ammunition in proportion to the notches on his pistol than any other captain in the Ranger service."[53]

Brooks is reelected in November 1910 and joins the Thirty-Second Legislature the next year as a wiser, more seasoned political operator. Last session, he advanced plans that took sections of several other counties, which effectively killed the bill creating a new entity. Focusing solely on Starr County land helps him cultivate much-needed votes but at the cost of good real estate. After the failure of that first session, any new county will by necessity be a sparse, landlocked place.

House Bill 94, which establishes a new county, is presented in late January and embarks on its own treacherous trail through committees. HB 94 survives a one-vote margin but passes the committees, finding an easier path in the larger session since Brooks and the separatist northern Starr County delegation are busy making compromises and lobbying support to ensure the bill moves to the Speaker. Rayburn signs off on the bill on the afternoon of March 9, and Governor Oscar Branch Colquitt signs the bill into law two days later.

Brooks returns to Falfurrias as a hero. Four hundred people attend a rally in his honor, during which he is literally carried by the crowd to a tea party in Garcia Hall.

The creation of what will be named Brooks County doesn't end the feud with the Guerra family and ironically helps their foes. Without the meddlesome northern Starr County dissidents, it's actually easier for Guerra to consolidate control over Starr County politics.

Founding Brooks County should be a positive coda for the lawman's life, with him enjoying the fruits of an undeniable political success that redrew the map of Texas. Indeed, Brooks's life can easily be canonized,

---

53 Kitty Barry, "Brooks Is a Peaceful Man," *Daily Express*, January 12, 1911.

if only seeing the high points. Author Robert Utley once wrote: "Tall, lean, and tough, he was also modest, quiet-spoken, and courteous, and possessed of a high sense of duty fortified by determination, courage, and a mind that grasped both the larger mission and the immediate task. A masterful marksman, horseman, and outdoorsman, Brooks proved smart, energetic, and persistent, and displayed his usual qualities of leadership."[54]

All of this is true. But his successful life is not necessarily happy.

The years of marriage have been lonely for Virginia. Her spouse's long weeks spent away from home as a lawman then became the never-ending travel required of a state representative. Now that he's a judge, Brooks is, for the first time, stuck at home. He's distant, restless, and prone to drinking.

"Even when Brooks had retired from the Ranger Force and concentrated his time at home, he is wont to take long trips 'on business' and ignore the family left behind," writes Brooks biographer Paul Spellman, a description provided by Brooks's children. "His traveling companion was always Jack Daniel's, often his son, and never his wife or daughter."[55]

Being a judge means enduring a litany of petty disputes. But the county commissioner's court, which he heads, is also busy creating county roads and bridges. Government buildings need to be budgeted. Brooks also founds a public school system and becomes its ex officio superintendent, drawing extra pay.

Brooks County is spared the ugly racial violence that swept through the valley between 1915 and 1918, in part because of the support of Lasater and county officials for the Hispanic populace and their reciprocal loyalty.

---

54 Robert M. Utley, *Lone Star Justice: The First Century of the Texas Rangers* (New York: Oxford University Press, 2002).

55 Spellman, *Captain J. A. Brooks.*

After Virginia dies in 1928, Brooks faces an empty ranch and the quietly sad downslope of his life. He cuts the perfect image of the publicly successful man who, at his core, has an empty existence. In the courthouse, he has stature and influence. At his quiet home in the South Texas scrub, he's reduced to just another lonely old man with a lifetime drinking problem.

Brooks clings to the judgeship over the next twenty years and never faces a real challenge from Republicans in a primary. But in 1932, a more real threat emerges from the Democratic Party in the form of former Falfurrias Mercantile Company general manager L. A. Dickey. The challenge from within the Lasater ranks must be serious because Brooks writes a cringeworthy letter in the local newspaper, the *Brooks County Texan*. "For the part I played in putting this county on the map, so far, my reward has been only honors and the respect of my fellow men," he says. "I am possessed of very little worldly goods, therefore, I need the office in order to be reasonably comfortable in these my last years. I appeal to you not for sympathy but for what is justly due me. After my long life of service and devotion to you I cannot believe that you will desert me now."

He also goes out of his way to extol his relations with Mexican Americans, a major voting bloc. "The Spanish speaking people have no reason for complaint," he writes. "I have looked after their interests, and fight for their just rights. For over forty years 'Old Captain Brooks' has never failed them, and I have no fear that they will desert me."

He's right. In the July primary, Brooks defeats Dickey 591–322; as usual, he's unopposed in November's general election. Six years later, he wins his fourteenth and final term.

As Brooks gets old, he gets sentimental and increasingly picks up a pen to gather his thoughts. Much of it is in third person, and he tends to ramble. On his eightieth birthday, J. A. Brooks even writes a piece of poetry:

I have often passed with the throng, sometimes right sometimes wrong, now destiny has seen fit my life to prolong, and
I still love to hear a good song. But if kind providence should
decree that it is time for me to pass on, and leave my place for
the strong, goodbye to the passing throng, and my heritage will
be happy, carefree, and long.[56]

In an interview with an uncredited reporter from *The Corpus Christi
Times* in 1937, Brooks, at age eighty-three, indeed seems reflective and
religious. "If there is no such thing (as Providence) then why did that
bullet that was intended for my heart clip off three fingers on my left
hand and split my rifle barrel instead?" he asks at one point.[57] His time in
East Texas was long ago, but it hasn't been forgotten.

Alcoholism continues to chew at the aging man. "June 27th, 1939,
at about 6:30 a.m. I drank my last alcoholic beverage," he writes in a testimonial. "It was done to please my two children Corrinne Kenny and
John Morgan Brooks, they both being strict prohibitionists and abstain
at any cost. Willpower, I find that I am blessed with it. Old Bourbon
whiskey has caused me many years of trouble, trouble that cannot be
atoned for in this world or life."[58]

He dies on January 14, 1944, and is laid to rest in Falfurrias, the seat
of the county that in 2021 still bears his name.

There's little but a sign to mark the start of Brooks County. It's just
another 942-square-mile section of nearly empty mesquite amid a sea of
identical brush. Agriculture never took here due to poor soil, leaving cattle as the chief ranching moneymaker. The result is the Falfurrias Butter

---

56 Spellman, *Captain J. A. Brooks.*

57 *Corpus Christi Caller-Times*, Empire Builders Edition, October 24, 1937. Thanks to
   newspaper archivist Allison Ehrlich for the help.

58 Spellman, *Captain J. A. Brooks.*

brand, which originally came from Ed Lasater's dairy here, but is now made in Winnsboro, Texas. Oil and gas help buoy the county's economy, but the area is sensitive to market changes. There's also a for-profit detention center in the county, housing hundreds of inmates waiting trials or facing immigration charges.

The county is quietly struggling in 2021, as it had through most of its existence. Nearly 40 percent of the population of seven thousand live under the poverty line. More than half are unemployed, according to the U.S. census data.[59]

Brooks County has stayed true to its political roots. It anchors South Texas as the oldest continual Democratic stronghold in the state; Brooks county voters have never favored a Republican presidential candidate in its entire history. During an election year, there are more yard placards simply saying PRAY than there are political signs.

There's little reason to stop at Falfurrias, the county seat. Road traffic flows in from U.S. Highway 281 and State Highway 285, while locals trickle in from Farm Roads 2191 and 1418. Most visitors are here to visit the shrine of the faith healer Don Pedro Jaramillo, on the outskirts of town. Devotees from across Mexico and the United States make pilgrimages to seek help from *"el mero jefe de los curanderos,"* who died in 1907. Stacks of crutches and photos of the healed adorn the man's simple roadside shrine and grave site.

The other draw in what locals call "Fal" is the Heritage Museum and Texas Ranger Room. This was once the Texas Ranger Museum, but the larger facility in Waco muscled the name from this small, county-funded facility, according to Lourdes Trevino-Cantu, a school librarian and museum volunteer. It would be too confusing to vie for grants sharing the name, she says.

Some of the Texas Ranger tenacity has clearly rubbed off on the diminutive museum director. After a burglar broke in and stole some

---

59 "QuickFacts: Brooks County, Texas; United States," U.S. Census, https://www .census.gov/quickfacts/fact/table/brookscountytexas,US/PST045219.

historic firearms in 2015, Trevino-Cantu tracked one of the missing pistols as it was being shopped around and returned it to the museum.[60]

The Heritage Museum runs on about $16,000 a year in city funds. Volunteers make the money stretch. The Ranger material isn't as tightly focused on J. A. Brooks as would be imagined. Inside reside artifacts from the county, including exhibits showcasing historic wedding dresses and profiling area veterans.

However, there are displays of Brooks family heirlooms, including the bow that Geronimo crafted for young John Morgan during the trip to the World's Fair and a somber, life-size painting of the Ranger captain gazing from a wall. The hidden treasure here is the well-maintained photo archive, which includes deep dives into area history, as well as files on Texas Rangers.

The Falfurrias Burial Park is within city limits. The cemetery has spread over the many decades, so the older plots are clustered near the road. Brooks's grave stands under the shelter of sweeping tree limbs. His son and daughter are buried to the left and right, at his side in death as they tried to be in life.

Decades after, the state of Texas planted a historical marker here, which contains a concise biography. But missing from the grave itself is any sort of honorarium. It's a simple marker, its surface etched only with his full name and some carved flowers.

J. A. Brooks was a husband, father, state representative, and long-serving judge, and as such earned any number of titles suitable for his gravestone. But only one would fit the man lying here. There's no doubt which experience amid a lifetime of challenge and achievement anchored his personality. From the moment he was promoted to the day he died, he preferred to be called "Captain."

---

60 Interview with author.

DRAMATIS PERSONAE

There are a lot of characters in *Red Sky Morning*, which may require a cheat sheet. Not content to just list the characters, I've first detailed key Sabine County folks separately, as a home for information about their later lives. After that is the comprehensive list of those who played a role in the story.

I. SABINE COUNTY ENDINGS

James I. Perkins

Sabine County judge who heard the Conner trials and lobbied Austin for Ranger involvement

Perkins loses the election to Howdy Martin, but enjoys long-term success. He's reelected to the bench in 1888, retiring in 1892 to open a branch of the law firm Wilson & Wilson in Rusk. But as always, he's eyeing the higher public office. In 1902, he wins a seat in the Texas Senate. In 1904, his term ends, and he's again elected as judge for a consolidated judicial district covering Cherokee, Nacogdoches, Angelina, Shelby, San Augustine, and Sabine Counties. He spends sixteen years in that position before returning to private practice. He buries a wife in 1905, marries another, and sires five kids. He dies in 1923 at age seventy-five.

W. W. Weatherred

Conner defense attorney, Community Committee posse leader

Weatherred will end his life away from Sabine County. He moves to Hillsboro, in Hill County. His ties there run deep, and he seems to have kept one foot there and another in Sabine County. As an example, his son W. M. Weatherred is born in Osceola, in Hill County, in early 1887. Not content to just relax, the old veteran practices law in Hillsboro with H. B. Short. He dies there in February 1897, gone but not forgotten in the deep Texas enclave where he spent most of his legal and political career. "The many friends in this county of the Hon. William W. Weatherred regret very much to hear of his death," reports the *Houston Post* from Sabine County.[1]

James T. Polley

Defense attorney and local leader of Community Committee posse hunting the Conners

Polley becomes judge for the Fourth Judicial District. He also founds a newspaper in nearby Shelby County called *The Champion*. Seven of his twelve children survive to adulthood. He lives in the town of Center and dies there in 1904 at just fifty-two.

J. O. Toole

Merchant and member of the Community Committee and Turner posses

The storefront partnership with his in-laws, the Pratts, dissolves in 1890 when Ed Pratt takes over his father's leadership role. Toole rebels against his brother-in-law and sets out on his own. Toole opens a rival store in downtown Hemphill's courthouse square, diagonally across from the Pratt store. In 1899, Toole expands into the adjoining lot and builds the first brick building in the town center. "While Hampton Pratt was satis-

---

1 "Hemphill Friends," *Houston Post*, February 18, 1897.

fied doing business the old fashioned way-informal agreements; casually kept records, Toole quickly put in place formal lending agreements that could be enforced legally," notes the National Park Service's registration of the Toole Building as a landmark. "With growing frequency, farmers put up their land as collateral for credit. If they were unable to pay their store debt, Toole would obtain legal title to their land. He was insensitive to crop failures or economic downturns, remaining intent on equaling and then exceeding the financial success of the Pratt family."

As a result of foreclosures, Toole becomes a large landowner. In 1921, the Temple Lumber Company buys the local sawmill and the railroad and invades Sabine County's forests. Toole profits from the cash that comes with the railroad's arrival but more so from the sale of his timber to the sawmill. He makes lots of money from this, even during the Great Depression.

J. O. Toole dies in 1940. "He was eulogized as a major force in the community, but although he was recognized as a very wealthy and important man, there were few mentions of contributions to the community," the NPS landmark document notes. "Many remembered him as a rapacious man who rose to power on the backs of the poor farmers who were his primary customers."[2]

Dr. John Wesley Smith

Sabine County doctor, witness during the Conner trial, tended to wounded Rangers

J. W. Smith continues to practice medicine in Sabine County his whole life. In February 1896, his son, Frank, marries Eva Clementine McDaniel, daughter of Bill Watson and Zerowine Joan Smith—Kit Smith's sister. He and Dr. Frank Tucker both practice medicine in deep East Texas for their entire careers, sharing caseloads and stories from the elder

---

2 National Park Service, "Toole Building," National Register of Historic Places Registration Form, October 1990.

doctor's time as a frontier medico. "John W. Smith of Hemphill" is on a list of twelve founding members of the Sabine County Medical Society, formed in June 1910.[3] He later serves as its president.

Smith dies in 1923 at age seventy-nine, putting an end to his fifty-two-year career. Dr. Frank Smith summarizes the life of a frontier doctor in Sabine County this way: "I have saddled my horse many times in all kinds of weather, put on slickers and overcoats in rainy and cold weather, stretched an umbrella, put my lantern on the bend of my elbow, sometimes not returning for a day or more. I recall one time my horse got scared of the stretched umbrella, threw me and medicine in every direction, but usually I managed to keep gentle horses."

Redden Alford

Conner family confidant who aided Company F in finding the Conner family campsite

Alford leaves Sabine County to live near Palestine, Texas, another roost of his extended family. He settles down on a farm near the town of Slocum, a predominantly African American hamlet in Anderson County. Delia dies on December 11, 1895. Alford remarries a woman named Susan Jane Teel, and they have a half dozen children. He has ten children in total but survives long enough to bury half of them.[4]

In 1930, census records show the elderly Susan J. Alford and Redin Alford (as his name now appears), born in Alabama in 1858, living on a piece of land in Anderson County worth $1,500. The old man is now ready to help spark a racial atrocity.

In July 1910, according to *The New York Times*, Alford ends up involved in a fight over a bad check: "The trouble originated between

3 *Texas State Journal of Medicine*, 1911.

4 For the easiest way to track the children, see "Redin Alford," Find a Grave, https://www.findagrave.com/memorial/16238409/redin-alford.

a white farmer, Redin Alford, and a negro, whose note Alford had endorsed some time ago. The negro left town and Alford was obliged to pay the note at one of the local banks. A few days ago the negro returned, when Alford called on him to account for his conduct. The negro grew insulting and trouble followed."[5] The spawns a conspiracy theory that causes a calamity for the African Americans of Anderson County. Word of mouth inflames the disputes with the Black community into a wholesale racial insurrection, and hundreds of white residents take up their weapons and prepare for a war. The mob soon becomes murderously aggressive and begins house-to-house raids, shooting Black property owners and burying the bodies in the woods.

"Men were going about killing Negroes as fast as they could find them, and so far as I was able to ascertain, without any real cause," Anderson County sheriff William Black tells *The New York Times*. "These Negroes have done no wrong that I could discover. There was just a hotheaded gang hunting them down and killing them. I don't know how many were in the mob, but I think there must have been 200 or 300. Some of them cut telephone wires. They hunted the Negroes down like sheep."[6]

Alford is not implicated in any of the violence, only in the initial seventy-dollar conflict that helped spark the outrages. This is his final contribution to awful Texas history; he dies on December 28, 1934, and is buried in Crawford Cemetery in Slocum under the name Redin Alford. Susan Jane, lying in an adjoining grave, follows him in 1948.

Thomas B. Anthony
Father of Milton Anthony, member of Turner posse, signed for bounty on Conners

The Civil War veteran is widowed for a second time but marries Mary Smith in 1902, who's likewise widowed when Samuel Dainwood dies the

---

5 *New York Times*, July 31, 1910.

6 *New York Times*, August 1, 1910.

year before.[7] She is the daughter of Caroline and Rev. Edward Smith—
tying the Smith and Anthony families even more tightly. He dies in 1917.

One hundred and six years later, in an article about the Fairmount
cemetery, Thomas Anthony is eulogized in an oddly revealing way. "One
of the best-known graves is that of Thomas B. Anthony, who in the
1880s volunteered to travel to Austin to collect a reward for the killers
of Texas Ranger Jim Moore," reads the *Newton County News* in 2007.
"It took considerable bravery on Anthony's part to make the long trip,
especially at a time when the Conners were still around."[8]

This is a pretty big misread, especially since the rewards that Anthony
signed for were collected via James Polley in Hemphill, after both Fed and
Willis Conner were dead. And if traveling to Austin is an exhibition of
bravery, Vernon Scott's solo travel to Hemphill is worthy of a medal.

Milton and Docia Anthony

*Brother-in-law to the Conner sons and murder victim Kit Low, helped the
Rangers locate the Conners*

Milton Anthony lives a seemingly unremarkable life, albeit one out of
Sabine County. He and Theodosia move to Jasper and proceed to have
five children, all of whom live to adulthood. Docia dies in 1930 at age
sixty-three and is buried in Hemphill Cemetery with the other Travises.
Milton dies in Jasper in September 1933 at age sixty-seven and is interred
in Vernon Parish, Louisiana, where his son Henry lives.[9]

---

7 "Fairmount Cemetery, Sabine County, Texas," Sabine County, Texas, https://sites
.rootsweb.com/~txsabine/burials/040–010414-Fairmount_Cem.htm.

8 Bob Bowman, "All Things Historical," *Newton County News*, October 3, 2007. The
article was distributed by the East Texas Historical Association.

9 Texas Death Certificates, 1903–1982, Texas Department of State Health Services,
Austin, TX, and "M. T. Anthony," Find a Grave, https://www.findagrave.com
/memorial/29016669/milton-t.-anthony.

Dan McNaughten

Search party, Citizen's Committee, and Turner posse member

Dan McNaughten remained in Sabine County. In 1920, the sixty-four-year-old speaks of the Conner feud to his family and his doctor, J. W. Smith, who is treating him for pellagra (severe niacin deficiency). Its symptoms are inflamed skin, diarrhea, mouth sores—and dementia. He tells his family, "If anything happens to me, don't blame the Conners," and shortly thereafter commits suicide with a knife.[10]

Isaac "Little Ike" Low

Brother-in-law to Fed Conner, married to Melissa Travis

Ike and Melissa have eleven children, and they don't farm any out. They do, however, accept help from Melissa's mother, Saphronia White-Travis (wife of Isaac Hickman Low, the uncle who raised Eli Low). The couple has a full house and need the help, but Little Ike also knows the old woman is struggling.[11] On August 1, 1908, Melissa dies and ends up in the Hemphill Cemetery. Ike Low, never one to be alone, remarries a woman named Emma Clark. They have three children, one of them named Dan. He gets engaged to a Smith girl, and the pair make local history. "The two attended church together. Apparently she got mad at him one day during a service and began beating on the poor fella, chasing him out of the church in front of everybody," recalls Blanche Toole. "From that day on the land the Lows lived on became known as 'Scrappin' Valley.'"[12] Given its hidden,

---

10 Mark Dugan, *Judge Not* (unpublished, 1982), quotes Smith and McNaughten descendants.

11 Sabine County Census, 1900 and 1910. Saphronia White-Travis finally moves in with her oldest son, William Travis, and lives with him until she dies in 1915.

12 Ed Wetterman, "1990 Interview with Blanch Toole, Sabine County Historian," East Texas Generations, August 1, 2010, http://easttexasgenerations.blogspot.com/2010

blood-soaked history, the idea that the nickname comes from an incident between those lovers in a church is bleakly ironic.

II. WHO'S WHO

Scott's Company F (1887 rank, first enlistment year)

William Scott (Captain, 1878)

John Rogers (Private, 1882)

James Brooks (Sergeant, 1883)

Henry Putz (Private, 1885)

Dee Caldwell (Private, 1886)

J. Allen Newton (Private, 1887)

F. P. Carmichael (Private, 1886)

Curren "Kid" Rogers (Private, 1887)

Bob Crowder (Private, 1884)

Ed Randall (Private, 1887)

J. B. Harry (Private, 1886)

William Treadwell (Private, 1886)

Carlton Hines (Private, 1887)

Jim Moore (Private, 1875)

Lawmen

Ira Aten: Texas Ranger lieutenant, undercover operations specialist

Winfred Bates: Company F sergeant under Captain J. A. Brooks

Jay Banks: Texas Ranger captain who served in the Rangers in the 1950s and opposed desegregation

John Formwalt: Sheriff of Runnels County

John B. Jones: Texas Ranger major, commander of the Frontier Battalion, foe of the outlaw Sam Bass

Thomas R. Knight: U.S. Indian Police agent lieutenant

Bill McDonald: Texas Ranger captain, peer of J. A. Brooks

/08/1990-interview-with-blanch-toole-sabine.html.

Charles "Girlie" McKinney: Texas Ranger lieutenant in Cotulla who recruited J. A. Brooks

Robert Owen: U.S. Indian agent, head of the agency and T. R. Knight's boss

Liam Sieker: Ranger captain and Frontier Battalion quartermaster

Sam Sixkiller: Deputy marshal and formerly the first captain of the United States Indian Police, T. R. Knight's father-in-law

A. J. Spradley: Sheriff of Nacogdoches County; Conner jailer and sympathizer

Ranger Friends and Family

Emily Virginia Scott Bower: William Scott's sister, married to Dallas County judge E. G. Bower

Corrinne and John Morgan Brooks: Children of Virginia and J. A. Brooks

Cornelius "Neal" Coldwell: Former Texas Ranger captain and ranch owner, family friend of Brooks's romantic interest, Virginia Wilborn

James Edward Pettus and T. Wheeler Pettus: Heirs to the Pettus Ranch, a.k.a. "Ranger Heaven"

Vernon Scott: Half sister of Captain William Scott

Edward Lasater: South Texas landowner and driving force behind the creation of a new county

Sabine County

The Conner Family

Willis Conner, "Old Man" (Husband)

John (Son), died unwed

Frederick, "Fed" (Son), married Nancy Travis

Piercy Conner (Wife)

Leander (Son), married Martha Smith

Alfred, "Alfie," "Bubba" (Son), married to Sallie

William (Son), died unwed

Charles (Son), married Julia Ann Scruggs

Nancy, "Miss Nan" (Daughter), married Elmore Harper

Catherine (Daughter), married John Williams, mother of Thomas Williams

Citizens

Octavine Cooper: Teenage witness in the joint trial of Fed and Charles
Conner for murder

Sam Everett: Down-on-his-luck hired hand, witness in the Conner murder trial

Joe Ford and John Marshall: Day laborers and controversial witnesses in
Conner murder trial

L. L. Loggins: Newspaperman, lawyer, jailbreaker, polygamist, and
scoundrel

Jack Low: Eli Low's father

Larkin Morris: Store owner, coroner's party member, and unindicted
jailbreaker

William Christopher "Kit" Smith and Eli Low: Murder victims and
Conner neighbors

William McDaniel: Neighbor who gave a home to young Kit Smith

S. H. Oliphint: Sabine County sheriff (after 1886)

William H. Smith: Sabine County sheriff

Frank Tucker: Medical doctor based in San Augustine

J. A. Whittlesey: Sabine County judge and coroner during the Smith-
Low murders

Elmer Harper: Conner family friend

Indicted Jailbreakers

Sterling Eddings

Wade Noble

W. E. T. Ogletree

Ike Gary

Sam Swan

Dutch Watkins

Leon Taylor

Modern Sabine

Weldon McDaniel: Sabine County Historical Commission president, descendent of Kit Smith

Captain Steve Scobie: Fishing guide, equipment working on the lakes of East Texas

Public Officials

José Tomás Canales: Texas State representative, spearheaded investigations into 1910 Ranger atrocities

Oscar Colquitt: Texas governor from 1911 to 1915

Augustus Garland: U.S. attorney general from 1885 to 1889

John Augustus Hulen: Texas adjutant general from 1902 to 1907

John Ireland: Texas governor from 1883 to 1887

Wilburn King: Texas adjutant general from 1881 to 1891

Lawrence Sullivan "Sul" Ross: Texas governor from 1887 to 1891

Indian Territories

Red Alexander: Owner of the store where St. John is killed; namesake of the town of Alex

Thomas Burke and Henry Witt: Love roundup cowboys, St. John murder trial witnesses

Price Fulton: Cowboy and St. John coworker and killing witness

Sam Gopher: Wanted by the Rangers for a bad mule deal, lives in the proto-town of Alex

Obadiah Love: Trail boss organizing a roundup in the Indian Territories

Albert St. John: Cowboy from a well-heeled family, working in the Indian Territories, shot by lawmen

Ridge Whitlock: Storekeeper in Alex, eyewitness to the St. John killing

Arkansas Legal Community

Thomas Barnes: Defense attorney for Brooks, Putz, and Knight

Elias Cornelius Boudinot: Defense attorney for Brooks, Putz, and Knight

George Maledon: U.S. deputy marshal and executioner

Isaac Charles Parker: Judge, U.S. Court for the Western District of Arkansas Court

Montgomery "Monte" Sandels: District attorney in Little Rock

Opponents and Outlaws

Sam Bass: Infamous armed robber and leader of a gang that William Scott infiltrated

George Bright: A horse thief captured by John Rogers

Billie Collins: Brother of Bass dead gang member, invited the outlaw to North Texas to commit crimes

John Wesley Hardin: Texas outlaw who once shot a deputy in Sabine County

John Gray: A gambler from McGregor County who was one of two men arrested as the Lone Highwayman

Jim Newsom: Sentenced to prison for a spate of stagecoach robberies near Ballinger as part of the Lone Highwayman case

Belle Starr: Famous outlaw and frequent target of authorities, dubbed "the Bandit Queen"

Brown County

William Adams: Brown County sheriff, fence cutter appeaser

W. M. and Lev Baugh: Prosperous ranchers, primary targets for local fence cutters

Will Butler: Brown County deputy, fence cutter sympathizer

Joe Copeland: Ranch hand and informant for the Baugh family

Fence Cutters

Jim Lovell (Brown County constable)

Bob Parrock

Amos Roberts

John Mathews

Wood Runnels

Frank Johnson

BIBLIOGRAPHY

Finding the best truth about the Texas Rangers deployments in 1886 and 1887 means parsing through many worthy earlier works, especially when it comes to East Texas. Here are some notable books and how they were instrumental in creating this book.

Captain J. A. Brooks, Texas Ranger and *Captain John H. Rogers, Texas Ranger* by Paul Spellman

For the Rangers' point of view, it's hard to get more comprehensive than Spellman. He understandably relies heavily on the organization's official records and sympathetic newspaper accounts. In Brooks's case, he also leans on his subject's journal, although it was written late in life and somewhat rambling. With COVID-19 shutting down government facilities during this book's development, having a fully sourced official version to rely on was a lifesaver during the early days of research. I found Spellman's discussions with Brooks's family members invaluable. Reasonable complaints can be raised when he leaves out the full legal disposition of Ranger cases.

Judge Not by Mark Dugan

In the early 1980s, this author embarked on a quest to find the truth of the Conner feud. It was finished but never published. Weldon Mc-Daniel, who helped him research the book, mailed me a copy after we met in Sabine County, when a very rough draft of *Red Sky Morning* was complete. Dugan's tenacity is inspiring; it took him four years to find documents and records that I'm able to locate almost immediately with a keystroke. His work tracing Conner property records and Willis Conner's movements in Florida proved invaluable. But even more precious are the details he recorded from now dead old-timers in Sabine County. Dugan clearly has an agenda to prove the Conners were more innocent than guilty—he even lobbied for a pardon for Alfie Conner in 1983—but he includes and considers other viewpoints in the work. (J. Allen Newton's testimonial is a notable exception.) I have cited *Judge Not* as if it were a published work, as it probably should have been. I'm grateful to Weldon McDaniel for entrusting me with a copy and happy to give a voice to those with whom Dugan spoke, who are now silent.

Trails and Trials of a Texas Ranger by William Sterling

If Paul Spellman offers a more clinical official history of the Texas Rangers, then Sterling is an emotional cheerleader. He introduces some great details about the Rangers as actual people, including unflattering tidbits about their past (I'm looking at you, Treadwell). However, he is also the source of seeming inaccuracies, like saying the Conners loosed their dogs on Company F during their firefight. It remains a great resource for Ranger lore of the era and an instructive glimpse of their attitudes toward each other and their prey.

Texas Gulag: The Chain Gang Years 1875–1925 by Gary Brown

This is a harrowing read filled with pathos and cruelty. But it's actually more smart than shocking. Brown presents each convict's stories in absolute context, historically and as sources. Having an expert writer point out the fault lines that exist between detail and aggrandizement is most appreciated. This should be required reading for anyone seeking to understand the law and order history of the Lone Star State.

Gunsmoke in the Redlands by Joe Combs

The Conner feud is discussed in one short chapter in this 1968 anthology of Old West shoot-outs, so it's hardly a comprehensive take. Still, it uniquely captures the pro-Conner views of old Edwin Harper, which is of value. Also, this book is what led to Combs later solving the mystery of what happened to John Conner, information he shared with Mark Dugan and Weldon McDaniel and finally published here.

Harris on the Pig by Joseph Harris

This book is never cited in this work, but it's required background material for anyone researching hog farming in the 1800s. Joseph Harris has a folksy way with words that is charming as well as educational. "Rough treatment and crowded sties have no place in the keeping of pigs," he says. "Fire any hired man who'd hit a pig."

The Cherokee Strip Live Stock Association: Federal Regulation and the Cattleman's Last Frontier by William Savage Jr.

This could be considered a bone-dry read if it were not so enlightening. The intersection of economics, regional politics, and race relations in the Wild West seems obvious but is very often misunderstood. Many of the things I thought I understood about the Indian Territories were wrong, or at least so simplistic as to be considered ignorant.

PLAYLIST

More books should include music playlists, I think, anyway, so here's mine for *Red Sky Morning*. This is also a way to thank these unwitting creative collaborators for their help in telling this story by acknowledging the soundtrack heard during its research and writing.

GANGSTAGRASS
"Red Sky Morning" and "I'm Gonna Put You Down"

An excellent blend of rap and bluegrass, Gangstagrass creates an intersection of modern, urban storytelling and traditional, rural instruments. I saw the band perform live in New York City a decade ago, after hearing the theme song to the TV show *Justified*, and I'm happy to say they are still putting out strong music. Much thanks to publicist Fiona Bloom and the members of Gangstagrass for confirming the lyrics quoted at the book's start and inspiring the title.

ENNIO MORRICONE
"A Fistful of Dollars—Main Theme" and "L'Ultima Diligenza di Red Rock" (from *The Hateful Eight*)

There's no need to explain why this epic composer belongs on this list, since he's the best at putting the glory and pain of manhunters on the trail to music. But why these songs, specifically? The first is the best spaghetti Western anthem to capture the long, lonely hours between dangerous encounters that defined the Ranger lifestyle. *The Hateful Eight*'s soundtrack generates a sense of inevitable doom that fits the colliding trajectories of the lawmen and outlaws in the book.

THE BUILDERS AND THE BUTCHERS
"Bottom of the Lake"

Told from the perspective of a drowned ghost, this brooding, dramatic song doesn't tell a story that fits neatly with any specific character. (Besides the Toledo Bend Reservoir, perhaps.) Still, the atmospherics and murder-soaked imagery suit the book's East Texas material. The so-called death country subgenre is fertile with talented artists that match the mood of the book; the music of the band Devil Makes Three also pairs well with a Western-crime-noir hybrid like *Red Sky Morning*.

JERRY GARCIA AND DAVID GRISMAN
"Whiskey in the Jar"

This is an old ditty, telling the tale (in its first incarnation) of Irish highwayman Patrick Fleming, executed in 1650. There may be no more enduring expression of the mythic appeal of outlaws. The song came to Colonial America and has been around ever since, covered in modern times by the likes of Michael Hurley, Thin Lizzy, the Dubliners, and Metallica. This is a particularly satisfying, toe-tappingly traditional rendition. Plus, Jerry.

TOM WAITS
"Sins of My Father"

The love of family drives many questionable decisions in this book, which is not surprising considering it explores feuding, interrelated clans. Many children paid the price of their parents' choices, some to their ruin. This plodding, spartan song presents a powerful expression of sin, regret, and redemption, all with a soft "goth country" vibe. For a mythic Old West feel, add Waits's "Black Wings" to the playlist.

INDEX

JOE PAPPALARDO is the author of the critically acclaimed books *Inferno: The True Story of a B-17 Gunner's Heroism and the Bloodiest Military Campaign in Aviation History*; *Sunflowers: The Secret History*; and *Spaceport Earth: The Reinvention of Spaceflight*. Pappalardo is a freelance journalist and former associate editor of *Air & Space Smithsonian* magazine, a writing contributor to *National Geographic* magazine, a contributor to *Texas Monthly*, and a former senior editor and current contributor to *Popular Mechanics*. He has appeared on C-SPAN, CNN, Fox News, and television shows on the Science Channel and the History Channel.